✎ **W9-BTQ-584**

B   19347
HIL   Hillary, Edmund Percival.

           Nothing venture, nothing
           win.

           AGNES IRWIN SCHOOL
           UPPER SCHOOL LIBRARY

Nothing Venture, Nothing Win

By the same author

HIGH ADVENTURE
NO LATITUDE FOR ERROR
SCHOOLHOUSE IN THE CLOUDS

With George Lowe

EAST OF EVEREST

With Sir Vivian Fuchs

THE CROSSING OF ANTARCTICA

With Desmond Doig

HIGH IN THE THIN COLD AIR

B
HIL

Nothing Venture, Nothing Win

by

SIR EDMUND HILLARY

COWARD, McCANN & GEOGHEGAN, INC.

NEW YORK

19347

First American Edition 1975. Copyright © 1975 by Sir Edmund Hillary. All rights reserved. This book, or parts thereof, may not be reproduced in any form without permission in writing from the publisher. SBN: 698–10649–0. Library of Congress Catalog Card Number: 74–24330. Printed in Great Britain.

Contents

Black and White Photographs

vii

Colour Photographs

List of Maps and Diagrams

Foreword

THE HEROES I ADMIRED IN MY YOUTH SEEMED TO POSSESS ABILITIES AND virtues beyond the grasp of ordinary men. My desire to emulate them was very great but I never succeeded in approaching their high standards. Fearful at heart in moments of danger, I found it difficult to produce the calm courage of the heroic mould. Having a certain rude strength, I lacked the quickness of hand and eye of the natural athlete. Well meaning enough and with a desire to help, I made few sacrifices in noble causes.

I discovered that even the mediocre can have adventures and even the fearful can achieve. In a sense fear became a friend – I hated it at the time but it added spice to the challenge and satisfaction to the conquest. I envied those who in success clung to a measure of peace and tranquillity – I was always too restless and life was a constant battle against boredom. But the compensations have been great – certainly more than I deserve. I had the world lie beneath my clumsy boots and saw the red sun slip over the horizon after the dark Antarctic winter. I have been given more than my share of excitement, beauty, laughter and friendship.

Chapter 1

Beginnings

I awoke to strangely mixed feelings of discomfort and anticipation. My air-mattress had deflated during the night and my hip was resting on the inhospitable ice. Reluctantly, to escape a rather too realistic dream, I opened my eyes and looked around the familiar surroundings of Camp IV. Our large tent presented a depressing scene in the early morning light. Scattered around the icy floor were the silent, sleeping bodies of my companions, all hidden in the depths of their sleeping-bags. A chaotic mass of oxygen apparatus, rucksacks, spare clothing, ropes, pitons, crampons, and iceaxes cluttered up the remaining room. With a feeling of uneasy distaste, I closed my eyes again. It was just another morning at Camp IV! Life at over 21,000 feet didn't leave you feeling too full of joy and happiness. Suddenly my mind cleared, and I remembered that this was far from being an ordinary day. Probably for me it was the most important day of all, for it was our turn to start on the long slow upward grind that might, with luck, end on the summit of Everest.

High Adventure

I WAS BORN IN AUCKLAND, NEW ZEALAND, ON JULY 20th 1919. As a child I never took much interest in family history but had drummed into me that my mother's family, the Clarks, were substantial people who owned a farm and ran the local store at Whakahara in the Northern Wairoa district, a hundred miles from the city. Grandmother Clark was born in New Zealand although her parents emigrated from Yorkshire. Grandfather, too, came from Yorkshire in the mid 1800s and must have been a reputable and hardworking citizen of some consequence. Unfortunately he came to an untimely end when in early middle age he was kicked on the head by one of his horses.

Grandmother never quite recovered from the shock of this experience and although I can remember her at over eighty years old as white-haired, upright and very dignified, her family contribution was more a moral one than an active participation in everyday living. But her twelve children rallied around and carried on as though no great misfortune had occurred. My mother was one of the youngest in the family and was brought up by her older sisters. Photographs show her to have been a pretty girl, slim and graceful. She played the piano well and had the social graces expected from a young lady in the Victorian era. But under her gentle exterior was a great deal of courage and determination – and she needed plenty of these qualities in her long life with my father. Conscientious and intelligent, she did well at school and later qualified at teachers college.

The Hillary side of the family didn't have the same secure place in the community. Grandfather Hillary was an adventurous sort of man and quite a family legend has built up around him; though how true it all is it is hard to know. He also originated in Yorkshire and learned a trade as a watchmaker. Later he travelled to India on business and sufficiently endeared himself to various Maharajahs to be well rewarded for his efforts – or so the story goes. Certainly he retired to New Zealand in the early 1880s with a useful financial nest-egg and married grandmother who was a great deal younger than himself. Ida Fleming came from Ireland and travelled to New Zealand on a sailing ship as governess for a well-to-do English family. My grandmother certainly had plenty of spirit: she took on another job as governess and sailed north up through the Pacific to Hawaii and as a child I listened enthralled to her tales about these long sea journeys.

After their marriage grandfather set up a watchmaker's and jeweller's shop in Dargaville, bought a few racehorses, and over the next few years successfully disposed of his fortune on the racetrack. By his middle sixties he was almost destitute. He concluded that he had contributed all he should to Society and went to bed for the next thirty years.

Grandmother accepted the challenge. She looked after grandfather without complaint and earned money for her family by any means she could: from performing menial tasks to using her artistic ability to create paintings and handicrafts that she could sell. She put her four children through school, gave them a solid background of character and independence, and then looked after herself with courage and dignity until she died at ninety-three – she was a remarkable woman!

My father's character was moulded by this uncertain environment into a mixture of moral conservatism and a fierce independence and pride which would not permit him to accept that any man or institution had the right to rule him – unless he himself thought fit. He was a keen thinker who disliked the family poverty with its lack of opportunity

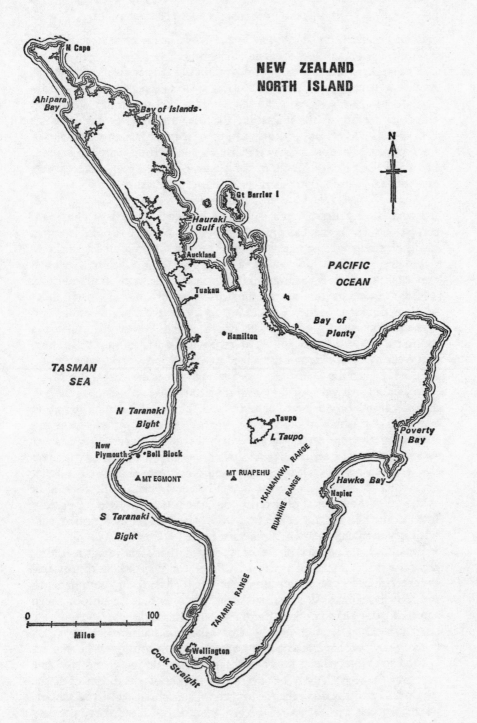

NEW ZEALAND
NORTH ISLAND

N

N Cape

Ahipara
Bay

Bay of Islands

Gt Barrier I

Hauraki
Gulf

Auckland

PACIFIC
OCEAN

Tuakau

Hamilton

Bay of
Plenty

TASMAN
SEA

N Taranaki
Bight

Taupo

L Taupo

Poverty
Bay

New
Plymouth   Bell Block

MT EGMONT

MT RUAPEHU

KAIMANAWA RANGE

RUAHINE RANGE

Hawke Bay

Napier

S Taranaki
Bight

TARARUA RANGE

0   100

Miles

Cook Straight

Wellington

and he became very interested in the social ideas that were gaining popular support in New Zealand at the time.

He started work as a copy boy for the local newspaper and found few outlets for his adventurous spirit – although he often told us how he used to creep on board the sailing ships tied up to the wharf and climb to the top of the masts just for the dare of it. English was his best subject and his opportunity to progress finally came when one of the reporters was sick and my father was told to handle the job instead. He made the most of his chance and later became a full-time reporter and journalist and a competent press photographer.

When World War One erupted my father was quick to volunteer for what he regarded as a worthy cause. He went overseas as a sergeant, served with the Australian and New Zealand Army Corps in the grim Gallipoli campaign, was shot through the nose and laid low with severe dysentery. He was finally invalided home more than a little disillusioned about noble causes. Soon after his return in 1916 he married my mother.

They moved to the little country township of Tuakau – forty miles south of Auckland–where my father had accepted the job of establishing a weekly newspaper, the *Tuakau District News*. Although he had the grand title of Managing Editor, he rarely had a staff of more than one, and over the years carried out virtually every job – reporting, setting up the type, printing the paper, and even at times delivering it himself.

My father was very capable with his hands and commenced building a family home on our seven acres of land. There were three children in our family – I had an older sister and a younger brother – and my memories of those early years are happy enough although my father was something of a martinet and there were few aspects of our lives that escaped his critical supervision. He was a tremendous story teller and when we were very young he held us enthralled night after night with endless adventures of 'Jimmy Job', the little man who supposedly lived in the hollow tree at the bottom of the farm. (I used similar tales with my own children when my turn came.)

Despite his considerable energy my father's enthusiasm didn't always last to the end of a project. Our house was quite a roomy one for this country community but it never had all its rooms completed or properly furnished. We had half a dozen cows grazing on our seven acres and my father milked them by hand morning and evening. He heartily disliked the monotony of this task and built himself a bookrack to hang over the back of a cow so he could read in comfort as he milked.

Tuakau Primary School was less than half a mile away, and wet, fine or frosty I walked barefooted every day to school – as did most of the children. I had the advantage of receiving coaching from my schoolteacher mother and benefited greatly from this. I didn't have the easy personality to be a teacher's pet but certainly received more than my share of teacher's attention and advanced rapidly through the classes. Being younger, I was generally smaller and weaker than most of my fellow pupils and never became fully involved in school sports or other activities. This lack of participation was aggravated by my mother's often repeated philosophy that 'you can judge people by the company they keep' and she didn't feel that most of my classmates had too much to offer. As a consequence I was permitted to play no games after school but had to return immediately home to the safety of the family circle. This attitude by my mother, who was so generous and kind in other ways, greatly irked me and I never knew if it was related to the substantial proportion of Maori pupils we had in the school.

I accepted our Maori neighbours as an ordinary and normal part of my life. For a year I shared a desk with a large and cheerful Maori girl who was no great shakes academically but who made quite clear to the bigger boys that anybody who pushed me around would have her to deal with and even the biggest boys weren't prepared to take that sort of risk.

My father had a close relationship with the Maori community through his newspaper activities and thoroughly enjoyed his many Maori friends (although I cannot remember any of them being invited to our home). Certainly we children listened avidly to his stories about Maori prowess on the rugby field and in the timber and flax industries. He was one of the few people to enjoy the friendship of Princess Te Puea Herangi, that formidable Maori figure who was renowned for her lack of enthusiasm for most Pakehas (white New Zealanders).

As I developed a personality and opinions of my own, I discovered that my father was a man of rigid rules who viewed with disfavour any breaches of his discipline. My childhood affection became dominated by fear of his displeasure and finally into outspoken resentment. We commenced the fierce arguments which carried on unabated throughout my teens. Mother was a woman of admirable character and gave me the affection and encouragement I needed. She played an important role in keeping our family together and her pride and courage made her our focal point. She maintained an astonishing balance between an energetic and dogmatic husband and her three rather independent children. When she died at seventy-three she had the pleasure of knowing that her children were all 'well established'. We were lucky to have such a mother.

Even during the worst days of the depression we were never short of food – our small farm saw to that with its cows, large vegetable garden, and extensive orchard – but I was increasingly having to escape into the realms of imagination and dreams to find the mental freedom I desired. Even matters of health were closely supervised and we operated on the philosophy that most human ailments were due to overeating. A common treatment for any disorder was 'dieting' – which meant a substantial reduction in our food intake – a very trying experience for a young boy with a hearty appetite. It did have the effect that I was most reluctant to acknowledge any illness unless I could hardly stand.

My father believed in the necessity of corporal punishment and we had many memorable confrontations in the wood shed. One of the most vigorous was in respect to my father's greatly prized grape vine. One evening he discovered that the best bunch of grapes was missing and I was accused of this misdemeanor. I denied it, and my incensed father told me he would punish me until I admitted my guilt. The beating continued for some time with frequent stops for me to confess (or for my father to regain his breath). He was not a man to give up easily but finally had to desist without getting the required admission. I can't remember whether I did in fact steal the grapes – probably I did.

There is nothing unusual, of course, about arguments between father and son, and despite our disagreements I always had a sense of loyalty to my father and indeed a well-concealed affection. He possessed many qualities that I admired and even in my most stubborn moments I was never blinded to the fact that I must have been quite a burden on his patience. He was certainly a conscientious parent – perhaps a little too conscientious at times.

I experienced a great deal of physical punishment both at home and at school but never became resigned to it or regarded it quite as casually as did some of my contemporaries. In my case it was aggravated by the appalling fact that tears came easily to my eyes – not from the pain which I regarded as nothing – but from the embarrassment and indignity of the whole miserable proceedings. I have been involved in outbursts of violence in my own life but I have always regretted it afterwards. I have yet to see the occasion when physical punishment achieved a really worthwhile result even under the best of motivation. Maybe there are occasions when as a last resort it is better than nothing, but generally it indicates an inability to handle the problem by more constructive means.

More than anything I liked to laugh and most of the time I found plenty to laugh about; even my father could be very entertaining at times. Although I used to smile very easily I suspect that this was more from embarrassment than natural cheerfulness (although I was cheerful enough most of the time). My most traumatic experience at primary school resulted from a smile. I had just been promoted to Standard IV from Standard II having bypassed the middle grade. The headmaster was a tall acid sort of man who gave the impression that he thoroughly disliked children. My first class was geography and he asked me to point out the Continent of Asia on the map. Overwhelmed, I had a mental block and couldn't say a thing about Asia or even a Continent. I stood there with an inane grin on my face getting more and more embarrassed. 'Don't stand there like a laughing hyena!' he bellowed at me and the class roared with pleasure at his witticism. I cringed inside and wished I could die.

I passed out of primary school at the age of eleven – two years younger than the average. My mother was determined that I should have a good secondary education, which in her view meant attending a big school in the city. My father was less enthusiastic – he already had the financial burden of educating my sister in Auckland and he thought I could be more usefully employed helping around the place. But when arguing about education my mother usually won. I was accepted as a pupil at Auckland Grammar School – regarded as one of the leading educational institutions in New Zealand. It was decided that for financial reasons I would have to live at home and each day travel by train to school. I became, in fact, the only pupil to travel regularly so far to a city school. For three and a half years my train left Tuakau station at seven a.m. and arrived back at six fifteen p.m.

Physically small and inexperienced, unaccustomed to mixing socially with anyone outside my own family, I descended on the world of the big city and found it a terrifying experience. During the summer holidays I had to take an examination at Auckland Grammar to determine my appropriate class. Forty years later I can still remember my overwhelming fear as I walked into the vast empty school building. When I emerged some time later I remembered nothing of whom I had met or what examination I had sat. I only knew I had failed miserably in every respect...

My first day at secondary school was a disaster! The twelve hundred boys gathered in school hall to be addressed by the headmaster and allocated their various classes. Long lists of names were read out and I listened ... and listened ... and heard no mention of my name. When the great hall was almost empty I gathered the courage to approach a passing master and ask what I should do. Thank goodness he was kind to me! He checked his lists – my name wasn't there – and then took me to the school office. I was finally led to my classroom, 3D – one of the lowest classes in the school.

For a month or more I was academically and emotionally lost and I rarely, if ever, spoke to anyone. The weather was gloriously fine and each lunchtime I slipped off into a quiet corner and munched my sandwiches in solitary fashion. I entertained myself watching the activities of a small ant colony and by the end of the month I felt I knew these ants better than I did my fellow students. I said nothing to my parents as I'd soon discovered that they were as out of touch with this different life as I was. At the end of the first term I was promoted to 3B – the second class – so presumably I must have been making some progress.

My confidence had received another blow. In the first week the muscle-bound gymnastics instructor cast his jaundiced eye over my scrawny physique, rolled his eyes to the heavens, and muttered 'What will they send me next?' He was no believer in sparing his victim any discomfort and told me my ribs flared out in most unnatural fashion, my back needed straightening and my shoulders were rounded. He placed me in the misfit class with the other physical freaks and devoted his main attention to the more adequately equipped schoolboys. I developed a feeling of inferiority about my physique which has remained with me to this day – it wasn't an inferiority about what I could achieve, but a solid conviction about how appalling I looked.

I filled my time with reading and dreaming. Books of adventure became my greatest support – Edgar Rice Burroughs, Rider Haggard, John Buchan – at one period I was regularly reading a book a day. In my imagination I constantly re-enacted heroic episodes, and I was always the hero. I died dramatically on a score of battlefields and rescued a hundred lovely maidens.

And then I started to grow – five inches one year and four inches the next. I became tall and lean with increasing strength. But the best part of school life still eluded me – the sports and social activities that commenced after lessons. I always had a train to catch!

The train became the most important part of my life – and here I gradually learned to excel. Leaping off while it was gaining speed, holding onto the handrails and running furiously alongside and then leaping tigerishly aboard at the last desperate moment – this was living! The horseplay and battles, the broken windows and smashed seats – nothing vicious about it – merely the side effects of violent youthful energy a little misdirected. I learned how to fight in the train, how to hurl my opponent into the corner of the seat and lie on him so he couldn't use any superior skill at boxing or wrestling. I learned how to push all the glass out of the broken window so the guard wouldn't see it and blame me. I learned how to collect 'Schoolboys Only' stickers from suburban carriages and place them on a choice carriage on the 4.20 express – and then travel home in uncrowded comfort.

At the age of fourteen my sudden growth proved to be too much for my clothes. In those depression years we had very little money and clothes had to last a long time. In the middle of winter it could be cold

in Tuakau as I rode my bicycle the mile from home to the railway
station and I was thankful for the warmth of my thick overcoat but
gradually the overcoat seemed to shorten, my arms poked further out.
One day a senior boy sarcastically referred to my 'waistcoat' – to the
delight of my fellow travellers. I never wore that coat again – or indeed
have possessed a heavy overcoat since.

The train became my little world and I spent many happy hours
there – reading, dreaming and skylarking – particularly on the way
home with school work finished and tomorrow a lifetime away. I
started getting boxing lessons and rather favoured my skill with a
long straight left. I persuaded one of the younger boys, a most cheerful
likeable lad to spar with me and duly pranced around him and showed
off my primitive skill. A couple of days later I was approached by the
guard on the train – the young boy's parents had complained that their
son was being bullied – he was coming home with his arms black and
blue.

A bully? Me? There was nothing I despised more ... And yet, to my
horror, I realised that the accusation was quite justified. Even the
guard saw my distress and told me not to worry, that no harm had been
done but to be a bit more careful in future. But it gave me a miserable
week!

I wasn't really a good fighter as I lacked the necessary 'killer instinct'.
In my last year at school I fought one of my few good friends. It
started perfectly harmlessly and then grew more serious when I
unthinkingly pounded him on the nose. Soon we were surrounded by
a hundred sadistic youths, all revelling in the bloody occasion. It
wasn't really much of a fight – I was taller and knew more about boxing
and soon blood was pouring from his nose and his eyes were puffing up.
But still he kept coming, and coming – hardly ever hitting me. I'd
back off until I couldn't back off any further and then have to go
forward and pound him again. I felt revolted – why was I doing this? ...
But I didn't know how to stop it. It was a long time before a master
appeared and called a halt – and took my friend to the clinic for treatment. My friend later became a pilot in the Battle of Britain and died
fighting over the English Channel.

Matriculation was the most important examination for secondary
school pupils and I managed to fumble my way through, doing reasonably well in chemistry and mathematics. We had now moved into
Auckland and my last year, in the sixth form, was the only year at
school I really enjoyed.

I was made a sergeant in the school military battalion – I can't quite
remember how it happened. My platoon included all the gangling
overgrown youths in the school – and I was the most gangling of the

lot. I spent my time trying desperately to stop my platoon (and me) from making complete fools of ourselves on parade – and as our normal position was at the head of the company this wasn't easy. Strangely enough my platoon members helped me generously with whispered advice at crucial moments. Somehow we managed to prevent ourselves from disgracing the school on important occasions – but discipline and devotion to duty were never our strongest points.

For a long time my father had been involved in keeping bees, first as a hobby and then as a profitable sideline. He didn't find it easy to accept the authority of his newspaper directors and finally decided to break free and go full time into commercial bee-keeping. It was the time of the great depression and life became more uncertain and we had a considerable financial struggle. It was the time, too, when food was being destroyed even though people were going hungry and we were swept along by my father's anger at such stupidity.

My mother, my younger brother and I all worked hard at the bees to make ends meet. Every weekend, all the school holidays and even during the long summer evenings I was fully involved in the business – I listened to some of my fellow students talking about sailing on the harbour or going off on their Christmas holidays to Lake Taupo and I hardly knew what they meant. By the time I was sixteen I was doing a man's work at home – and enjoying it too – but there wasn't much time for holidays.

In this final year at school I was desperately keen to go with the school winter party to Mount Ruapehu. I'd heard glowing tales from other boys about skiing and it sounded very good fun. The honey crop had been a good one, I'd worked hard for some years in the business without receiving any pay – not even pocket money. My father considered my request at some length and then agreed that money could be spared on this occasion for my trip – seeing it was the slack time of the year.

I saw my first snow at midnight when we stepped off the train at the National Park Station. There wasn't much of it but it was a tremendous thrill and before long snowballs, as hard as iron, were flying through the air. As our bus carried us steadily up towards the Chateau Tourist Hotel perched high on the mountainside, its powerful headlights sparked into life a fairyland of glistening snow and stunted pines and frozen streams. When I crawled into my bunk at two in the morning I felt I was in a strange and exciting new world.

For ten glorious days we skied and played on the lower slopes of the mountain, I don't think I ever looked towards the summit. We had been told the upper parts of the mountain were dangerous, and I viewed them with respect and never dared to venture on them.

Actually there was little need. It was a year of exceptionally heavy snows (although I wasn't aware of this at the time) and the Chateau had a couple of feet of snow on its lawns. The main public ski centre at Salt Hut was deep under snow and you could actually ski over its roof. In these days of glacial retreat and warm winters it is hard to imagine that we did all our skiing on slopes which nowadays are passed by car on the way to the ski grounds.

I was intoxicated by the whole experience, the hurling of our bodies uncontrollably down an almost vertical slope; skiing through forest and rocks to the Chateau, the magnificent food; even the freedom and the lack of regular tasks.

After a fresh fall of snow a competition was held on the front lawn of the Chateau for the best snowman. A companion and I built a 'Hitler' – very much in the news in those days – and we won – the first and only time I have received a prize in a public competition.

I showed little natural skill at skiing but plenty of strength and energy and I returned home in a glow of fiery enthusiasm for the sun and the cold and the snow – especially the snow!

For two years I became a university student and found it difficult to adapt to this new environment. I lacked interest and concentration and didn't seem to be able to make any friends – or maybe I was too selfconscious to try hard. During the winter – the off-season for bees – I filled my time with reading, dreaming and long energetic walks. To have a few pennies in my pocket I'd save the tram fare by walking the five miles to university each morning and then walk back home again in the evening. I was adopted by a group of young trampers who spent their winter Sundays walking through the dense rain forest of the Waitakere Ranges. They were a cheerful, pleasant lot and I was thankful for their friendship and happy to carry any load, push anybody up hills, rush off on any reconnaissance, make any trail . . . I knew I had more physical energy than most and I revelled in driving myself to the utmost. I still found it difficult to believe that anyone in their right mind could get pleasure out of my company. I felt stiff, insecure and socially insufficient – and no doubt I was!

Gradually I became more and more involved in bee-keeping – largely, I suppose, because I felt more at home there. My father was a tremendous worker although his energies were too widely spread to ensure his economic success. He helped organise the New Zealand Beekeepers' Association and became Secretary and then President. For years he battled for the improvement of honey marketing methods and founded and edited several bee-keeping journals.

Finally I dropped out from university to work full time for my father – as my brother did too. It was a good life – a life of open air and sun and hard physical work. And in its way a life of uncertainty and adventure; a constant fight against the vagaries of the weather. We had 1600 hives of bees spread around the pleasant dairyland south of Auckland, occupying small corners on fifty different farms. We were constantly on the move from site to site – especially when all 1600 hives decided to swarm at once. We never knew what our crop would be until the last pound of honey had been taken off the hives; it could range from a massive sixty tons down to a miserable twenty or less. But all through the exciting months of the honey flow the dream of a bumper crop would drive us on through long hard hours of labour; manhandling thousands of ninety pound boxes of honey comb for extracting . . . and grimacing at our daily ration of a dozen, or a hundred, beestings. We were incurable optimists. In the summer we worked seven days a week from dawn until dark – and frequently late into the night. We accepted cheerfully that this was the right thing to do and even at Christmas thought nothing of working right through the night so that we could get half a day free to go window shopping in the city.

In winter time we were still busy but there was more time now for other pursuits. I took lessons in fencing, jujitsu and in boxing. I remember the excitement when my gymnasiam was used by Vic Calteaux the New Zealand professional welter weight boxing champion who was preparing for a defence of his title. Calteaux was an immensely powerful man and a bruising fighter and several of us were invited to give him some sparring practice. I was under no great delusions about my skill but was both taller and heavier than Calteaux and was quite keen to give a hand. We pranced around the ring for a while, largely shadow boxing, when I noticed his guard was rather slack so reached out and thumped him rather firmly on the nose. Calteaux's temper was never particularly well controlled and he set about me in furious fashion and duly lowered me to the canvas with a terrific hook to the solar plexus. I was helped from the ring by my concerned instructor who muttered, 'Why didn't you stick to sparring?' From this experience I learned a couple of useful lessons – not to punch professionals on the nose . . . and that it is no disgrace to be beaten by a champion.

Like many young people I was passing through a stage of religious questioning – trying rather desperately to combine some sort of faith with the facts of life as I saw them. I found it increasingly difficult to believe that anyone or anything was likely to go to the trouble to 'save' me or to create at some specific moment in time a 'heaven on earth'. I didn't know that I wanted to be 'saved' anyway and was very doubtful if I would qualify for any variety of heaven. I could see some logic in praying for the welfare and protection of my family and friends, but had the feeling that it was rather cowardly to be constantly calling for help in solving my own problems – a rather youthful and arrogant view no doubt – but I was developing a conviction that most of us would have to solve our personal and social problems for ourselves.

My parents, too, had been drifting away from the formal activities of the church and were clearly seeking different answers in their own minds. A number of speakers on 'new' religious thought visited Auckland and my parents took us to hear some of them. Most impressive was Dr. Herbert Sutcliffe – an accomplished speaker with an expert and lively stage presentation. In his philosophy of 'Radiant Living' he emphasised the importance of physical, mental and spiritual health and gave a great deal of advice on how to achieve a balanced and successful life. We went away from his first lecture feeling highly stimulated and wanting to hear more.

As a family we attended further courses of lectures and when Dr. Sutcliffe established a branch of his school in Auckland we became foundation members. 'Radiant Living' was rather an astonishing conglomeration of ideas, culled from a multitude of religions and philosophies. It included much practical psychology of the 'think and grow rich' variety; there was great emphasis on healthy foods and a balanced diet; on a variety of rhythmical and relaxing exercises; on moderation in things of the flesh rather than abstinence or excess. I suppose that my grasp of this was oversimplified and frequently rather shallow but it was undoubtedly helpful to me at the time. I learned to speak confidently from the platform; to think more freely on important topics; to mix more readily with a wide variety of people.

At various times I tried hard to study religious matters but I gained little long lasting satisfaction from them. There seemed to be so much that was sanctimonious and orientated to the next world. I read voraciously of theosophy, anthroposophy, and half a dozen other unorthodox philosophies. I tried desperately to understand the profound writings of Rudolph Steiner and Krishnamurti; I toyed with meditation, concentration, positive thinking. From all of them I gained some immediate inspiration, then slowly my enthusiasm faded. After a few years it faded for 'Radiant Living' too. I had the feeling I'd been trying to escape from life – and that I should go out into the world and get on with ordinary living.

Chapter 2

Wartime in New Zealand

ON THE DECLARATION OF WAR I IMMEDIATELY APPLIED TO JOIN THE air force and train as a pilot – to fly had always been an ambition of mine and the independence and freedom of a pilot's life seemed very attractive. But in those first days of the war there was a very long period of delay before an applicant was taken in for training. I had plenty of time to be harassed by my religious conscience and I was greatly troubled over the approach a Christian should have to killing – and I regarded myself as an enthusiastic Christian at the time. I wasn't too impressed with the arguments put up by some clergymen and Christians to justify the support of war and I had no doubt that equally devout people in Germany were convinced that God was on their side. I decided that I would have to make a decision one way or the other – either to remain a Christian and refrain from killing or forego my beliefs and get on with the war. After much agonising reflection I withdrew my air force application.

I was very restless and unhappy and the first few years of the war were the most uncertain and miserable of my life. I was working very hard and had little time to spare for entertainments but I tried to get some small outlet for adventure in the hills and mountains. In the summer of 1939/40 I was still only twenty but felt so weighed down by mental turmoil that I persuaded my father to give me some time off and I spent my meagre savings on a short trip to the Southern Alps with an older friend. We planned to stay for two days at a famous tourist resort, the Hermitage, right in the heart of the giant peaks of the Southern Alps.

We had a magnificent drive through the mountains and arrived at the Hermitage in the early afternoon. It was a perfect day and the great peaks seemed to tower over our heads. I looked on them with a growing feeling of excitement – the great rock walls, the hanging glaciers, and the avalanche-strewn slopes. Strangely stirred by it all I

28

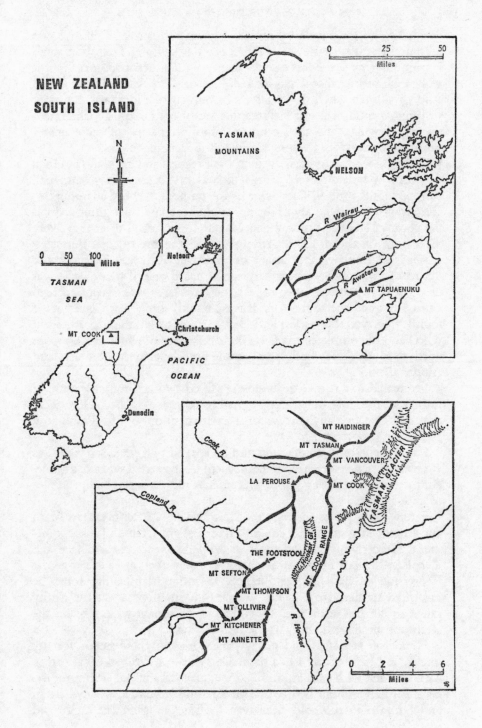

NEW ZEALAND
SOUTH ISLAND

N

0   50   100   Miles

TASMAN
SEA

MT COOK

Christchurch

PACIFIC
OCEAN

Dunedin

Nelson

0   25   50
Miles

TASMAN
MOUNTAINS

NELSON

R Wairau

R Awatere

MT TAPUAENUKU

MT HAIDINGER

Cook R

MT TASMAN

MT VANCOUVER

LA PEROUSE

MT COOK

TASMAN GLACIER

Copland R

THE FOOTSTOOL

MT SEFTON

MT THOMPSON

MT OLLIVIER

MT KITCHENER

MT ANNETTE

R Hooker Gl

MT COOK RANGE

R Hooker

0   2   4   6
Miles

decided to go for a walk by myself. The nearest snow I could see was high up in a gully in the Sealy range behing the hotel. I set off towards it stumbling over the loose rocks in my light shoes. I soon realised it was much further than I had judged, but for some reason I kept going. And at last I reached it – a tattered remnant of old avalanche snow spanning a mountain torrent. In an excess of enthusiasm I kicked steps up and down it, and then with an astonishing sense of achievement stumbled back down the long slopes to the Hermitage.

Sitting in the lounge that evening I felt restless and excited. And then the hum of voices hushed, and I looked up to see two young men coming into the room. They were fit and tanned; they had an unmistakable air of competence about them. I could hear a whisper going around the room: 'They've just climbed Mount Cook.' And soon they were the centre of an admiring group with all the pretty girls fluttering around like moths in the flame – or so it seemed to me! Keeping well out of the way, but straining my ears, I heard one of them say 'I was pretty tired when we got to the icecap, but Harry was like a tiger and almost dragged me to the top.' It wasn't until some year s later that I found they were Stevenson and Dick, a famous climbing partnership who had just completed the first Grand Traverse of Mount Cook from north to south. (They both later became Presidents of the New Zealand Alpine Club.)

I retreated to a corner of the lounge filled with an immense sense of futility at the dull and mundane nature of my existence. Here were chaps who were really getting some excitement out of life. Tomorrow I must climb something!

I approached my companion and he agreed to give it a try. But as we had neither experience nor equipment he suggested we take a guide. All the necessary arrangements were made and I went to bed in a fever of anticipation.

Fate was kind to us and next morning was fine. After breakfast Brian and I met our guide and I couldn't help a slight feeling of disappointment. He certainly looked the part with his weatherbeaten face and Tyrolean hat but his mature years and excess weight didn't give the impression of dash and endurance. In rather dampening tones he informed us that we'd tackle Olivier – a small peak on the Sealy range above the Hermitage. 'Of course, if it's too far we can spend the afternoon boiling the billy at the Sealy lakes!'

He led off at a slow and steady pace – too slow and steady for my liking, and before long I had dashed on ahead. I climbed up the steep narrow track with a feeling of freedom and exhilaration. I'd been at the lakes for half an hour before our intrepid guide hove into view. Brian and I swam in the cold clear water while our guide lit a fire and boiled a billy. We attacked our lunch with ravenous appetites.

A thousand feet of snow stretched between us and the crest of the range. At my impatient movements our guide sighed deeply and reluctantly stirred himself. He led off up the slope. This was real mountaineering! The snow was pleasantly firm and an easy kick produced a comfortable step. The long slope underneath gave an impression of exposure and despite my eagerness I followed docilely behind. We reached the crest of the ridge and looked over into a magnificent valley of great glaciers and fine peaks. A few yards along the ridge was a high rocky outcrop. I couldn't restrain myself any longer – our guide felt the need for a rest but I scrambled quickly upwards. In a few minutes I was climbing onto the summit of my first real mountain.

I returned to the Hermitage after the happiest day I had ever spent. And now, more than thirty years later, after months and even years spent on snowy peaks and icy glaciers I can still remember the intense pleasure of that day. Despite all I have seen and experienced over several decades of exploration I still get the same simple thrill out of glimpsing a tiny patch of snow in a high mountain gully . . . and feel the same urge to climb towards it.

When conscription was introduced in New Zealand the strength of my convictions was about to be tested. Then the matter was taken out of my hands. My father had never approved of my going into the air force – he considered I could be better employed in honey production which was a reserved occupation like ordinary farming. Unknown to me he applied to have me retained in this essential work and when his application was immediately granted I didn't know whether to be glad or sad.

As time passed my thoughts turned increasingly to the air force again. While I realised that I was doing a useful production job I was becoming bored with hard routine work. My school friends were overseas in the services and my religious convictions were receding. Finally my father could stand my importuning no longer and at the end of 1942 agreed to institute action to get me released. I applied again to the air force and was accepted – but learnt to my sorrow that I might have to wait a year before commencing training.

In 1942 and 1943 New Zealand was deeply concerned with the Japanese attack through the Islands to the north of Australia – particularly as the majority of our young fighting men were embroiled in Europe and Africa. A Home Guard was formed of all those physically capable of attending lectures and doing military training at the weekends. I was issued with a clean but rather battered uniform and a rifle classified as 'dangerous to fire'.

One of our first tasks was to help at a United States Marine ammunition dump. Thousands of explosive shells had to be carried from the field where they had been dumped to a new concrete platform. Our officer led us to the job, explained what had to be done and told us there was a day's work ahead of us. My eye was trained to the moving of the maximum number of sixty-pound tins of honey in the minimum of time and I couldn't see us spending the full day on such a task. Our officer disappeared to more important responsibilities and the platoon leisurely started the moving project. I carried my first shell the only way I knew how – at a half jog, as my brother and I always did when we were moving boxes or tins of honey. But one shell seemed hardly a worthwhile load. Next trip I took two and this was more satisfactory.

My older Home Guard companions looked on in astonishment but gradually the pace increased and towards the end a dozen of us were carrying two each and virtually racing against each other at a fast jog trot. By lunch time the job was done – and I can still remember the accusing glare of the officer who returned to find us ahead of schedule. What was he going to do with us all the afternoon?

For month after month I attended these parades only to find them incredibly boring and non-productive. Many of my companions were important members of the community so there was no likelihood of me being given any responsibility. Brought up as I had been to hard physical labour I found the pace of the older men too slow. The final blow came one Sunday when we carried out some war exercises. My platoon was given the task of stalking another platoon established on the summit of a high wooded hill. Somehow, we were told, we had to creep up on the defenders and surprise them.

My platoon spread out well apart and commenced the stalk. My sector contained dense brush and many rock bluffs. Full of enthusiasm I wriggled and squirmed my way upwards, making the minimum of sound, dodging every dry twig, allowing no revealing branches to sway. Three hours later – at one p.m. – I poked my head through the last cover to see the defending platoon, and my own, sitting together and resting after lunch. 'We always stop at twelve o'clock for lunch,' I was told. This was too much and I never attended another Home Guard parade. I received a number of warning notices but as I was due to enter the air force in a few months' time I ignored them.

At the beginning of 1944 I was called up by the Royal New Zealand Air Force. This was the commencement of a new life – a life which gave me a lot more leisure to do the things I wanted to do and many more opportunities for adventure. But despite my keen anticipation of the exciting days ahead I still had a nagging concern that my parents might find it difficult to keep the business going without my help. For a while at least there was nothing I could do about it.

Our initial training was carried out in a series of camps called Delta in the Wairau valley of Marlborough. For five and a half days each week our noses were kept to the grindstone but from midday Saturday to Sunday night we had a great deal of freedom. The camp food was excellent, there was much emphasis on sport, and the academic work wasn't too demanding. I came to regard it all as a glorious holiday – particularly as both sides of the valley were lined with tall mountains.

On the first free Sunday I set off for the mountains by myself, fording the Wairau river and climbing to the top of a line of foothills. The higher I got the more mountain peaks I could see and my enthusiasm to get amongst them became overwhelming. Dominating the hills to the south was the massive summit of Mount Tapuaenuku 9,465 feet – a superb sight and I determined to climb it whatever else I did.

The temperatures became very cold with the onset of winter and great was the excitement when we had a dusting of snow on the camp – most of us had never experienced snow on our homes before. I devoted every spare moment to walking and climbing on the lesser peaks surrounding the camp – but 'Tappy' never left my thoughts for long. I could see its snowy summit from the parade ground, from my sleeping hut and from the playing fields.

We were given psychological tests to determine our suitability for aircrew. My interest in mountaineering must have emerged for the young doctor carrying out the tests confessed to a similar enthusiasm. He wanted to climb 'Tappy' too – why didn't we join up? He had another officer friend who would want to go and he could undoubtedly organise transport over the eighty miles to the foot of the mountain? It sounded too good to be true . . . and so it proved to be! I made all my preparations for a three-day weekend and then received a message that the officers couldn't get leave so the transport wouldn't be available.

I decided to go by myself. One of my fellow trainees had a motorbike. He wouldn't lend it to me when I admitted I'd never ridden one before but he agreed to take me on the back as far as he could. After dinner on the Friday night I collected my heavy pack and clambered on the bike behind him. We roared off into the darkness with quite a flourish, out through the gates of the camp and onto a road slick with ice. By the time we had picked ourselves out of the ditch I realised the driver knew as little about motorbikes as I did. No major damage had been done so we pushed on. The further we went the sicker the bike became and we finally stopped with only a third of the distance covered. By this time I was happy to be on my own feet, so said goodbye and headed along the road in the dark. It was five miles before I reached the nearest sheep station and asked rather nervously if I could use a spare bunk in the shepherd's quarters for the night. The owner's wife invited me inside, fed me generously and gave me a comfortable bed – it was my first experience of generous South Island country hospitality.

I was away very early on the Saturday morning, prepared to hitch-hike up the valley. Traffic was negligible and I only managed to get two short lifts and had to walk on foot at least fifteen miles – not much fun with my heavy pack. The few people I met tried to discourage me from going on but the snow covered peaks were looking even more tremendous. At two thirty p.m., somewhat footsore, I reached the Hodder river where I had to leave the road for the mountains.

Feeling a little lonely I climbed down from the road and commenced the uneven plod up the shingle river bed. Soon I was in the depths of a gorge, fording the river through freezingly cold water, and winding backwards and forwards in the bowels of the mountain. The shadows were lengthening when I reached the Shin hut and thankfully stopped for the night.

I cooked myself a simple meal and settled down to sleep. For a while I dozed peacefully as the fire sank to a pile of embers. Then I became painfully aware that there were other living creatures in the hut. My mattress was a pile of dry grass and out of it came hordes of jumping fleas – they didn't actually bite me but they were crawling everywhere. I had resigned myself to this when I was disturbed by an unusual rustling sound. I investigated and found the hut was alive with mice, no doubt attracted by my food. I put the food away more carefully and then settled down again. I awoke a little later with the impression that some-thing strange was going on. I lay rigid for a while trying to identify the problem and soon I got the answer – a mouse was sitting between my eyebrows and tugging at a lock of my hair. I sat up with as good a squeak as any Victorian maiden.

By four a.m. I'd only had four hours' sleep but prepared a quick breakfast and was away from the hut before five o'clock. It was dark and very cold as I groped my way across the river bed and up the side of the main ridge. If I hadn't examined the ground carefully the evening before I'd have never made it. The early morning light found me al-ready high above the hut and grinding slowly up the long ridge with a heavy frost crunching under my feet. Then the sun came up and warm-ed me a little and I started appreciating the glorious morning.

I reached the snowline at 5,000 feet and plugged steadily on . . . now there was only 4,000 feet to go. At 7,000 feet heavy cloud came over the peak and it snowed quite heavily. I wondered if I should turn back. I was startled to hear what sounded like a thin human voice calling for help . . . and then realised it was the eerie wail of the native parrot, the kea. I pushed on through the clouds and was rewarded at 8,000 feet when it became clear and sunny.

There was heavy snow everywhere now and a great deal of knobbly ice. A strong cold wind had sprung up and I worked my way very slowly up to the Pinnacle at 8,800 feet. It was close on twelve o'clock so I searched out a sheltered spot and had a bite of lunch. I was in a spectacular position. To the west above heavy clouds towered a range of snowcapped peaks. I didn't know what mountains they were. To the east was the blueness of the sea stretching all the way to Wellington.

I set off again and the climbing became a lot harder. I had to make my way across the side of the Pinnacle – a tall rock tower – and I was very much aware of the steep drop on my right. I cut hundreds of steps in the icy surface, and felt isolated and a little frightened – and exhilarated too! I was glad to get off the traverse and reach the slope beyond, and then head upwards once more. It was a steep slope and all the rocks were festooned with great bulges of ice. I kicked my way upwards, sweating a bit now as I was out of the wind and the sun felt quite warm.

Halfway up I felt hot and tired so made a little shelf in the snow and sat down for a rest. Suddenly I heard a swishing sound and next moment received an appalling whack in the middle of my back. I teetered on my seat and almost fell off; then hastily clawed my way to safety again. A huge chunk of ice had come loose from a boulder and had almost wiped me off the slope.

I felt a little shaken; maybe some more would come down? I had to move but should it be up or down? I started on again and slowly made my way to the top of the slope. To my disappointment I saw that clouds were rolling up again and they looked thick and dark. I quickly took a few bearings with my compass and jotted them down in my notebook – something I'd been doing all the way up.

I crossed an easy flat section and arrived at the last big bump at the same time as the heavy cloud moved in. I was half blinded by drifting snow and from then on didn't see very much. I fumbled my way upwards for quite a distance until there was nowhere else to go and then realised I must be on top. It was rather disappointing really – it didn't feel like being on a mountain at all – but I couldn't afford to wait for the cloud to clear. Time was passing and I felt some concern about finding my way down the mountain in the mist.

I turned downwards and commenced the long descent. The slope to the saddle was slippery and unpleasant with soft snow sliding everywhere. But the traverse along the Pinnacle was much easier now I couldn't see the big drop underneath. To my relief I came out of the cloud at 7,500 feet and commenced the long trudge down the ridge. I was very tired and knew I hadn't a hope of getting down before dark and the clouds were chasing after me. It got dimmer and dimmer and finally as black as pitch and I was going slower and slower. I reached the place where I thought I should drop off the ridge but I couldn't be quite sure. Then I stumbled over a rock that I seemed to remember stumbling over in the morning. I decided to go straight down and tumbled and slid over steep snowgrass slopes hoping I wouldn't find a bluff in the dark. My guess proved right and I reached the riverbed without striking any difficulties. I staggered across to the hut feeling dead weary – I'd been going for fourteen hours – and I wasn't interested in food. I just crawled into my sleeping bag and neither the fleas nor the mice kept me awake this time.

I set off again at four a.m. – somehow I had to get back to camp that day. I shuffled down the river in the dark and felt much happier when I reached the road . . . at least now I had a chance of getting a lift if any vehicles came along. After a few miles I found good water and firewood and cooked myself a huge breakfast. There were still no vehicles so I started walking again. For six hours I tramped down the road and covered at least twenty miles and there wasn't a single vehicle going in my direction. I met two cars coming up valley and both stopped to pass the time of day and to cheerfully inform me that I'd become a common topic of local conversation and the betting had been that I'd be dead by this time – they almost seemed disappointed.

Finally my luck changed when a truck came down valley and the driver willingly offered me a lift. I knew my troubles were over when he said he was going all the way into Blenheim. He even stopped at a friendly homestead and we were given a huge meal. I reached Blenheim late in the evening dirty, unshaven and very tired. I waited for the bus to leave for camp and listened to the young airmen discussing their social conquests of the evening. But I didn't care! I'd climbed a decent mountain at last.

As was to be expected in New Zealand, rugby football was our main winter sport. My team won the Squadron championship and some of us were selected to represent our Squadron against other teams, and we won these games too. With my height of 6 ft 2 in. and weighing nearly 190 lbs I played in the forwards and usually did rather well in the lineouts. When aggravated, I found my bony elbows could be used to advantage in tight play and I think we all accepted that rugby was a pretty rough sort of a game any way.

My team carried on to win the seven-a-side championship as well and our reputation as a fit and energetic group was rapidly growing. Sufficiently so that two of us, Pax Hickson and myself, were approached by a visitor from a neighbouring camp with a rather unusual request. This large camp was holding the finals of their own rugby competition in a few days' time and the teams were very evenly matched. One of the teams had just lost two of its best members through sickness – would we come along and take their places? We were unconcerned about the ethics of such an idea and accepted the invitation.

It proved to be a torrid game and a very close struggle at first. I was able to get the ball back in the lineout with such success that the opposition concentrated their efforts on me and it became pretty lively at times. Pax Hickson scored a fine try and we ended with a resounding win. As I came off the field grinning with satisfaction I was accosted by an angry supporter of the other team who informed me in no uncertain terms that I was the roughest player he had ever seen. He was obviously planning to complete what his team had been unsuccessful in doing – putting me out of action – and I was relieved when a surge in the crowd swept us apart. In thinking over his comment I had to agree there was some truth in it . . . and it took a little of the edge off my pleasure.

In the mountains at least I could thrash around and do nobody any harm. Every weekend, wet or fine, I set out for the hills. Getting regular companions proved to be my most difficult job – few of them lasted more than one trip. It wasn't so bad when the weather was fine but often we were combatting floods and snowstorms – and nearly always the weekend of climbing concluded with a fifty-mile bicycle ride back to camp.

For quite a while I relied on solo climbing and scrambled up a number of peaks by myself. It was quite an experience to be alone in the hills, and I had a few frights too. I found that getting spreadeagled on a steep bluff without a rope wasn't so funny when you were by yourself and you felt rather nervous about fording a flooded river. But at least it was better than having a poor companion or doing no climbing at all. My luck turned when I met Jack McBurney. Jack was a Corporal Gunnery Instructor who was a keen hunter and loved the hills. Tough and strong he was having the same problem as I was – getting companions to go out regularly week after week. But once we got together that problem was solved for both of us. We climbed peak after peak – and in the process we learned quite a lot from each other. Jack was an excellent bushman and hunter and I supplied the climbing enthusiasm – we were a happy team. The last few months of the course went all too quickly. Before long we had our final exams and I was writing home:

Our examinations went reasonably well. Some of the papers were fairly tough but I managed a fair mark. I was a bit careless in some things but it cannot be helped now. Two hundred and sixty chaps sat the exam and I got a total of 936 out of 1,000 and came 14th in the course. We now know what is happening to us. I am going to New Plymouth to be trained as a navigator. This suits me very well as I am keen on navigation and my age makes me a bit old for pilot training.

Last weekend I went up to the Kaikouras with Jack McBurney. I don't think I've ever spent a harder weekend. We biked the sixty miles to Mt. Tapuaenuku on the Saturday. It was up hill all the way against a strong head wind and it nearly killed us. It took eleven hours of hard riding with packs on our backs and then an hour's tramp up to the lower hut. The next morning we were still very tired but we climbed up the ridge to Tapuaenuku and reached 8,500 ft before turning back in deep snow. We found the deep snow just a bit too much. On the Monday we rode all the way back to camp through Blenheim, a total distance of about 80 miles and mostly against a head wind. Our shoulders got very tired from our heavy packs but, funnily enough, when we came to the last long hill we quite unconsciously started racing each other to the top. It was a great adventure even if we weren't completely successful.

I was sad to leave my friends and the mountains that had given me so much pleasure but at least I knew I was going to a good mountain at New Plymouth – Mount Egmont 8,260 feet rising straight up from the sea coast. By now I found it much easier to fit in with a new group of people and our navigation class at New Plymouth was small, compact and friendly. It was quite a thrill when we commenced our practical navigation course and started flying day after day – although the thrill wore off rather quickly as we bumped around at low altitudes in the spring turbulence. I found it a good deal harder to apply my knowledge in the plane than in the class-room but gradually improved my skill and technique.

Every weekend I was back on the mountain – climbing it solo or with anyone I could persuade to come along. I usually borrowed someone's bicycle and after lunch on Saturday rode the twenty miles to the foot of the mountain, pushed my bike up to the end of the road at 3,000 feet and then trudged to the Tahurangi hut at 5,000 feet. Next morning I'd climb the mountain, then race down again and bicycle back to camp.

On one occasion I was asked to take a party of nine up the mountain and it turned into quite an interesting day. This time we drove to the

end of the road in an air force truck and then hiked up to the Tahurangi
hut in an hour's hard work. It was a showery windy cold day and pretty
miserable. Two of the boys had had enough by the time we got to the
hut and decided not to go any further. After a hot cup of tea and a bite
to eat the eight remaining of us set off again. We clambered up through
unpleasantly soft snow and it got steadily colder and ultimately became
very bitter. After an hour's climbing we struck ice and had to start
cutting steps. Two more of the party decided they wanted to turn
back so I conducted them down to the soft snow which was reasonably
safe. The last six of us roped up and set off again. We had with us an
air force doctor, Flying Officer Auld, who was an experienced mountaineer. I went at the head of the rope and chopped the steps and the
doctor came along at the end to keep an eye on the other four boys.
We had about a thousand feet to go and it was quite a laborious job
cutting steps all the way up the steep icy slope. It was so cold our
clothes and the rope were frozen stiff and became covered with icicles.
I had an icicle about five inches long hanging from the strap of my
ski-cap.

The visibility was nil due to clouds and when we finally chopped
our way onto the top we quickly turned around and came down again.
After getting off the ice we had a marvellous glissade for several
thousand feet down to the hut. Another cup of tea and we rushed down
to the truck and back to camp where a hot shower and some tea soon
put us right again. Next day the party was staggering around camp with
wind-burnt faces and stiff and bruised muscles but I was more used to
it and didn't feel any ill effects.

Christmas 1944 was approaching and I could expect a ten-days'
holiday. I was tempted to go off climbing in the Mount Cook area but
knew I should probably go home and help with the bees. My mother
was keen that I return home but my father had several men working
for him and gave no sign that he would appreciate my assistance. In the
end I went to the mountains.

I had arranged to meet another climber in Christchurch so we
could go on the trip together but I was already discovering that with
many people there was a big gap between talking about doing something and actually setting about doing it. My prospective companion
never did turn up and I heard nothing further from him. So off I
went by myself.

As the bus steadily approached the mountains my excitement grew
There was a great deal of snow around and the scenery was magnificen.
I had all sorts of plans about what I would do by myself and some ot
them were very ambitious indeed. When I stepped out of the bus at the
Hermitage and looked on the great ice-clad faces of Mount Cook and

Mount Sefton my ideas shrank rapidly down to size. I'd built up quite a lot of confidence over the previous year but now I realised how little I really knew. I'd become an energetic mountain tramper but what about crevasses and avalanches and things like that?

By morning my confidence had partially returned. There were no climbers at the Hermitage so if I wanted to go anywhere I'd have to do it by myself. With a heavy load of food I staggered up the valley to the Hooker hut and spent a few days scrambling further up the valley and visiting the Sefton bivouac on the slopes of Mount Footstool. My idea of climbing Footstool rapidly faded when I saw the crevasse fields I would have to cross. I was descending below the bivouac when I suddenly shot through the snow up to my waist and only the lucky chance of a boot catching on a rock prevented me from jamming down another eight or ten feet. I was rather shaken and a lot more careful after that.

I decided to cross to the Meuller glacier and had a delightful scramble up to the Sealy Lakes and over the ridge. I even went to the top of Mount Olivier – the peak I had climbed on my first visit to the area. There was a lot more snow around this time and the slopes seemed quite unstable as I dropped down the other side to the Meuller hut at 5,500 feet.

The hut was a bit disreputable as it had been half filled with snow during the winter but fortunately the stove worked satisfactorily. On the whole I was pretty comfortable. I had a satisfying meal and then made up my bed. Most of the blankets were damp but I found four that were dry and these plus my sleeping bag kept me warm despite the altitude. When I was making up the bed I found a huge weta (a large unpleasant looking insect) in one of the blankets – so I went through all the bedding again very carefully. The weather had been deteriorating during the day and didn't look very promising when I went to bed.

I had an excellent night's sleep but woke to find a howling gale blowing, and rain and snow coming down with great force. I was very content to stay in bed as I'd found a couple of thrillers in the hut. I got up about ten thirty and cooked myself a stew – dried soup, onions, dried peas, barley and lentils, and a tin of lamb and green peas. It was a great success and feeling quite distended I retreated back to bed. When the rain eased in the late afternoon I climbed a small peak above the hut and returned soaking wet. I had been by myself now for nearly a week and I was finding this about as much as I could stand. I decided to return back to the hotel next day.

Next morning dawned beautifully fine with clear skies and a blazing sun. I packed my gear and set off up the slopes with quite a heavy load.

I reached the summit of Mount Kitchener without much trouble and had a pleasant rest in the warm sun. Being by myself I was very much aware of the dangers of the area – as can be judged from the rather verbose letter I wrote to my family:

I descended from Kitchener with difficulty down steep rocks where I kept my mind occupied by giving forth a great speech to the elements. You should have heard the speech – it was a beauty! The more precarious the position I was in the more outstanding the flow of words! When handholds were at a minimum, feeling and emotion were at a maximum! I really surprised myself at the rapidity and ease at which I descended. If I'd allowed my mind to dwell on the prospect it would have taken me twice as long.

Once more back on the snowy slopes I trudged along to the summit pyramid of Annette (7,300 ft) and after a stiff bit of rock climbing in which I found my pack a constant drag I clambered up on top. It was now midday so I gazed around from this exalted position while I had lunch. From Annette a long and formidable ridge runs down to Sebastapol, a 4,000 ft peak right behind the Hermitage. I intended forcing a way down this ridge. However, it was still early so I left my pack at the foot of Annette and set off to try and scale Mount Seally (8,600 ft).

I had to wallow for a mile across a snowfield in which I sank up to my knees with each step and then up a steep jagged ridge. At about 8,000 feet the climbing was becoming pretty severe and as time was getting on I decided not to take any more risks but to return to Annette – which I duly reached after another long wallow through the snow.

Next I had the job of getting down onto the ridge towards the Hermitage. It was approached by an extremely steep snow slope several hundred feet in extent and broken by two great crevasses. The only way I could see to get past the crevasses was to hug the cliffs on one side. Here there was a groove about three feet wide and two feet deep made in the snow by avalanches of rock from the unstable cliffs above. I guessed that as the rocks hadn't gone through into the crevasses the covering of snow should be thick enough to stand me. So, with a silent prayer that no rocks would come down the groove while I was there I sat down and let her go!

I shot down that groove like an express train and didn't give the crevasses a chance to get nasty. I got up such speed I had great difficulty in pulling myself up but managed to do so in plenty of time to prevent myself going a few thousand feet in the wrong direction. After a long and sometimes difficult scramble down the ridge I reached its lowest point and then had an eternity of ups and downs to cross before reaching the summit of Sebastapol. From here it was a simple matter to glissade down some lovely scree slopes and I reached the Hermitage at 6 p.m.

At the end of January 1945 we completed our training at New Plymouth and sat our final examinations. I came second in the course and acquired an 'above average' in the practical aspect. The air force had stopped their normal procedure of giving the top half of the class commissions so we all remained sergeant navigators – not that it seemed to make any great difference in the free and easy atmosphere of air crew.

To complete our aerial education we were given a month's air gunner's course and blazed away thousands of rounds of ammunition at drogues towed by another aircraft. I found it difficult to display much interest and proved an indifferent performer. My greatest success was to shoot away the drogue itself – and I even managed to put a few holes through the tail of the towing plane which brought me a certain amount of criticism.

To complete our preparation we carried out a period of survival training in the Waitakere Ranges outside Auckland – my old stamping ground in fact. With fiendish glee we ambushed tired columns of sweating ground staff, established secret camps in the bush, and ranged far and wide around the countryside. The last day's programme was a cross-country jaunt – travelling over hills, rivers and forest from our starting point to the given destination – about a four-hour trip. We were broken up into small teams of half a dozen members, each with its own leader.

Our instructor was a hardy and confident corporal who was always telling us not to worry about things.

'Constantly check your route with map and compass,' he told us. 'And stick together whatever happens. Remember it is the responsibility of the group leader to see that the members of his party arrive *together* at the Cascades.' And there was no doubt that he was looking at me when he said this.

'What will we do when we get to the Cascades?' I asked.

'Don't worry about it! I'll be there before you.'

'What say you don't get there first?' I enquired politely.

'Don't worry about it! I'll be there when you arrive,' he said very firmly.

We were duly taken to our departure location and pointed in the right direction – then off we went. All my party were fit and keen and I was determined to get them there first even if it meant carrying one of them. We went across the hills like a tornado – it was terrific fun! When the corporal, hot and sweaty, jogged into the Cascades we were relaxing in the shade trying to look casual. He didn't say anything but I noticed a fleeting grin twitch his face . . .

Chapter 3

Fiji

IT WAS AN EXCITING MOMENT FOR ME WHEN OUR SUNDERLAND FLYING boat took off from Auckland Harbour bound for Fiji. This was my first trip out of New Zealand and I was all set to enjoy every moment of it. For the first hour or two we bumped our way through billowing clouds with only infrequent glimpses of the foam flecked ocean below. Then we ran out of the bad weather – out into the sunshine – and floated along between the blue sky and the bluer sea. My first sight of Fiji fulfilled all my wildest dreams. The dark green of the jungle-covered hills, the white surf rolling across the jagged reefs, and the whiter sand beyond – all seemed straight out of an adventure story.

It didn't take us long to get established in our new home at Lathala Bay. The quarters were very comfortable and the food superb. The only drawback was the heat. Most of the chaps spent their spare moments lying panting on their beds but I found far too much else to do. We were formed into crews and were kept very busy doing our conversion course onto Catalina flying boats but most weekends I managed to arrange some interesting activity. The country behind Suva was heavily covered in bush and there were some rugged looking hills, but at first I couldn't find a way to get into them. Instead I teamed up with my special friend among the other navigators, Julian Godwin, and we bought a little yacht. She was only 11 feet 6 inches long but was in excellent condition and had a full set of sails.

Every night for a week Julian and I went sailing for an hour or two in the *Gremlin* as we called her. Julian had a deep love for the sea. He was something of a 'loner' – like me – and although he hadn't been the top student academically in our navigation class, I had always felt he had the greatest natural talent in our group. He'd lived in yachts practically all his life and spent his idle moments dreaming about them and designing new models. He had no great enthusiasm for tramping and other sports but he certainly had a tremendous devotion to sailing.

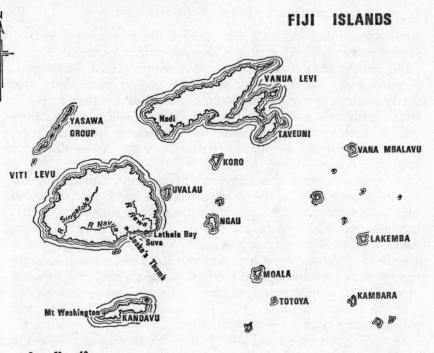

After lunch on Saturday we loaded our vessel down with plenty of provisions and set sail across the lagoon. Five miles away was the pretty little island of Nukulau and we tacked our way back and forward into a fresh headwind and a choppy sea. The clear water and the cool breeze quickly wiped away our tropical lethargy and we settled down to enjoy ourselves. Early in the evening we anchored the *Gremlin* in a sheltered cove underneath the coconut palms and strolled ashore.

The island was only about ten acres in extent and we soon explored it and found the only inhabitant. He was an old Hindu who very decently said we could sleep in a little two-roomed building on the shore of the island facing out to sea. It was a delightful place and the sea breeze kept it cool and fresh. We didn't have any beds but we heaped armfuls of dry springy grass on the floor and put a canvas cover over that. There was plenty of driftwood around and we grilled some chops over an open fire and then washed it all down with a tin of peaches. After a stroll on the sand in the moonlight, we thankfully sank onto our grassy couches and didn't stir until morning.

The following day we were up early for a refreshing dip in the sea and a substantial breakfast. Then we sailed up the coast towards another island some distance away. It was quite rough and the *Gremlin* bounced all over the place and shipped quite a lot of water. I bailed out furiously while Julian calmly and expertly handled the tiller with a look of great contentment on his face. When we entered a channel that led through the reef to the open sea we wallowed up and down on the great ocean billows, but at least we stopped taking in water. We were nearly swamped getting ashore on the island and dried ourselves out with a brisk walk around the shoreline. We saw no sign of habitation and knocked down a few coconuts for a refreshing drink. The wind was behind us on the way back to base and we planed over the waves in great style.

In this fashion we filled in many pleasant days and explored a number of islands along the coast. We made another weekend visit to Nukulau Island but were rather disappointed when the old Hindu told us that the house we had used before was already occupied by an Indian school teacher. We started preparing a bivvy out in the open but after a while the caretaker came and said the school teacher was only using one room and would be pleased to have us use the other. The teacher proved to be a most impressive looking man, about forty years old with very expressive eyes and a short curly beard. His name was Muhammad Abdullah and he was a Moslem.

During the evening I had a long talk with Muhammad about the problems in India and he expressed his belief that the conflict between the Hindus and Moslems was less a matter of religion than of economic difference. The Hindus were generally better off, had most of the Government positions, and controlled more of the financial life of the country. The Moslems on the other hand were fairly poor and had a low standard of living. Muhammad believed that if the great undeveloped resources of India were brought into development and applied to the economic improvement of its poorer peoples then many of the problems would disappear.

When Muhammad started talking about religions in general I was greatly impressed by the breadth of his knowledge. He certainly knew far more about Christianity than I did and he could quote freely from the Bible to illustrate his points. He referred to the one God of all – of Hindu, Moslem and Christian – and said that all these religions were only different ways of approach. I went off to bed feeling incredibly narrow minded and insular. Before Muhammad went to bed he washed his hands, face and feet and then performed his prayers. About five o'clock in the morning he came out of his room (I happened to be awake) washed again and went back to his prayers. He started singing very musically and after a while I drifted off to sleep. When I awoke he had gone.

The Catalina was a fine aircraft rugged and dependable with a tremendous range, but it was very slow. Frequently we were averaging only a hundred and ten miles per hour and with a strong head-wind it could be much less than this. Accurate navigation was very important as a beam wind could blow the aircraft far off course on a long flight. I thoroughly enjoyed the responsibility of being navigator on these long ocean trips and was pleased to find that my training at navigation school worked out very well in practice.

The trips I enjoyed most were the long night flights when we had to rely almost exclusively on astronomical navigation. On one eleven-hour flight we crossed 600 miles of empty ocean to three small islands near New Caledonia. We cruised at 9,000 feet and it was quite cool but very calm. The sea was completely blanketed out by tumbled layers of cumulus cloud sharply outlined in the bright moonlight. I spent a good deal of my time shooting the stars with my sextant and plotting fix after fix. The air was so still that it was difficult to believe that we were moving at all and it was a simple task to make accurate astronomical observations. We came in over our first landfall with impressive accuracy – impressive to me, anyway.

We turned onto a new course and flew along a chain of islands, completely clear of cloud and shimmering in a moonlit sea. One of the islands was an active volcano and the crater was like a great glowing cigarette end with every now and then sparks flying up as red hot boulders were hurled in the air. I found it strange as we flew along in the cool still air to accept that on the little islands lying dark and quiet beneath us people were sleeping and dreaming. We seemed almost unlimited by time or space while these people spent their whole lives on tiny specks of dust surrounded by hundreds of miles of ocean. No doubt my existence in New Zealand looked just as restricted to an inhabitant of New York.

We were sometimes required to carry out mercy trips. On the island of Ono-i-lau, about 220 miles from our base, a Fijian had been very ill for several weeks and the authorities had radioed Suva and asked for a plane to take the man to hospital. We flew to Ono-i-lau and landed in the large central lagoon and immediately a boat shot out to meet us – followed by a whole succession of them. The outrigger canoes made a great sight as they raced towards us with their big triangular sails drawing well in the stiff breeze. They came alongside our aircraft very expertly and most of my crew and an air force doctor jumped aboard.

It was my turn to stay and look after the aircraft so when a cheerful looking Fijian boy asked if he could wait on the plane with me I nodded my assent. While the boats were dashing madly for the shore I became better acquainted with my companion. He told me that he was fourteen years old and that he had been to school in Suva and he certainly spoke English quite well in a rather broken fashion. I showed him over the Catalina to his great interest and delight. When he saw some white bread he said quite calmly, 'Me like piece of white bread – it good taste', and he rubbed his stomach at the same time. I could hardly refuse his request and prepared a great slice of bread and butter for him. He told me he wanted to go back to Suva and get a job with white men so that he could earn some money. 'Me very poor boy,' he told me, so I said, 'in New Zealand me very poor boy too,' but somehow my statement lacked conviction. Any money he could get, he explained, was being saved for the passage back to Suva on the rare boat that visited this island. I suppose the fare for a 220-mile trip was a pretty big sum to him.

When we saw the boats returning to the plane he made his last plea. He was clad in a very disreputable pair of khaki shorts so he pointed at them and said, 'You fine man! Me love you very much! You give me money to buy new pair of pants so I can go to Suva?' He said it all with a huge grin and although I was embarrassed at his request I was sufficiently impressed to fumble around in my pocket for any loose change. To my consternation I discovered I didn't have any money at all – there wasn't much need for it when we were flying – but when I told the boy, I could see he thought I was lying. I was mighty relieved when the boats returned and the sick man was loaded aboard.

We flew back into a glorious sunset but I was feeling quite depressed. As I relaxed in the mess after a substantial dinner and clad in fresh clean clothes my thoughts kept returning to the boy at Ono-i-lau who had said, 'Me very poor boy'.

Things were going so well with my navigation that I was building up quite a lot of confidence – until the day we had a low level exercise. For six hours we had to fly a few hundred feet above the sea following a series of complicated search patterns. We took off from Lathala Bay in a choppy sea and strong wind and flew under a heavy layer of low cloud. The start of our search was the prominent headland on the island of Kandavu, a hundred miles or so to the south of Suva. As we flew towards it we were buffetted unmercifully by severe turbulence. I had felt a little queasy on other trips but had never been airsick so didn't take these rough conditions too seriously.

We set course from the great cliffs of Kandavu and as we bumped along I concentrated hard over my navigation table working out the great variety of course changes necessary. The crew had become very quiet and there wasn't the usual cheerful chatter over the intercom – and I noticed a couple of crew were stretched out on the bunks looking rather pale.

For two hours we jostled along only 200 feet above the waves and half the crew were airsick. I was too busy to think about such matters until I suddenly noticed the map was getting a little hazy and I felt a cold sweat breaking out on my face. I had a strong feeling of nausea and realised with horror that I too was being affected by the motion. My first reaction was shame – I still had my boyhood belief that any sort of sickness was a deplorable weakness – and I determined to stick it out and not let anyone know how I felt.

Backwards and forwards we turned on each new leg of the search and I grimly hung on. I handed up the last course which would bring us back forty miles to the north of our starting place on Kandavu and then slumped forward onto the table. I had twenty minutes before the Captain would need a new course to start the next search pattern to the north. For fifteen of the minutes I lay there fighting the desire to vomit and then I became conscious of the Captain's voice speaking to me over the intercom.

'Kandavu ahead.'

Kandavu ahead? What had gone wrong? We shouldn't be anywhere near Kandavu. I staggered up to the pilot's cabin and peered out over the white capped waves to the dimly seen headland looming up through the low clouds. My God! It did look like Kandavu. Too ashamed to say anything to the Captain and suspecting that he didn't realise that we weren't meant to be off Kandavu, I groped my way back to my table and desperately started to re-work my courses.

The next few hours were grim ones for me. Racked by airsickness, tormented by doubts, and just generally miserable I made no attempt to discuss the matter with the Captain – or even to get an accurate radio bearing. At last it was time to turn for home and I thankfully handed up a course and an expected time of arrival – and collapsed over my table again.

Fifty minutes later a puzzled Captain called me up. 'No sign of land yet, Ed. I think we'd better have a radio bearing!' His concern was understandable as according to my advice he should have been landing at base by now. The radio bearing was unbelievable – we were to the north of Fiji still a hundred miles from base. Another bearing confirmed this and a somewhat irate Captain swung the aircraft south. It was a relief when familiar headlands rose up out of the sea and we were able to steer confidently for home. As we slapped down in the choppy bay I reached depths of misery that I had never experienced before.

What had gone wrong? Next morning the senior navigation instructor and I went through my flight records and replotted it all. The answer was quite simple. Those fateful words 'Kandavu ahead', had started me going. Of course it wasn't Kandavu at all – it was an island forty miles to the north and we were just where we should have been. But for me it had become Kandavu. This forty-mile error accumulated during the course of the day and with no astronomical checks possible due to the weather, and radio bearings unreliable due to our low altitude I had ultimately put us a hundred miles off course.

In the following weeks this experience gave me a few nightmares in which Kandavu figured prominently but it taught me a good lesson and I made certain there wasn't a repetition of such foolish errors. Strangely enough I never suffered airsickness so badly again even in the most turbulent weather and when we joined our squadron for operational duty I came to rather pride myself on my navigational skill. From then on I succeeded in guiding our plane around the Pacific without, I believe, too much further worrying by the crew. This navigational experience certainly stood me in good stead twelve years later when I used it to plot our way over the flat snowy wastes of the Antarctic plateau to the South Pole. Some day I'd like to go back to Kandavu and see that great headland again.

The most prominent peak around the Suva area was a large pinnacle of rock shaped like a giant thumb – and indeed 'Joske's Thumb' was its name – (strangely enough this mountain had been named after a relation of my future mother-in-law). It had only been climbed a couple of times and I discovered there was an officer in camp who had taken part in the last ascent. My interview with him wasn't exactly a cheerful affair. He pointed out the difficulties and dangers of the climb in no uncertain fashion and, although he didn't say so, he left me with the very strong impression that I would only get into trouble if I attempted it. However I still intended to go so he finally unbent enough to scribble out a rough sketch map giving the direction from which to approach the peak.

I needed a companion and some means of getting to the Namburu River which was twelve miles from Suva. I went to work on Julian Godwin and he finally agreed to come as long as we sailed the first part in the Gremlin. After lunch on Saturday we loaded our boat with provisions, added a couple of blankets and a mosquito net, and then set sail along the coast.

There was a pleasant breeze blowing and we crossed Suva Harbour without difficulty. We then entered an extensive area of coral reefs and as the tide was very low we had to follow any deep channels we could find and make frequent changes of course. Several times the centre-board bashed violently against up-jutting lumps of coral and it seemed a wonder to me that the Gremlin wasn't split wide open. It was five o'clock before we arrived off the Namburu River. When we entered the broad mouth of the river the wind dropped right away and we found it difficult to make any progress at all. By the time we'd covered half a mile darkness was approaching and we knew we'd have to camp. We could see no sign of habitation in any direction – only extensive swamps stretching away on either bank.

We pulled into the shore and started constructing a little bivvy. On the swampy ground we laid down a heavy layer of leaves and then covered this with eighteen inches of springy fern. The jib laid on this made our floor and a couple of blankets completed the bed. At each end of the bivvy we pushed sturdy uprights into the mud and spanned them with a strong ridge-pole. We hung our mosquito net from the ridge-pole and draped the mainsail over the lot to give us some protection from the rain.

We were ravenously hungry by now. It was pitch dark but I soon collected some dry wood and started a roaring fire. Before long we were munching hot pork and beans on toast and following it with the usual tin of peaches. It was a good repast and I felt thoroughly contented as we crawled into our bed and pulled the mosquito net carefully into place around us. We lay listening to all the multitude of night noises in the swamp – the quiet twittering of a bird; the creak of the rushes as something pushed through them; and then a tiny splash as an insect dropped into the water. Dominating everything was a steady and growing hum. At first I didn't realise what it was so grabbed my torch and switched on the light. It shone on a solid wall of blood-hungry mosquitoes searching for the slightest gap in our netting. They must have come from all over the swamp to be in at the kill. For a while we lay uneasily waiting for the insects to penetrate but our net was a good one and as nothing happened we became accustomed to the angry hum and drifted off to sleep.

The first light of morning woke us from a deep sleep. We had a quick breakfast from a tin of grapefruit and some toast and jam and then repacked the boat. I knew we didn't have time to really get to grips with Joske's Thumb – we had to sail our boat back to base by dark – but at least we could do a worthwhile reconnaissance. We carefully perused our scribbled map and then got under way.

For hours we tramped up hills and over valleys; pushed through dense bush; scrambled up steep rock faces; wallowed across swamps up to our thighs, and waded up rocky streams. At mid-day we emerged on top of a 1000 ft. hill after five hours of extremely tough going. At no stage had the route we were taking seemed to correspond with our map but now the whole countryside was spread out beneath us and we could identify our position. A couple of miles away was the river we should have followed – our precious map was a dud. We could see Joske's Thumb not too far away now and looking immensely impressive from this angle.

But time was getting short. With our new knowledge of the country we took a faster route and panted our way back to the *Gremlin* by two thirty p.m. We heaved everything on board and pushed out into the stream. The leisurely current carried us down to the mouth and out into the lagoon but the wind was coming from straight ahead and we had twelve miles to go.

We tacked backwards and forwards seeming to make little progress. A meal of cold tinned meat and another tin of fruit helped my morale, but when darkness came my spirits were at a low ebb.

We had now broken through the reef but were still a couple of hours from home. To make matters worse a strong wind had come up and the sea was decidedly choppy. We started shipping quite a lot of water and I had to bail furiously. Julian was magnificently calm but I was thoroughly jittery. It was an enormous relief to see the lights of Lathala Bay and when I finally stepped into the water to drag the boat ashore it was with some firmness I informed Julian I didn't plan any more such experiences. However we did a great deal more sailing together and I always enjoyed his company and admired his skill. After the war I spent a day with Julian sailing in his yacht on the Auckland Harbour and I have no doubt that wherever he is now, the sea and boats will not be far away.

I didn't get another opportunity to examine Joske's Thumb until much later in the course – in fact just before we flew off to join our squadron in the Solomons. I had managed to interest two other members of my crew in the project – Ron Ward and Trace Moresby, both very active and energetic people. It was to be a one day affair and I was thoroughly disgusted when I dived out of bed at six o'clock to find the rain streaming down. This made our chances negligible but as it was our only opportunity I thought we had better go anyway. I aroused the others and we had some breakfast and cut some sandwiches for our lunch. At seven o'clock our new form of transport drew up outside – the milk truck. We scrambled on the back amongst the milk cans and after a hectic forty-minute trip were deposited at the Namburu River. The truck disappeared in a cloud of water and mud.

I knew the track for the first few miles as I had come back over it with Julian. We plunged off the road and the first stretch was through a particularly loathsome swampy piece of bush. The mud was black and sticky, ankle deep all the way and knee deep in places. The air was heavy and musty with a strong odour of decay. On either side of the track were deep, slimy looking pools. It was altogether a very unpleasant little stretch and not a good start for the day. We were greatly relieved when we finally climbed up a narrow clay gully and emerged on a small wooded ridge. But not for long. Down we went again into the next stretch of swamp. But this wasn't quite so bad; much like the ordinary New Zealand swamp but with a lot of trees. Due to the heavy rain the track was under water in places and we were wallowing up to our knees. Finally, after an hour or so, we came out on the Naikoro-koro River.

Here an unpleasant surprise awaited us. When Julian and I had visited this river it could be crossed in many places without the water going much above the knees but now it was a brown and turgid flood. We'd have to swim. We were so wet that it was almost a waste of time to remove our clothes but we did it anyway and tied them in a bundle on top of our heads. Then we waded across with the water coming up to our necks. We only made a few hundred yards up the other side before we were forced to ford the river again. This was the pattern over the next few hours and we made frequent crossings and in many cases had to swim to safety. The current was now becoming so vigorous that we were frequently buffetted off our feet.

A couple of hours up the Naikorokoro we struck the tributary river we were looking for and headed off to the right. The hills and jungle were blanketed in rain and we had seen nothing of Joske's Thumb and didn't have much idea of its true direction. We scrambled up the rocky side stream slipping on the greasy boulders and wading through deep pools. Then the stream branched again.

We decided to gamble on the ridge between the two streams and hope for the best. The bush was very dense, and forced us to hack a rough path with a slasher. The ground underfoot was slippery and treacherous and the three inches of slush that lay on top slithered away at every step. But we kept driving up the ridge and after a time came to the foot of some great bluffs – fifty feet high and streaming with water. For the first time we felt a little encouraged for the Thumb is all rock and it looked as though we might be getting close. We sidled around the bluffs on the left-hand side and continued up the ridge. It was getting much narrower now, and steeper, and in places dropped off in great precipices.

We were halted by a great rock face over a hundred feet high. The only route seemed to be out to the right and we made our precarious way up the slippery wet rocks of a long narrow crack. We wriggled to the top and then carried on up a very narrow and steep ridge to come face to face with the last stupendous rock pinnacle of the Thumb. Our hearts sank! The rock face above us was an enormous overhang and looked quite unclimbable. We had come up the wrong side – underneath the ball of the Thumb.

Fifty feet above us and a hundred feet from the top of the peak was a ledge about three feet wide which disappeared around the corner out of sight. There was a chance it might take us onto an easier face of the peak but it was very exposed. The only ropes we had with us were pieces of strong clothes line but we roped up onto one of these. With a great deal of struggling and scratching around we managed to ease our way up onto the ledge. And there we sat – for the first time in the day protected from the rain by the great rock bulge above. Anxious to see what happened to the ledge around the corner I carefully worked my way along to the end and then poked my head around. Phew!

The ledge fell away sheer for three or four hundred feet. Several hundred yards away across an impossible gulley another ridge abutted onto the Thumb and this was at a much more modest angle. It was in fact, as we found later, the route that had been used by the successful parties.

I wriggled around on the ledge and looked up towards the summit. Above me was a narrow crack in the face that looked as though it might lead somewhere. I jammed myself into it and managed to climb about thirty feet until I was stopped by a verticle section. A bit further on the climbing didn't seem too bad but now I was out in the rain and the crack was streaming with water. Bitterly disappointed at being rebuffed I was much too conscious of the four hundred foot drop below me to take any more risks – and I hadn't much confidence in our length of clothes line. It didn't need the urgent cries from my companions to persuade me to turn back. I cautiously lowered myself back down the slippery holds and onto the ledge. The Thumb had beaten us again.

A few hundred feet down we found a cave that was reasonably dry. The temperature was warm and humid so we stripped off our dripping clothes and ate our soggy sandwiches. A couple of tins of fruit (my favourite diet), followed in quick succession and then we were ready for the descent. On the way up the river we had seen some very large bamboo poles four to five inches in diameter lying in the bush. They appeared ideal material for a raft and that's how we planned to use them.

With our hunger appeased we quickly dressed and then glissaded down the ridge, wriggled down the bluffs, and hurtled down the creek to the main river. It was in full flood and the current was tossing branches and tree trunks around in every direction. We set to work to manufacture our rafts. We had two pieces of rope with us – a long piece and a short one. Trace and I decided to make one big raft while Ron used the shorter rope to make a smaller raft for himself. In half an hour we were ready. The big raft had two layers of bamboo poles all lashed together and measuring about ten feet by four feet. We tied our clothes high up on our shoulders, grasped a long pole each and leapt aboard.

The current gripped us and whipped us away. Shrieking with delight we surged towards the first corner. Within a hundred yards Ron struck a fierce eddy which tossed his raft over. He disappeared under the muddy brown water and then he and his raft were swept into the bank. But we sailed on. The weight of the two of us on the raft forced it deep into the water and most of the time I was sitting with the water over my hips. Every few hundred yards we'd strike another rapid in the river and we'd go tearing down these at a fearful pace, trying to guide ourselves frantically with our poles, but as often as not striking a stump or hidden root and being tipped out into the flood. Soon we were wet again from head to feet and even our packs had water sloshing around inside them – but we didn't care.

For two hours we sailed down the river, our rafts slowly disintegrating underneath us from the constant collision with stumps and tree trunks. We hit a particularly steep rapid with a sharp turn at the bottom and started hurtling down this at an alarming pace. Despite our frantic poling we were unable to make the corner and crashed with a fearful wallop into a large dead tree trunk. The raft could stand no more and it collapsed beneath us. Now our frolic took a much more serious turn.

Trace and I found we were being forced by the fierce current hard against the log and we were getting tangled up in the branches. For a moment or two we had a desperate struggle to stop being dragged under the log by the current but finally managed to force our way to the side and climb out of the river. Ron soon joined us – his raft had come to pieces a little further up.

Caked in mud from head to foot we arrived back in camp well after dark. As we luxuriated under hot showers we agreed it had been one of the wettest but most enjoyable days we had spent. Some time in the future, I assured myself, I'd return to Fiji and complete the climb of Joske's Thumb.

Chapter 4

The Solomon Islands

ON COMPLETION OF OUR OPERATIONAL TRAINING IN FIJI WE WERE posted to the Solomon Islands to commence routine Search and Rescue duties. Our first hop was to the New Hebrides and after a comfortable night there we were away again from Santos at six a.m. and climbed rapidly to 8,000 feet. The cloud formed a great unbroken sheet below us and on our left were some massive mountains reaching towards our height. In the dim light they looked like grim black islands in a white sea. Then we saw a spectacular tropical dawn. The rim of the sun pushed above the horizon and the clouds gleamed like burnished silver while the volcanic peaks were tipped with gold. With the abruptness of the tropics it was full daylight with the blue sky above and the blue sea below and we really felt we were now in the action zone, although the war had largely moved to the north of the group.

Our Captain was determined to make a good impression with his first landing to join our new Squadron at Florida Island. Down we came like a bird to gently tip the waves outside the reef, and then softly squelch into the sea. The base was still a mile away across the water and we taxied energetically towards it. I had moved to the back of the aircraft and was idly watching the water rush by and already starting to sweat in the hot sticky humidity. Suddenly the colour of the water changed to a lighter blue and next moment there was a rending crash on the hull beneath and we came to a shuddering halt – we were aground on the reef.

The intercom started crackling with reports from the flight engineers that we'd been holed in the bow, not too badly but water was coming in freely and then yells from the Captain for a couple of men overboard to push us off the reef! Ron and I, clothes and all, were soon in the water. The aircraft had only just caught the edge of the reef and we were easily able to push it back into deeper water. 'All aboard,'

SOLOMON ISLANDS

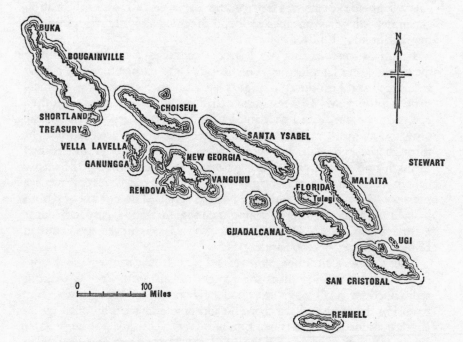

yelled the Captain and gunned the motors. As the plane rose up through the water onto the planing step the gaping hole was lifted clear of the sea. We approached the ramp at great speed and when it seemed we must surely run ashore the Captain cut the motors and the plane sank back into the water. The sea started gurgling in again but quick action by all concerned had us safely hauled to dry land before our craft could sink beneath us. So much for our impressive arrival on station!

We quickly settled down into the camp routine. The station at Halavo was in a wide and colourful bay protected by reefs and small islands. Spread out amongst the trees were a number of large huts and half a dozen Catalinas were pulled up on the shore. It looked very pleasant and peaceful. Life wasn't too bad, either, for the accommodation was simple but comfortable enough and the food palatable most of the time. Our clothing was minimal – a pair of shorts and sandals and we rapidly developed magnificent tans. At night it was compulsory to wear long-sleeved shirts and slacks to combat the malarial mosquito. Swimming was the main sport and with the water always over eighty degrees fahrenheit you could stay in as long as you liked and never get cold. The climate was hot and enervating, I suppose, but in many ways it was the sort of life that tourists pay large sums to enjoy. But enjoyment was far from the thoughts of most of the station personnel – they lay on their beds and dreamed about home. I found it the best holiday I'd ever had.

The giant trees shading our barracks contained a multitude of birds including some fat pigeons. This inspired me to manufacture a bow and arrow and I produced a mighty weapon after several days of energetic whittling. My first test was carried out inside our hut – I set up a target on the flimsy end wall and let fly. With the deep 'twang' of the bow the arrow shot through the target and disappeared from sight through the end wall. In consternation I chased after it and rushed through two more huts milling with people before finding the arrow deeply embedded in an upright pole. How it missed everyone is a mystery – and why I should have been so careless I do not know – but I have noticed that a group of young men together find it easy to become a little irresponsible. Despite great efforts I was never successful in bringing down a pigeon for the pot.

There were a number of private boats at the station and before long we were making plans for a yacht of our own. Ron Ward, our radio operator, a tall tough independent character had brought with him from Fiji the mast and sail from his old boat and we'd all been rather abusive about it at the time. But now we were quick to appreciate Ron's foresight. Someone discovered the framework of a fourteen-foot boat awaiting completion. It didn't seem to belong to anyone so we took it over. We decided not to waste time in sheathing it in wood but to use canvas instead. Every spare hour between patrols was spent on the yacht and it was a great moment when the last coat of paint dried and we were able to launch the craft. In light winds she moved slowly but steadily and was beamy and stable. We went for a trial sail out to sea in a stiff breeze and we fairly flew along with three men on board.

Ron and I recognised that we had a lot in common – we were both robust and restless – and at the first opportunity we went off together on a full day's trip in the yacht. We loaded aboard plenty of food and water and sailed off into a vigorous breeze. Our objective was a small island about six miles away and we had to do a lot of tacking to make any progress. It was a glorious day with the sun blazing down and only the breeze making it bearable, and despite our tanned skins we could feel the sun cooking our bare backs. After a three-hour sail we came to the island and pulled on to a glittering white beach.

This was the loveliest island I had yet seen. The palm fringed shore, the white sands, the surrounding sea, blue beyond belief, made the perfect story book South Sea Island. We rested on the cool green grass under coconut trees and drank refreshing coconut milk. The island appeared deserted but there were signs of earlier habitation; crumbling brick walls, paths nearly overgrown by the voracious jungle, and a large spacious garden long gone to weeds. We could only surmise that this idyllic spot had been a victim of the Pacific war.

The island rose in the centre to a bush clad peak 500 feet high. Despite the gruelling heat Ron and I scrambled to the top, bathed in sweat. The view in every direction was superb. The coral reefs below us were coloured in every imaginable shade of green, blue, pink and purple. We rested in the shade of a tree and agreed that this island was just about the ideal place for a couple of beachcombers like ourselves. The heat produced extreme lethargy but as the afternoon progressed we dragged ourselves back through the jungle to the boat and set sail for home. We had a following wind and drifted effortlessly along with palm trees, headlands and coral reefs slipping by. We reached camp as the sun was setting, drugged with the sun and all that we had seen. Night came like turning off a light, and the fireflies glowed and pulsated amongst the trees. We had only the strength left to collapse on our beds and lie sweating under our mosquito nets.

After a few weeks we developed quite a craving for fresh food and Ron and I turned our attention to subsidising our diet. One evening I went for a paddle in my light canoe and trailed a line and spinner along the reef. I almost fell out of the canoe when there was a sudden and almighty bite and I found it necessary to drop the paddle and grab the line. After quite a struggle I landed an eight-pound trevalli. We cooked it for supper and found it quite delicious.

There were many good fish to be caught in these waters and we used most methods to get them. We even tried taking a rifle along the beaches and looking for the mullet that frequently swam just off shore. A well placed shot in the midst of a school could stun a fish or two and then we'd rush into the sea and scoop them out. This particular sport officially came to an end one memorable evening when the camp Commander was taking a peaceful stroll. A ricocheting bullet snapped a twig a few inches above his head and a new regulation was posted prohibiting the use of rifles for this purpose – a prohibition we observed only when in sight or sound of camp.

Despite such activities, filling in the long hot days and sweaty evenings wasn't always easy. I tried rather ineffectively to study a book on geology and did a lot of reading – light novels mostly, but some non-fiction as well. I enjoyed Mawson's *Home of the Blizzard* and Admiral Byrd's *Alone* but perhaps my most treasured books were *Camp Six* by Frank Smythe and one on the Himalayas by James Ramsey Ullman which included excerpts from the writings of many famous mountaineers. I'd found this book in the air force library in

Fiji and without too many qualms carried it on with me to the Solomons. I had received a bundle of New Zealand Alpine Journals and I read these from cover to cover – and then read them again. My letters home at this time reflected my reading. 'I wouldn't mind a trip to the Antarctic' I told my family 'although I'd much prefer going to the Himalayas.' In describing our various activities to my sister I jocularly mentioned that some day I planned to write a book and call it 'Battle against Boredom'. . . .

Every second day we had some sort of a flying task – a patrol, a search, or a mercy trip. On one occasion we flew to the mission station at Ugi to unload medical supplies and pick up the Bishop of Melanesia. As soon as we touched the water some canoes shot out to meet us and in the biggest one was the Bishop himself – a tall impressive Englishman. At his determined invitation we all went ashore and walked the mile or so to the Mission Hospital. We had lunch with the staff and an excellent meal it proved to be.

The hospital was mostly for maternity purposes and we were told that the death rate amongst children under one year in the Solomons was 400 in every 1,000. The senior nurse, Miss Field was a remarkable person. As the nearest doctor was thousands of miles away she frequently had to perform major operations. On one occasion she amputated a gangrenous leg and on another she removed a tumour from a native's abdomen, in both cases saving their lives. We were most impressed with Miss Field's kindness and courage.

There was a high school at Ugi which drew its students from other missions in the islands round about. There were 120 pupils from fifteen to eighteen years old and I was astounded and impressed by them. I recorded at the time:

> Generally speaking the natives I have seen in the Solomons are a pretty miserable looking lot but at the mission school the boys seem to have thrown off this dull uninteresting appearance and are a very bright, intelligent and cheery group.

We were invited to play a game of cricket against the school team and to our astonishment were thoroughly beaten.

As we flew back to Halavo I had a long talk with the Bishop and enjoyed his practical comments and good sense. He clearly regarded his charges as human beings and remembering how well they had played cricket I thought he was probably right. This visit impressed me quite a lot and I admired the missionaries and the nurses for their unselfish efforts in education and health, although I found it more difficult to be enthusiastic about the religious aspect.

Much of our routine flying was necessary and useful but we also experienced frustrating searches and non-existent emergencies. On one occasion we were called out to search for an American Catalina that had crashed on Rennell Island about 150 miles away. The survivors were apparently signalling from the ground and we were even given the registration number of the Catalina.

We rushed to Rennell and commenced our search. Every village signalled us with some sort of mirror and the island was a blaze of lights. We flew around for several hours and could find nothing. We landed beside a native village near the reported area but they knew nothing of any crashed aircraft. Finally the Americans sent out the DC3 that had originally reported the disaster to lead us to the spot, and it took us to the wreck of an old plane that had been under water for years – we had just ignored it as a familiar part of the scenery. The missing Catalina had been parked the whole time beside the airfield on Guadalcanal.

We arrived back in Halavo after dark, tired and hungry. We scrambled into a jeep – four in front and two of us in the back and set off to our eating quarters on top of the hill. The parking area was on the edge of a steep sixty-foot drop which went down almost sheer. Phil Warnes swung the jeep around with a rush and jammed on the brakes. Nothing happened – someone's foot was underneath the brake pedal. For one horrible moment we teetered on the edge and then slowly toppled over. Phil baled out to one side and Ron Ward out the other. But the remaining four of us were wedged in and couldn't move. We went crashing down the precipitous drop at a terrific pace just missing a big tree. My only thought was, 'Well you've had it this time for sure!' We were thrown about the jeep but amazingly it didn't turn over. Next thing we knew we crashed into a pile of logs at the bottom and came to a halt with a terrific thud.

A dozen airmen had been looking on in horror and they rushed over to pick up the battered remains. But we stepped out safe and sound apart from a few bruises, although none of us did justice to dinner that night. When I examined the spot in daylight it was unbelievable that some of us hadn't been seriously hurt or killed.

To improve the performance of our fourteen-foot yacht we installed a two and a half horsepower engine and a propeller. Our auxiliary yacht delighted us with its performance and we estimated that in calm conditions we could do six knots with two of us on board. This modification enabled Ron and me to carry out a project we had planned for some time – to go crocodile hunting. Crocodiles were a rarity around our base although there were still plenty of them in the less visited areas of the Solomons. At one mission station they had told us about shooting a sixteen-foot monster that had consumed a number of the local inhabitants.

We made all the necessary preparations for our hunting trip – two rifles and ammunition, a big harpoon, and a canoe towed along behind. For hours we chugged up muddy inlets, eased our way around corners, always hoping for a crocodile. To our great excitement we saw one slither into the water as we entered a small bay but by the time we grabbed our rifles it was too late.

Half a mile further on we pushed our nose into another bay and searched the area carefully – there was nothing to see. On the far side was a little inlet, obviously very shallow and half filled with weed. We examined it rather hopelessly and noticed a half submerged log in the middle. Then Ron and I realised it wasn't a log – it was a crocodile. Slowly we brought our rifles to our shoulders and fired. There was a terrific splash and the writhing form of a crocodile appeared on the surface, its contortions getting slower and slower until it finally subsided into the water and disappeared.

Elated with our success (each of course claiming the hit), we debated how best to collect the crocodile. We didn't want to risk the canvas walls of our big boat in the shallow water – there might be other crocs around and we were a long way from home. We decided on a better solution. I transferred to the canoe with a rifle and paddle. Ron tied the rope onto the harpoon and then gave it to me. I paddled cautiously into the inlet – decidedly apprehensive about meeting an infuriated crocodile face to face. There was nothing to be seen so I started prodding around with the harpoon. Next moment I felt something on the bottom – but what? Taking a firm grip on the harpoon I speared fiercely downwards – there was a violent thrashing as I backed hurriedly out of danger and Ron pulled in the rope and brought the dying crocodile to the back of the boat.

Our return to Halavo with the crocodile was something of a triumph. We strung the creature up on the mast – all eight feet of it – and admired its powerful jaws. Out came Ron's camera and appropriate shots were taken ... and then virtually everyone on station came down to the boat and had their photos taken with the crocodile too.

Over the next month we became more and more daring in our attempts to shoot another crocodile, but although we fired at a number of them and scored a few hits we never did succeed in bringing any more back to base. It became clear that most of the crocs were hiding in the mangrove swamps where our big boat couldn't go. Ron and I took to penetrating the mangrove streams in our canoes with a paddle in hand and a rifle across our knees. It was an eerie business making our way down the long mangrove tunnels with their smell of salt and decay. I came around one corner to look straight into the eyes of a crocodile resting on a large root. I picked up the rifle and fired but in the same moment the crocodile dropped off the root and disappeared into the water. I waited breathlessly, with rifle ready – where would he reappear? But he never did and as I saw no blood on the water I concluded I had missed him.

Our final search for crocodiles caused us quite a few problems. We motored to an inlet some distance from base, armed with a rifle and my .38 service revolver. We were crossing the inlet when we saw a crocodile some distance away – certainly too far for a shot. I put my revolver down on the stern of the boat and leaned forward to close the engine throttle. When I sat up again the revolver had gone.

This was a major calamity, as the RNZAF had very strict regulations about weapons. We quickly identified our position – it appeared as though the gun must have dropped on the edge of a muddy reef. While one of us stood on constant guard with the rifle against possible crocodiles Ron and I took turns at diving overboard and fumbling around the bottom in the murk. It was rather deep and we couldn't stay down for long so in the end had to give up the search.

We returned to base to make other plans. We remembered that the marine section had a diving helmet and air pump and felt this would make all the difference. The sergeant in charge of the marine section proved very co-operative. For half a day Ron and I practised with the helmet off the wharf – one of us walking under water while the other pumped. It was great fun to wander around on the sandy bottom in clear water trying to spear fish – as long as nothing distracted the attention of the pumper up top.

We were now ready for our major search. We recruited a third member and then headed back to the inlet. We anchored over the spot and while one of us stood on guard, another pumped air and the third went overboard. We searched the place for four long hours and I spent two of them below myself. It was very murky and unpleasant as the bottom was covered with about a foot of slushy ooze and all around were deep black holes and jagged coral lumps. On one occasion, while I was below, the man on guard fired at a large stingray and frightened it away – but we didn't see any crocodiles. Finally we had to admit defeat.

There was a Court of Enquiry into the loss of the revolver but it was quite a cheerful occasion. We were mildly censured for diving in crocodile infested waters and yet complimented on making such energetic efforts to retrieve the gun. The final decision was that I must pay the twenty-seven dollars cost of the weapon – and I didn't feel too happy about this as it was possible to pick up a similar gun for a couple of dollars at any American base.

The end of the war with Japan signalled the run down of air force activities in the Pacific and the Catalinas became very busy transporting men back to New Zealand. Our crew was chosen to stay in Havalo as standby for search and rescue and all ideas of a weekly trip home to Auckland faded away. To celebrate VJ day the Commanding Officer decided to give some of the ground staff a picnic flight to a scenic spot and we were sent to reconnoitre it.

We flew to Rekata Bay which had previously been a Japanese seaplane base and tied up to one of the Japanese mooring buoys. The inflatable boat was being prepared for the trip ashore but Ron and I decided not to wait, so dived overboard and swam the couple of hundred yards to the beach. We spent a happy two hours ashore wandering around in this very pretty place and when we discovered an old ammunition dump half a mile from the aircraft we tried unsuccessfully to blow it up. As we walked along the beach we noticed a shark following us with its triangular fin sticking up out of the water. We were fairly used to sharks and when we returned to join our companions we thought nothing of plunging into the water again and swimming back to the aircraft.

Next day another crew went to Rekata Bay with a load of passengers all set for a pleasant break from routine. Some of them started swimming ashore – as we had done. Suddenly one of the airmen was attacked by a shark. He had the presence of mind to punch it on the nose as it came towards him and it turned away – and he swam furiously for the beach. The shark came at him again and once more he punched it on the nose. He was getting close to shore now and when the shark made a third attack he kicked it with his foot and got a nasty cut in the process. He needed only a few more strokes to reach shallow water and staggered out onto the beach.

This experience took the heart out of the picnic and everyone returned to the plane in the boat. They were on their way back to Halavo when a check showed that a man was missing and though they returned and searched they couldn't find him. The following day a full search party went to Rekata Bay in another aircraft and anchored at the same buoy. They immediately noticed an immense crocodile swimming around and though they fired a number of shots it refused to go away.

The Court of Enquiry came to the conclusion that the crocodile had caught the poor airman and pulled him under. They believed the body must be hidden under the water in some old sunken aircraft and this seemed the logical answer. It was a sad ending to a happy picnic.

Grandmother Hillary—
a remarkable woman.

The author's parents on their
wedding day.

The young Edmund, aged
1 year and 8 months.

The author with crocodile he shot in Solomon Islands.

On the summit of Mount Seally in 1947—one of Edmund Hillary's first major summits.

With his great climbing friend, Harry Ayres, his first ascent of Mount Cook.

Breslauer hut in the Austrian Alps.

Eric Shipton and Amadablan Col after the first crossing in 1951.

George Lowe and author leaving Auckland in March 1953 to join Mount Everest Expedition.

Edmund Hillary and Tenzing being welcomed on arrival in Kathmandu valley after their ascent of Everest.

At Base Camp—Everest 1953.

John Hunt.

Tenzing, Hunt and Hillary greeted by Pandit Nehru in Delhi.

With George Lowe and author on the way to a State banquet in London.

We were released from our search and rescue duties for one trip back to New Zealand carrying passengers and then returned to Havalo to swelter in temperatures of 100° or more. The station was greatly reduced in strength with only two aircraft and about fifty men. I took turns with the other navigator at being operations officer, meteorological officer, and intelligence officer – which all sounds a great deal more impressive than it really was. My main task was to give take-off and landing instructions which wasn't a very demanding duty as we only had about two aircraft movements each day.

With the war ended we all felt very restless and the various activities that had seemed such fun in the past had lost most of their appeal. We were on constant standby for search and rescue so could not at any time be far away from base. Someone discovered an abandoned motor boat with a seized-up engine and we set to work to get it back into operational order. Our flight engineers did great work on the engine and got it running smoothly again while we calked and painted the hull, and renamed it *Jolly Roger*. When we relaunched the boat and carried out trials we were very happy with its speed – it was an ugly brute of a boat but its 180 h.p. marine engine gave us a speed in excess of thirty knots. The boat kept us entertained for a couple of weeks and gave us a few moments of triumph when we were able to surge past the Commanding Officer's official runabout.

One Sunday morning Ron and I arose very early to take one of the airmen across the bay to the American Naval Base at Tulagi to attend a Catholic church service. It was a pleasant sunny morning with a fresh breeze putting quite a chop on the sea. Ron and I pumped out the *Jolly Roger* and filled the two tanks with petrol. These tanks were suspended above the engine and I noticed that one of them was a bit loose but didn't bother too much about it. When the airman joined us we shot off across the bay at full speed and did the four-mile journey in eight minutes.

We deposited the young airman at Tulagi and then turned around for the trip back to Havalo. We were now heading straight into the sea and it was quite bumpy so I eased back on the throttle. After a mile or so we came into the lea of Palm Island where the seas were flat calm and I opened out to maximum speed again. When we emerged from the shelter of the island the sea was quite rough and we hit the waves with a succession of mighty thumps. The next moment we heard a loud crack behind us and a sheet of flame shot through the holes around the engine compartment – the petrol tank had broken loose!

The fire was well beyond our control although the engine was still roaring merrily on. Ron and I had both been scorched already and knew we'd have to bale out before the other tank exploded. I yelled to

Ron to jump and then let go of the wheel and stood on the seat. Next moment the boat hit a big wave and veered sharply. I was thrown off balance and fell on my back on the engine covers through which the flames were spurting. I wasn't wearing a shirt and could feel my flesh sizzling and the pain was quite considerable. I remember thinking, 'Now I know what it's like to be a rasher of bacon'. I had just enough energy to roll off the engine hatch into the water. The *Jolly Roger* charged on for another hundred feet and then exploded in a great sheet of flame.

The salt water was extremely painful on my burns and we were a long way from shore – at least 500 yards. I just flopped around for a while not worrying too much about going anywhere until Ron yelled at me to get moving and then I started swimming slowly towards the shore. I kept going through a fog of pain and the choppy sea didn't make for easy swimming anyway. Every now and then I'd feel myself giving out and I'd flop over on my back and float and try and do back stroke but I'd just go around in circles. Ron wasn't as badly burnt as me – although badly enough – but even he was tiring and he'd give me a yell and I'd flop over again and start paddling once more. I didn't have much clothes on anyway but to help my swimming I tore off pretty well everything.

After what seemed like an eternity I felt my foot touch the bottom but I was past caring too much by this stage. We staggered up the shore and collapsed on the sand. The sun was beating down now and its heat on our burns was too much to stand so we got back on our feet and staggered the half mile over the reef and along a road to the nearest habitation on Tanenhoga Island. The sun was so unpleasant on our backs that at times we had to walk along the road backwards.

The only people in residence were two U.S. sailors who were still in bed and were clearly flabbergasted at our appearance. We tried to explain that we were burnt and needed some assistance but they just sat there with their mouths open. So we asked if they had any tannic acid and they finally produced a big tube. I put some on Ron and he put some on me and it seemed to ease the pain quite a lot. By now they realised we were in trouble and said they'd run us across to the Tulagi Naval Base in their boat.

The boat trip was only a mile or so but it seemed much longer as I was feeling pretty hazy by this time. The Americans had called ahead by radio and there was an ambulance to meet us at the wharf and we were soon being taken into the Naval Hospital and people were fussing around. The doctor gave each of us three quarts of blood serum as well as numerous shots of morphine, penicillin and glucose. He seemed pretty worried about me as he was having the greatest difficulty in finding a vein to get a needle into, but after a while he was successful and the haziness cleared and everything came back to normal again. I suppose the drugs were having their effect.

Our New Zealand CO turned up and I could see by his face that he wasn't too happy about my condition. He didn't tell me but he sent a message back to my parents warning them that I was 'critically' ill. They decided that Ron and I should be shifted to the much better equipped U.S. hospital on Guadalcanal and as an American destroyer was just about to leave we were carried on board and placed on deck in the shade of a four-inch gun. I can remember a succession of faces coming along to look us over and then I went off to sleep.

I woke up in the hospital in Guadalcanal as I was being taken into the operating theatre and I seemed to spend a long time there. The doctor was a very pleasant person and seemed to know just what he was doing. He told me I had forty per cent of my skin burnt off and I was lucky to be alive but if they could prevent infection I'd be O.K.

By this time I hadn't the slightest doubt that I would survive – but kept thinking what a blasted nuisance the whole business was. Even so that first week was pretty miserable with the extreme discomfort of heavy bandages in the hot sticky conditions; being woken night and day for penicillin injections (I had a hundred and forty of them) and the fact that the only comfortable way to lie was on my stomach.

The doctor told me I would be in hospital for many months and the way I felt the first week I suspected this might be true. But by the second week my burns were healing well and I was staggering out of bed for short walks. By the third week I was bored to tears and making a thorough nuisance of myself. Then Ron Ward was classified as being well enough to leave hospital and return to New Zealand – and I didn't see him again for many years (and by then he was a school principal and a senior inspector). I couldn't understand the attitude of most of the patients who seemed perfectly happy to relax in the comfort and attention of the hospital. I must have been an appalling patient to have around.

My importuning of the doctor finally bore results. He expressed his astonishment at the rapidity of my healing and agreed he would be pleased to see me go. After three weeks I emerged from the hospital still swathed in bandages, a bit shaky and a lot thinner but with few signs of infection. I knew I could largely thank my fitness for that, plus my luck in striking an excellent surgeon who later became very distinguished in his profession in the United States.

All I wanted now was to return home. I found it infuriating to be kept waiting several weeks for 'observation and treatment'. Finally some intelligent person decided I could just as well have my 'observation and treatment' at home. To my joy I was flown back to Auckland and given my discharge with sick leave. In the cooler temperatures and with good fresh food I made a rapid recovery although for a long time my skin was very tender and I still have a few minor scars – but nothing of any consequence. I considered I'd had a lucky escape and I've been careful with fires of all types ever since.

Chapter 5

New Zealand Climbing

I RETURNED TO CIVILIAN LIFE WITH THE DETERMINATION TO GET BACK to the bees as quickly as possible and help my family with harvesting the honey crop. My stay in the air force had been generally such good fun that I felt rather guilty about my parents having to work so hard in my absence. My attitude of course had changed in many ways. I had enjoyed the taste of freedom and a regular income and didn't want to return to a system where my finance depended solely on the whim of a parent. I was now twenty-six and I wanted to cram quite a lot of activity into the next ten years. Anticipating a warm welcome back into the business, it was something of a surprise when I discovered that I really wasn't needed – my father was employing a number of staff and he was already half way through the honey season.

At first I didn't know quite what to do. The air force doctors had told me to take it easy for a few months but I was rapidly regaining strength and vigour. I was at something of a loose end when I received a note from my old climbing friend Jack McBurney saying he was being demobilised – what about both of us heading off to the hills again? I had saved some money while in the air force so finance was no problem. I decided to go immediately.

In the middle of January 1946, only two and a half months after my accident, I met Jack McBurney at Mount Cook and we went off climbing together. We were strong, energetic, and immensely enthusiastic with quite a lot of experience of travelling in bush and rough country. But our knowledge of mountaineering techniques was culled almost entirely from books and alpine journals. Compared with the young climber of today we were lacking in technique and confidence. The whole emphasis in those days was on 'safe' climbing and anyone foolish enough to break the rigid rules was regarded as stupidly irresponsible. Sound and sensible methods are indeed highly desirable and should be encouraged but it is true that over-emphasis on safety can impair confidence and greatly affect performance. Our interest in safety was perhaps understandable. We had no radios in huts to transmit calls for help and no helicopters to supply instant rescue.

With the *Alpine Journal* route guide in one hand and an ice-axe in the other we clambered up a few good peaks – Mount Seally which I had attempted solo the summer before; Mount Hamilton; and our first 'ten thousand footer' which was Malte Brun. Undoubtedly our most exciting climb was the ascent of De La Beche – a peak generally regarded as being only of moderate difficulty. We left the De La Beche hut at four thirty a.m. and made our way up through the crevasses of the Rudolph Glacier and up towards Graham Saddle. Our route guide then indicated that we should cross the low ridge to the right onto a broad plateau which gave access to a number of the local summits. Unfortunately the crevasse at the bottom of this ridge was very wide and deep and the upper lip formed a formidable ice wall.

The summit of De La Beche was almost directly over our heads and the face above Graham Saddle didn't look terribly difficult from our position so we decided to try it. We struck poor conditions almost immediately – the steep slope leading up to the rock face was hard green ice covered by a two-inch layer of loose flaky ice – and we had to cut hundreds of steps. After several hours of this arduous work we reached the rock face only to find it was a good deal steeper than it had appeared from below and with many of the holes and hollows filled with ice. We were very much aware of the exposure beneath us and had little desire to descend our line of steps – so on we went.

The wind was freshening and with every gust we were showered with icicles from above. I started clawing my way up the rocks and cutting steps across short stretches of hard ice. I had the greatest difficulty in finding any sort of a belay and for hours we had a complete sense of insecurity. For a while I followed a steep rib but this petered out and the only route was into an evil looking gully. I kicked and cut steps up this until finally the angle eased a little; the snow improved and I was able to kick good steps with one blow of the foot. Twenty minutes later to our enormous relief we emerged onto the ridge only a short distance from the summit. It had taken us six hours for the last thousand feet.

The summit was safe and comfortable and we relaxed in the sun – enjoying the extensive views of mountain, glacier, and ocean. Our rest was rudely interrupted when we became unwilling participants in one of the swift weather changes for which the Southern Alps are notorious. One moment the weather appeared to be perfect and in the next clouds were pouring over Graham Saddle and a nor' west storm had descended on us. We hastily cramponed down the ridge being increasingly buffetted by the wind and enveloped in clouds. The temperature had risen appreciably and next moment we were lashed by freezing rain – a very unpleasant experience on a high mountain.

Jack was leading down the ridge with great care; he was far from happy with the conditions. Suddenly his ice-axe slipped on some hard ice and he swayed unevenly for a few seconds before steadying himself. This was the final straw to breach his taciturn exterior; he raised his ice-axe towards the heavens and waved it at the storm. 'By the powers. . .!' he bellowed in unaccustomed fury . . .

With such poor visibility we did not fancy carrying out our plan to go direct down the heavily crevassed east face of the mountain. We resolved instead to cross the ridge and return to our upward route of the morning. The steep snow on the side of the ridge was soft enough for the kicking of steps and we climbed down to the huge crevasse that had previously barred our way. I cut a bollard in the ice and hitched the rope around it. Then Jack and I lowered ourselves down the ice wall into the depths of the crevasse and pulled the rope down behind us. We had observed a broken section of ice on the lower lip and were able to hack a stairway up this and climb out onto the glacier.

The glacier here was split by long crevasses and in the morning we had zigzagged our way backwards and forwards through them. But now we could see very little and route finding was most tedious through the driving rain and fog. It took us a long time to find a way past the biggest of the crevasses but when they started decreasing in size we were so cold and wet that we decided to plough straight down the middle and jump everything as we came to it – frequently a dangerous procedure in poor visibility. Before long we were surrounded in a labyrinth of crevasses with no easy way out. After a lot of prodding and step cutting we came to the fringe of the area and only one big crevasse barred us from open ground. It was too wide to jump but I noticed that eight feet down there was a small plug of snow which might possibly take a man's weight.

An even more violent gust of wind helped us make the decision to use this route. I lowered Jack over the lip of the crevasse onto the snow plug and, protected by the rope, he cautiously eased his way across. It was a relatively easy climb up the other side for Jack to get onto safe ground. Now it was my turn. I could see nothing to hitch the rope around – how could I get down onto the bridge? I was too cold and tired to be cautious any longer and decided to jump onto the plug and trust it would support me. Jack was well belayed with the rope around his ice-axe.

I took a nervous glance or two into the green depths of the crevasse and before I could lose heart I jumped out and down. I hit the snow with a wallop and went right through. Next moment I was up to my armpits in snow and my chin had rapped sharply against the icy surface crust. My legs were hanging clear into the gaping hole but the remnants of the bridge were giving me tenuous support. Spreading my weight as widely as I could I wriggled cautiously out of the hole and then writhed across the bridge on my stomach. I was glad to sink my ice-axe into the firm snow on the far wall of the crevasse and clamber up the steps to join Jack. We reached the hut at seven thirty p.m. wet, cold and very tired but with a considerable sense of achievement. As far as I can discover we were the first party to have used this direct face route on De La Beche.

We completed our trip with a useful bag of ascents and although we hadn't exactly set the world on fire we had developed a lot of confidence and I was determined to do a great deal more mountaineering. I found that the honey crop had been disappointingly small and the family finances were rather strained – which was a fairly normal situation for us. My father was happy to dispose of some of the staff and thus reduce the regular payment of wages. I took their places on a 'work now and pay later' basis. My family gave me board and lodging and it cost me very little to live as I neither smoked nor drank and had a limited social life. It sounds frightfully boring, no doubt, but I didn't regard it as such at the time. I became more and more involved in beekeeping and increasingly responsible for organising the business.

With the onset of winter and the decrease in outdoor work I felt rather restless and my father was happy to give me time off without pay. I used some of my carefully hoarded air force money to head back to Tapuaenuku again.

My plan was to traverse over the range from the Awatere Valley to the Clarence River and to put in some high winter camps. I didn't have much in the way of equipment, obviously a tent was an essential requirement. No alpine tents were available in Auckland in those days so using information from alpine journals I had a tent made by the local canvas goods manufacturer to my own specifications. (The first of a large number of tents I've been responsible for producing over the years). This model was an astonishing contraption, heavy and subject to streaming condensation, but at least it had a sewn-in floor and was reasonably robust. My companions weren't terribly experienced – Allan Robb had done a little climbing on the northern volcanoes but my younger brother, Rex, had no mountaineering experience at all.

We made our approach to the mountain up the Hodder River which twists and turns in the depths of a great gorge and necessitates a continuous succession of fordings – some enthusiast has recorded that more than a hundred crossings of the river are necessary. It was impossible to keep boots and socks dry and we just charged through the bitterly cold water boots and all – and then sloshed up the bank until the next inevitable crossing. The rocks lining the river were encased in ice, and very tricky, and our shoulders ached from the heavy loads. After many hours we reached the last clump of trees at 3,000 feet. It was a beautiful site and we were tempted to camp there but it received little of the winter sun, the ground was frozen hard and the river almost completely covered with ice. We continued on a little further and reached our first snow. In a more open section of the valley amongst the snow drifts we pitched our tent and cooked a sparse meal over a miserable fire. It was so cold that we soon crawled into our sleeping bags and settled down for the night. I had previously spent many nights under tent flys in the bush but this was the first time I had camped in a tent on the side of a mountain.

Considering the inadequate nature of our gear we slept surprisingly well and awoke reasonably warm but rather stiff from our exertions of the previous day. We agreed to spend an easy day in reconnaissance and wandered up the ice-clad valley towards Mitre Peak. We were already learning that frozen streams in the bottoms of deep gorges made extremely difficult travelling and turned back after a fruitless few hours.

We had another very cold night and it was a miserable business next morning packing our cold gear plus the frost-encrusted tent. By eight a.m. we heaved on our loads and laboriously climbed the ice and snow to the foot of a ridge where we swung left into the valley which drained the high saddle between Tapuaenuku and Mount Alarm. Snow conditions were quite good at first and we gained a lot of height on the firm surface. The wintery sun finally reached us to counteract the chill wind flowing down from the ice above. We stopped for lunch in the shelter of a great boulder but soon got cold and moved on again.

Then we struck a series of great basins in which the snow was very soft and trail breaking became a most arduous procedure. It was a long time before we reached the last basin beneath the saddle at an altitude of about 8,000 feet and decided this would serve as our camp site. We stamped out a place in the snow and then erected the tent with frozen fingers. It was a lonely spot but the views were quite superb – below us now were many ranges of snowcapped peaks stretching to the horizon. When the sun dipped behind a ridge it became freezingly cold and we hastily crawled into the tent. Before long our primus stove was humming fiercely and there was plenty of time to cook ourselves an excellent meal. Full and contented we pulled on every piece of clothing and wriggled into our sleeping bags.

We were warm at first and quite comfortable but the cold from underneath started creeping through (we had no insulated mats or air mattresses), and the second half of the night was thoroughly miserable – frozen condensation inside the tent was hanging down in six-inch icicles from the roof. By morning we were stiff with cold and didn't have the courage to move out of our bags until seven a.m. when it was fully daylight.

We prepared a quick breakfast and then set off from the tent with the intention of climbing Mount Alarm to the west of us. With cold-stiffened limbs we kicked steps up the hundred feet to the crest of the saddle and poked our heads over the top – and were greeted by a howling southerly wind, bitterly cold and straight from the Antarctic. There were great banks of cloud over the sea and the outlook was decidedly ominous.

Having no desire to weather a storm at this altitude we rushed back to our camp and packed all our gear. By nine thirty we were away again with heavy loads on our backs – this time bound for the higher summit of Tapuaenuku. The climbing was easy at first and not unpleasant as we were out of the wind but when we emerged onto the ridge we met the full force of the gale and very cold and tedious it proved to be. The snow became harder and harder and the kicking of steps increasingly difficult so that frequently I had to cut a staircase with my ice-axe. To save weight we had decided not to bring crampons and now we bitterly regretted this. We laboured slowly upwards – driven only by the need to reach the summit before the storm broke.

At three thirty p.m. we kicked our way onto the top to find the view largely obscured by cloud. Wasting no time we moved down the icy slopes towards the head of the Dee River and then plunged down a long snow gully. Roped together we glissaded down the steep slopes in exhilarating fashion. Darkness caught up with us as we were negotiating a frozen slope above the Dee River. The route ahead didn't look very promising so we decided to bivouac where we were.

We could find no spot flat enough for our tent and as this slope was subject to rock barrage from above we considered ourselves lucky to discover some little hollows in the shelter of a great boulder. Getting water involved a major expedition down to the river but a hot brew on our precious stove was a lifesaver. Rain and slushy snow had started falling and we retreated into our sleeping bags and covered ourselves as best we could with the tent and our parkas. As I was settling down for the night I noticed that one of my big toes was throbbing and found that it was swollen and dark. Further investigation showed that the upper part of one of my boots had come away from the sole, probably with all the violent step-kicking I had been doing – and a touch of frost bite was the result.

Despite our cramped position and the miserable weather we awoke refreshed and ready to cover a lot of ground; but the Dee River had other plans for us. Our route led through deep gorges with many waterfalls and the spray had encased the rocks in ice and made the vertical sections almost impassable. Our journey became a series of ascents and descents of bluffs above the river as we climbed around impracticable stretches and by nightfall we were clambering down a spur in heavy mist with just over a mile on the map to show for a hard day's work. To our disappointment the spur came to an abrupt end and dropped off in a six-hundred-foot bluff to the river below. There was no water anywhere so we couldn't camp – we'd have to climb down. Fortunately the clouds cleared for a moment and in the last light I was able to locate a possible route down the face. Every here and there I could see stunted trees clinging to little shelves or emerging from cracks in the rock. It should be possible to rope down from one of these to the next, I decided.

Complete darkness came and before long we were enveloped in cloud again. I knew we'd have to move extremely carefully – there was a lot of loose rock around and it would be very easy to dislodge some of it on a companion's head. Morale wasn't terribly high but my brother proved invaluable to me at this stage. Although lacking mountain-eering experience he had confidence in my judgment and was prepared to co-operate in any way.

I tied Rex on one end of the rope and looped the rest of it around a handy tree trunk, then suggested he step into the blackness below. Not without trepidation he did so and soon was bumping down the cliff face with a flashlight in his hand seeking a ledge and another belay point before the rope ran out. I was vastly relieved when the weight eased on the rope and his faint cry floated up to tell us he'd found a good location. I quickly lowered the rucksacks down to him and lowered Allan too. Then it was my turn to hitch the rope over the tree trunk and slide down the doubled line to join them. For three hours we moved slowly but safely in this fashion and were always lucky enough to find another stance when we needed it. We descended a short vertical section into a rock-filled gully and then stumbled our way down a shingle fan to the bed of the river. We were parched with thirst and a drink of fresh clear water tasted like paradise. Rain was falling as we trudged down the riverbed looking for a camp site and thankful that we now seemed below the ice level. At nine thirty p.m. we pitched our tent on a terrace beside the river and collapsed into our sleeping bags. Two days later we emerged on the east coast and through a gap in the clouds could see heavy snow mantling the upper slopes of Tapuaenuku.

My toe was causing me some discomfort so on arrival in the city of Christchurch I went to the casualty ward of the Public Hospital. The young doctor on duty examined the black swollen mess with obvious disinterest, then quickly covered my whole foot with cotton wool and a series of bandages until I looked like an amputee. When I mentioned to him that I still had some walking to do he commented, 'That's your problem,' and called out 'Next!' Carrying my shoe I hopped into the waiting room, removed all the bandages except a light cover, cut a hole in my shoe over my big toe and replaced the shoe. The doctor passed through the waiting room as I was completing this task but he refrained from comment. For the next couple of months I travelled and worked with a hole in my shoe until the toe finally healed.

My life started to assume a more regular pattern as I found ways and means of indulging my enthusiasm for the mountains. I worked long and hard at the bee-keeping life and received a modest income from so doing. My ordinary financial needs were small and I saved every penny for use on mountaineering trips. With some reluctance my father had agreed that the long hours we worked in the Christmas and New Year periods warranted me taking an unpaid holiday at the end of January for summer mountaineering. In the middle of winter when maintenance work kept us only at half pace it was easier to get time off.

I kept on climbing, skiing and tramping at every available moment. Perhaps the most important step in my mountaineering life happened when I became friendly with guide Harry Ayres. Harry was New Zealand's outstanding climber with a tremendous reputation for brilliant icecraft and a formidable ability to complete the biggest and most challenging climbs. Harry was already something of a legend to me when I first got to know him well in the summer of 1947. We met in the Malte Brun hut and I was immediately impressed by his personality. Smallish, sinewy and incredibly quick and strong, Harry looked as tough and competent as he was. He was climbing with Susie Sanders and despite his great reputation he worked harder than anyone else in the hut on cooking and all the unpleasant chores. My companion was Allan Odell and early next morning the four of us left the hut together with different objectives in mind. By the time we had climbed a couple of thousand feet together in most convivial fashion Harry and Susie had decided to abandon their peak and join us instead on Aiguille Rouge. We crossed the west ridge together and struggled up the Beetham Glacier in the teeth of a very strong wind. The final face of the mountain was protected from the wind and we had a most enjoyable scramble with frequent rests. Harry actually went to sleep on one warm ledge as we basked in the sun. The wind on top was very strong so we didn't stay long before beating a hasty retreat but it had been a very happy and successful day. I was enormously impressed with Harry's professional ability and realised with sinking heart how far I still had to go in climbing technique.

The four of us did another climb together – Mount Haidinger – and we had a chance to see Harry at his best when the last steep rise to the summit proved to be eighteen inches of powder snow over solid ice. Harry gave a fine exhibition of step cutting up this face, brushing off the snow and hacking out bucket steps in the green ice underneath. Halfway up the face he was startled by an abrupt movement from Susie and it was an eye-opener to me to see the immense power and speed with which he slammed his ice-axe pick into the hard ice for an emergency belay. I kept thinking what a thrill it would be to climb on the same rope as Harry, and chance finally played into my hands. A

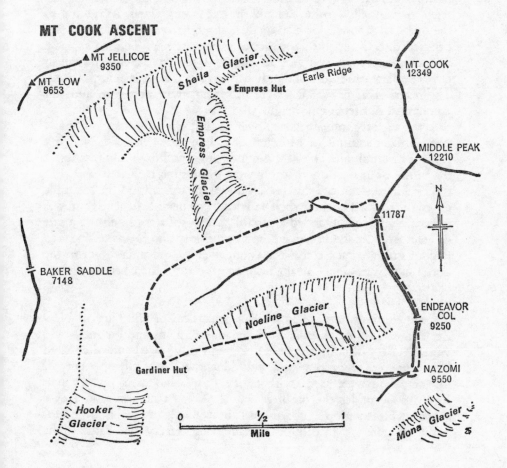

MT COOK ASCENT

MT JELLICOE
9350

MT LOW
9653

Sheila Glacier

Empress Hut

Earle Ridge

MT COOK
12349

Empress Glacier

MIDDLE PEAK
12210

N

11787

BAKER SADDLE
7148

Noeline Glacier

ENDEAVOR
COL
9250

Gardiner Hut

NAZOMI
9550

Hooker
Glacier

0   ½   1
Mile

Mona Glacier

client cancelled at short notice leaving Harry with a spare week and he agreed to go climbing with me.

We went up to the Haast hut at 7,000 feet with plans to tackle Mount Cook, 12,349 feet, the ambition of all local climbers. The alarm clock got us up just before midnight – it was fine and clear. We gulped down some food and by one a.m. were on our way. In crisp conditions we climbed the long snow slopes of Glacier Dome and then twisted through the crevasses of the Grand Plateau. Our pace slowed as we reached the contorted ice of the Linda Glacier but even in the dark Harry showed an almost uncanny sense of direction. Eventually a bad crevasse held us up for some time and we were forced to wait half an hour until dawn showed us the way through a maze of ice blocks. The upper Linda Glacier was almost free of breaks though well-littered with avalanche debris, and we proceeded on crampons directly along the snow shelf to the foot of the summit rocks which were clear of snow and a delight to climb. We moved together all the way on the steep rock revelling in the sun and the expanding views. At the top of the rocks we stopped for a meal then, donning crampons once more, climbed directly up the long slopes of the ice cap. The ice cap is a fantastic place, steep and very exposed, but we were lucky enough to have excellent conditions and only had to cut a few steps in icy sections. The other great mountains were dropping away below us and this emphasised our feeling of height.

It was a great moment to step over the last small crevasse and finally stand on the summit of Mount Cook. It meant I had achieved my first major ambition. The strong wind made conditions unpleasant but the views both north and south were quite superb. Elated with our success I hardly noticed the descent down the ice cap and the scramble down the rocks. The snow shelf had now considerably softened and was quite unstable so demanded a careful packing of steps to ensure a safe descent. The Linda Glacier was soft and slushy and it was a long and tedious struggle back across the Grand Plateau and then down to the hut. But my tiredness meant nothing; for me it had been a day of triumph.

Over the next few years I did a great deal of climbing in New Zealand both in summer and winter, in crampons and on skis – and with a variety of companions. I was frequently scared and often tired but there were few moments I would have willingly missed. Many of my best days were spent with Harry Ayres, and many of my best climbs done under the umbrella of his skill. At no time did I ever approach his technical standard but I absorbed a great deal of his philosophy of safe but forceful mountaineering. Harry was later to be invited to join the 1953 Everest expedition – but the invitation was rescinded with the change in leadership. We have no way of knowing how Harry would have performed at high altitudes – other factors apply here as well as technical ability – but his presence on the expedition would certainly have strengthened it immeasurably. I have no doubt that Harry would have been somewhere around the summit when the great moment came.

It was always difficult to get away in summer so I started spending more and more time in the mountains each winter. I was only a mediocre skier but discovered that a competent grasp of traversing, sideslipping, and kick turns could handle even the steepest of country. I tasted the joys of ski mountaineering and revelled in cross country skiing over snow covered glaciers. If an ice slope or cornice barred our way I was eager to unlimber my ice-axe and hack a line of steps to the other side. I hearned something about the dangers of avalanche and quite a lot about survival.

One winter Jack McBurney and I spent several weeks shooting deer and backpacking their skins out for sale – a common and profitable hobby of young New Zealanders at the time. We even panned for gold in the cold swift waters of the Cook and Balfour Rivers – and had precious little to show for our labours at the end of three weeks. We waded over mountain passes in the middle of winter and hunted chamois and thar on steep mountain slopes.

To save a little money for skiing I worked for six weeks on a hydroelectric construction project at Lake Pukaki and found this a new experience in itself. At the time this was a low priority project and much of the labour force could be classified as decidedly scruffy. We had almost daily visits from the police to arrest fellow workmen and take them back for trial in the city courts. My job was surveyors' lineman for one of the younger engineers (who happened to be a well-known mountaineer). The pay was good; but not good enough, I decided, so I did a second job at night and became a tally clerk with a pile driving gang. This left me eight hours out of the twenty-four for sleeping and eating – more than enough considering the easy work I was doing and the good money I was making.

My job as tally clerk supplied a few interesting moments. The first night I joined the four-man gang after dinner and we walked through the frosty air to a large muddy pond on the down river side of the dam. There was a dinghy on the shore of the pond and we used it to row out to a floating platform supporting a tall tower. The task was a simple one; to test the depth and consistency of the clay in the pond by driving a succession of steel pipes into it. The hammer was a great iron contraption suspended from the tower and pulled up by hand. My job was to take a tally of the number of blows required to drive a foot of pipe into the clay.

The four-man team was not an impressive group – they ranged from a small wizened character with a bitter debauched face to an enormous Maori workman who seemed to lack the customary good nature. Work commenced – if you could call it work – and the four men pulled the weight to the top of the tower with the greatest of ease and duly let it fall with an almighty clunk – and I made a notation in my book. At the end of an hour nobody had achieved a sweat and they had driven a pipe down a total of twelve feet.

'O.K., that's the lot for to-night,' said the little man and the four of them got back in the dinghy. 'Coming, mate?'

Somewhat dazed I asked for an explanation – and got it. They were working on contract – so much a foot of pipe – and someone had made a mistake. Twelve feet of pipe in a night was enough to give them all a substantial pay packet so that's all they did. No point in spoiling a good contract was there? What they did was really none of my business – I got paid wages for an eight-hour shift irrespective of how much pipe was driven – so we rowed ashore and went to a small hut which was already crammed with a dozen other men (I don't know what sort of contract *they* had). A stove was red hot in the corner and a game of cards was going strong. For six hours I listened to crude stories and idle chatter and I have rarely been more bored. At the end of the eight-hour shift I was more than happy to escape back to bed.

The second night was as cold and frosty as the first. Out we went to the platform and this time it took us nearly two hours to knock a pipe down twelve feet. We rowed ashore and the gang headed for the hut but I stayed behind, I couldn't stand another six hours of dirty jokes; and didn't I have some sort of responsibility to my employers? I jumped into the dinghy and rowed out to the platform again. In the next six hours I operated the hammer by myself and drove in another thirty feet of pipe, recording it all in my notebook. At the end of the shift I went off to bed feeling a lot happier.

I was back on the survey job next morning and felt none the worse for the night's work. During the afternoon I felt a jab in the ribs, and there was the little man.

'The fellas aren't too happy about last night,' he hissed out of the side of his mouth in best Mafia fashion. 'If you do it again they say they are going to throw you in the lake.'

I grabbed his jacket and pulled him close until we were eyeball to eyeball. 'You plan to throw me in the lake?' I queried.

'Not me, mate!' he hastened to assure me, 'it's the other fellas.'

Thyangboche monastery with Everest behind.

The children meet Tensing in
January 1963.

Children at Thami school.

Makalu from the foothills of Nepal.

I released him and he slunk off back to his hut.

Nobody said anything that night as we rowed out to the raft but there was tension in the air. It took two and a half hours to drive the pipe down twelve feet – the clay was getting much tougher – but finally the job was done.

'Let's go ashore,' said someone, but nobody moved.

'Coming, mate?' one of them asked me.

This was it, I knew, and I braced myself.

'Not me, friend!'

For a few seconds nothing was said and the atmosphere quivered with violence. It was the big Maori who made the first move.

'Let's knock the bloody thing down a bit further,' he suggested. 'I've had a gutsful of sitting in that hut . . .'

And knock it down we did – eighty feet that night. I can't say I ever became bosom friends with this quartet but over the next few weeks we didn't spend another hour in the hut. Finally the 'bosses' caught up with the contract and had it modified – but the men had made a fortune before the change came.

Chapter 6

South Ridge

THINGS THAT ARE FAMILIAR TEND TO BE TAKEN FOR GRANTED. IT WASN'T until I travelled widely overseas that I came to fully appreciate the mountains of New Zealand both for their beauty and for the challenge they presented to the enthusiastic climber. The Southern Alps run north and south for hundreds of miles and present a mighty barrier to the damp westerly winds sweeping off the Tasman Sea. The upper limit of the bush is only 3,500 to 4,000 feet and above this height the terrain becomes increasingly precipitous and is heavily glaciated. From the ice cap of Mount Cook 12,349 feet to the terminal faces of glaciers on the West Coast which descend to within a few hundred feet of sea level the whole environment is dominated by ice under constant movement. The weather can be warm and balmy one moment and wild and tumultuous at the next – and a full scale nor' west storm is more to be feared than any Himalayan blizzard. Access to the mountains is often long and difficult – or used to be before the development of ski-planes and helicopters – and the competent climber in New Zealand must become skilful in bushcraft, the crossing of swift flowing rivers, and in the carrying of heavy loads.

By the end of the Second World War most of the major summits had been reached except for a few virgin peaks in inaccessible positions. There were still a number of great ridges that hadn't succumbed and of these the south ridge of Mount Cook seemed to attract the greatest discussion and interest. Swooping up in a series of steps from the lesser peak of Nazomi it had a dominant position above the Hermitage Tourist Hotel and so could be seen by everyone. Lying away from the sun it was frequently plastered with ice and then regarded as hazardous in the extreme.

Many mountaineers of this period made their plans to 'have a look at the south ridge'. Some tried but were rebuffed by bad weather before hardly getting to grips with the ridge. Only one party in fact by 1948 had set foot on the ridge and they retreated from the top of the first step reporting that the way ahead appeared difficult but climbable.

I had looked at the ridge the same as everyone else and dreamed a little about having a try at it. At the end of January 1948 I joined up with Harry Ayres and we agreed that the climb might be on. The weather was unusually settled, the south ridge looked remarkably clear of ice, and I was very fit after a couple of weeks of climbing with other companions. Harry was always fit, anyway.

On February 4th we arrived at the Gardiner Hut on the Hooker Glacier. Our companions were Mick Sullivan, an energetic young guide whose family owned the Fox Glacier Hotel, and a slim and comely young medical student, Ruth Adams, who had a reputation for fitness and speed in the mountains and a fine record as a skier. We had brought with us a variety of camping gear for we planned to bivouac on Endeavour Col – a prominent dip in the ridge between the summit of Nazomi and the foot of the south ridge.

The morning of February 5th was pleasantly fine apart from some high cloud. We made leisurely preparations, assembling sleeping bags with waterproof covers; a methylated spirits cooker; a little food; and all our spare clothes. At one p.m. we left the hut and climbed in soft snow up the Noeline Glacier, zigzagging on a long rope through the central crevasses. A difficult bergschrund and an ice slope that needed step cutting made us work a little harder before we could get onto the rock of Nazomi but soon we had climbed into a long rocky couloir running up to the ridge within a few hundred feet of the summit. An easy scramble up the ridge saw us on top of Nazomi at five forty-five p.m. after an enjoyable afternoon.

Sweeping up in front of us was the south ridge, rising in a succession of abrupt rock steps to the icecapped lower peak of Mount Cook. My first impression of the route was favourable – the rock seemed clear of ice and the first two steps didn't appear terribly difficult even though steep in places. Only the long third step looked formidable and even this we decided might be tackled by a traverse out to the left. We noted that the final band of rock below the ice cap could also be turned out to the left should it prove difficult to scale directly.

We debated where we should put our camp. For some hours the weather had been looking unsettled and we had no desire to be caught by a storm in an exposed position. It would be difficult to retreat from Endeavour Col – perhaps it would be better to bivouac on Nazomi itself? We chose a spot at the head of the rock couloir about thirty feet down on the western side and felt sure we could descend from there even in the worst of weather. For the next couple of hours we laboured mightily to produce a platform large enough for all of us and a rock wall to give some protection from the wind. In our determined efforts to save weight we had brought very little solid food and our evening meal was spartan in the extreme. When I wriggled into my sleeping bag and stretched out on the hard and uneven rocks I missed the warm feeling of internal comfort that comes from a full stomach. Lying on this airy ledge high above the glacier I could see the south ridge with all its steepness and difficulties outlined against the sky.

I didn't sleep very well. In the early hours of the morning the wind freshened and came whistling through the cracks in the rock wall and we all suffered from varying degrees of cold. The weather was still far from promising and a glance over the ridge showed ominous clouds massing on the Malte Brun Range. We shivered in our bags until four thirty a.m. and the weather didn't seem to get any worse. Finally we sprang into action. Breakfast didn't take long to prepare – Mick Sullivan, with his wry humour, described the main ingredients as 'a breath of fresh air and a good look around'. By five thirty a.m. we had everything packed and we left our bivouac site with few regrets and started down towards Endeavour Col. The rock on the ridge was easy at first but we were stiff and clumsy and it wasn't until we warmed up that our standard improved. We had to cut steps across an ice slope to reach Endeavour Col by six thirty a.m.

The weather was now looking much better and many of the ominous clouds were dissolving in the morning sun. Without much conviction we discussed throwing our sleeping bags in their covers down a steep narrow snow gully descending a thousand feet to the head of the Noeline Glacier, but finally decided against it. The bags could have easily snagged on a rock and in any case it would be a long climb to retrieve them. We carried everything on with us.

At six forty-five a.m., climbing on two ropes, we first set foot on the south ridge and I could feel a growing sense of excitement. We were now moving smoothly and well and made good time up the loose rock of the first step. Keeping below the ridge on the east side we moved together all the time and though we were always aware of the tremendous exposure beneath us we struck no great difficulties. A large finger of rock barred our way on the ridge and we dropped over onto the ice slope on the east and Harry cut a line of steps up it. When we returned back onto the ridge we found that the rock tower could have been turned quite easily on the west or even traversed. Only a little time had been lost and by seven forty-five a.m. we were on top of the first step.

By now the skies had cleared and there was hardly a breath of wind. So far we had been following in other people's footsteps . . . from now on the ridge was completely untouched and this seemed tremendously important – why it should be I don't know. Talking and laughing in rather over stimulated fashion we moved on to the second step. To our delight the rock improved in character. Still keeping a little down on the east side we found the climbing exhilarating with only a couple of steep pitches slowing us to any great extent. Our packs were rather bulky and heavy for rock climbing and after a while we could feel them taking the edge off our early energy. It took us an hour and a half to climb the second step and we were glad to rest in the sun and have a bite to eat.

It was now nine fifteen a.m. Our viewpoint was a superb one. To the east we were looking across the mighty Caroline face of Mount Cook (not climbed until twenty-two years later); to the west great bulges of ice hung over the Noeline and Hooker Glaciers; far below were the contorted ice fields lapping the bottom of the mountain; and in the distance we could see the golden brown grass of the McKenzie country and the milky blue of Lake Pukaki. We were elated at our progress – but what would the third step be like?

We debated how we should tackle this problem. The route we had seen from Nazomi still offered the best possibility – a traverse out to the left, then up and back to the ridge. Harry had been doing most of the leading; he now waved to Mick Sullivan to go through and we watched Mick and Ruth moving slowly but steadily up the bottom rocks of the third step. Harry was still examining the face above us. 'I think we might do a direct route, Ed,' he said. 'Would you like to try it?' I looked at the line he suggested – it was like the prow of a great battleship with a tremendous drop down the Caroline face. I imagined it would be both exciting and a little terrifying. Feeling rather dry in the throat I nodded.

'Let's go.'

We swung to the right on to our route and our companions disappeared from view. As we gained height on the third step we thanked our good fortune that the rock was firm and sound though very steep and indeed in places overhanging. Good belays were few and far between but some excellent leading by Harry brought us two thirds of the way up the face before we were stopped by a very difficult pitch, towering above our heads. I had a most insecure location with little chance of checking any fall, and Harry was spreadeagled on the face. He inched his way up a smooth slab until he was stopped by a nasty holdless bulge. Three or four times he tried to make another move but each time he was forced to abandon it.

'I have to come down, Ed, and it's not going to be easy!' Desperately I clung to my minimal belay and tried to jam a section of the rope into a small crack. For a moment Harry just clung there – and then, fully balanced, he let himself slide back over the slab; I could hear the grating of his boot nails on the rock. He was sliding fast as he reached the bottom of the slab and I half expected him to go tumbling over. But Harry was his usual expert self – he had remembered a hold on the way up and grabbed calmly at it as he went by. Next moment he was safely on a ledge and looking for an alternative route.

We considered going out to the right into a very steep ice couloir – it had vertical ice steps in it and looked mighty technical. We edged around a narrow corner onto a ledge about four inches wide – I have rarely been in a more exposed position. And then we struck an unexpected blessing. At chest height there was a crack a couple of inches wide and into this crack a small rock was firmly wedged – it was a perfect belay. Some distance above the belay was another crack which offered a good hold and a possible lead onto easier rock. From here the ice couloir looked very unhealthy – was it possible instead to go direct up the rock?

Balancing like an acrobat Harry somehow got himself on top of the belay and spreadeagled himself against the face. But stretched to his fullest extent he was still a foot short of the top crack – one more step would do it but there were no more steps to take. Standing behind him, and leaning out over the face I had my right arm firmly around the rock belay. I reached up my left hand and called out, 'Take a step on my hand, Harry'. I thought my suggestion reasonable enough, but Harry was less than enthusiastic. What if I couldn't hold his weight or if the crack was still beyond his reach?

He pondered for a moment and then decided to take the risk. He put his left foot on my outstretched hand, poised himself for a moment, then sprang like a tiger. I hardly noticed his weight and to my delight saw he had grabbed the crack with both hands. With a fearful effort he pulled himself up higher and then wriggled his way into a safe position. For a few moments he rested, getting back his strength, and then pulled the rope in tight and called to me to come on up.

Even with the rope from above I found it hard enough to get on top of the belay. I was too heavy for Harry to drag up the next holdless section – I'd have to climb the rope myself. Contary to the impression one may get from western movies, climbing a thin alpine rope overhand in a difficult situation isn't terribly easy. It was only after a colossal effort that I was able to get myself up this section and join Harry on his ledge. In another ten minutes we were on top of the third step.

We heard the sound of voices and Mick and Ruth climbed up to join us. Their traverse to the left had brought them to the foot of a shallow couloir and they had to tackle some very steep rock on its righthand side. They had found the final pitch very difficult and made three unsuccessful efforts at it before they found the solution and finally reached the top.

The worst of the climb was now behind us – of this we were sure. We strapped on crampons with a certain light-hearted confidence and climbed good firm snow to the band of rock below the ice cap. A goodly number of steps had to be cut in the ice between the rocks but we were soon resting on the last ledge and enjoying the fantastic views. We suddenly became aware that we were being signalled from the Hermitage Hotel 9,000 feet below. As we learned later we had been seen crossing the snow and a dozen mirrors were now sending messages of congratulation.

We cramponed the final ice cap and onto the summit at one forty-five p.m. We devoted a few minutes to photographs, gave a wave or two to the Hermitage and then rushed down the ice cap to the west to find a sheltered place out of the wind. We were very thirsty and sadly lacking in food. We melted ice on our small stove and boiled some water. Ruth added a bar of chocolate and we waited anxiously for the delicious cup of hot chocolate she had promised us. Alas, the result wasn't quite up to expectations. I forced down a mug of browny looking liquid with lumps of chocolate sticking to the bottom.

At three p.m. we commenced the descent of the west ridge – one of the classic routes on Mount Cook. Getting off the ice cap onto the rock proved difficult but then we climbed down fine warm rock for thousands of feet. The crevasses at the foot of the ridge looked very formidable and we were hardly now in the mood for major problems. Harry did an inspired lead and we crept along a snow ledge under a great rock cliff and almost miraculously emerged on to open snow. We romped into Gardiner hut at seven forty-five p.m. after a tremendous day. I was still finding it hard to believe that I had actually been on the first ascent of the south ridge.

The weather deteriorated over the next two days and we were happy to rest and eat and cheerfully argue about our climb. When the weather cleared we were eager to go again and ready to tackle our next objective, La Perouse, 10,101 feet, a massive peak at the head of the Hooker Glacier. There hadn't been many ascents of La Perouse due to its inaccessibility. The traditional route was very long and involved climbing to the Divide Ridge and then traversing a number of intermediate summits before reaching the final peak.

At four a.m. we left the hut, strapped on our crampons, and set off up the Hooker Glacier. There was a very hard frost and the surface was excellent so we had no difficulty in finding our way through the shattered centre of the glacier. Following a route that Harry had pioneered the previous season we dodged under a nasty icefall and then worked our way up heavily crevassed slopes to the foot of a long steep ice slope which led to the divide. Cramponing wherever possible and cutting steps where necessary, we moved up this slope and finally stepped on the ridge at seven a.m.

It was still very cold so we pushed straight on. The crest of the ridge was rock, steep in places and very unstable. Our two ropes kept well apart to prevent any trouble from dislodged rocks but it was a constant worry. The small peak of Jellicoe was particularly unstable, and a shower of rocks descended at each fresh foothold or hand grip. It was hard to understand how rocks could pile in place at such a steep angle and rather disconcerting to find enormous boulders rocking gently at the touch. I didn't enjoy this stretch and was glad when we reached the summit of Mount Low. Here the ridge was ice and snow and a great deal broader, dropping off at a gradually increasing angle to the west.

We commenced cramponing down to the col between Low and La Perouse and to our disgust found the ridge cut completely by a very large crevasse. The bottom lip of this had fallen away leaving an ice wall at least thirty feet high. I established a good belay and Harry cut a series of hand and foot holds down the face. When I climbed down to join him I found it quite a tricky section, steep and exposed. Harry and I could now see that the crevasse abutted against a rock outcrop and the ice wall there formed a fairly continuous slope. This looked an easier proposition so we called to Mick and suggested he use it. He and Ruth went off to investigate while Harry and I climbed over to the col and relaxed in the sun, watching them.

We'd been making good time on the climb and it was still only ten a.m. Mick was cutting steps and we could see by their size and angle that the slope was much harder and steeper than had appeared from below. To save time it would probably be easier to rope down the slope from the rock outcrop and then we could all climb back on our original route. Mick took a stance on the rock and Ruth walked out onto the few steps he had already cut. We expected her to swing across the slope until she was in a direct line with the belay and then descend straight down. She took another step, her weight came on the rope and next moment she was away – sliding down the slope completely out of control and at great speed – the rope had broken!

We watched, aghast, and I heard Harry shout 'No! No!' Ruth shot down fifty feet and then dropped over an eight foot ice wall onto a steep frozen slope which funnelled towards tremendous precipices. It seemed that nothing could save her, until she crashed into a half-embedded boulder which effectively – and very fortunately – stopped any further progress. Harry and I dropped our packs and sprinted across the hundred yards or so to Ruth – probably the fastest hundred yards cramponing on steep slopes ever performed in these parts. We found her unconscious, rather gory due to superficial cuts, and generally rather battered. I held her in place on the steep slope – she was moaning gently – while Harry hacked out a large step in the ice and then we moved her onto it. A brief examination showed possibly a broken arm and maybe even a broken back; at the least she had severe bruising plus concussion and shock. Mick now arrived having done a hair-raising descent by our original route. With some difficulty we moved Ruth off the slope and on to a safer spot. Here we dressed her in our spare clothes to minimise the effects of shock and made her as comfort-able as we could.

It was quite obvious that we would have no hope of getting Ruth back down the difficult unstable ridge up which we had just come. In fact, we were in such an inaccessible place that we'd have to get considerable assistance if we were to get her out at all. If the weather deteriorated there was small chance of survival for any of us unless we had shelter, warmth, and food. After a brief conference we decided that one must descend to the Hermitage to organise rescue proceedings; another return from Gardiner before the weather had a chance to break and bring Ruth's sleeping bag, a stove and some food; while the third remained with Ruth and dug out an ice cave for shelter and warmth.

Harry and Mick were the natural choices to go down the mountain and get the rescue under way – and they agreed that this was the sensible procedure. When they roped up and departed I admit to an initial surge of loneliness and even despair – Ruth was groaning deeply and I realised only too well how far we were from the comforts of home. But there was work to be done, and I started searching for a suitable site for an ice cave. After a while I found a place at the end of a large crevasse. It wasn't ideal but there was a natural roof and floor and I was able to cut a path down into it. I set to work to enlarge the hole and very hard work it proved to be with only an ice-axe as a tool.

Soon after mid-day we were enveloped in mist, and a cool breeze lowered the temperature appreciably. Ruth regained consciousness about two o'clock, and although she must have been very cold and uncomfortable she displayed good spirits and much fortitude. Her main complaint was at having missed all the 'fun' over the previous three or four hours. She asked if she could have some aspirin to combat the pain in her back and I carefully issued out three pills. (Later Ruth didn't remember anything about this part of the day). At four p.m. the mist cleared and I climbed up through the crevasses to the crest of the

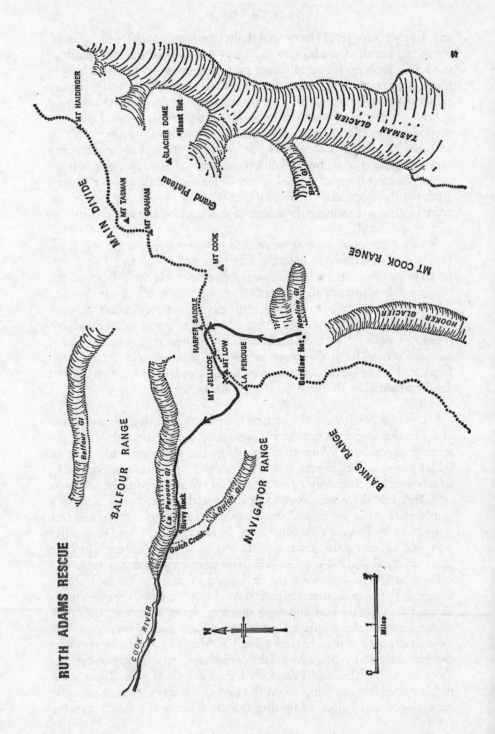

RUTH ADAMS RESCUE

MT HAIDINGER

MT TASMAN

MAIN DIVIDE

MT GRAHAM

GLACIER DOME

Haast Hut

Grand Plateau

Bell Gl.

TASMAN GLACIER

MT COOK

MT COOK RANGE

HARPER SADDLE

Noeline Gl.

MT JELLICOE

MT LOW

LA PEROUSE

Gardiner Hut.

HOOKER GLACIER

Balfour Gl.

BALFOUR RANGE

La Perouse Gl.

Bivvy Rock

Gulch Gl.

NAVIGATOR RANGE

BANKS RANGE

Gulch Creek

COOK RIVER

N

Miles
0   1   2

ridge and looked down the tremendous ice face of La Perouse. I was excited to see a clearly defined track going all the way down the Hooker Glacier to Gardiner Hut – a most comforting sight.

By five p.m. I had finished the ice cave, having chopped out a hole six feet long, four feet six inches high and four feet in width. I carried Ruth into our private ice box and we settled down in relative comfort. I had paved the floor of the cave with flat rocks and found this helped considerably by keeping our bodies off the ice. I had also blocked the entrance with ice chips and when I lit a candle there seemed an immediate improvement in the temperature – and in our morale. I can't say I was particularly comfortable but could hardly complain when I compared my situation with that of Ruth. Poor Ruth dozed off at times but in her sleep tossed and groaned in distress – when she woke she was incredibly courageous and cheerful. Her back was proving very painful and periodically she'd get me to prop her up a little as this seemed to give her some relief. Now and then I'd crawl outside and stamp around trying to get warm – I was only wearing a woollen shirt under my parka as all our sweaters had gone on Ruth.

I was not expecting Mick Sullivan back until eleven p.m. at the earliest. It was a very pleasant surprise when a cheerful face appeared at the door just before ten and Mick clambered in with a bulging pack. We soon had Ruth resting in her sleeping bag and the primus heating up some soup. Mick had done a very fast trip from Gardiner – not much over five hours and the last hour of this had been in the dark. He hadn't been able to carry sleeping bags for us but he did have windproof covers. After a hot drink we crawled into these and spent a somewhat crowded but reasonable night.

Tuesday morning was again fine and clear. We were heating up some water on the primus when we heard the roar of an aircraft and rushed out to greet it. Rocking about in a most alarming manner, the plane came in over the west ridge and we could see a large bundle suspended underneath. The aircraft was piloted by Harry Wigley, a renowned local airman and ex-fighter pilot, and despite the extreme turbulence he dropped the bundle very accurately on the frozen slope above us. (Harry Ayres was in the aircraft, too, acting as navigator and being thoroughly airsick.) Three more trips were made by the aircraft during the morning and all of the bundles fell within thirty feet of each other in a remarkable exhibition of accurate flying under very difficult conditions. Two of the bundles slid down into a large crevasse, but we had no difficulty in getting them out. We had scratched out on the snow the words 'O.K. All well' and apparently these were seen on the second or third run. The gear was packed in chaff sacks and padded liberally with straw. It included an alpine tent, stretcher, sleeping bags, a huge bundle of rope and tinned food, bread, butter, biscuits, etc. Apart from a few tins which had burst only the bread, biscuits and Weetbix had suffered from the fall.

It was a beautiful day with practically no wind so we moved Ruth out of the ice cave into the sun and she was soon asking to have some of her excess layers of clothing removed. Mick and I spent a little time enlarging the ice cave and then pitched the tent in a snow-filled crevasse. The chaff sacks and straw made excellent mattresses for the floors of the tent and ice cave. We were feeling much happier now – Ruth seemed stronger, the weather was still miraculously fine, and we had enough supplies to survive a spell of bad weather.

That evening we moved into the tent and at nine p.m. were just settling down for the night when a tremendous shout sent us tumbling out again. Lights were coming towards us off the summit of Low and we were soon welcoming Chief Guide Mick Bowie and three of his guides. That was the turning point in the rescue for me. Mick Bowie was a powerful man of tremendous personality and experience and with his arrival everything seemed to come under control. It wasn't that he said or did anything more than anyone else but his quiet presence welded us into an effective team. Mick Bowie told us that plans had been made for us to retreat down the west ridge of La Perouse – a less technical and safer route and then we'd have to walk down the turbulent Cook River to the West Coast. Harry Ayres and a strong party of ten climbers from Christchurch were camping back along the ridge and would reach us in the morning. The weather report wasn't particularly good and the big priority was to get Ruth down to lower levels before a storm could break. We squeezed into the tent and the cave and settled down for a good night's sleep.

Wednesday morning, February 11th, was still fine but ominous hog's back clouds were hovering over Canterbury. Mick Bowie and his party left just after nine a.m. to reconnoitre a route up onto the west ridge. Between ten a.m. and noon the various ropes of the Christchurch party came into camp after a very uncomfortable bivvy on the ridge. It was tremendous to see Harry Ayres again.

Dr. Jerry Wall was with the party and he gave Ruth a thorough examination and prepared her for the long trip. He said she was badly bruised and had severe concussion, but to our relief, her back was not broken. Looking pale but cheerful, with a first-class black eye, Ruth was strapped into the stretcher – a contraption made of bamboo slats and canvas with rope handles. Spurred by our fears of the weather we heaved our cumbersome packs on our backs and picked up the stretcher. The first stage of the journey involved us going uphill; climbing the steep crevassed slopes towards the summit of La Perouse. The first half hour was notable for its confusion of advice, but an efficient system was soon perfected and, with slight modifications, used successfully throughout the trip. Two alpine ropes were tied on the front of the stretcher, which was dragged over the snow like a sledge. On downhill grades the ropes were used for anchoring and lowering, while two men guided the stretcher. When going uphill one man guided the stretcher and anchored it where necessary, while three men on each rope would go out the full length and then tow the stretcher up hand-over-hand. We found it impracticable for the party to be roped together and used the towing ropes and stretcher as our only personal belay.

Good progress was made in hauling the stretcher up until we reached an ice wall where Mick Bowie had fashioned a primitive rope ladder. We all scrambled or were dragged to the top of this and then hauled the stretcher up from above. For a while the country was very broken and in many places the stretcher was suspended over large crevasses. This could have been very nerve racking for Ruth but she was heavily drugged and didn't have too much idea of what was going on.

The last slope leading up to the west ridge was a very long one and here we used a 400-foot rope, dragging the stretcher to the top in one operation. It was four p.m. and we were only thirty feet from the summit of La Perouse. The weather looked exceedingly ominous, with Cook and Sefton both blanketed out by heavy clouds.

We decided not to linger but started the descent of the west ridge. A tricky bit of traversing was first necessary in order to cut along the top of the big slope on to the flatter ridge beyond. A rough handrail of rope was improvised and using this the stretcher was carried to flatter ground. The grade was quite a lot easier, now, and although the west ridge was narrow in places there was a hollow between the steep rock faces on the north and the snow slopes on the south and this made an excellent road. The west ridge took a sharp turn to the left and dropped off. Our route lay down a very long steep snow slope, more than 400 feet in length. The long rope was belayed securely on the crest of the ridge and then the stretcher lowered down with two men guiding it. When the rope was nearly fully out, the two men anchored the stretcher and the rest of us cramponed down to join them, using the big rope as a handrail.

In this fashion we worked our way downwards until eight p.m. when we reached some moraine covered ice on the edge of a long drop. It was somewhat exposed but relatively flat and there were plenty of pools of water on the ice. It was about 7,500 feet – a much safer altitude – and here we pitched our tents. Mick Bowie issued our food ration – a couple of slices of bread, a lump of bully beef, and a third of a tin of fruit, all washed down with a mug of ice cold water.

We had a last gloomy look at the weather and then crept into our bags and settled down for the night.

In the early hours of the morning it began to rain but to our relief there was very little wind. At five a.m. we were aroused into a wet and miserable world but another slice of bread and bully beef was a great help to our morale. By six a.m. the rain had almost ceased and we were on the move. The route lay down a long narrow rock couloir; a most unsalubrious place where it was almost impossible not to dislodge loose rocks. We cut an ice bollard at the top and hitched the rope around this and around two men as well. Then two at a time the party climbed down the couloir, using the rope as a handrail; each pair waiting until the previous pair was down and in shelter before commencing their descent. Finally the stretcher was brought down and the worst of the morning was over.

A succession of snow slopes were handled in routine fashion and by mid-day we were having lunch amongst the moraine by the side of a pleasant little lake. Then we had a long sidle on snow grass slopes above the La Perouse glacier, working in relays on the stretcher and then some pretty rough ground and dense undergrowth. It must have been very unpleasant for Ruth in the places where we had to drag the stretcher – but she seemed to sleep through most of it. Finally we reached Gulch Creek and made contact with a party who had cleared a track up the Cook River. Soon all the tents were pitched, everyone was well fed, and a general air of contentment spread over the gathering. The exciting part was now over and tense nerves could relax. We had carried an injured girl in a stretcher almost over the summit of a major peak; the remainder of the trip would just be plain hard work.

And hard work it certainly proved to be. For the next three days we manhandled the stretcher through incredibly difficult bush on steep gorgy terrain. The West Coast team had done a great job in slashing a track for us but it was still very rough indeed. There were many bluffs and a rope was in constant use, the stretcher and its six bearers being hauled and lowered where necessary. Underfoot the surface was appalling. We were constantly slipping into holes between rocks and roots or sliding down moss covered rock faces. A good deal of the time we had to pass the stretcher from hand to hand.

Seven days after leaving the Gardiner hut we reached the West Coast road – ragged, lean and very tired. Seventeen of us had crossed over La Perouse and all had made it safely – although there had been a few close calls. Ruth was flown to Christchurch hospital and ultimately made a complete recovery.

It had been a considerable experience for me personally. Our rescue team had included many of New Zealand's finest climbers and I had plenty of chance to see them in action – and very impressive many of them were too. I noticed that some of the liveliest and most energetic weren't always the most reliable when the pressure came on. It helped confirm my growing belief that technical skill was not the only worthwhile characteristic of a first-class mountaineer – I was also learning to admire the soundness and mature judgment that came from wide experience.

Chapter 7

European Alps

1949 WAS AN IMPORTANT YEAR FOR THE HILLARY FAMILY. MY SISTER HAD
gone to England to complete a Master's degree at London University
and was about to marry an English doctor. There had been a bumper
harvest of honey from the bees so the family was more financially
affluent than it had ever been. It seemed a good opportunity for my
father to retire and let my brother and myself commence buying the
business with a long-term loan. Mother was in favour of this move – she
was anxious to be present at her daughter's wedding and see something
of Europe – also she had quite a lot of confidence in her sons. After
protracted discussions my father reluctantly agreed on the basis that he
retained some of the bees and all the buildings, vehicles and property.
My brother and I commenced operating the business on our own
account and with the minimum of equipment.

My parents duly went to England and were present at my sister's
wedding. They bought a new car and we waited to hear the good
news that they were setting out on their tour of Europe – but nothing
happened. By the end of the New Zealand summer – in April 1950 –
my brother and I had completed the honey crop and had a little money
in hand. I then received a letter from mother saying that dad had lost
all interest in going anywhere or doing anything. Would it be possible,
she asked, for me to come to England and drive them around the
Continent? At short notice I decided to go, and booked myself the
cheapest berth available on a ship from Sydney to London. Two of my
friends were leaving for Cambridge University at a similar time and
we agreed to join up somewhere and do a bit of mountaineering
together. I packed my climbing boots and ice-axe and set off to see the
world . . .

I crossed the Tasman Sea to Sydney in one of the old flying-boats
and then loaded my gear on a taxi and drove from the Rose Bay
Terminal to the P & O *Otranto* at the main wharves. I'd never been

Putting the roof on Kunde hospital with Tamserku behind.

Opening of Khumjung school by the Head Lama of Thyangboche.

Thami school.

School kids.

on an ocean liner before and just stood beside my baggage and looked aghast at the milling throng. I hadn't been there long when a large powerful man with a great air of authority came up to me and brusquely enquired if I was a boarding passenger. On confirming that I was he said, 'Leave your baggage here. Go over there, fill out a form and present your tickets.' I was mighty thankful for his generous help – obviously he was in charge of the wharf – although I was vaguely puzzled by the fact that he wasn't wearing a tie and he could have done with a shave. I duly returned with my documents completed.

'That's the lot,' he told me. 'Go on board now and your baggage will be taken to your cabin.'

What service, I thought, and with effusive utterances of thanks I turned towards the gangway.

'Hey!' shouted my impressive friend, 'how about paying the porter!'

I had never paid a porter or tipped anyone before and I was horrified at having made such a simple mistake. I looked anxiously around. 'Where's the porter?' I enquired.

He jabbed a huge thumb in his chest and roared, 'I'm the porter, mate!'

The *Otranto* was an ancient 20,000-ton liner in its last year of service and my six-berth cabin was down in the bowels of the ship. The boat was crammed with young Australians and New Zealanders travelling to Europe and a lively time was had by all – even by me. Time slipped quickly by and we revelled in the relaxed life at sea. We visited Colombo, Aden and the Suez Canal and I saw a little of how the rest of the world was living.

At the end of May I drove my parents through France, Italy, Switzerland, Austria, Germany and Holland. I was resigned to being bored – who would choose to see Europe with elderly parents? – but to my astonishment I enjoyed every moment of it. Mother was completely in her element and even dad gained a new lease of life. Restrictions on taking funds out of Britain made our finances rather tight but never desperately so. Each morning mother purchased food in a village market – she had only a few words of the local languages but this never seemed a problem. At lunch time we'd choose a beautiful corner off the main roads and cook a simple but adequate meal on our camp stove. We usually ate and slept in cheap 'pensions' but sometimes we'd treat ourselves to a meal at a good restaurant. Everything was made easier by the glorious spring weather, I cannot remember a single day of rain. In Italy I walked up the Leaning Tower of Pisa, and visited more art galleries than I ever hope to see again. Switzerland was glorious with spring flowers, and Austria a dream – with its tall church spires against a backdrop of forest green and mountain ridges. I was enthralled with the beautiful old buildings.

Back in England the weather continued fine and I left my parents in London and started exploring the country by train and double-decker bus. How I enjoyed the green rolling countryside, the glorious trees, and the ancient history! I spent many happy hours within the century old walls of cathedrals and churches. One morning I disembarked very early from a train in the town of Ely and searched out the venerable cathedral. It was well before public hours but I found an unlocked door and wandered inside. The great building was completely empty and very quiet. The morning sun streamed through high windows and my footsteps echoed from the paved floors. Ely Cathedral was built by the mother of Hereward the Wake – an old hero of mine – and in imagination I peopled the place with the warriors and maidens of a thousand years before. For an hour I was completely transported into the past.

In London I made the usual pilgrimage to Westminster Abbey and other ancient and venerable institutions. The royal tombs made history come alive for me and so did a hundred other relics of a mighty past. As a citizen of a new country with little history I felt I was being accepted back into the ancestral fold – it gave me an astonishingly warm feeling. In those days, like most of my fellow citizens, I was British first and a New Zealander second – it is only in recent years that we have been thrust firmly out of the family nest.

I saw a little of the other side of life too. For my age I was still rather naïve. While waiting in the Piccadilly tube station I was approached by a large and rather menacing character and listened with concern to his story of misfortune and hardship. It was quite a shock when I suddenly realised he was a beggar, and a mighty persistent and aggressive one too. It was very late and there were few people around; he kept crowding up on me and giving me the full benefit of his liquor laden breath. In the end I had to make it quite clear that I intended to thump him if he didn't desist and he shuffled off with a mighty sour expression. On another occasion I was having a haircut and the rather unattractive barber's assistant recognised my accent as antipodean and started whining about the problems of living in London and expressed his intention of striking it rich in Australia or New Zealand. I expressed my belief that a 'loser' in London could well prove to be a 'loser' in New Zealand, too, and he wholeheartedly agreed but felt that all doors would open for a man of such obvious talents as himself.

My days were passing all too quickly. It was soon time to leave on my last project – a climbing trip to Austria and Switzerland. With two fellow New Zealanders, Cecil Segedin and Bruce Morton, I boarded the train at Victoria Station in company with hundreds of holiday makers. I was surprised how many of them were laden with backpacks, ice-axes and ropes and suspected they were heading for a mass invasion of the north face of the Eiger. We felt rather ashamed of our less ambitious plans – until we eaves-dropped on the experts and discovered that most of them were tramping through France or were planning a camping holiday at the Riviera. We rattled into Paris and had to change trains and stations – and discovered how energetically the Parisien taxi driver despised foreigners, particularly country cousins like ourselves. Our train left the Gare de l'Est at ten thirty p.m. en route to Innsbruck and it was crammed to capacity. The wooden seats in the third class-carriage were extremely uncomfortable and we gave relief to our sore bottoms by climbing into the commodious luggage rack and having a quiet snooze – having no difficulty in ignoring the complaints of passengers and guard who only spoke French anyway.

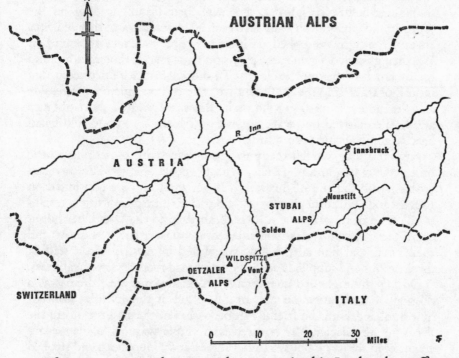

After a twenty-two-hour marathon we arrived in Innsbruck scruffy, dirty and tired. Our unshaven faces were turned firmly away from several of the better-class hotels but we finally obtained rooms in an unexciting boarding house much more suited to our pockets. We had little knowledge of the Austrian mountains and when we discovered an impressive pamphlet on the Stubai Alps we decided this would be as good a place to start as any. Clean, rested and equipped with a selection of colourful Austrian clothing we travelled by bus to the village of Neustiff.

As our initial objective we chose an easy peak called Hoher Burgstal, 8,571 feet, which had a track leading all the way to the top. We followed a well-graded path through pleasant open pine forest for three and a half hours and then reached the Starkenburger hut at 7,300 feet. The weather had unfortunately deteriorated by this time and we were surrounded by cloud. Feeling in need of a rest after our strenuous efforts we entered the hut and found it full of cheerful young schoolgirls, looking a good deal fresher than we did. After lunch we pushed on into the mist and despite some difficulty in knowing which path to take we finally reached the large cross indicating the summit. Heavy fog restricted our view so we scribbled our names in a large book thoughtfully provided on top and made our plans for the descent. We decided to pioneer a little so ignored the many broad paths leading off the summit and plunged instead down an ill-defined track that led into an easy rock gully supplied with a wire rope to hinder the climber. We then glissaded down some easy slopes for several thousand feet and finally emerged below the clouds. To our chagrin we discovered that instead of traversing the mountain we were still on much the same side and the same group of giggling schoolgirls was only a short distance away. We enjoyed our walk down through the forest and felt it had been a good get-fit programme.

Next morning we felt ready to get to grips with something a little more demanding and preferably with fewer schoolgirls. We travelled by bus up to the end of the valley. In the light rain we continued on foot through beautiful pine forests and passed some delightful waterfalls to the head of the valley and then climbed up to the Dresdener hut at 7,570 feet. This hut was well situated amongst a circle of snow and rock peaks and like all the huts we visited in Austria had a staff of three or four and supplied accommodation and food at very cheap rates.

During the night it rained again and in the morning there was a dusting of fresh snow on the tops. We left at the civilised hour of nine a.m. and with the friendly good wishes of the staff set off up the Fernauferner Glacier. We had received ample warning of dangerous crevasses in this area, but we found it pleasantly innocuous and strolled to an easy pass at the head. From the pass a long rock ridge ran up to the Schaufelspitz, 10,932 feet, and this we ascended in the hot sun with much loss of perspiration but little technical difficulty. We reached the top in the early afternoon and after a brief rest to enjoy the very fine view we descended the standard route to the south and returned to the hut over a couple of easy snow passes. We were welcomed back like conquering heroes and as we sat in comfort, sipping cool beers, we agreed that Austrian mountaineering had some distinct advantages over its rather more rugged New Zealand counterpart.

Next day we traversed a couple of pleasant summits and crossed the range to the delightful village of Solden in the Oetztal Alps. As a celebration we treated ourselves to a luxurious lunch in the best hotel and noticed a magnificent Rolls Bentley parked in front. We were halfway through our meal when there was a commotion at the door and a young couple entered, glanced around the room, and came over to our table. Speaking in a rather stilted English voice the man introduced himself and then asked if he and his wife could join us for lunch. We were puzzled at this interest – the girl was handsome and well dressed while the man gave an impression of affluence; we could hardly refuse to eat with them. We quickly realised we had little in common, but the couple's geniality never faltered. Finally we discovered the solution – they were under the impression that the Rolls Bentley belonged to us. When I gleefully informed them we were only impecunious colonials they hastily completed their meal and departed.

We had an exciting ride in a jeep up valley to the village of Vent and our cheerful driver informed us he had driven a tank for Rommell in the Western Desert. We shouldered our loads and climbed to the substantial Breslauer hut at 9,314 feet and were warmly welcomed by Frau Christine Egger and her two beautiful daughters. Before long we were comfortably installed in the kitchen with its delicious smells and glowing stove. For a few glorious days we climbed mountains and helped with the chores. We were very reluctant to leave this friendly haven.

We decided to return to Solden by way of a high pass to the west of the Wildspitze. Bowed down with all our gear we trudged up the approach glacier on a crisp and beautiful morning. The usual route to the pass crossed the bottom of a steepish snow slope, entered an icy looking gully and then followed up some easy rocks. At the bottom we met a party of three Italians who were arguing violently amongst themselves. The leader had crampons and was climbing rapidly up the firm snow. The other two were without crampons and seemed distinctly apprehensive. Realising their predicament we started chipping steps up the slope ahead of them and they thankfully followed after. This snow slope ran in a single great sweep to the ridge above the pass and offered an interesting variation to the standard route. Satisfied with our good deed for the day, we ignored the traverse to the left and continued straight up the slope to a barrage of frenzied but receding cries. The snow was beautifully firm and we made fast time, enjoying the sense of exposure. Near the top it became very steep and icy so we scrambled on to good sound rock and moved up to the ridge above the pass. The view of glacier and peak was magnificent.

Stimulated by the climb we started down an easy ice slope to the pass and with much flourishing of my ice-axe I hacked a trail in a flurry of chips – just as our Italian trio emerged on the pass by the more conventional route. I confess to a glow of self-satisfaction when the leader commented, 'I see you have been on a mountain before!'

Our route lay across the fine glacier draining the north-west face of the Wildspitze and we soon struck tracks leading in the right direction and had no difficulty in winding across a heavily crevassed glacier and lightheartedly slid down steep slopes on the seats of our pants. We passed a party climbing the mountain by the standard route and watched with interest as a member fell through into a crevasse and was hauled out by the guide with a casual nonchalance that indicated plenty of practice. We reached Solden in the late afternoon – hot, tired but very content. We had enjoyed our Austrian trip enormously. Very little of the climbing had been difficult but we had crossed some beautiful country and had been warmly welcomed by the local inhabitants – and everything had been incredibly cheap.

I was looking forward to visiting Switzerland with immense enthusiasm and great respect. This was the home of mountaineering and of epic climbs. In a way the contrast with Austria was a disappointing one. The mountains were magnificent, the facilities superb, the scenery groomed to perfection, the prices astronomical, and the welcome eager but condescending.

We started at Grindlewald under the great north face of the Eiger. Cecil Segedin had only a few days left and we wanted to climb the famous Jungfrau before he returned to England. We studied our maps and route guides and decided to start our climb from the Bergli hut. The easiest approach was to use the famous railway which winds its way through the rocky heart of the Eiger up to the Jungfraujoch station at 11,333 feet. It seemed that the Bergli hut could be approached from the Eismeer station and this suited us as the train ticket was much cheaper to Eismeer.

We caught the eleven a.m. train at Grindelwald and were soon clacking slowly up the steep hillside with many glorious views of famous peaks – Wetterhorn, Schreckhorn and Eiger. At Kleine Scheidegg we transferred into the Jungfraujoch railway and disappeared into the dark cold bowels of the mountain. We told the guard of our plan to get off at Eismeer and he expressed considerable surprise – the route to the Bergli hut hadn't been used for some time, he informed us curtly, we would be better advised to carry on to the Jungfraujoch.

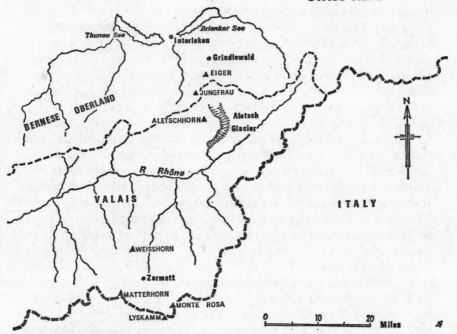

We had a brief discussion – our plans were made and we didn't want to waste money – why not try the Eismeer route? Eismeer station was a large chamber hollowed out of the rock with a tunnel leading to an observation window set into the cliff and a mighty view of glacier and mountain, We enquired about access to the open air and were rather grumpily directed down a narrow ill-lit tunnel to a small steel door. We pulled the door open and received a blast of cold air – then stepped out onto a narrow rocky platform high above the snows.

Below us was a vertical thirty foot rock face polished smooth by the glacier. At the bottom was a large crevasse. How did one usually get down? Help was at hand. A railway employee appeared carrying a rope ladder over his shoulder. In lugubrious tones he warned us about using this route, then shrugged his shoulders, attached the ladder to a steel hook set in the wall and threw it down the bluff. We hastily donned our boots, descended to the snow and scrambled rather uncomfortably over the crevasse. Standing forlornly with rucksack in one hand and my shoes in the other I watched the ladder being rapidly withdrawn and heard the door slam with a positive finality.

We moved out into the sun and produced some food to bolster our sagging morale. By the time we were ready to carry on, our good spirits had returned. To reach the Bergli hut it was necessary to cross a broken ice fall nearly a mile in width. We set off in the soft afternoon snow and wound our way past crevasses and seracs, often having to backtrack but slowly making height and distance. Our main problem appeared to be a big crevasse near the top of the icefall and we traversed to the left as it looked easier to cross there. On reaching the crevasse we found our easy way was an illusion and that nothing remained but to try and scale the ice wall direct. Fortunately a good snow bridge stretched from the lower lip to the upper wall, leaving only a fourteen foot vertical section to be surmounted. By standing on the bridge I was able to cut a large step about seven feet up. Cecil then belayed us and Bruce climbed onto my shoulders and somewhat nervously scrambled into the step. The step proved unequal to the task, gave way with a rush, and we both landed on the snow bridge with a substantial thump. I returned to the ice face and reached high above my head to enlarge the damaged step and remove some of the ice above so that it would be possible for Bruce to stand upright. The ice chips tumbled merrily down into the depths of the crevasse. Once again Bruce climbed onto my shoulders and put his weight tentatively on the step – this time it held. He cut himself a handhold and then hacked a stairway up the top part of the face. We were glad when he wriggled out of sight and securely anchored himself in firm snow. There was much pulling and grunting before we all ascended this obstacle and safely reached easier ground beyond – and by then we had realised why this glacier was no longer classified as a tourist route. The Bergli hut was deserted and devoid of fuel or food – we had expected to obtain both there, so went to bed hungry.

The morning was beautifully clear and we left the hut at five a.m. and were delighted with the crisp snow underfoot. We crossed several small saddles and two large snowfields under the face of the Monch until we arrived at the Jungfraujoch station. This station, hollowed out of the rock, was really a small village with hotel, restaurant, post office, and souvenir shop. Here we deposited most of our gear and then set off again for the Jungfrau, 13,642 feet. It was now becoming very hot and we were soon breaking through the crust and making heavy work of it. The route lay through a large snow basin steep in its upper slopes, and slightly corniced at the top. The soft snow and very hot sun made our progress laborious in the extreme. There had been a recent snow fall and there wasn't another track to be seen, but this made things more enjoyable. On crossing the ridge we met a cold wind which improved the surface, and our energy, and we were soon scrambling up the last few hundred feet which was quite exposed. It was a thrill when we finally set foot on the summit – a picture of the

Jungfrau had been a treasured possession when I was a child – and now I was standing on top of the mountain! The view was magnificent but the wind was very cold. We cautiously descended the steep upper section and crossed back over the ridge. Out of the wind it was unbearably hot and we found it a tiring journey back to the Jungfraujoch. I think we were suffering a little from our lack of food over the previous twenty-four hours.

As a special treat we had lunch in the restaurant. We were eating a fine meal when an American tourist approached and asked if he could take our photograph. He had followed our climb all the way, he told us, with his powerful binoculars. He complimented us enthusiastically on our performance and I felt a bit embarrassed as we had really been rather slow over the last section.

'Say, Bud!' he said generously in reply to my protestations 'you've got to go slow out there else you'll fall down dead!'

When we emerged into the observation room we were objects of great interest. Deluded no doubt by my Austrian hat and unshaven countenance a pretty auburn haired girl approached me and asked politely if I spoke English. I rose to the occasion and replied 'Yawohl, a leedle . . .' but could not continue the act and burst out laughing. When she discovered I was only a New Zealander she departed flushed and furious.

Cecil clambered aboard the train which would take him down the mountain and finally back to London. Bruce and I plunged down the five miles of the Aletsch Glacier to the Concordia hut. The hut was being repaired by a large group of workmen and as we still didn't have any food we managed to persuade the hut-keeper to let us eat with them. I found the constant diet of spaghetti and garlic sausage rather monotonous. The next two days were fine and warm and we climbed the Finsteraarhorn on one day and the Monch on the next. It was quite a relief when the following morning was sufficiently unpleasant to give us a good excuse to crawl back into bed.

During the day we had long and friendly discussions with the large group of Swiss climbers who were based on the hut. One handsome girl asked me what I thought of Switzerland and I was enthusiastic about its beauty. 'Yes,' she agreed, 'Switzerland is the most beautiful country in the world!' I discovered she had never been outside the borders of her own country but she spoke with complete conviction.

As our last big effort in this area we planned to climb the Aletschhorn 13,784 feet by an interesting route over the summit of the Dreickhorn, 12,500 feet. We left the hut at three a.m. and although we didn't have much trouble crossing the glacier in the dark we unfortunately struck the side of the ridge rather far up and had a steep and difficult face climb over good rock before reaching the crest. We found the ridge quite easy and made excellent progress. At 11,500 feet we reached a section of snow that had looked very steep and exposed from below. It was certainly steep but the morning sun had already softened it and we were able to kick safe steps up to the foot of the summit rocks. Stimulated by our progress we tackled the rocks with enthusiasm and emerged on top of the Dreickhorn at eight a.m.

Before us stretched almost two miles of ridge to the higher summit of the Aletschhorn – and the first mile of this looked narrow and interesting. Far ahead we could see two parties ascending by the ordinary route. Strapping on our crampons we charged along the ridge in perfect snow conditions, traversing steeply to avoid some cornices and cutting a few steps when necessary. Halfway along the ridge there was a steep dip and we descended this with care kicking our crampons well into the icy crust. Then the ridge broadened and we came onto the tracks of the other parties.

The route was now a series of snow and rock bumps – easy climbing technically but tiring in the hot sun. We were making fast time and soon caught and passed one of the other teams, judging by the strong smell of spirits, they had been celebrating their climb the night before. We scrambled up the final rock ridge to the summit to be welcomed by the second party – a friendly middle-aged Englishman and his Swiss guide.

It was very pleasant on top and we had the usual round of photographs. We were in no particular hurry to depart but the guide enquired rather abruptly about the route we planned to use for the descent. When I said we intended going down his upward line he suggested we should leave first as we would travel more quickly. We were agreeable and I said it would only take us a few moments to put on our crampons down the ridge a bit. 'You will not need your crampons,' he commanded us brusquely but we duly strapped them on all the same. I felt a certain coolness as we shot past his party and raced on down the ridge.

At mid-day we reached the spot where we had to leave the ridge and drop directly down to the glacier some 2,500 feet below. From above, this route looked quite spectacular. It was composed of a steep rubble ridge running down between two great ice couloirs which were obviously subject to a lot of rock fall. We gingerly commenced our descent and to our relief found it easy going. We simply walked down the steep soft rubble losing height rapidly but taking considerable care as any fall would have been difficult to check. Soon an added danger commenced as the other party started showering rocks from above. These channelled into the icy slopes on either side of us but made uncomfortable companions as they whizzed by. I realised then why the guide wanted us to go first.

The ridge seemed interminable in the hot sun but finally ended in a precipice. Our route led across to the right under the ice slope and much shouting went on between the two parties before the rock falls stopped and we made an undignified but rapid crossing to safer ground. Further scrambling took us down to the glacier by two o'clock and after a certain amount of dodging amongst large crevasses we reached easier going and were soon back at the hut. To our surprise we received a rousing cheer from the workmen who had followed our climb throughout.

Despite our long day Bruce and I decided to leave the hut and descend to the valley – a walk of several hours. We had a short rest and packed our gear – then I went to find the hut-keeper and pay the bill. I had just completed this task when a very worried guide came rushing in the door and started talking quickly to the hut-keeper. 'Where is the Englishman?' I enquired, wishing to say goodbye.

'He is down a crevasse!' I was informed by the chagrined guide. While crossing a very large ice bridge it had collapsed and precipitated the Englishman into the depths. The guide was a strongly built man and had managed to hold his companion after he had fallen about fifteen feet, and had in fact dragged him to the top on two occasions. But the climber was too shaken to help himself out. The guide had no alternative but to lower him down the crevasse to a snow bridge and then leave him there while he hurried off for assistance. A party of carpenters, bricklayers and guides was quickly assembled and laden with ropes, blankets and a sledge they set off up the glacier. I had offered our services only to have them gruffly declined.

After the rescue party had departed Bruce and I decided we couldn't go down valley and leave a compatriot in a crevasse – maybe the chap would appreciate talking to another English-speaking person? Despite our rebuff we quickly set off after the team and soon caught up to them. We were approaching a group of big crevasses at the foot of the ridge and as the trail was now fairly obvious Bruce and I raced on ahead. The unfortunate victim had been down the crevasse for several hours and I didn't know what to expect as I crawled carefully up to the shattered ice bridge – blood and injuries, possibly even death from exposure? I poked my head over the edge and looked down. A small neatly dressed figure with hat on head was stamping around on a snow bridge fifty feet below and swinging his arms across his body to keep warm. I shouted a welcome and in formal fashion he expressed his pleasure at seeing me. He was perfectly all right, he said, but rather chilly.

The rescue team was very expert! One of the men was lowered and the Englishman was soon hoisted out on three ropes. He was dragged down the glacier on the sledge and assisted into the hut. Next morning, although very stiff and sore, he was not much the worse for his adventure. When we departed his grumpy guide actually waved us goodbye.

It was a great thrill to arrive at Zermatt in the heart of the Swiss climbing area and be able to look on the famous slopes of the Matterhorn. The town was full of tourists and we were approached by a number of guides offering to take us up the peak. We decided instead to visit the Monte Rosa area and travelled there by train and on foot. Our efforts to get information in the hut were once again frustrated by suggestions that we take a guide, and we had depressing accounts of the difficulties and dangers ahead of us. On the first fine day we left the hut at three a.m. bound for the Lyskamm. The route lay up the broken Grenz glacier for something over five miles and despite the warnings we found the climbing pleasant and not too arduous.

After four hours of steady going we reached the Lysjoch – the saddle between Monte Rosa and the Lyskamm – and were rather taken aback to find large numbers of tourists wandering around the place, they had travelled by cable car from Italy.

The narrow corniced ridge running up to the Lyskamm looked most impressive and I remembered reading about disasters that had occurred there. We approached the ridge up a steep face and did some energetic cramponing to bring us out onto the ridge some distance up. This was exhilarating climbing and we carried energetically on, taking great care in the section with large cornices. The ridge now broadened into a steep face which proved quite icy and I started cutting steps. Before long we could move freely again and at nine thirty-five we climbed onto the narrow summit after a most enjoyable ascent.

There was a cold wind on top and we were finding our clothing wasn't terribly effective. We moved off quickly and descended straight down the ridge – kicking our crampons hard in. We didn't find it difficult although it probably looked quite spectacular to the tourists who were shouting and pointing at us from the Lysjoch. Once down on the saddle we decided to finish off the day by traversing over the top of Monte Rosa. The ridge running up to the mountain from the saddle didn't look very steep and we knew the standard route on the other side was considered quite easy.

It was a long trudge across the saddle, and very tiring work breaking trail in the soft snow. I was happy for Bruce to take a spell in the lead. As we approached the ridge I instinctively let out a little more rope and then, without thought, thrust my ice-axe deep into the snow as a belay. Next moment there was a great Woomph! and Bruce and a huge piece of cornice disappeared in slow motion out of sight down a great drop. I whipped a loop of the rope around the shaft and hung on grimly; the weight came on with a great jerk, but held; and I listened to the cornice rumbling further and further down the mountainside until all was quiet.

I called out into the silence and after a long wait I heard a faint reply, weakened by the wind. Bruce was O.K., he said; he hadn't stopped too abruptly; he'd held on to his ice-axe; he'd swung against a slope and could anchor himself to ease some of the pressure on the rope. 'Can you take enough on the belay so I could pull in the rope a bit?' I bellowed down to him. He'd try I finally heard. I wasn't terribly happy about my own position. Strain marks on the snow came back to my belay – maybe some more might peel off? With a considerable physical effort I got the rope over my shoulder and lifted hard . . . the rope moved up. I quickly extracted my ice-axe and plunged it a couple more feet further back, into safer ground. For half an hour we worked and ten feet of rope came in as Bruce eased up the slope. At one stage I heard voices and a party came down the ridge above. I waved to them and they waved back in friendly fashion, then dropped out of sight.

Twenty feet of rope was now in and I could speak to Bruce much more readily. We were only making slow progress but would in the end undoubtedly have succeeded. Fortunately, quicker help was at hand. Down the ridge came three climbers – two guides and one client. I called and waved – they stopped, looked, and then moved over towards us. I was glad to see them! I explained the situation and one of the guides, well belayed, wriggled forward on his stomach and dropped a rope with a loop in the end for Bruce's foot. Then it was only a matter of time and soon a snow-clad figure came writhing over the top gasping for breath. Bruce had been down the slope for more than an hour. The guides pulled him to safety and told him to lie down. In due course, they said, a stretcher would be obtained and a rescue undertaken.

'How are you, Bruce?' I enquired, horrified at the thought of such complications.

'I'm O.K. but a bit shaken up,' he told me.

'Think you could walk down?'

'Give it a try!' he said.

I thanked the guides for their help and told them we'd be on our way. They protested vigorously but we were off. Our descent of the Grenz Glacier was easy at first but became more laborious as the shock started to affect Bruce. We were very slow over the last section and very glad to get to the hut. It had been an eventful day.

Bruce was bruised and sore next morning but we descended to

Zermatt in deteriorating weather. We weren't sorry when rain gave us a day of rest, and snow on the tops prevented any climbing for a few days. We made our way leisurely up to the Weisshorn hut with the intention of climbing that famous mountain. For a couple of days we could do nothing but then the weather cleared and we set off early in the morning towards the standard route up the East ridge. We had easy travelling over the glacier approaches and then up a rocky shelf. The route guide informed us that this approach was sometimes subject to stonefall but now everything was frozen firm. We chipped up a hard-packed snow slope towards a great loose rock face and in the dim light had quite a job getting access onto the first steep rock. Then we traversed backwards and forwards up loose shelves and as the light improved our confidence grew and we made faster time. We emerged onto the east ridge and saw a fine rock arete stretching above us and now well plastered with fresh snow. The sun was tipping the peaks and we started to really enjoy ourselves although two steep pitches had ice on the rocks and forced us to take some time and much care.

For the last thousand feet the ridge was largely snow and the sense of exposure increased. The surrounding summits were dropping below us and the views were most spectacular. A light layer of snow covered an icy undersurface and it needed a lot of hard kicking before a decent grip could be obtained with the crampons. The ridge broadened into a face, quite steep in its upper part and we climbed steadily up this. We were a hundred feet from the top when some figures started descending towards us – they were two parties who had traversed over from the north ridge. We met about fifty feet from the top and we were only too pleased to use their tracks for the final stretch.

It was an exciting moment for us – the summit of a famous peak, and in the distance the great finger of the Matterhorn reaching towards the sky. But the wind was cold and we didn't stay long. We chased down after the others and on the rocky part of the ridge all three parties stopped and had lunch together. The sun was now obscured by cloud and we were surrounded by driving mist so no one felt like taking too long over the meal. We descended the ridge with caution and once I had warmed up again I started to really enjoy it. At the point where Bruce and I had joined the east ridge we all stopped and had a discussion. It was agreed that we would use the shorter route – our route of ascent – even though it wasn't recommended by the guide books as this part of the mountain was rapidly falling away. Keeping close together to minimise the danger from loose rocks we moved steadily down the face – releasing a barrage of rocks in front of us. We soon reached the much steeper and more difficult lower portion. With no obviously easy way down, all three parties commenced prospecting for routes on either side of a large rock couloir. Suddenly there was a rumble far above and as everyone ducked for cover an enormous rock avalanche swept the couloir and the ridges on either side. Half-ton boulders were crashing around and we were peppered with dust and rubble. From my haven under a bulging rock I saw a wave of giant boulders sweep right over one pair and gave up all hope of their survival. When the dust cleared they were still there – an overhanging rock had proved their salvation and they emerged unharmed but very shaken by their experience. We helped them down to the snow and then glissaded quickly out of the danger area. Bruce and I rushed ahead back to the hut for a quick meal, then packed our gear and descended to the railway in the valley. Our European climbing trip was over.

It is interesting to look back after twenty-five years. Face climbs are now the normal procedure and even beginners are festooned with front point crampons, jumars, and enough rope to berth a battleship. Judged by modern standards our climbs in Austria and Switzerland were very modest – we, in fact, regarded them as being modest at the time. Conditions and standards have changed much in the quarter of a century. We were using nailed boots and heavy manilla ropes; we didn't have the advantage of warm down jackets; and although we had read about pitons and other climbing paraphernalia we certainly didn't possess any of them. Nearly every party we saw was conducted by guides and we struck a great reluctance to give any information or advice; very different from the more informal and helpful atmosphere in our own sparsely populated mountains.

But it had been a marvellous experience all the same; even to see some of the famous classic mountains had been a thrill. Our equipment was second rate and our techniques no doubt mediocre, but we were strong and energetic and the guided parties were always moving too slowly for our liking. I returned to England and New Zealand very content with the use I had been able to make of my time. My horizons had been greatly broadened and I was determined to do more travelling in the future.

Chapter 8

To the Himalayas

WHENEVER I THINK OF MY EARLY DAYS IN THE HIMALAYAS, GEORGE LOWE automatically comes to mind. George was a primary school teacher in New Zealand and a born entertainer. I have never laughed longer and louder than I did in his company. He was tall and strong and a formidable climber with an effective ice-axe and bouncing energy. For quite a few years in New Zealand George and I didn't actually climb together but we were always meeting in huts or on glaciers and seemed to get on particularly well. We even talked about the possibility of organising some sort of a trip to the Himalayas and it was agreed that I should try and find out how we should go about it.

Towards the end of my visit to Europe I received a letter from George saying that a well-known climbing foursome in New Zealand had also decided to organise a Himalayan trip. Their objectives were very ambitious – Kangchenjunga or even Everest. They had invited George to join them and on his suggestion they were inviting me too – was I interested? Interested in going to the Himalayas? I certainly was even though I knew a score of climbers in the country who were technically more competent than I was. Despite such feelings of inadequacy I was confident I could make a worthwhile contribution. I wasn't foolish enough to believe it was only my climbing abilities that were being considered – you had to be prepared to take the time, too, and raise your share of the cash.

Over the next few months the membership of the party changed and shrank in size – and so did the objectives. Only one of the original group remained, Earle Riddiford, but George Lowe and I were still there and we had a fourth member, Ed Cotter. Money was hard to come by and so indeed was mountain permission. In the end we settled for a shoe-string expedition, very largely financed out of our own pockets. Our main objective was the unclimbed Mukut Parbat, 23,760 feet, in the Gawhal Himalaya. Although several other New

Zealand climbers had gone on Himalayan expeditions before, we were the first all New Zealand party and we had to start right from scratch.

Our organiser was Earle Riddiford, a young lawyer with a shrewd brain and tons of drive and ambition. Bespectacled and not particularly robust looking, he hardly filled the image of a rugged mountaineer but he had an impressive record of good climbs. His enthusiasm never faded and it was only due to his persistence that we managed to get away.

In January 1951 we had a test run in New Zealand – an attempt on the formidable unclimbed Maximillian ridge of Mount Elie de Beaumont. We backpacked seventy pounds over high and difficult passes, weathered a torrential northwest storm, and established a base camp on the remote Burton Glacier. I was quickly learning to appreciate the qualities of the others; Ed Cotter's whimsical humour; George's boisterous competence; Earle's cool intellect. In one glorious day we battled our way up the magnificent Maximillian ridge and reached the summit of the mountain. George and I had teamed up for the first time and George led most of the climb in impressively calm and confident fashion. Apart from Harry Ayres who had no equal, I thought George the most competent climber I had been with and it was a happy and successful trip.

We left New Zealand at the beginning of May 1951 and travelled by flying boat to Sydney where we joined the P & O *Orion*. The ship was crammed with young people travelling to Europe and we revelled in the relaxed and lively atmosphere. I believe our foursome made some small impact on the life of the ship – certainly Ed Cotter's remarkable ability to walk on his hands along the rail of the ship in heavy seas attracted the attention of the young ladies – and the ship's master-of-arms. As my previous trip had made me familiar with the ports we visited I quickly acquired the title of 'Cosmo P' being short for Cosmopolitan Percival. It was with great reluctance that we left the ship in Colombo and left our friends and romances behind. There was a sorrowful atmosphere on the train as we rattled through the glow-worm speckled night towards the tip of India.

May is a bad month for travelling in India – or it was in the days before air-conditioned trains. Everything was dry and dusty before the monsoon rain and the temperatures were very high. This was reflected in barren fields and drying water holes and gave a desolate effect to the very flat countryside. But there was plenty to see – the many villages and the amazing variety of people kept our interest at a high pitch.

On May 25th we arrived at Madras and spent the day there while waiting for our next train. As we wandered around the city I couldn't help contrasting the magnificent buildings and fine roads with the pitiful multitudes of deformed beggars and poor people. I even saw a dead man lying unnoticed in the gutter. Our train departed in the evening but the setting sun brought little relief from the heat and we were soon enveloped in dust again. We had the luxury of a shower in our compartment and this gave us a little relief – until the water supply ran out.

For days we travelled on. One morning we watched dozens of small children laden with bags of rice stealing free rides on the train. They clung on the sides, on the roof, and even underneath on the bogeys. At every stop police chased them with sticks, but for every child that was driven off two more clambered on behind the policemen's backs. With amazing fortitude these children hung on the sides of the train for a non-stop run of nearly fifty miles and we allowed some into the carriage where they sat on the floor with a patient resignation which struck me as a common feature of Indian life. On reaching their village the children darted for cover receiving many hearty blows from the band of police-men awaiting the train's arrival.

After five days' travelling from Colombo we arrived in India's largest city, Calcutta, and were impressed again by the fine buildings in the modern part of the city. However a short walk down a side street landed us in an area of unimaginable squalor filled with seething masses of the local inhabitants. Never had the contrast between riches and poverty seemed so great to me. I felt the stirrings of conscience – life was pretty easy in New Zealand – what were we doing about such problems?

We left the slums of Calcutta behind and raced through the dust-choked night in the 'Bombay Mail', crossing the river Ganges at Benares. Then it was on to Lucknow and a temperature of 113 degrees in the shade and finally the terminal of the railway in the town of Kathgodam in the foothills of the Himalayas. Tired though we were of train travel it had been an amazing experience; now we could feel a growing excitement at the knowledge that we would soon be amongst the mountains.

We chartered a bus, loaded our gear on board, and drove slowly up the fifty-eight miles of well formed road that twisted its way to the famous hill station of Ranikhet at over 6,000 feet. We broke through the pine forests onto the crest of the ridge, and there were the moun-tains – Nanda Devi, Trisul and a host of others. Our hearts were filled with wild enthusiasm and we were impatient to be on our way up into them. I felt a rush of emotion at this first sight of the Himalayas and wandered off by myself in the dust to revel in the great peaks lining the horizon and to soak up the exciting sounds and smells.

The Himalayan Club had arranged that four Sherpas would be

waiting in Ranikhet for us and it was equally exciting to meet them. Their reputations as high altitude porters were well known to us from Himalayan literature and now we would be working with some of these famous men. Passang, Tondu, Nima and Tenzing immediately impressed us with their air of cheerful efficiency and we were soon working together as a happy team.

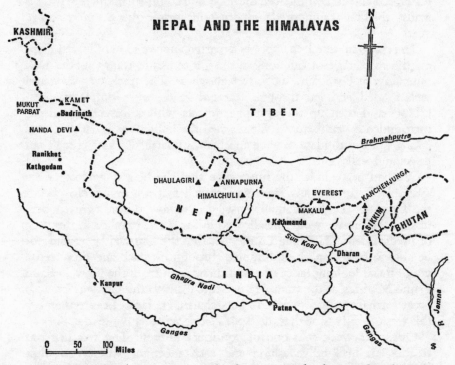

Our immediate objective was the famous Hindu shrine of Badrinath, a trip of over one hundred miles across many deep valleys and high passes. In a fury of activity we repacked all our luggage into sixty-pound loads, bought more food, and signed on thirty local 'coolies' for the ten-day march. We added an unexpected member to our party for the walk into the mountains—a young Indian student, Keki Bunshah, who was on holiday in Ranikhet. Keki was later to become deputy leader of an Indian Everest expedition and a distinguished lawyer; we found him pleasant company and a most useful interpreter.

Two incidents brought home to me that we were now in a strange new country, very different from our peaceful New Zealand. I picked up my shirt one morning and a five-inch scorpion fell to the floor and scuttled away into a dark corner. The same evening we were walking through the forest when a lithe dark shadow shot across the road ahead of us – it was a black panther, stalking its favourite food, a domestic dog.

On June 2nd all was ready and we loaded our luggage, four Sherpas, thirty porters and ourselves into two buses for the fifty-mile journey to the start of the walking track. Nearly all of our porters became sick on the winding mountain roads and they were a sorry sight by the time we reached our destination. Back on solid ground they quickly recovered and we commenced the noisy and colourful business of issuing loads – the first of a hundred such occasions for me over the next twenty years.

The chaos subsided, the porters departed and we soon followed them on the first stage of our long walk – a ten-mile tramp to the Dak bungalow at Gwaldam, 2,000 feet above us. The track was wide and well graded and led through terraced fields, over simple wooden bridges and then up through pine forests with a few small villages surrounded by cultivation. We reached the bungalow as darkness was falling but not too late to have another wonderful view of Himalayan peaks and valleys.

We had been under the impression that the Dak bungalows were available for use by any legitimate traveller at a nominal charge but the Chowkidar was adamant – we must have official written permission before we would be allowed inside. Earle excelled in this type of predicament. Gambling on the fact that the Chowkidar would not be able to read English he fumbled through his pack and produced a very official looking letter of recommendation from the New Zealand Prime Minister of the time. He presented this to the Chowkidar with great formality and it worked like a charm. As far as I can remember this was the only time that the P.M.'s letter was of any use to us.

Our next week was one of continual interest. The weather was treating us in kindly fashion and each morning we set off after breakfast into glorious sunny skies. We were carrying packs of thirty-five pounds to help with our acclimatisation and they didn't affect our appreciation of the beautiful hill country. We had a series of great ridges to cross and we'd climb steadily up through miles of rhododendron forest into pine woods and finally into open grazing country, carpeted with wild flowers. A steep grind over a 10,000 or 12,000 foot pass would be followed by a wild plunge 6,000 feet to the river far below. In the late afternoon we'd pitch our tents in some secluded spot and sit writing diaries or reading, with a background of cheerful shouts from our porters as they cooked their chapatties over small fires or prepared a bed for themselves under overhanging rocks.

We started to experience the porter trouble which so many expeditions had mentioned in their accounts. It was the inevitable conflict between our wish for the porters to travel as far as possible each day and their natural desire to do no more than a normal day's work. On one occasion we pressured them into a long seventeen-mile day over a high pass and we went to bed that night with cries of 'murderers! slave drivers!' ringing in our ears.

We had no idea of what was reasonable but ultimately adjusted to local standards and appreciated that ten miles a day with a heavy load over steep country was a fair effort. For this we were paying the porters three rupees a day (about 40 US cents).

On June 8th we arose early after a cold night spent at 10,000 feet. We had a quick breakfast, packed our small tents and were away by seven fifteen a.m. Ahead of us was a steep rise of 2,000 feet and as we were now very fit it took only an hour to reach the top of the famous Kuari Pass (12,400 feet). This was considered one of the finest viewpoints in the Himalayas and the view was certainly stupendous. Far across great valleys and ridges towered dozens of mighty giants. Fascinating names such as Nanda Devi, Dalaghiri, Gauri Parbat and Nilcanta were excitedly shouted about as we quickly identified some of the better known peaks from maps and photographs.

Our porters had taken much longer to reach the pass and they now displayed some reluctance to move on again. One of the porters was an exceptionally large man, heavily muscled, and he seemed to be the natural leader of the group. He also seemed to be something of a wit and we became the butt for many of his jokes – or so we suspected. We couldn't understand his comments but they brought ecstatic laughter from his companions. At first I found it easy to be philosophical about the matter but as our relationship with the porters deteriorated his comments became increasingly irritating.

From the Kuari Pass we wanted to drop 6,500 feet down to the valley below before camping – a big descent, it is true, but we'd had an easy morning. The porters refused and said they planned to stop in an hour or so and we seemed to have reached a stalemate. Grinding my teeth with frustration I was walking away from the group when the tall man chose to make another of his sharp comments ... and the porters roared with laughter. In a fury I swung around, grabbed his shirt front and made quite clear that I intended to let him have a king-sized uppercut. The reaction was astonishing – 'No! No, Sahib!' he pleaded, shrinking miserably away. My anger evaporated and I walked away leaving a very quiet group behind. Without much further complaint the porters carried on down the long hill to our destination.

After my first flush of triumph I started feeling a little poorly about my violent reaction. I remembered the social background of the porters and how unlikely it was they would defend themselves against a 'Sahib' – even such a lowly 'Sahib' as I was – let alone attack in return. I clearly had a social advantage and had been acting like a bully. I still lose my temper at times but I have learnt a lot since then . . .

On the eighth day we arrived in the large village of Joshimah, perched above the Aleknanda River on the main pilgrim route to Badrinath. The shrine at Badrinath, at 10,000 feet, was considered by the Hindus as one of the most sacred in India. All devout Hindus, we were told, tried to visit this shrine once in their lifetime. The long difficult trek at high altitudes was a great test for religious enthusiasm but we learned that 40,000 people were crossing this route on foot each year as soon as the winter snows melted. Certainly our two-day trip from Joshimah to Badrinath was an amazing experience. Pilgrims of all ages and social classes were moving steadily up valley filled with undoubted fervour. Most were walking; some rode on sure-footed ponies; others were carried in litters by four coolies; some were sitting in a woven bamboo seat on the back of a single porter. There were many old people making their last journey – happy to die in this holiest of Hindu shrines. The track was frequently hollowed out of solid rock and wound up and down the precipitous walls of the great Aleknanda Gorge. The confined air on this jostling route with no sanitation made travelling a trying business in the heat of the day and most of the pilgrims started well before dawn and rested during the mid-day hours.

Early on the morning of June 11th we came around a corner in the track and Badrinath lay below us – a shanty town with corrugated iron roofs. Dominating all was the giant temple with its gilded dome. We were seeing a sight which was the ultimate dream to millions of devout Hindus. What were their thoughts at reaching the same spot? Did they consider all their struggles and trials were being rewarded by this scene? An examination of nearby pilgrims failed to show any variation in their air of passive resignation. But many of the pilgrims we had met on the track returning from Badrinath had been shouting and singing, and bubbling over with enthusiasm. Apparently their visit to the sacred temple had worked some great change. High over the town towered the wonderful ice spire of Nilcanta (21,600 feet). It was a remarkable sight with its saw-toothed ice ridges and terrific rock faces. This was to be our first objective and my heart sank a little at the prospect.

We sorted out three weeks' supplies and engaged some men from the local village of Mana to act as porters. These Mana men were very hardy types – great carriers and excellent over rough country. They were terrifically independent and had strong views on their rights – firmly believing in a four-hour day with time off for lengthy puffs of the communal pipe. They were dressed in plain, heavy homespun woollen garments held together by constant mending and rarely, if ever, washed. On their feet they wore clumsy leather shoes but over difficult country they removed these and travelled in bare feet. Their dress was in contrast to our four Sherpas who had been supplied by us with much the same gear as we ourselves wore – heavy boots, warm woollen clothing, windproof outer garments, ice-axes and rucksacks.

After a short day's march from Badrinath we camped in a lovely open glade at the foot of the Satopanth Glacier. The next morning we climbed up the glacier along the lateral moraine. Sheer cliffs with great bulging rock faces closed in on us and when we turned the corner and saw the immense ice-clad north face of Nilcanta it looked impregnable and impossible. We established our base camp amongst the boulders at about 13,500 feet and then discharged the Mana men just as steady rain commenced falling. The temperature dropped, the rain turned to snow, and our tiny tents were soon sagging under the weight.

For five days the bad weather continued. During one brief clearing we made a reconnaissance to 15,000 feet across the north face of Nilcanta then retreated when we realised we weren't going to get much higher in that direction. By the time the weather showed signs of clearing on June 19th we were feeling very bored and frustrated so made quick preparations to establish a camp on the 18,000 foot saddle on the west ridge of Nilcanta.

We left camp at six a.m. and kicked steps up a steep snow slope into a large snow basin which was already very hot under the fiercely shining sun. The Sherpas were carrying forty-five to fifty lbs apiece and we had at least thirty lbs each; our progress was very laborious. We put on the rope and started to climb a long and steep slope of old avalanche snow. The altitude was draining our strength and each man could only kick steps for a few rope lengths before gaspingly giving way to a replacement.

We had nearly 5,000 feet of steep snow slopes between us and the west col, a formidable task in an alpine region and an over-ambitious one when working at these altitudes. We had many lessons to learn about altitude and acclimatisation and we learnt a lot of them on this venture. A sudden crash on our right made us jump with alarm and we watched some ice pinnacles tumble over a cliff and fan out on the snow far below. The slope was steepening considerably and making steps in knee deep snow proved an exhausting business. The Sherpas were carrying their heavier loads magnificently but could give us little assistance with the trail breaking.

After a time the weather clouded over, heavy mists surrounded us and snow commenced falling. Obviously a blizzard was brewing. Pushing on as hard as we could we drove our weary bodies upwards and at five p.m. dumped our loads just below the col. We had been moving for eleven hours. Little could be seen through the driving snow except ice-encrusted rock bluffs and snow slopes dropping steeply off into nothing. We quickly took the loads off our Sherpas and sent them back down our tracks to the relative comfort of base camp. They disappeared into the mist. Cold, miserable and very tired we used our two light shovels to excavate a narrow platform on the slope. With numb hands we pitched our two tents and tied them well down into the snow. Thankfully we crawled inside our tiny homes, shed our outer clothing, and scrambled inside our sleeping bags. Before long the gentle purr of our pressure stove and the scent of cooking food filled our tired bodies and minds with contentment. The raging blizzard outside was quickly forgotten.

All next day the bad weather continued with much snow falling. We kept warm in our double sleeping bags but had to resign ourselves to the cramped discomfort of our tents, reading, talking and cooking to pass the time. The following morning a temporary lifting of the weather enticed us outside. One look at the steep west rock ridge of Nilcanta was sufficient. Plastered as it was with fresh snow and ice we doubted if we would ever get up it. We decided instead to attempt an unclimbed snow peak of 20,500 feet to the west of us as we could see an obvious approach up a long corniced snow ridge.

Roping up we commenced slowly climbing, kicking steps in the deep soft snow. Several steep stretches required extensive step-cutting in ice and used up a lot of our limited energy. After three and a half hours of careful moving we had reached over 19,000 feet but were still a long way from our peak. Once again we were surrounded by clouds and snow commenced falling. We were very tired so returned to camp. What was wrong with us we wondered? We were proud of our strength and energy – what had happened to it now?

Next morning patchy weather and snow showers again delayed us but we finally crawled out of our tents, dressed in all our warm clothing and windproofs, and commenced climbing up our track of the previous day. We were going a little better and soon reached our previous furthest spot. Heavy mist obscured our route but we continued cautiously along the heavily corniced ridge. With the shafts of our ice-axes thrust deep in the snow as a belay we groped our way along, keeping well down the steep south face to escape the great cornice. The visibility was so poor that at times the top of the ridge was difficult to see. Soon we crept over 19,500 feet. I was leading at the time, laboriously kicking and cutting steps on the steep slope. Suddenly there was a great Woomph! An enormous cornice twenty five-feet wide dropped away on my right. Without hesitation I leapt quickly down the slope to my left and slapped my ice-axe deep into the snow. I knew the other three members of the party must have been on the cornice as it fell. Looking around as I jumped I saw three agile figures in the air at the same time. They too had instinctively leapt to safety as this great mass of snow and ice thundered down 4,000 feet to the glacier below. Leaning on our ice-axes and panting for breath we had no difficulty in deciding that under the conditions we would be better off to retreat.

After a long and cautious descent we arrived back at camp to find two of our Sherpas awaiting us. A brief conference followed. The monsoon had obviously broken. Fresh snow every day was making climbing difficult and dangerous, also we were insufficiently acclimatised and lacked the strength and energy to get very far. We struck camp and carrying very heavy loads struggled down through heavy snow to base camp. Even after the magnificent meal prepared by our other two Sherpas I went to bed with a feeling of futility and defeat.

We retreated back to Badrinath and at the lower altitude our confidence returned. To escape the monsoon snows we would go north to the Tibetan border, we decided, and tackle our major objective Mukut Parbat 23,760 feet. We should be much fitter by then. On June 27th Lowe and I left Badrinath and followed the Saraswati River up a great gorge and into an open valley lined with rugged peaks. At mid-day we stopped by a pleasant stream for lunch and watched great eagles circling above us with contemptuous ease. Far across the valley came the thin sound of a shepherd's flute and we could see a mixed flock of sheep and goats grazing on the lean pastures.

In late afternoon we reached the grazing alp called Gastoli. Here we expected to cross the Saraswati River but to our dismay found the bridge had been taken down during the winter months and had not yet been replaced. There was a surging mass of water sweeping through the thirty-foot gap. Our efforts to bridge the gap with great beams proved unsuccessful and we were forced to camp for the night alongside the river. Next morning two of us went back down the river for a couple of miles and crossed on a great pile of avalanche snow. We returned up the other side to drag several of the beams into place and make a shaky but adequate bridge.

We continued on up the valley and saw two men coming towards us. They had swarthy Mongolian countenances, great knives in their belts, and long red cloth boots. Our Sherpas greeted them cheerfully. They were Tibetans, we discovered, the first to cross Mana pass since the winter snows. They were driving a flock of long-haired sheep and goats, each carrying saddle bags containing salt for trading purposes.

We turned off the main valley and climbed the terminal face of the West Kamet glacier. By mid-afternoon we could look up miles of rock covered glacier to the great 25,000-foot bulk of Kamet but we still couldn't see Mukut Parbat. We camped at 15,500 feet in misty weather. We awoke with the sense of excitement that a good reconnaissance can bring. It was clear that we wouldn't see much from the floor of the valley so we climbed a steep rock and snow spur to over 19,000 feet. Gradually the great rock precipices of Mukut Parbat unfolded and to our intense disappointment we could see they offered no easy approach from this direction. We retreated back to the Saraswati river to meet Cotter and nineteen porters carrying three weeks of food and equipment. In misty cold weather we huddled around a smouldering fire of yak dung and discussed our plans.

Our only chance now was the Shamro glacier so we moved up valley again. As we approached the Tibetan border the terrain became increasingly barren and windswept. Mana pass into Tibet was clearly in sight ahead of us when we turned to the right and started climbing the heaped up moraine of the Shamro glacier. To save their shoes from ill-treatment our porters removed them and went barefooted over the sharp rocks. After several hours of travelling we chose a flat but uninteresting site to pitch our tents and established base camp at 16,000 feet.

For the next few days the weather was very unsettled with poor visibility and we were only able to establish that a great ice fall was blocking our way up the Shamro glacier. To our delight we discovered a grassy spot at 17,000 feet with a small stream of clear fresh water. We decided to move camp to this idyllic spot and pitched our tents on a carpet of mountain flowers. All around towered ice clad peaks – and none of them had been climbed.

At last a fine day arrived. Lowe, Cotter and I set off into a clear cold dawn. We went quickly up the glacier to the foot of the ice fall and then strapped on our crampons and wound our way past crevasses and seracs along a route we had chosen some days before. We got through the ice fall without too much difficulty and continued up the glacier which was split here and there by deep crevasses. We were soon in a position to see the whole of the approaches to Mukut Parbat and could pick what appeared an excellent site for our next camp at about 19,000 feet. Indeed, the route as high as 21,000 feet looked broken but certainly feasible. We felt a surge of optimism.

An impressive snow peak of over 20,000 feet was near at hand on the left branch of the Shamro glacier. Cotter did a fine lead up a steep ice gully onto a small glacier and then it was an easy walk to the foot of the peak. We chose a ridge of broken rock and laboriously made height. Just before mid-day we reached the summit ridge and could feel ourselves weighed down by the enervating effects of altitude. The ridge was heavily corniced and looked very unstable. In difficult snow conditions and feeling very concerned about avalanches we eased our way across the steep slope under the cornices and clambered up the last few hundred feet. With a burst of excitement we moved onto the top, 20,330 feet – we had climbed our first twenty thousand footer.

Our elation was tempered by fears that the snow would deteriorate and become more dangerous in the strong heat of the sun. We paused only for a few photographs and then Lowe started down the opposite ridge. The ridge was steep, narrow and crevassed but the snow here proved to be in good condition. Held on a tight rope from above, Lowe kicked and cut a safe route down the steepest part.

The ridge now ran for some two and a half miles with little loss of height to a peak directly above Camp I. We hoped that the snow along the ridge would give us good travelling but were sadly disappointed. The snow had a light crust which would almost hold our weight and then collapse and precipitate us hip and even waist deep. Our struggles along this ridge became a desperate procedure. We were enveloped in cloud and lashed by wind-driven snow. We found difficulty in keeping on the narrow ridge as it was heavily corniced and we were forced down on the steep south face. Cold, miserable and not a little worried we plunged along with frequent rests. An improvement in the weather came just as we struggled onto an easier part of the ridge.

Climbing up onto the summit of the subsidiary peak required a great effort. It was now five p.m. We had nearly 2,000 feet of steep rock and scree to descend and little energy left for the task. We reached camp just before dark and were greeted by Riddiford and the Sherpas with a strengthening cup of hot tea. To celebrate our success we opened a precious tin of peaches and talked with unabated enthusiasm until late in the night. It had been a long and tiring day but a great success and I felt that some of our confidence had been restored.

Two days later we set off to establish Camp II on Mukut Parbat. Heavily laden with gear we found the heat very trying as we climbed the ice fall and noted where an ice avalanche had swept over our previous tracks. Plugging slowly along we reached the head of the glacier and then cut steps up a steep slope onto a rock and snow saddle between the Shamro and west Kamet glaciers. Here there was an excellent camp site, well protected from the wind and with a good flat position for our tents. Our altitude was 19,000 feet and we had wonderful views of mountain and valley on all sides. We sent the Sherpas back down to Camp I for the night and we were soon driven into our tents by the cold.

The morning sun hit our camp at eight and made life pleasant again.

Above us was a great ice fall split by enormous crevasses and ugly ice cliffs. Somehow we had to get through this ice fall to reach the summit ridge of Mukut Parbat. Cotter and I set off on a reconnaissance and were able to make a safe route through the lower portion before the heat of the sun and tiredness from our previous day of heavy backpacking sent us scampering back to camp.

We returned to the attack at six a.m. next morning. It was particularly cold and we pulled on all the clothing we had. Our bodies kept reasonably warm but our feet gave us a lot of trouble – none of us had particularly effective boots and the higher we went the more we suffered. On the steep upper slopes George and I took turns at chipping a safe stairway in the hard frozen snow. Winding in and out amongst giant crevasses and great pinnacles of ice we were always seeking a safe route. We were suffering agonies with our feet. Just before eight o'clock we managed to cross out to the left on an ice shelf into the rays of the early morning sun. With cries of thankfulness we sat down, took off our boots and massaged our feet. It was at least an hour before we could continue with safety and comfort.

We moved on upwards, crossing several snow bridges over wide crevasses, and then entered a large snow basin before swinging to the right through a particularly broken area. A very shaky snow bridge was crossed with careful belaying of the rope around a well sunk ice-axe shaft. We cut up a steep ice slope and emerged on a snowy saddle at over 21,000 feet. We could look straight out onto the high plateau and the barren mountains of Tibet while above us towered the great ridge of Mukut Parbat. Our reconnaissance had been successful and the problem of the ice fall had been solved.

Bad weather intervened again but two days later we returned up this route with our four Sherpas and established Camp III on an ice shelf just under the Tibetan Col. Room was very limited and on one side we had a creaking ice cliff and on the other a great drop. Three of our Sherpas returned back to Camp II while Passang remained with us. I shared a tent with Passang and halfway through the night I woke to see him dimly crouched on his knees and murmuring some repetitive phrase I couldn't understand. I knew he had been trained as a Tibetan monk and could only suppose he was devoutly performing his religious observances. Several hours later I woke to see Passang on his knees once more, murmuring gently, and had difficulty in repressing my ire at such enthusiastic devotions. When it occurred a third time I felt I had grounds for complaint. I was about to express some modest criticism when something about his actions caused me to hesitate. I looked a little more closely and discovered that Passang's devotions were in fact his efforts to inflate a faulty air mattress.

July 11th dawned fine and clear but very cold. With our inadequate footwear we were afraid of frostbite and didn't dare leave our tents until the sun reached us at eight a.m. Then we roped up – Riddiford, Cotter and Passang on one rope and Lowe and myself on another. We climbed our ice steps onto the col and were once again greeted by a freezing wind. Lowe forced a fine route through deep, cold powder snow up a steep face and finally onto the main ridge of Mukut Parbat. The snow on the ridge was frozen hard and gave an excellent grip to our crampons but the strong wind made conditions very unpleasant. At 22,500 feet George and I reached a rocky outcrop where we could shelter from the wind. George was having a lot of trouble with his feet and mine didn't feel too comfortable. We cut a couple of seats in the icy slope, tied ourselves securely to a belay, and then removed our boots and massaged our feet back to life. Riddiford, Cotter and Passang climbed up to us and carried on through.

When our feet had recovered George and I moved on again – all set to get to grips with the upper part of the mountain. We crossed an icy bump and saw that the ridge narrowed appreciably and dropped away in a shallow dip before sweeping up again towards the summit. Perched in the dip, cutting steps in hard ice, was Earle Riddiford and his progress was very slow indeed.

For a while George and I waited getting colder and colder. We were so accustomed to being the leading pair that we felt rather frustrated. It wouldn't be easy to pass on the ridge even if Riddiford was agreeable which we now realised was rather unlikely. George and I had a brief discussion – the other team were not as fit as we were and we frankly doubted if they would have time to lead the apparent difficulties of the icy ridge and reach the summit before dark – and meanwhile we would get mighty cold waiting behind them. Shouting across the wind the two parties debated the matter. It was now after mid-day – should we retreat now while still fresh and return to the attack to-morrow? In the end Lowe and I decided to return while the others went on.

All afternoon we watched them high on the ridge making apparently little progress. Then the cold drove us back to our tents. Throughout the evening we waited impatiently to hear their voices but as darkness descended we became very worried. Lowe went up onto the col with a torch while I prepared a hot meal. What could have happened to them? Finally after nine p.m. the sound of their approaching voices dispelled all doubt and they crept exhausted but triumphant into the tent. Displaying great persistence and courage they had pushed on along the ridge despite a very strong wind and had finally reached the summit at a quarter to six.

Everybody had a poor night and Riddiford's feet and hands required much rubbing to restore them to life. I had a feeling of deep disappointment that George and I hadn't gone on to the summit. We'd done most of the work on the lower parts of the mountain but then we'd made a wrong decision. I was astonished at Earle's stubborn determination. He had been far from well throughout the trip and I couldn't imagine how he had found the strength to persist. He had shown how a tremendous will could dominate most bodily weakness.

In deteriorating weather we retreated off the mountain and back to Badrinath for a period of rest. There was mail waiting for us and some interesting news. Our financial problems were eased when Earle received a substantial draft from one of his relations and generously offered to put it towards our meagre expedition funds. And someone had sent a cutting from a London newspaper saying that the famous British explorer, Eric Shipton, was to lead a reconnaissance party through Nepal to the south side of Everest in a few months' time. What a trip to be on, we all thought. Inspired into action I wrote to a friend in Britain who was on the Alpine Club Committee suggesting that some members from our party should be considered for this reconnaissance (and unbeknown to me the New Zealand Alpine Club had sent a similar letter).

After five days of rest at Badinath I wrote in my diary, 'Boredom setting in! I can't sit around writing and resting with the same ease as George and Earle. My main desire is to get back up and climb a few peaks and then hurry off home to the bees.' By this time I had re-sorted all our supplies and everything was ready to go. Some vigorous prompting finally got the party moving and we headed back to the Shamro glacier leaving an unwell Riddiford behind.

That first night we weren't in the best of moods as we cleared a site to pitch our tents. A huge rock was blocking the way and I braced myself to move it. 'Don't bother,' said George grumpily. 'I've tried to move it and can't. I don't imagine you can!' I looked at him in surprise, then grabbed the rock and heaved it out of the way. I was prepared to concede that George was better than me at many things but brute strength wasn't one of them.

On the west side of the Saraswati river we met a group of Tibetans camped beside the narrow track with their sheep grazing the steep hillsides. One of them possessed an ancient rifle of enormous bore which looked like a relic from the battle of Waterloo. Apparently the barrel was blocked by a bullet and they asked for our assistance in removing it. We accepted the weapon rather doubtfully and managed to tap the bullet loose and clear the barrel. The owner then fumbled in his tattered garments and triumphantly produced a live round. He placed it in the gun and then offered us the honour of first shot – which we firmly declined. He then offered the gun to our Sherpas and porters in turn, none of whom accepted it. Finally he realised he would have to test it himself, so closing his eyes, took aim in the general direction of a large boulder and pulled the trigger. To our surprise the gun went off with a resounding bang and a spurt of dust some six feet in front of the barrel proved it was once again in working order.

The weather in the Shamro was still very unsettled but for two weeks we explored and climbed to our hearts' content. We were very fit and well acclimatised and we rushed around the country with great vigour and made a number of new ascents. As a culminating effort George and I decided to return to Camp III on Mukut Parbat and climb the fine snow peak of 22,180 feet to the north of the Tibetan col. With three heavily laden Sherpas we set off up the glacier and pitched our tent at the old Camp II site, just as snow commenced falling. The monsoon was on us with a vengeance. All night it snowed and next morning we had an extra foot of it around the tents. All day we lay in our sleeping bags with the soft patter of the snow for company.

We woke at five a.m. next morning and discovered it was clear outside. We quickly sorted five days' food and set off for Camp III. The fresh snow made extra work for us on the steep upper slopes, and extra risks too, but we were going particularly well and made height rapidly. I was making trail along the lower lip of a huge crevasse when I dislodged an enormous cornice with my ice-axe and we jumped to safety as it collapsed inward and rumbled down into the depths. The whole ice-fall quivered and it took us a while to steady our own breathing. The shaky snow bridge that had caused us concern on our previous visit was now completely gone and a wide crevasse separated us from our former camp site. A long detour down and around was necessary before we returned to our old Camp III to find the two tents we had left there were half buried in snow and ice. We commenced digging them out as snow started falling again. When the Sherpas arrived we took their loads and sent them quickly back to Camp II. We settled into our tents, crawled into our sleeping bags, lit our primus and commenced the thankless task of cooking ourselves a stew.

In the evening a clearing in the mist made us poke our heads out of our tent door. An amazing sight met our eyes. Camped as we were at 21,000 feet we were higher than most of the surrounding peaks, only the giants challenging our height. Far across the valley enormous cumulo nimbus clouds were floating steadily up from the south. Every few seconds one of them would be completely illuminated by a brilliant flash of lightning. With each flash all the surrounding peaks would glow into sharp relief and then slowly fade. Bad weather was obviously approaching so we tested our tent fastenings and then crawled shivering back into our warm sleeping bags.

All that night and for the next two days the snow fell and the wind blew without ceasing. Snow piled up against our tent. On the slopes below us great avalanches were rumbling down. Beneath us the ice creaked and groaned in its slow but relentless progression down the mountainside. We were completely cut off. All we could do was stay where we were. The only view outside the tent door was the driving snow and the long fingers of ice streaming from our tent ropes. George seemed able to rest and sleep more easily than I did although he emerged on one occasion and announced that 'Some people wouldn't think this was fun!'

On the evening of the second day the weather showed signs of lifting and colder temperatures froze the snow into greater stability. We woke next morning to a very windy day with storm clouds drifting around. In desperation we dressed in all our clothes and windproofs and decided to attempt our peak. With little hope we kicked up through the fresh snow to the Tibetan col and the wind whistled about our ears. Suddenly the wind dropped completely, the sun shone and we were sweltering in the heat. Much encouraged we pushed on up the steep slope taking turns at kicking and cutting steps. We had many uneasy thoughts about the dangers of avalanche and we kept as direct a line as possible to prevent any likelihood of us cutting the slope and starting a slide. Forcing our way upwards at considerable speed we were soon approaching the large crevasse separating the long slope from the summit cone. We did some careful belaying with the rope and another bout of step cutting – then we were on top at 22,180 feet. The view on all sides was breathtaking. Below us to the north east stretched the barren and uninviting hills of Tibet, to the west lay the Saraswati valley and Nilcanta still wreathed in angry storm clouds. Above us towered the great masses of Mukut Parbat and Kamet. Revelling in the warmth and the view we took many photographs until gathering clouds warned us that our spell of fine weather was to be brief.

Moving down our steps we hurried back to our tent just as the clouds closed in again and a terrific hail storm struck us. The tent shook under the impact and almost collapsed under the weight of the hail-stones. We were very thankful when the storm passed. The evening was misty and cold and windy again but we went to sleep well satisfied with our day.

With tremendous loads we evacuated the camp next morning and staggered down the ice fall. We were halfway down a steep smooth snow slope when there was a great shudder, and a thump, and the whole slope subsided a few inches around us. Avalanche? I put in a quick shaft belay but the slope was deep and soft – giving no security. We could only carry on straight down the slope with our hearts in our mouths. Twenty yards further the slope subsided again – but it didn't slide! The next half-hour was agonising as we pussy-footed down the slopes under considerable tension and were subjected to two more subsidences. We were mighty relieved when we reached a line of seracs and the avalanche danger was behind us.

By August 14th we were all back in Badrinath organising ourselves for departure. We said reluctant farewells to our Indian friends – the Doctor, the postmaster, and the Secretary of the Temple. On August 16th in pouring rain we set off down the Alaknanda Gorge to Joshima on the first long stage of our journey home. Continual rain gave us many problems with slips and washouts on the track but finally on August 25th we arrived dirty, shaggy and in tattered clothes back in civilisation at Ranikhet. We'd had a magnificent introduction to the Himalayas and a good measure of success – and now, as a climax to months of enjoyable travel and good companionship, there was a telegram waiting from Shipton inviting two of us to join the British expedition to Mount Everest.

Chapter 9

Prelude to Everest

FOR THIRTY YEARS MOUNT EVEREST, 29,028 FEET, THE HIGHEST MOUNTAIN on earth, had resisted the efforts of a succession of tough mountaineering expeditions. Everest represented the ultimate in achievement; the supreme challenge for flesh and blood and spirit. Would it ever be possible to overcome the forces of nature and reach this remote summit? Men had already died in the attempt – and many more were yet to die. Should one even try?

And now two of us could go to Everest – but which two? I knew I should go home and get on with my business, but Everest was an enormous attraction for any mountaineer. I pushed conscience aside; the chance to go to Everest outweighed everything else.

I was very fit and there were no arguments about my inclusion. But would George Lowe or Earle Riddiford be the other member? Comradeship was forgotten and bitterness crept into the discussion. George was more robust physically and he was technically more competent but Earle was an aggressive climber and he had the money that might make the trip possible. I could see the point of Earle's argument even if George couldn't; Earle had climbed Mukut Parbat and he had the money – you couldn't really argue against that. In the end Earle went but I can still remember George's accusing face as he watched us depart by bus to the railhead.

We took with us two of our Sherpas – Passang and Nima – and travelled back down the railway to Lucknow. Then it was a mad rush – cashing a draft from the New Zealand Alpine Club and purchasing supplies for our time in Nepal. In the evening an Indian friend took us to the 'Club' which must have been a grand place in the days of the British Raj but was now delapidated and sad. We sipped a small nip of whisky poured ceremoniously from a bottle standing in lonely splendour on the empty bar and talked nostalgically about the 'good old days' – or at least the others did. I thought the 'old days' sounded rather privileged and pathetic.

We had a desperate few moments next day getting all our purchases
on the train but finally rolled east for twenty-five hours to Katihar and
then north to Jogbani on the Nepalese border. Most of the way it
rained but the countryside was lush and beautiful. We arrived at
Jogbani after midnight and puddled through streaming rain to a suitable
verandah where we slept the remainder of the night amongst the frogs
and mosquitoes.

Shipton and party, we learned, were five days ahead of us and would
take quite a lot of catching. The thirty miles of road from Jogbani to
Dharan was a muddy morass and even our four-wheel drive truck
had the greatest difficulty in getting through; on a number of occasions
we had to unload our equipment and manhandle it through knee
deep mud. It was a memorable day in many ways; I saw Everest for the
first time (or so I was told), a small white pyramid on the far horizon
and I watched a dozen vultures tearing to pieces a half dead cow.

In Dharan we had torrential rain and it was a terrible business
getting the seventeen porters we needed. When we finally moved on
we had lost another day but had the consolation that Shipton would be
having the same problems. It took us two days to reach the hill town of
Dhaunkuta where we were given a warm welcome by the local
Governor. I was already developing a liking for the cheerful and
handsome Nepalese hill people who seemed to be made of tougher
fibre than the crowded millions down on the muddy plains.

For the next four days we battled our way across the rain-soaked
hills. All local travelling was at a standstill with every river and stream
a raging torrent – but Earle and I simply had to keep moving if we
were to have any hope of catching Shipton. Using our experience of
river crossings in New Zealand we forced our way over every flood
and brought our porters over too. On the fourth day we heard the
news that the other party were only a short distance ahead of us. Earle
and I raced up the long hill in the dusk to the village of Dingla where
they were camped, hoping they hadn't moved on. What would they be
like, I wondered? Would they be 'pukka sahibs' – frightfully formal
and decent?

We entered the outskirts of the village and were met by a smiling
Sherpa who conducted us to a large house and upstairs to a pleasant
room. Four men scrambled up to meet us and my immediate impression
was of large bodies in solid condition – I suppose it was the contrast
with our thin and hungry frames. Eric Shipton came forward to greet
us and I felt a sense of relief at his unshaven face and scruffy clothes.
This was an exciting moment for me. I had read all Shipton's books
and followed his tough pioneering expeditions with enormous interest.
Now I was not only meeting him but going on an expedition with him

too. His companions seemed a likeable group: Bill Murray, a dour Scotsman with a mature and agreeable personality; Michael Ward the doctor, young and well built with an easy impetuous manner; and the massive Tom Bourdillon, formidable and quiet with a warm smile.

When I look back on that first trip of ours into Everest I can appreciate the many problems we had. It was still in the height of the monsoon rains and the local people were deeply involved in their crops – few of them wished to be far away from their home villages. No Europeans had been through this part of Nepal and we had little information about it. Shipton had chosen our route from the map – it looked the most direct approach to Everest – but it proved to be exceptionally steep and little used. For eleven days we moved slowly forward with overloaded porters – slithered forward would be a better term. We were pestered by hordes of bloodsucking leeches; cut off by washed-out bridges; attacked by stinging wasps; struggled along overgrown and ill defined paths. We were wet most of the time and so were our tents, while our clothing was stained with blood from our leech bites.

But there were many great moments too; the morning the clouds lifted and we had a superb view of Chamlang and Makalu; and the many chances I had to get to know Shipton and understand why he was such a redoubtable explorer. On September 21st we had our first really fine morning and we could hardly believe it. We had reached the great trench of the Dudh Kosi river and the peaks around us were superb. We climbed rapidly up to a pass at 10,000 feet and looked into the valley ahead. It was magnificently wide and deep and with great excitement the Sherpas pointed out their villages – we were looking into the famous district of Khumbu, the home of the Sherpas.

We camped the night at Phakding beside the wild Dudh Kosi and dined magnificently on freshly harvested fruits and vegetables. It was one of the pleasantest valleys I had ever seen. In the morning I pushed on ahead of our party and commenced the long climb up the hill towards Namche Bazar. I came out on a little spur and saw the immense mountain wall joining Nuptse and Lhotse and the mighty triangular summit of Everest thrusting into the sky – it looked beyond comprehension. Sherpa Dannu came down the track – he had been sent on ahead – and he produced a flagon of *chung* (beer) and a bag of hot potatoes.

Reunited and replenished we climbed slowly up the track which traversed a steep hillside covered in tall pines and overshadowed by enormous rock bluffs and sharp snow summits. We turned a corner to see the village of Namche Bazar nestling in a hollow in the side of the hill – more than sixty houses and a superb spring of fresh water. We were welcomed with *chung* and Tibetan tea and moved into a large dark house specially vacated for our use.

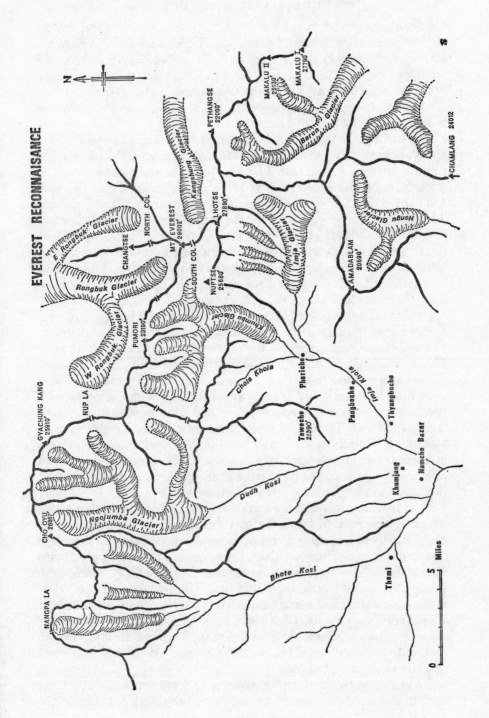

EVEREST RECONNAISANCE

N

NANGPA LA

CHO OYU
26867'

GYACHUNG KANG
25910'

NUP LA

Ngojumba Glacier

W Rongbuk Glacier

E Rongbuk Glacier

Rongbuk Glacier

CHANGTSE

NORTH COL

PUMORI
23190'

MT EVEREST
29002

Kangshung Glacier

SOUTH COL

NUPTSE
25880'

LHOTSE
27890'

PETHANGSE
22080'

MAKALU II
25130'

MAKALU I
27790'

Barun Glacier

CHAMLANG 24012

Hongu Glacier

AMADABLAM
20690'

Imja Glacier

Khumbu Glacier

Chola Khola

Pheriche

Imja Khola

Pangboche

Teweche
21390'

Thyangboche

Khumjung

Namche Bazar

Dudh Kosi

Bhote Kosi

Thami

0   5   Miles

We spent several days at Namche, paying off our porters and sorting all our food and equipment. I developed a high temperature and dysentery and was so thin that I wondered if I would ever be able to do anything on the reconnaissance. To my shame I had to be left behind when the main party moved on and spent a couple of days recuperating. As I grew stronger my optimism returned and I was soon bursting with energy again.

I moved up the valley with only Sherpas for company and I have always been thankful that I saw the area first in this way. I left at eight a.m. on September 27th with Passang, Angputer and two porters. The track from Namche traversed the steep hillside above the Dudh Kosi and I could feast my eyes on the tremendous summits of Kangtega and Tamserku. I came around a corner and ahead of us was the unbelievable shape of Amadablam – surely the most dramatic of all great mountains. (Over the years my expeditions have climbed all three of these peaks). We arrived at the village of Tesinga and had a delicious drink of hot *zum* milk and then dropped down to the Dudh Kosi and started the long climb up to Thyangboche Monastery.

I walked through the archway at the entrance to Thyangboche and climbed over the crest of the spur – and looked in wonder at the view filling the head of the valley – the greatest wall in the world between Nuptse and Lhotse, and Everest behind it with a long plume of snow streaming from the summit. I was warmly welcomed by the head Lama with food and drink and invited to see the Monastery temples with their superbly painted wooden panels and impressive statues of the Buddha and Guru Rimpoche. It was three hours before I could move on and wander through a gloriously beautiful valley with the trees tinted in autumn colouring – certainly, I was sure, the loveliest place I had ever seen. I crossed the river over a delightful bridge and climbed slowly up to Pangboche – revelling in the scenery.

Next morning was fine again and I left Pangboche early, then chose a comfortable rock to await the arrival of the Sherpas. After an hour and a half there was still no sign of them so I raced back to the village and found Passang sitting in the place of honour and being plied with tea and food. They were soon on the move again and we reached the grazing village of Pheriche by mid-day. The peaks lining the valley were quite terrific and I was sure they would be almost impossible to climb. For the first time I felt I was looking at mountains that over-shadowed my own New Zealand summits. We spent the night in two rock huts at the terminal face of the Khumbu glacier and it snowed steadily for hour after hour.

It had cleared by dawn and we carried on into a fresh and sparkling world. The sun soon melted the snow on the grassy flats beside the glacier and we enjoyed pleasant travelling and exciting views. At one o'clock we reached the camp site at Gorakshep beside a large lake and were surprised not to find the main party there. I carried on up the glacier and found the new base camp in a lateral moraine hollow beside an excellent spring. It was good to meet the others again and share their experiences. I hadn't really missed anything by being late – Tom, Mike and Bill were all having trouble with altitude although Earle and Eric seemed in good form. In the late afternoon Eric and I went for a climb up some high moraine bumps and examined the approaches to the mountain with binoculars.

From this position the south face of Everest looked a most appalling jumble. The early expeditions had approached Everest from the north through Tibet and what little they had seen of the south face had seemed quite impossible. The Nepalese side of the mountain had been closed to foreigners until 1950 when the first party under Tilman visited the Khumbu glacier. For some reason they didn't go far up the glacier before returning and reporting that there was no sign of a reasonable route. We had some rather dramatic photographs taken by the 1933 flight over Everest and these seemed to confirm the Tilman view. Certainly from our viewpoint above base camp the south face looked very formidable. At this angle the ice fall squeezed out of the narrow gap between the buttresses of Everest and Nuptse like toothpaste squelching out of a tube. The lower slopes didn't look too difficult but even these seemed to be menaced by avalanches.

On September 30th we commenced our full-scale investigation of the ice fall. Mike and Tom tried to push a route up the right-hand side but were soon rebuffed by dangerous ice. Earle and Passang approached the ice fall in the centre and in five hours of slow but steady movement made useful height. Shipton had invited me to accompany him in an attempt to get a look into the valley above the ice fall; the Western Cwm as it was named by Mallory. We skirted the Khumbu glacier and started climbing a ridge leading towards the peak of Pumori. We were now square on to the ice fall and the higher we went the better our view became. From nearly 20,000 feet we were able to look right into the Western Cwm and to our amazement we realised that there was in fact a possible route on to Everest from this side; up the ice fall, through the Western Cwm, traverse to the left up the Lhotse face to the South Col, and then up the ridge to the South Summit and the top. It was one of the most exciting moments I can remember and we returned to camp bubbling over with the news.

For three days it snowed and life was thoroughly miserable. Then it was clear and cold again with everything blanketed in dry powder snow. We made a big effort and pushed up the ice fall, passing the point reached by Riddiford, and threading a way through a badly shattered middle section. We zigzagged under leaning seracs and toppling ice cliffs until only a big slumped crevasse seemed to separate us from the top of the ice fall. The snow was loose and unstable but we didn't feel like stopping now. We started across the last steep slope above the crevasse when suddenly the whole slope avalanched. Shipton and I managed to jump clear, and so did Passang, but Riddiford was being carried relentlessly towards the crevasse. Passang put in an excellent belay and Earle was pulled to a stop while the ice blocks carried on past him and tumbled in to the depths. Shaken by this incident and unhappy with the condition of the snow we retreated down the ice fall and decided to give the snow a couple of weeks to consolidate.

We split into two parties – to my great delight Shipton had asked me to accompany him on a trip of exploration to the east while the remainder of the party were exploring to the west. It was a marvellous adventure for me. We travelled up the Imja valley under the great south face of Lhotse and struggled over a high pass into the head of the Hongu glacier system. On the east side of the Hongu we climbed another 20,000-foot pass and looked across a wide snow plateau towards Makalu and the Barun glacier. It was all new country, completely unexplored, and I quickly caught Shipton's fervour for such untravelled places.

We made our way out of the Hongu by a new pass, later called the Amadablam Col. We found it very easy to approach from the Hongu side – I rushed up the glacier by myself in exuberant fashion, dodging around the few dangerous crevasses. When I looked down the other side my attitude changed – it was very impressive – 600 feet of fluted snow and ice dropping abruptly to the head of a heavily crevassed glacier. When Eric and the Sherpas joined me there was a long discussion. The Sherpas didn't like the look of this slope – why not return by the original route, they asked? In the end we persuaded them to continue.

Eric waved me through and I started hacking a zigzag pathway down the face. I was roped to Angputer and he belayed me from above and then I belayed him down to me. It took a long time but I was enjoying every moment of it. Halfway down the face I struck a very icy stretch and took particular care with the steps. I found a crack in the ice and established a secure belay before calling Angputer down to me and then I watched him carefully as he could be a little clumsy at times. Even as I watched, he slipped and fell and shot past at great speed. I clung to the belay with all my strength. It seemed a lifetime before the the rope came tight with a twang; the belay held, and Angputer was spreadeagled on the slope. For a moment there was no sound only our deep panting and then I heard the noise of laughing. I looked up and saw the other two Sherpas hanging on to the slope and almost bursting with good humour at Angputer's predicament.

It was well after dark before we were off the slope and down through the ice fall to the floor of the valley. We were very dehydrated and desperate for something to drink, but stumbled for hours across boulders and bluffs before we arrived at the banks of the Mingbo river. There was firewood there too and a good cup of tea made life bearable again. We bedded down in the scrub and slept peacefully under a full moon.

Shipton and I were back at Everest base camp on October 19th – just over two weeks after we had left. There was no sign of the other team so we spent three days moving the camp over to the foot of the ice fall – and then set to work reestablishing the route. We found that considerable changes had taken place. The snow was now much firmer and safer but the ice fall more shattered and in places decidedly unstable. In the central sector we had quite a fright when a large area quivered like a jelly at our passage and we gave it the name of the 'Atom Bomb' area.

On October 25th the western party returned. They had crossed into the Ngojumba glacier and tackled the steep ice of the Nup La pass on the Tibetan border. The difficulties had been considerable and they were forced to abandon the attempt. They were now very much fitter and better acclimatised so we joined forces for a last examination of the ice fall. We were away from camp early in the morning and made very fast time. We approached the 'Atom Bomb' area with considerable trepidation but to our relief it was much more stable than on our previous visit. We penetrated through the seracs and ice walls without too many problems and came to the last slope where we'd had our fright with the avalanche. Tom Bourdillon did an aggresive lead up the lip of a corniced crevasse and we emerged on top of the ice fall. We were still separated from the Western Cwm by a giant crevasse but the ice fall itself was below us. Delighted with our success we turned downwards and descended at great speed – Shipton and I racing each other the whole way. Although Shipton was forty-four years old he was still very fit and strong and highly competitive.

Over the next few days we discussed the problem of the ice fall and there was much talk about 'unjustifiable risk' and 'unsafe for porters'. But I think we all realised that these were attitudes from the past, that nobody was going to get up Everest without taking a few risks, that the ice fall would never be a place for the cautious or the fainthearted.

With our main task completed, my conscience started troubling me – not before time, of course. I'd been in the Himalayas for nearly six months and I was getting increasingly concerned about my brother and our honey business. Riddiford and I decided to leave the main party and cross the Tashi Lapcha pass to the west of Namche Bazar and make a very direct route back to Kathmandu. It proved an exhilarating journey. The pass was technically demanding and the Rolwaling superbly beautiful. We crossed the Nepalese hill country in the height of the harvest season and it was throbbing with music and laughter. For ten days we travelled through country that no European had visited before and we were warmly welcomed in every village.

The city of Kathmandu had its own charm too. We were guests of the British Ambassador, Mr. Summerhayes, and we couldn't have been more comfortable. There was only one piece of news to mar our pleasure. The Swiss had been granted permission to attempt Everest the following year so all our ambitious plans could be forgotten. It was strange how we resented this news; as though Everest belonged to us and no one else had any rights to it.

On the evening before I left for India I attended an Embassy dinner and became very friendly with a distinguished Nepalese guest. We were discussing my walk over the hills in order to get to the railhead – in those days Kathmandu had no air or road connection with the outside world – all the vehicles in the valley had been carried in by porters. My companion announced that he would lend me a suitable horse for the journey – a terrifying prospect for such an indifferent horseman as I was. I consoled myself with the thought that this was just idle talk engendered by the good food and wine.

In the morning I said farewell to my hosts and was taken in the Embassy limousine to the commencement of the hill track. To my horror there was a great white horse waiting for me, rearing up in very spirited fashion – my friend, alas, had not forgotten his promise. It was only pride that got me on the horse and for a few moments I could feel him trembling beneath my weight. I grasped the reins and gave a firm tug. The reaction was immediate. The horse swung around and galloped at full speed back towards Kathmandu. I tried sawing furiously on the reins but all to no avail; our relentless progression continued and we were fast approaching the outskirts of the town. With a hopeless gesture I dropped the reins – and the horse stopped in its tracks. Using my knees I gently coaxed him around, and around he went. A gentle 'geeup' seemed worth a try – and back we jogged towards the hill path. We had clearly reached an understanding – I was to leave the reins alone and he would get me to my destination and this he duly did.

On November 24th I sailed from Bombay for Sydney. I shared a cabin with an agreeable Irish Australian who rarely appeared except to go to bed. I was twenty-eight lbs lighter than when I had left New Zealand and seemed ready to drop off to sleep at the slightest chance I, carried on board a bunch of fifty huge and delicious bananas and slept and ate my way through the Indian ocean.

One of my tasks in Nepal had been to keep a careful note of all the expenses that Earle and I incurred during the expedition as these were to be refunded to us by the Alpine Club. My list included the cost of the large number of cups of tea we had purchased from 'char shops' as we travelled through Nepal. We received a note from the Honorary Treasurer in London (a millionaire who was renowned for his careful watch over Club funds), saying that 'gentlemen are expected to pay for their own cups of tea.' We advised the Treasurer by return mail that we were New Zealanders and not 'gentlemen' and regarded the cups of tea as part of our standard diet and all our expenses were ultimately refunded. When I met the Treasurer in London in 1953 he insisted on buying me a drink in memory of this argument.

I hadn't been long back in New Zealand before it was announced that the Everest Committee was planning an expedition to Nepal in 1952 to serve as a training run for the team they intended sending to Everest in 1953. The objective chosen was Cho Oyu, 26,870 feet, the seventh highest mountain in the world and a formidable challenge in its own right. Eric Shipton was leader and both Earle Riddiford and I were in the party. To my delight George Lowe was also included on this occasion. My brother displayed his usual good nature and agreed once again to carry the burden of the business while I was gone. This expedition produced some substantial results, I believe – the five British who went highest on Everest the following year had all been on Cho Oyu – but we failed miserably on Cho Oyu itself.

Shipton had an irrepressible urge to see as much new country as was possible so decided on a new approach to the Everest region. We crossed the Nepalese border in a desert-like region at Jaynagar and climbed up through Okaldunga and the Solu valley to the Dudh Kosi river. We were rather an unusual collection – competent enough technically according to standards in those days but with a wide range of ages, philosophies and idiosyncrasies. We arrived in Namche Bazar soon after the Swiss had left for Everest and then moved up valley towards the Nangpa La on the Tibetan border.

Our base camp at Lunak was arid and uninteresting, and the atmosphere there tended to be rather depressing too. We had received news from some itinerant Sherpas that the Chinese had moved a garrison into the town of Tingri only a short distance away on the other side of the border. The most promising approach to Cho Oyu was up the Kyetrak glacier which was in Tibet and there were long and heated discussions about the dangers of being apprehended by the Chinese soldiers. Shipton and Bourdillon seemed particularly concerned by the dangers; I felt the risk was very small, and anyway above 17,000 feet we ought to be able to keep ahead of any soldiers. By the time the matter had been thrashed out the whole party was filled with uncertainty and we were constantly looking over our shoulders for the Chinese bogeymen.

In the end we compromised – we travelled over the Kyetrak glacier but we put no permanent camps on it. From an advanced base well down on the Nepalese side of the border we crossed the Nangpa La, travelled up the Kyetrak glacier, climbed the ridge splitting the north side of Cho Oyu and established a camp at 21,000 feet – six climbers and six Sherpas with five days' food. The rest of the party retreated back over the border. With our eyes constantly swivelling towards Tibet we felt mighty lonely during the next few days.

Bad weather harassed us and so did ill health. Our food was unimaginative and nobody ate much of it. We pushed up the ridge to nearly 22,500 feet where it merged into a series of great ice cliffs. Out to the left there was a slope of solid ice sweeping up through the cliffs but access on to it looked rather dangerous. Above the slope hung great fractured fingers of ice. I ended up cutting steps towards it with half the party shouting out not to be a fool but to come down. So down I duly went; we seemed to have lost the spirit to attempt such a place. Afterwards I had a terrible sense of shame that we had given up so easily but I suppose it is difficult to succeed on a mountain like Cho Oyu when you are constantly looking over your shoulder. This was the way by which the mountain was ultimately climbed – and a couple of climbers later died on the same ice slope.

I was very fit during this Cho Oyu period, and George and I climbed four good peaks over 20,000 feet. But we were now very happy to retreat back over the Nangpa La to base camp and then move off down valley. Some tests were to be carried out on oxygen equipment but Shipton agreed that George and I should head off on a trip by ourselves – I think he realised we weren't very happy about our Cho Oyu efforts.

For a long time I'd been thinking about trying to cross the Nup La. The stories told by Earle and the others when they were rebuffed the previous year made it sound a mighty interesting place. If we could get over the pass we'd be able to visit the north side of Everest and this would be the trip of a lifetime – to see the Rongbuk Glacier and the traditional camp sites of the famous expeditions of the 20s and 30s. Our Sherpas warned us that the Chinese were now in occupation of the Rongbuk Monastery but we had no intention of going that low and our escape route over the Nup La couldn't really be cut off. In 1952 the Nepalese Government was not terribly concerned about its northern border – once you had permission to visit an area you could climb anything or go anywhere – a very different situation from the rigid limitations of the present day.

With three Sherpas and six porters we moved up the Ngojumba valley and established a base camp at the foot of the series of great ice falls that filled the head of the valley. It was a tremendously impressive place. The porters returned, leaving our compact and mobile team of five. The right-hand ice fall – the one attempted by Riddiford's party – was very broken and we observed a huge section subsiding in a thunderous avalanche. I tried to push a way between the ice and the rock but it proved a futile effort. Next day George and I tackled the rock buttress splitting the main ice falls but found it steep and unstable and retreated in disorder. We returned to camp feeling rather discouraged.

Only one possibility now remained. Late in the afternoon Angputer and I went for a walk up the left-hand valley to examine the smaller ice fall that had always looked by far the worst. To my surprise and delight I noticed a possible line giving access to the heavily crevassed central sector. For four days George and I battled with the crevasses and ice walls of the Nup La ... cutting hundreds of steps, wriggling over shaky snow bridges and falling into a terrifying number of crevasses. The warm temperatures of the approaching monsoon season made the snow soft and unstable and we had to fight every inch of the way. On the fourth day we broke through and climbed to the crest of the Nup La and looked with excitement down the West Rongbuk glacier to the mighty bulk of Everest. We had a tremendous sense of achievement and I felt I could now shrug off my feelings about Cho Oyu.

Carrying heavy loads we raced around the north side of Everest, down the West Rongbuk glacier, across the main glacier with its towering ice pinnacles, and then around the corner to the East Rongbuk glacier. We were very fit indeed and made relatively light work of the distance and the difficulties. We had many exciting moments – our first glimpse down valley of the renowned Rongbuk Monastery; getting to Camp I (still littered with old batteries and other rubbish from the early British expeditions), and the sight of the famous North Col and its snow approaches – which in all honesty didn't look terribly difficult. For five days we galloped around the lower slopes of Everest but there was always one nagging thought – in these warm conditions what was happening to the Nup La?

On June 3rd we were camped back on the West Rongbuk glacier. We had planned a day of exploration to seek out a new route over the divide into Nepal but ominous black clouds were sweeping up from the south. We struck camp and covered the six miles to the pass in one and a half hours. In driving snow and cloud we loaded up the rest of our gear and plunged down towards the ice fall. For six hours we fumbled our way over crevasses and ice walls. The snow fall was incredibly heavy and new avalanches were sweeping down the slopes above us. Heavily laden and fearful for our safety we were afraid to camp and struggled on as best we could. We were enormously relieved to emerge from the active section and trudge wearily down the moraine peppered ice. I have never felt happier to crawl into a warm sleeping bag in a stout tent and know that the dangers were behind us.

One big question now filled our minds – what had the Swiss done on Everest? We decided to go and see. We clambered up the tributary Guanara glacier and camped at the foot of the high pass at its head. A sudden clearing in the weather had produced very cold temperatures and when we moved off again early in the morning the ice on the glacier exploded under our boots. We climbed rapidly to the crest of the pass and rested on a rock in the sun, enjoying the magnificent view of Everest and the Khumbu Glacier area. Soon after mid-day we were at Gorakshep beside the lake where we expected to find the Swiss party in residence but there was no sign of life although warm ashes in the fire showed they were not long gone. We rushed up the glacier to the foot of the Everest ice fall but it was deserted and silent; only empty cans and the other debris of modern man showed that people had been living here for a couple of months.

In the morning we carried on down valley. I had a restless night thinking about Everest; today we must get an answer. At Phalong Karpo an old Sherpa herdsman mumbled that seven Swiss had reached the top. It seemed hard to believe and we felt quite depressed. At two p.m. we arrived at Pangboche and were soon talking to Shipton. He gave us the news – Lambert and Tenzing Norgay had reached 28,000 feet before turning back; the mountain was still unclimbed! I would be a hypocrite if I suggested that we weren't delighted, but there was admiration, too, for the terrific effort that the Swiss had made.

There was a definite holiday air about the party as Shipton, Evans, Lowe and I headed east into the Hongu and then over into the Barun valley. We climbed and explored with great energy and had a very happy time. With the cares of a large expedition off his shoulders Shipton was a new man and revelled in the type of expedition in which he excelled. We retreated before monsoon snows and waded knee deep in flowers down the lower Barun. We crossed a 14,000-foot pass in torrential rain and descended into the warmth and leeches of the Arun valley.

We followed the track down the Arun river and it was hot and sticky all the way with frequent showers of rain. The river and its tributaries were in spate so George and I made a raft out of two air mattresses and floated down long stretches of lively water – until a fearful battle with a huge whirlpool made us lose our enthusiasm – and nearly our lives. Shipton was now in a great hurry to get back to England and help with the planning of the 1953 British attempt on Everest and pushed relentlessly on. With no such sense of urgency George and I reluctantly kept pace. We were thin, hot and rather scratchy when we emerged at Dharan and hired a truck to take us to the railhead at Jogbani.

In October and November 1952 the Swiss made another attempt on Everest. They had a very strong party and plenty of equipment and oxygen – but the temperatures were very cold and the winds viciously strong. Despite all their efforts they were unable to get far above the South Col and ultimately the second attempt was abandoned.

Chapter 10

Top of the World

THE 1953 BRITISH EVEREST EXPEDITION WAS LAUNCHED IN AN ATMOS-phere of excitement and optimism. Eric Shipton had been asked to lead the attack and duly selected his party which included George Lowe and myself. It was to be a fairly large and elaborate expedition for those days (although very modest by modern standards) but nothing much happened for quite a while. I just accepted this as part of Shipton's lethargic approach to big expeditions and felt that all would come right in the end.

Then came the bombshell! I read in the newspapers with disbelief that Shipton had been replaced with a new leader – Colonel John Hunt – someone I had never heard of. The report said he was a distin-guished soldier with a couple of Himalayan trips to his credit. 'Everest will be unthinkable without Shipton,' was my immediate reaction, 'and who wants an Army man anyway?' I seriously considered pulling out of the party.

But John Hunt soon showed he was no 'Colonel Blimp'. I received a letter from him concerning my selection in the team and making no attempt to conceal that the change of leadership had been badly handled by the organising committee. A note from Shipton expressed his disappointment but gave support to the main objective and this helped overcome my reluctance.

In fairness to the Everest Committee I must agree that Shipton was not happy as leader of a big expedition. He didn't enjoy large-scale organisation and he disliked having to make decisions which might affect the safety and lives of many of his friends. In exploration however he had few equals. He had a relentless urge to cross the next pass or to look into the next valley, and he had a remarkable ability to withstand boredom and discomfort. With Shipton as leader our expedition would not have been as well prepared before departure but it might still have been successful on Everest. We had a strong affection and loyalty for

Nima Tashi—a renowned
Sherpa leader.

Mingmatsering's wife
Angdoule with all her
jewellery.

Masked dancer at Mane
Rimdu.

Amadablam with Khumjung
in foreground.

The author is welcomed at
Bakanje school.

him and there was a considerable organisational ability already present amongst the members of his team.

I first met John Hunt in Kathmandu and despite my pre-conceived prejudices I was immediately impressed. He greeted me with great warmth; told me he was expecting much from me and that he wanted me to share with Charles Evans the advisory tasks of his 'Executive Committee'; and how he personally intended to 'lead the expedition from the front'. I suspect he used a similar approach with all of us but I found it effective all the same. John had great energy and drive and expressed a complete conviction that our party could get to the top – an approach I always viewed with caution. He handled most of us with considerable skill – we were all individualists with a dislike of military procedures but we received no orders, only suggestions or requests which were generally so soundly based that we were happy to agree and give our loyal co-operation.

I learned to respect John even if I found it difficult at times to understand him. He drove himself with incredible determination and I always felt he was out to prove himself the physical equal of any member – even though most of us were a good deal younger than himself. I can remember on the third day's march pounding up the long steep hill from Dologhat and catching up with John and the way he shot ahead, absolutely determined not to be passed – the sort of challenge I could not then resist. I surged past with a burst of speed, cheerfully revelling in the contest, and was astonished to see John's face, white and drawn, as he threw every bit of strength into the effort. There was an impression of desperation because he wasn't quite fast enough. What was he trying to prove, I wondered? He was the leader and cracked the whip – surely that was enough? I now know that sometimes it isn't enough – that we can be reluctant to accept that our physical powers have their limits or are declining, even though many of our best executive years may still be ahead of us.

I was eager to meet Tenzing Norgay. His reputation had been most impressive even before his two great efforts with the Swiss expedition the previous year – and I certainly wasn't disappointed. Tenzing really looked the part – larger than most Sherpas he was very strong and active; his flashing smile was irresistible; and he was incredibly patient and obliging with all our questions and requests. His success in the past had given him great physical confidence – I think that even then he *expected* to be a member of the final assault party on Everest as he had been with both the Swiss expeditions although I am sure that neither John Hunt nor any of the rest of us took this for granted. I didn't have much to do with Tenzing on the march in, he was very busy with the many responsibilities of a *sirdar* (foreman) and we had a very large group of Sherpas and porters to be organised, but I was impressed with his competence and pleasantness, although I can't say I rated him more highly as a *sirdar* than some of the other famous Sherpas I had met. He was very kind-hearted and at times went too much out of his way to do things for his friends or relations. One message came through, however, in very positive fashion – Tenzing had substantially greater personal ambition than any Sherpa I had met excepting perhaps Passang Dawa Lama who was also a mighty formidable individual. Tenzing would be keen to see us successful, that I felt sure, not that he had any particular liking for the British, but because this would mean that he too would be successful.

It was a thrill to return to Thyangboche and camp on the snow in these glorious surroundings and know that this time we had the equipment and the men to really thrust towards the summit. I have never had a conviction of success in any challenging project – certainly not on a big unclimbed mountain. What's the point in starting if you always know you're going to succeed? I felt we would give Everest all we had – but there was no certainty of success – and that's the way I liked it.

For two weeks we travelled up the glaciers and climbed on the lesser peaks, trying to adjust to the thin air and get as fit as possible. Most of the time we could see the great triangular summit of Everest with its long plume of wind-blown snow and we knew that soon we would have to get to grips with this problem. I found it a terrifying and yet exciting prospect.

The whole party returned to Thyangboche on April 6th after a succession of successful acclimatisation trips and we had a happy and boisterous reunion. The five of us from Cho Oyu formed the solid core of the team and we were all going particularly well. Charles Evans with his calm and sensible temperament and great charm was the man to whom everyone turned if they wanted advice or help. He was a competent and experienced climber, determined and yet unselfish . . . though behind his calm exterior there lurked as competitive a spirit as any of us possessed. He teamed up most of the time with Tom Bourdillon, who combined great strength and formidable determination with considerable skill on rock – they were a redoubtable pair. Alf Gregory was a bit of a contrast – small, neat and efficient, he knew how to conserve every bit of his strength and save it for the big moments. George Lowe didn't conserve anything whether it was making us laugh, filming a flower or just sleeping – there were no half measures – but George sometimes had to be prodded into the lively action he was capable of in the mountains.

I had started to enjoy the other members of the party too. Mike Ward was back again as Medical Officer with his raffish grin above a coarse black beard; Charles Wylie handled the Sherpas and porters with kindly competence; George Band and Mike Westmacott were young and skilful rock climbers; and Wilf Noyce was a tough and experienced mountaineer with an impressive record of difficult and dangerous climbs. In many respects I considered Noyce the most competent British climber I had met.

We had three other members in the party – non-climbers really but they all went to more than 21,000 feet. Tom Stobart, tall and blond was the film cameraman; Griff Pugh, lean and red-headed, was the physiologist and although his tests caused us much discomfort he kept us amused with his sardonic absent-minded humour. James Morris, correspondent of the London *Times*, was a slim and sensitive intellectual. We were a happy group.

John Hunt had displayed tremendous drive and energy. He frequently exhausted himself with his efforts and looked completely drained – but from somewhere he'd produce enough extra strength to still keep going. Nobody worked as hard as John or was as ferociously determined that we should succeed. Like many leaders he was a lonely and withdrawn figure at times, but he could produce at will a warm and powerful personality. John's instant charm was a formidable weapon in his armory; it affected some of us more than others – but none doubted his unflagging devotion to our major objective.

To my great satisfaction John asked me to take a party up the Khumbu Glacier to establish Base Camp and then to reconnoitre a route through the ice fall. It was the job I was hoping to do, and when I managed to persuade John to let George join us too I could not have been happier. With thirty-eight porters we made our way up the Khumbu valley and over the moraine and bare ice of the Khumbu Glacier. On April 12th we pitched our tents amongst the great ice pinnacles at the bottom of the ice fall and Base Camp was established.

On re-reading my diary after twenty years I get the impression that I must have been a rather uncomfortable person at times on the expedition – restless, competitive and a little argumentative. Yet my memories of the expedition have revolved about the good times ... about the people I liked and laughed with; the tough jobs we did together and the feeling that everyone was giving of their best – according to their strength and temperament at the time. We were a good team – of that I am convinced – and it was this team spirit more than anything that ultimately got Tenzing and me to the summit. If you accept the modern philosophy that there must be a ruthless and

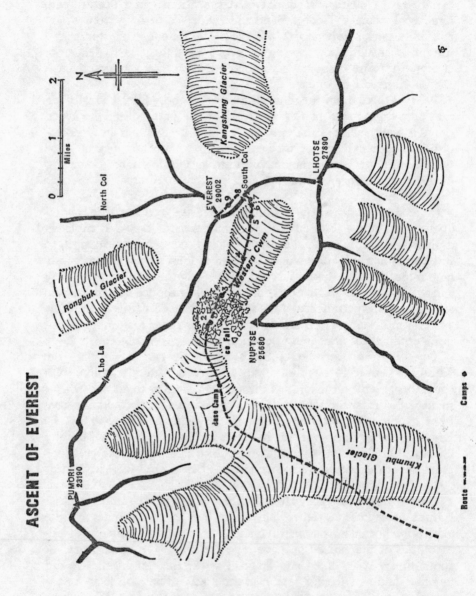

ASCENT OF EVEREST

Route ━━━━ Camps ◆

selfish motivation to succeed in sport then it could be justly claimed that Tenzing and I were the closest approximations we had on our expedition to the climbing Prima Donnas of today. We wanted the expedition to succeed – and nobody worked any harder to ensure that it did – but in both our minds success was always equated with us being somewhere around the summit when it happened.

On April 13th Mike Westmacott, George Band and I made a first reconnaissance of the ice fall. We had hoped to establish a camp part of the way up and were accompanied by four Sherpas carrying tents and food, but we found the ice fall so broken that we sent the men back to base and pushed on alone. After five hours of creeping amongst crevasses and great blocks of tottering ice we reached within a few hundred yards of where the Swiss had established their Camp II the year before . . . but it had been quite a struggle. I returned next day with Mike and Ang Namgyl and we were a bit shaken to find fresh ice blocks littered over our tracks on the worst section. We made a few variations to the route and ultimately established a reasonable path to the site of Camp II although it was still rather menaced by ice cliffs.

I thought it advisable to investigate a route through the middle of the ice fall especially now that George Lowe was back on his feet after a few days of dysentery. The two Georges and I made quite a good route up the middle until we came to a most appalling line of shattered seracs. Even as we watched one of them tilted over and crashed down in a terrifying avalanche – fortunately a few hundred yards to our right. We abandoned the reconnaissance and went back to work improving our original route. Next day the three of us plus three Sherpas carried gear up and established Camp II. The top part of the route had subsided during the night which gave a feeling of uncertainty to the whole area. We pitched two tents in the safest place we could find and then sent the Sherpas back down to Base. It was quite eerie in this camp at night – we were always aware of movement as the ice fall shuddered its way downwards – and aware too of the unstable ice above us.

April 17.
   The two Georges and I set off from Camp II and made our way through a startling crevasse and serac area. We reached a difficult section we called the 'Ghastly Crevasse' but managed to find a route through. We crossed the last crevasse by putting one foot on a sliver of ice and a quick leap. Ice blocks above looked most ominous. We tried a route up to the right towards the Nuptse ice cliffs but got into the most dangerous serac country I've yet struck. We then followed

a lead to the left and this took us finally to a little saddle and we could see the first big snow shelf guarded by great ice cliffs. We could see no direct assault so squeezed around to the right through vertical slabs of ice – the 'Nutcracker' – and then climbed the ice wall firstly up a reasonable angle and then by jamming up a vertical ice crack. I was quite pleased with my lead here. This great block was joined to the next by a bridge and we were on the brink of the Cwm. We returned down the crack and the 'Nutcracker' and then followed a long traverse which landed us at the 'Ghastly Crevasse'. We met John Hunt and Ang Namgyl at Camp II and I conducted John up to the 'Ghastly Crevasse' again to give some idea of the route. We all descended to Base. I consider the route is rather dangerous but feel well satisfied with our efforts.

Activity on the ice fall over the next few days was confined to improving the route and putting in various bridges with pine logs and ladders. On April 22nd we established Camp III on top of the ice fall and Mike Westmacott, Da Namgyl and I spent the first night there. It was a roomy and pleasant stretch of flat snow on top of a huge block of ice and there was no danger from hanging ice. It was a pleasant change to have a place to sleep without any sense of impending doom. Mike and I made some substantial improvements to the upper part of the ice fall route and a couple of days later heard on the radio schedule that John Hunt and a large group were coming up to join us. This was to be Tenzing's first trip up the ice fall and we didn't discover until later that he had rather resented being confined to organisational duties (however important they might be) rather than sharing the excitement up front as he preferred to do. This was certainly no deliberate action on our part – I was thoroughly enjoying the problems of the ice fall and so were the others – but I don't think the thought entered any of our minds that Tenzing could help us to any great extent at this stage.

April 25.
    We set off early on a lovely morning to try and find a route through the breaks directly ahead. I had a lot of hard cutting and tricky work and made enough progress to know that we could put a fixed rope route through if absolutely necessary. Mike was going very badly and we returned to the tent very slowly. John arrived with a large group from Camp II. It snowed in the afternoon but about 4 p.m. John, Charles Evans, Wilf Noyce, Tenzing and I carried the bridge along to the big crevasse, bolted it together so it was 18 feet long and then put it across. I christened it by crossing first. John was very keen to go on so sent Wilf and Tenzing back for the 5 o'clock radio contact

(Tenzing wasn't at all happy about this) and the other three of us pushed on. We had to make one rather dangerous tack under the West Spur ice cliffs but then cut well out into the middle of the Cwm and were greatly jubliant to find no obvious difficulties ahead. We returned to Camp III feeling fine.

April 26.

John and Charles on one rope and Tenzing and I on another set off for Camp IV. We followed our old track and crossed the aluminium bridge. Tenzing and I broke off to examine the Swiss dump for Camp III and found about a load of food, mainly pemmican. We caught up to the others and then took over the brunt of step plugging in deep snow. A tricky bit of ground followed with many concealed crevasses, then some deep plugging until finally Tenzing and I, taking turns, arrived at Camp IV, 21,000 feet, well ahead of John and Charles – John being very tired. At Camp IV there was a good deal of Swiss food in boxes and round casks. We spent some time unearthing this and it came to six or seven loads of useful stuff. After a couple of hours Tenzing and I departed for Base Camp. We reached Camp III in one hour, passing Greg and Wilf and their Sherpas who had dumped their loads half an hour from Camp IV. We descended to Camp II in 33 minutes on a perfect track. We met George Lowe with a team of porters at II and had a pleasant yarn. It was good to see him looking so well again. Tenzing and I left Camp II with a great rush which was suddenly checked when under the weight of a hearty jump from me a large ice block sheared off and descended with me down a crevasse. Only lively work with my flailing crampons and a fortunately quick rope from Tenzing stopped an unfortunate experience. We continued to Base in 55 minutes. Tenzing is an admirable companion – fit, energetic, capable and with excellent rope technique.

This was the first time I had climbed with Tenzing and I was impressed with his strength, his sound technique, and particularly his willingness to rush off on any variation I might suggest. For the first time I had the germ of an idea that I might team with Tenzing as much as possible. My natural inclination was to climb with George Lowe but John Hunt was definitely opposed to this – he preferred to share our vigorous New Zealand icemanship around the team. If George and I had not been so separated we might well have ended up on the summit together.

For five days I was closely involved in the carrying of supplies through the ice fall to Camp III. Meanwhile preparations were under way for an

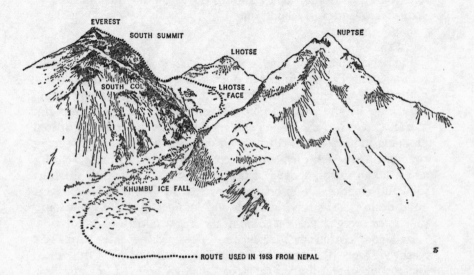

examination of the Lhotse Face using the closed circuit oxygen being operated largely by Charles Evans and Tom Bourdillon. In fact there was so much interest and attention being devoted to the closed circuit oxygen that I felt this might be to the detriment of those of us who were using the traditional open circuit equipment. I suggested to John Hunt that Tenzing and I should do an energetic test with the open circuit set to see if there were any snags that should be corrected. John was very concerned about supplies of oxygen but to my relief he finally agreed.

May 2.

Tenzing and I did a long oxygen trial. We used the pack-frame and an RAF oxygen bottle unit weighing 27 lbs odd and with 1400 litres capacity giving just over 5 hours on 4 litres a minute. We each had a total load of about 40 lbs. We departed from Base on a perfect fresh morning at 6.30 a.m. and felt first class operating on 4 litres. We moved steadily up the hill and there was no effort entailed in arriving at Camp II after 1 hour 28 minutes. Everyone was in bed but we got a quick cup of coffee and were away in 14 minutes. We wandered up the hill with a couple of inches of snow on the track and arrived at Camp III in another 50 minutes, feeling wonderfully fresh. We had a pleasant chat and another drink and then were away again at 9.32. We crossed the aluminium bridge and were then most appalled to strike deep fresh soft snow and commenced plugging steps. Absolutely no track remained. It was frightfully hot but taking turns we pushed on with determination. The deep snow made going very difficult but we arrived at Camp IV at 11.36 having taken two hours from Camp III. We were rather tired from our plugging efforts but soon recovered and felt first class. We had a long wait before Mike Ward and Charles Wylie arrived from Camp III using 2 litres a minute – Mike carrying 55 lbs and Charles about 40. Then six Sherpas rolled in with gear and a larger camp was set up. Finally at 4 p.m. when we were getting rather worried Tom Bourdillon and Charles Evans with an exhausted John between them came very slowly down the Cwm with frequent sit downs and reached camp. John said 'For the first time I really feel a bit done in.' Charles' comment on the closed circuit was that it was too heavy and made you feel far too hot. They had reached some 500 feet above Camp V and realized there was a good deal of work to get to Camp VI. John had planned to come down with us but was too tired to descend so Tenzing and I rushed off into a colossal snow storm at 4.20 p.m. The Cwm tracks were wiped out, the flags were invisible, avalanches thundered down the great rock walls and we fumbled our way along. We finally found the bridge above Camp III and then in driving, painful hail made very slow progress to the Camp III dump and then down the rope ladder and through the 'Nutcracker'. In the deep snow I plunged ahead down the track but progress was funereal as I was up to my waist in holes half of the time. The light was fading but a fortunate easing of the heavy snow fall enabled us to make slightly better speed to the tents of Camp II. We debated whether we should stay here but decided to risk it and go on. I had a ghastly time finding a route over the gully and 'Atom Bomb' area but managed to get through. Then Tenzing took a lead and we plunged up and over ice blocks in a flurry of snow, chasing flag after flag. We emerged in 'Hell-fire Alley' in semi darkness, plunged down it, raced over 'Hillary's Horror' variation and then dashed over the last bridge just as darkness fell. Our fumblings around for the track were pretty annoying but we finally reached camp at 7.40 after quite a day. We were tired but far from exhausted.

Tenzing and I had made a highly successful run and showed what could be done with the open circuit equipment. Over the next few days a group of us were sent down to Lobuje for a rest off the mountain.

I disliked going away from the scene of the action but was persuaded that it was for the good of the team. While we were resting the closed circuit party worked on the lower part of the Lhotse Face but they experienced quite a few problems with their equipment. We all gathered at Base Camp on May 6th and next day had long discussions about plans and personnel. It was only at this stage that the final parties were selected for the various tasks on the upper part of the mountain. Charles Evans and Tom Bourdillon were to use the closed circuit oxygen equipment in the first assault and their main objective was to reach the south summit. Tenzing and I were to try for the top with the open circuit.

We moved back onto the mountain and in three days I conducted three successive lifts of supplies up to Camp IV, having to break fresh trail each time – on the last day I broke trail through eighteen inches of new snow. On May 14th most of us moved to Camp IV (Advanced Base Camp) to be in position for the final stages of the climb. George Lowe and Ang Nima had moved a camp from V to VI and were working on the upper half of the Lhotse Face.

The next week was the most frustrating time of the expedition for me. Day after day we watched the Lhotse Face through our binoculars but progress was very slow and sometimes minimal. I felt that time was passing and we weren't getting much closer to the South Col. On several occasions I suggested to John and Charles that Tenzing and I should go up and give a hand on the route but John insisted that we conserve our strength for the final assault.

May 15.

Wilf Noyce and I left Camp IV and went to V where Mike Westmacott was lying in bad condition. He couldn't get any higher so we sent him down. We took three laden Sherpas, Da Tenzing, Ang Namgyl and Passang Phutar and went on up to Camp VI to greet George Lowe and Ang Nima who were having a rest day. Wilf Noyce was going very well but I put on the pace a bit and the rope came tight so I had to slow down. Wilf remained with George but I took three Sherpas on up the Lhotse Face and we established Camp VII with a tent, cooker and food. Drifting snow had obscured a lot of George's route. It was hard work carrying a load up to 24,000 feet without oxygen but not unduly so. Wilf Noyce was staying on to give a hand so I returned down to Camp V and spent the night there with Charles Evans.

By May 19th George Lowe, Mike Ward and Ila Tenzing were in Camp VII at 24,000 feet but the Lhotse Face attack had almost fizzled

out, and we were already being warned about the approaching monsoon snows. The weather had not in fact been very satisfactory but there
was also a clear lack of vitality in our thrust at this stage. I knew from
experience that George needed someone to stimulate him into the
considerable action he was capable of – and he simply wasn't getting
this stimulation. I felt quite grumpy that I wasn't allowed to go up and
give him a hand. Next day John decided that George should come down
and he returned to our camp as relaxed and cheerful as ever. Wilf
Noyce had gone up to Camp VII with nine Sherpas and we were
desperately hoping that they might push a lot higher and on May 21st
we watched eagerly for any sign of action. Finally only two figures
(Wilf Noyce and Sherpa Annullu) moved above Camp VII and with
immense excitement we watched them climb slowly across the Lhotse
face to the South Col at 26,000 feet. It was a tremendous step forward
for the expedition. In a backing up movement on the same day Charles
Wylie and another group of Sherpas went from Camp V to VII. This
meant that fourteen Sherpas (our entire high altitude team) were at
Camp VII and it was absolutely essential that on the 22nd the whole
bunch should go to the South Col or food would run out and the
attack would break down.

May 21.
    . . . We had discussed the unfortunate likelihood of no one getting to
the South Col the next day and finally decided that Tenzing and I
should scream up as a booster party to make sure that the Sherpas
got there. We left at 12.15 using oxygen and arrived at VII after
4 hours and 15 minutes. Tenzing was invaluable and he and Charles
Wylie organised all the loads in the evening ready for an early
start in the morning. With 17 people in camp we found that cooking
facilities were inadequate and food and water insufficient.

May 22.
    Cooking started at 5 a.m. but only a cup of tea had been produced
by the time we departed at 8.30 a.m. Tenzing and I were using
oxygen, as was Charles Wylie . . . but not the porters. Tenzing and I
went ahead, kicking and cutting steps. We made height quite well to
the top of the Lhotse glacier but the Sherpas were already finding the
altitude quite a problem. We had a lot of work to do preparing the
route across the traverse and most of the Sherpas were going slower
and slower . . . some even lying down on the slope and all very tired.
Two of them were in considerable distress so Tenzing and I each took
an oxygen bottle from their loads. We continued making the trail
and finally breasted the Lhotse ridge. Meanwhile one of the Sherpas

had given up and Charles Wylie took from his load a 20 lb bottle of oxygen.

Tenzing and I descended to the desolate windswept South Col and dumped our loads beside the wrecks of the Swiss tents. What a place! The South summit looked absolutely terrific from here. Three of the hardier Sherpas arrived and got rid of their loads and Tenzing and I left the remainder of our oxygen on the Col too. We climbed back up the little slope to the top of the face and met the rest of the Sherpas and Charles Wylie with a solid load. We then plunged down across the traverse picking up the exhausted Sherpa on the way. We ground down to Camp VII and had a brief rest and a drink . . . then six of us carried on down to Camp IV, passing John Hunt, Tom Bourdillon and Charles Evans at Camp V on their way for the first attempt on the summits. It had been a tremendous and successful day . . . we now had 14 loads of 30 lbs each on the South Col.

Tenzing and I had two rest days at Camp IV before going back up the mountain and we took them with reluctance. We were eager to be under way as the assault phase was in full cry and morale was now very strong. On May 24th Bourdillon and Evans, the closed circuit team, with John Hunt and two Sherpas as support party went from Camp VII to the South Col in very slow time due to the bad conditions. We realised that their arduous seven-hour trip would make an attack the next day impracticable – and so it proved. The following day they had to rest on the Col while Tenzing and I climbed up to Camp VII with our support group of George Lowe and Alf Gregory and eight strong Sherpas. Tenzing and I reached the camp in three and a quarter hours and it seemed to get easier each time we went up. It was a beautiful afternoon for a change and we appreciated the ample room and sense of security in this camp.

May 26.

The whole group of 11 of us got away promptly in the morning for the South Col. I led all the way and Tenzing and I went pretty quickly. Things seemed to be going all right behind so we carried on fairly smartly. At 9.30 we saw our first view of two ropes on the South-east ridge above the couloir. John had left at 7 a.m. with Da Namgyl – John on 4 litres and Da Namgyl on 2 litres. Tom and Charles had a lot of trouble with their closed circuit oxygen and didn't get away until 7.50 a.m. We got a great thrill out of watching their progress. Tom and Charles surged ahead but John soon stopped and dumped loads about 150 feet above the Swiss ridge camp – at about 27,350 feet.

Tenzing and I reached the South Col in two and three-quarter hours. We saw John and Da Namgyl descending and went up to meet them and assisted them back to camp. John was very exhausted. The rest of our party duly arrived including the five Sherpas who were only carrying to the South Col – unfortunately the three Sherpas who were meant to carry loads up the ridge for us trailed the field by miles. At 1 p.m. Tom and Charles disappeared over the South Summit – what an achievement!

A great achievement it was indeed! They were higher than men had ever climbed before; but to my shame the delight I felt at their success was tempered with secret thoughts of envy and fear. Would they go on towards the top, I wondered? They had already done so much better than I had expected – perhaps they would have the strength to continue? Tenzing was more obviously concerned than I – he felt sure they would now reach the summit and felt some bitterness that a Sherpa had not been given the opportunity to get there with the first party. The South Summit was shrouded in cloud – we had no way of knowing what the men were doing.

Our unworthy thoughts were wasted effort. At three thirty p.m. Evans and Bourdillon appeared again out of the mist on their way down the ridge – they had turned back from the South Summit 28,700 feet. Absolutely exhausted, their descent of the ridge was hazardous in the extreme. They had a number of tumbles in tricky places and then fell from top to bottom of the great couloir – it was a miracle they survived. They reached the South Col more exhausted than any men I have ever seen. Tom was still bitterly disappointed they hadn't tried for the top – but Charles knew they would never have returned. Too tired almost to talk, they painted a gloomy picture of the ridge running on towards the summit; and expressed their doubts about us making it. By mid-afternoon it was blowing furiously and life on the Col was an extreme of misery.

May 27.

One of the worst nights I have ever experienced . . . very strong wind and very cold, −25 centigrade . . . and particularly uncomfortable. Tenzing, George, Greg and I were in the pyramid tent and breathing a little oxygen. John, Tom and Charles were crammed into a Meade and the three Sherpas in the small dome. It was a very windy morning indeed and I couldn't get warm. Tom and Charles were completely exhausted. They finally decided they must get away. Angtember had been sick all night so he too was to go down. John, after some rather pointed discussion decided to descend too.

It was a pathetic sight to see the bunch climb the slope above camp. Tom was on his knees on numerous occasions and we had to give him an oxygen bottle. John, too, was very tired and the determined Charles seemed the only rational member of the party. They finally disappeared and had a most difficult descent to Camp VII where Mike Ward was fortunately in residence and was able to give them help.

May 28.

A fine but windy morning, —25 centigrade. The first blow was that Pember was sick leaving us only one Sherpa . . . Ang Nima. We decided we'd have to carry up the camp ourselves. George took 3 oxygen cylinders which made up a load of about 41 lbs; Greg carried oxygen plus a primus and food . . . about 40 lbs; Ang Nima had 3 oxygen bottles . . . 41 lbs; Tenzing had two oxygen bottles and so did I . . . plus all our personal and camping gear, camera and food . . . at least 49 or 50 lbs each. The other three departed at 8.45 and had made a lot of height up the couloir by the time Tenzing and I left at 10 a.m. Our loads slowed us down but we were going very well. The couloir was hard windpacked snow and had to be cut for many hundreds of feet and George did most of this work.

Tenzing and I caught up to the others on the ridge by the Swiss tent at 27,200 feet aproximately. After another 150 feet we came to the dump made by John and Da Namgyl of a tent, fuel, food and oxygen. After some discussion we decided to push on carrying all the gear. I took on the tent making my load to over 60 lbs and the others divided the rest and probably had over 50 lbs. We continued on up the ridge with George doing most of the leading and plugging. The ridge was steep with a little snow over the rocks but the upward sloping strata gave easy going. We continued for some time but found no sign of a camping site. Oxygen was running low and we had to switch over to assault supplies. The position was getting a bit desperate when Tenzing did a lead out over deep unstable snow to the left and finally we found a somewhat more flattish spot beneath a rock bluff. We decided to camp here at 27,900 feet and gave the others a little oxygen and sent them down. It was 2.30 p.m.

Tenzing and I took off our oxygen and started making a camp site – a frightful job. We chopped out frozen rubble with our ice axes and tried to level a suitable area. By 5 p.m. we had cleared a site large enough for a tent but on two levels. We decided it would have to do so pitched the tent on it. We had no effective means of tying down the tent so I hitched some ropes to corners of rocks and to oxygen bottles sunk in the snow and hoped for the best. At 6 p.m.

we moved into the tent. Tenzing had his Lilo along the bottom level overhanging the slope while I sat on the top level with my feet on the bottom ledge and was able to brace the whole tent against the quarter hourly fierce gusts of wind.

The primus worked like a charm and we consumed large amounts of very sweet lemon water, soup and coffee and ate with relish sardines on biscuits, a tin of apricots, dates, and biscuits with jam. I had made an inventory of our oxygen supplies which were inevitably low due to the reduced porter lift and found that we only had one and three-quarters light alloy cylinders each for the assault. By relying on the two one-third full bottles left by Tom and Charles about 500 feet below the South summit I thought we could make an attack using about 3 litres a minute (I had adjustments for this on my set and fortunately Tenzing's set was faulty and on 4 litres a minute it was really only delivering a little over three litres).

We also had a little excess oxygen in three nearly empty bottles and this could give us about 4 hours of sleeping at 1 litre a minute. The thermometer was registering —27 degrees C. but it wasn't unpleasantly cold as the wind was confined to casual strong gusts. I spread the oxygen into two two-hour periods and although I was sitting up I dozed reasonably well. Between oxygen sessions we brewed up and had lemon juice and biscuits. It was very noticeable that although we had used no oxygen from our arrival at the camp site at 2.30 p.m. until we went to sleep at 9 p.m. (six and a half hours) that we were only slightly breathless and could work quite hard ... certainly harder than I expected at 27,900 feet.

May 29.

At 4 a.m. the weather looked perfect and the view superb. Tenzing pointed out Thyangboche Monastery far below us. We commenced making drinks and food and thawing out frozen boots over the primus stove. I got the oxygen sets into the tent and tested them out.

At 6.30 a.m. we moved off and taking turns plugged up the ridge above camp. The ridge narrowed considerably and the breakable crust made plugging tedious and balance difficult. We soon reached the oxygen bottles and were greatly relieved to find about 1100 lbs pressure in each. The narrow ridge led up to the very impressive steep snow face running to the South Summit. Evans and Bourdillon had ascended the rocks on the left and then descended the snow on their return. Their tracks were only faintly visible and we liked neither route. We discussed the matter and decided for the snow. We commenced plugging up in foot deep steps with a thin wind crust on top and precious little belay for the ice-axe. It was altogether most unsatisfactory and whenever I felt feelings of fear regarding it I'd say to myself, 'Forget it! This is Everest and you've got to take a few risks.' Tenzing expressed his extreme dislike but made no suggestions regarding turning back. Taking turns we made slow speed up this vast slope. After several hundred feet the angle eased a little and the slope was broken by more rock outcrops and the tension eased. At 9.00 a.m. we cramponed up onto the fine peak of the South Summit.

We looked with some eagerness on the ridge ahead as this was the crux of the climb. Both Tom and Charles had expressed comments on the difficulties of the ridge ahead and I was not feeling particularly hopeful. The sight ahead, in fact, was impressive but not disheartening. On the right long cornices like fingers hung over the Kangshung face. From these cornices a steep snow slope ran down to the left to the top of the rocks which drop 8,000 feet to the Western Cwm. I thought I saw a middle route by cutting steps along the snow above the rocks and sufficiently far down from the crest to be out of danger from the cornices.

Our first three-quarter bottles were finished so we discarded them and set off with a light 19 lb apparatus – one full bottle of oxygen which we were using at 3 litres a minute. We dropped off the South Summit and keeping low on the left I commenced cutting steps in excellent firm frozen snow. It was first class going and as I was feeling very well we made steady progress. Some of the cornice bumps proved tricky but I was able to turn them by dropping right down onto the rocks and scrambling by that way. Tenzing had me on a tight rope all the time and we moved throughout one at a time. After an hour or so we came to a vertical rock step in the ridge. This appeared quite a problem. However the step was bounded on its right by a vertical snow cliff and I was able to work my way up this 40 foot crack and finally get over the top. I was rather surprised and pleased that I was capable of such effort at this height. I brought Tenzing up and noticed he was proving a little sluggish, but an excellent and safe companion for all that. I really felt now that we were going to get to the top and that nothing would stop us. I kept frequent watch on our oxygen consumption and was encouraged to find it at a steady rate.

I continued on, cutting steadily and surmounting bump after bump and cornice after cornice looking eagerly for the summit. It seemed impossible to pick it and time was running out. Finally I cut around the back of an extra large hump and then on a tight rope from Tenzing I climbed up a gentle snow ridge to its top. Immediately

The bridge we built over Dudh Kosi below Namche Bazar.

Mingbo airfield at 15,500 feet with Mount Taweche behind.

Snowmobiles with Mount Herschel in background.

Towards the summit of Mount Cook while on the Grand Traverse.

it was obvious that we had reached our objective. It was 11.30 a.m. and we were on top of Everest!

To the north an impressive corniced ridge ran down to the East Rongbuk glacier. We could see nothing of the old North route but were looking down on the North Col and Changtse. The West ridge dropped away in broad sweeps and we had a great view of the Khumbu and Pumori far below us. Makalu, Kangchenjunga and Lhotse were dominant to the east looking considerably less impressive than I had ever seen them. Tenzing and I shook hands and then Tenzing threw his arms around my shoulders. It was a great moment! I took off my oxygen and for ten minutes I photographed Tenzing holding flags, the various ridges of Everest and the general view. I left a crucifix on top for John Hunt and Tenzing made a little hole in the snow and put in it some food offerings – lollies, biscuits and chocolate. We ate a Mint Cake and then put our oxygen back on. I was a little worried by the time factor so after 15 minutes on top we turned back at 11.45.

The steps along the ridge made progress relatively easy and the only problem was the rock step which demanded another jamming session. At 12.45 we were back on the South Summit both now rather fatigued. Wasting no time (our oxygen was getting low) we set off down the great slope in considerable trepidation about its safeness. This was quite a mental strain and as I was coming down first I repacked every step with great care. Tenzing was a tower of strength and his very fine ability to keep a tight rope was most encouraging. After what seemed a lifetime the angle eased off and we were soon leading down onto the narrow snow ridge and finally to the dump of oxygen bottles. We loaded these on and then, rather tired, wended our way down our tracks and collapsed into our camp at 2 p.m. Our original bottles were now exhausted. They had given us four and three-quarter hours and allowing 800 litres in these very full bottles our consumption had averaged two and five-sixth litres per minute.

At the ridge camp we had a brew of lemon and sugar and then picked up all our personal gear and connected up our last bottles – one-third full. At 3 p.m. we left the ridge camp and although we were tired we made good time down the ridge to the Swiss camp and the couloir. The snow in the couloir was firm and we had to recut all the steps. We kicked down the lower portions and then cramponed very weakly down to meet George...

George met us with a mug of soup just above camp, and seeing his stalwart frame and cheerful face reminded me how fond of him I was.

My comment was not specially prepared for public consumption but for George . . . 'Well, we knocked the bastard off!' I told him and he nodded with pleasure . . . 'Thought you must have!'

Wilf Noyce and Pasang Puta were also in Camp and they looked after us with patience and kindness. I felt a moment of sympathy for Wilf – he was the only one left with the strength to try for the summit; but now he wouldn't get the chance. It was another foul night with strong wind and very cold temperatures but Tenzing and I were given oxygen and the time passed amazingly quickly. Reaction was starting to set in next day and I felt very lethargic as we traversed the long slopes of the Lhotse face and then tramped slowly down the Cwm towards Camp IV. The party drifted out of camp towards us, not knowing if we had been successful or not. When George exuberantly gave the thumbs up signal of success they rushed towards us and soon we were embracing them all, and shaking hands, and thumping each other on the back. It was a touching and unforgettable moment; and yet somehow a sad one too.

Chapter 11

Aftermath of Everest

BASE CAMP HAD NEVER BEEN MY FAVOURITE CAMP SITE – IT WAS COLD, uncomfortable and rather sordid – but now it seemed a home away from home. I felt a great relief to be safely off the mountain and already our success was becoming remote and unimportant – until on June 2nd we tuned into the BBC for a description of the Queen's Coronation and to our great excitement heard the announcement that Everest had been climbed. Somehow hearing it officially over the radio from half the world away made the climb sound far more important and real.

The expedition moved down valley to Thyangboche and we revelled in the mild temperatures and the green grass and flowers. There were frequent monsoon showers and we could see fresh snow on the high summits. I was extremely thin and completely lacking in energy and did little more than write letters and sleep whenever I could. The others weren't much better and we were a lethargic but happy crew. John decided to go ahead to Kathmandu to make travel arrangements leaving the rest of us to walk out more slowly with the main baggage.

We moved across the great ridges of Nepal through monsoon rain and blood hungry leeches. Every day we were met by mail runners from Kathmandu with bundles of congratulatory telegrams and it was becoming clear that the climb of Everest had attracted world-wide attention. Late one afternoon George Lowe and I were walking along a narrow path above the valley floor when we met still another mail runner – the second that day. George opened the mail bag and sorted out the letters. 'A letter for you from John Hunt,' he said, and burst out laughing. I took the letter and saw it was addressed to Sir Edmund Hillary, K.B.E.

'Very funny joke,' I commented sourly, then read on . . . John and I had both been given titles by the Queen – I was now officially Sir Edmund Hillary, K.B.E.

It should have been a great moment, but instead I was aghast. It was a tremendous honour, of course, but I had never really approved of titles and couldn't imagine myself possessing one. I had a vivid mental picture of myself walking down the main street of Papakura dressed in my torn and dirty overalls. 'My God!' I thought, 'I'll have to get a new pair of overalls.'

John's letter told me that the K.B.E. had been accepted on my behalf by the Prime Minister of New Zealand – it would be thoroughly impolite to turn it down now. I went to bed that night feeling miserable rather than pleased.

As we approached closer to Kathmandu the flood of letters and telegrams grew greater and greater. The world Press was still full of inflated stories about our activities and there were even a few signs of discord. John Hunt was asked by elated Indian Press men for his assessment of Tenzing as a climber and cautiously commented that 'Tenzing was a competent climber within the limits of his experience,' which I imagine was probably true of all of us but could hardly be called an enthusiastic endorsement. It was not well received by the Indian Press – and I don't blame them too much for that. John was determined to present the climb as a success of the whole team – as indeed it was – and resisted strenuously the efforts by the Press to pick out Tenzing and myself.

John rejoined us on the last night before our arrival in Kathmandu and told us that it had been reported that Tenzing had reached the summit first and that this was causing great excitement in the valley of Kathmandu. Tenzing assured us he had made no such claim – we had operated as a team and the question of who actually placed a foot anywhere first was of no consequence to us – or to any mountaineer. I completely agreed with this and refused to take the matter very seriously, and was stupid to have resented it later.

Next morning we climbed the long hill to Banepa and there was a growing feeling of excitement. Groups of Press and officials had come out to meet us and the crowd increased rapidly in size. I was approached by an Indian reporter who represented a large London daily newspaper. He told me he was authorised to offer me £8,000 for my story of the summit day on Everest. 'The expedition has sold all press rights to the London *Times*,' I told him, 'What would the members of the expedition think if I ignored this agreement and sold my story to someone else?'

'My newspaper,' he informed me, 'feels that the sum offered is large enough to enable you to withstand a little bit of criticism.' He never knew how close he came to getting thumped by an incensed mountaineer although, strangely enough, I became very friendly with him in later years. He was like many reporters – a very decent sort of chap personally but completely cynical about human behaviour as far as press matters were concerned.

We arrived at the commencement of the road and were surrounded by a milling, hysterical throng all wanting to touch Tenzing. He was obviously terrified at this determined attention. Tenzing was pushed into an open jeep and made to stand upright holding on to a cross-bar. John and I were squeezed into the back seat. Then we were off in a clamour of sound followed by a second jeep crammed with young Nepalis. (No transport had been arranged for the rest of the expedition and they had to thumb rides into Kathmandu with the Press Corps.)

We rocketed through the countryside past waving and shouting people. Our companions in the two jeeps were constantly extolling Tenzing's virtues. '*Shri* Tenzing!' one of them would shout. '*Zindabad!*' (Long life to you!) would come the massive refrain. It was tremendously colourful and exciting. In every village the crowd had gathered to honour Tenzing and the streets were gay with banners. I noticed one banner was much more common than any other – it depicted a mountain with a man on the summit waving the Nepali flag and a rope going down the mountainside to another climber who was resting on his back with arms and feet in the air. I didn't have to be very bright to realise that the recumbant character was me but at first I found it quite funny.

We arrived at a big town and drove into the main square which was packed with thousands of people. Tenzing was conducted with great ceremony on to a big dais and John and I followed cheerfully after – we were lucky to get a couple of seats at the back of the official group. The speeches of welcome brought tumultuous applause ... and then Tenzing was ushered forward to speak. Obviously overwhelmed he said only a few hesitant sentences, but it didn't matter. The heavens rocked with the response. John Hunt was taken to the microphone and spoke to a suddenly subdued crowd. He confined himself to some complimentary words about Tenzing which produced a wave of applause.

The official party was now split by a fierce debate. One group rushed up to me and led me towards the microphone, then another group led me back to my seat again. Finally the senior official waved his companions aside and took me firmly forward. 'Everyone,' he told me in English, 'would like a few words from the second man on Everest!' As I opened my mouth to speak a deathly hush fell over the whole huge gathering and I realised to my horror that it wasn't just a disinterested silence – there was an enormous and active dislike flowing towards me.

My comments were short, complimentary and inoffensive. As I

withdrew to my seat in the rear the only sound to be heard in the whole square was my footsteps echoing on the dais – there wasn't a clap or even a cough. Everyone in that vast crowd was pouring out hate towards me, not for what I was or had done – they'd probably never heard of me before – but because they feared I might not be happy to remain 'the second man on Everest'.

The next few hours were quite a trial for John Hunt and me. At each large town the welcome was repeated and so was the reaction. My ears were deafened with the constant cry of 'Zindabad' and I had become a little irritated at the succession of banners displaying my recumbent figure. When our motorcade was slowed down to a walk by a muddy stretch a young man rushed forward, clambered on the jeep and sitting half on top of me started bellowing 'Zindabad' in my ear. I pushed him very firmly back into the mud.

On the outskirts of Kathmandu we were met by a group of senior Government officials and immediately the atmosphere changed. John and I were resurrected from the back seat and joined Tenzing in places of honour, while the banners seemed to have disappeared and the vast crowds were smiling and friendly. As we entered the city it became a triumphant progression and my warm affection for Nepal returned. Over the next few days we were honoured by the King and Queen of Nepal, had a tremendous civic reception and were greeted everywhere with great warmth and friendship.

'There are some bad people in that part of the valley,' we were informed when we commented on our unusual reception, 'and they like to create trouble whenever they can.' I still get asked 'who got to the top first,' even after twenty years. The answer has been given, of course, but still people keep asking. Tenzing and I now say that we, 'reached the summit together'. We shared the work, the risks, and the success – it was a team effort and nothing else is important.

We flew down to the steaming plains of India and to a tumultuous welcome. In Calcutta the Governor of Bengal had a huge reception in our honour and we attended a succession of official functions. We visited the University and spoke to the students, and emotion ran high. As we were drawing away in our limousine through tight-pressed ranks of students I lowered the window and reached out to shake hands with one smiling young man. There was an immediate surge forward and my arm was nearly wrenched off by twenty other students. I took care to keep the window closed after that.

We landed at Delhi airport and could see a vast crowd being kept back by barriers and a line of policemen. As Tenzing emerged from the aircraft the crowd swept forward and twenty thousand excited people came running towards us across the tarmac – a terrifying sight and Tenzing went white as a sheet. Somehow we got Tenzing (and ourselves) into the limousines. 'If this is a friendly crowd,' was my thought, 'heaven protect us from an angry one!'

The Prime Minister of India, Pandit Nehru had arranged a great welcome for us. At an open-air function in the centre of the city and with all the pomp and ceremony for which Delhi is renowned we were presented with special gold medals honouring our achievement.

At a State reception we were mobbed by fifty cameramen wanting a group photograph of Nehru, Tenzing and myself. 'We will stand on the steps here,' Nehru announced to the group. 'You have ten minutes to get your pictures.' For ten minutes there was absolute bedlam and then Nehru clapped his hands and quietly said 'Enough!' To my utter astonishment the cameramen disappeared. I have had the chance to talk to many heads of State over the years – kings, presidents, and prime ministers – but the one who impressed me most with his personality was undoubtedly Pandit Nehru.

We were welcomed at London Airport like conquering heroes. Even Eric Shipton was there – thrusting into my hands a bunch of the bananas I have always enjoyed (I ate them all on the way up to London). For weeks I moved in a completely different world – drifting through a succession of parties, official functions, a State banquet and a Buckingham Palace garden party. My diet seemed to be largely smoked Scotch salmon and champagne, I started waking every morning with a mild hangover.

I met the well-connected, the powerful and the rich; it was tremendously entertaining although I saw little to envy or, indeed, much to admire. I was knighted by the Queen in a simple private ceremony with only the expedition and the Royal Family present. It was an amazing month – I will never have one quite like it again.

Early in August 1953 George Lowe and I flew back to New Zealand to visit our families. I made one stop on the way – in Australia – to see a young musician who was studying at the Sydney Conservatorium of Music. Louise Mary Rose was the daughter of J. H. Rose, a reputable lawyer in Auckland and the past president of the New Zealand Alpine Club. I had known the family for many years and had respected and liked them. I had been enamoured of Louise for some time, even though I was eleven years older. I asked her to marry me and go to England for the lecture tour I had agreed to undertake. Somewhat in a daze she consented and I was overjoyed – it certainly proved the most sensible action I have ever taken.

When George and I flew into Auckland in a Solent flying boat we could see a huge crowd gathered at the sea-plane base. We had experienced large crowds before, but always in foreign countries where it was difficult to take them very seriously. But these were our own people; they had been to the same schools and watched the same football matches. They knew all our weaknesses and wouldn't easily be deluded by the heroic guff that had been flooding the newspapers. What were they doing here in such numbers? We looked at each other in wild alarm. The plane landed in a cloud of spray and taxied to the unloading pontoon. We emerged into a sunny winter afternoon to handshakes, hugs, cheers and even a few tears – and all because we'd climbed a mountain! It was unbelievably emotional and it was with difficulty that I suppressed my own feelings.

The next few weeks were frantically busy. Public lectures throughout New Zealand; civic receptions; and getting an overdraft at the bank so I could fly Louise with me to Europe. On September 3rd (her twenty-third birthday) Louise and I were married and next morning we were on our way back to London.

The introduction of a romance into the Everest story certainly kept the public interest at a high pitch. When we landed in Sydney there was another big crowd to see us with flashing cameras and inquisitive press men. I was delighted to discover that Louise's bubbling enthusiasm and fresh open personality which had appealed so much to me seemed to have the same effect on everybody she met. At official functions I found I could leave a great deal of the talking and entertaining to her – while I relaxed and admired. Her first letter home after our departure showed how much she was enjoying her new life.

> Government House,
> SINGAPORE.

Dear Hillary and Rose parents,
    I'm not really sure if I'm dreaming everything or not, but anyhow I'll tell you all about it and you can decide for yourselves.
    Well first of all after we left you we had a long and boring trip in the plane which took over 8 hours, and when we got to Sydney there was a terrible crowd of people at Rose Bay to meet us – mostly hysterical women. Before lunch on the plane we were offered a drink with the Skipper's compliments. I had a gin and squash and because of the altitude it went straight to my head and poor Ed and George were quite amused and worried. I have decided never to have anything alcoholic in a plane again, it obviously isn't right for me . . .
    When we left Sydney we were taken to a private room where

supper was served for us and our friends. There must have been about 20 people there and it was very pleasant. Then we were told to go into the plane after everyone else. Oh the joys of flying in a Constellation! It's glorious and they are so huge and powerful, it's impossible for me to describe, but really it's a terrific sensation. They are also very comfortable and you are put on a terrific fuss. The view of the lights of Sydney was magnificent. It made the city look bigger than ever. We had a glorious trip and slept most of the way. Darwin was hot and steamy. A Quantas official met us and took us in his car to Berrimah, the Quantas Lodge 9 miles out of Darwin. We had two hours there discussing serious things with this most serious of officials. Going back to Darwin Airfield was very interesting as it was light and we saw a bit of the country which is flat, barren and pretty awful with all houses on stilts. The only really enjoyable feature of our stay was a bird that started singing at sunrise, its tone was like a bell bird and it kept on singing bits of Italian opera arias with great rhythm and precision.

Then away we swooped in the plane over the Timor Sea. It was a very interesting trip to Java with many islands and huge volcanoes. Two were over 12,000 feet high. The pilot flew round and almost into the crater of one, and during the whole trip he gave us a commentary about the interesting things. I went up in front and had a lot of fun and also had a good look at the kitchen and admired their potato chips so much that the pilot arranged for a big bowl to be sent to Ed and me for morning tea. I ate so many I felt quite sick, but after a big lunch with wine, nuts, fruit and all the trimmings I felt much better.

Djakata was so hot that I gasped like a fish for half an hour after getting back on the plane. Shortly after we crossed the equator, which was most satisfactory as I am now the complete traveller. We got to Singapore at 3.30 and were met by the A.D.C. and others and taken to a cool air-conditioned room where I was presented with a bouquet of glorious orchids and we had the usual press business. Then we drove in a Daimler with all the vice-regal frills to Government House, were met by bowing servants etc, and also everyone at the gates presented arms, and I just sat and giggled. We were taken to our rooms and had a bath and rest. Our room consists of an air conditioned bedroom, a sitting room, writing room, changing room, one verandah and bathroom. As fast as I put my things down the 'Amah' or whatever you call her, took them away and washed them. Well, after a bit of a rest we went downstairs and met His Excellency and Commander Clark the A.D.C., and had drinks in the garden until I started to scratch my legs furiously because of ants. So His Excellency took the hint and we went in. We had dinner at 8 with 10 of us. It was a rather frightening affair but I got through. We sat and talked until about 10.30 and found it very hard to keep awake in the heat. Commander Clark was a great help and told us exactly what to do. Sir John is a rather shy and diffident person but very charming and dignified.

. . . Next day we went to the Commissioner General's, Mr. Malcolm Macdonald, for lunch. There were some very interesting Dutch diplomatic people there and also Sir Anthony Abel and Sir Hubert and Lady Graves. Malcolm Macdonald is a magnificent fellow and when he appeared for lunch he just sat on the edge of a chair and asked me if I thought Ed would like to take his tie off, so I said yes. It was a most glorious informal affair and his home is very beautiful. After lunch he showed us his collection of pottery and rugs. He has the most beautiful Sung Ming Chang Dynasty stuff, a lot of it in light cream and yellow and both Malcolm and I agreed that yellow is the perfect colour for china. After that we spent the afternoon wandering round G.H. grounds and taking photos and movies. Then in the evening there was a terrific dinner party with two Sultans etc. (wore my wedding frock, up to this I had been wearing my black daisy frock). After dinner we rushed off to the theatre. The acting was very good and everyone was dressed well and it was most exciting. Malcolm Macdonald introduced the boys and whilst doing so said the most terrifically flattering things about me in his speech. He is a real orator. I was really amazed at his short talk. He invited us all to stay with him next time we come through. Ed's really thrilled. I seem to have made rather a hit with these govs. etc. At the end of the lecture I went home with Ed and the Gov. in the Rolls!! Cheers. Usually we go in the Humber which is equally good . . .

Really life is too good to be true. Now we are feverishly trying to fix finance and packing. We are having dinner up here in our room tonight as the boys have a lecture and there is an official dinner with the Gov. starting at 8. Am staying up here to write my diary and generally catch up with myself.

Lots of love
Louise.

In London we rented a small flat in South Kensington and I commenced a series of lectures all over Britain. We made a quick trip to Brussels for the European premiere of the Mount Everest film and I learned by heart a short speech in French which commenced, 'Je suis très hereux d'être ici . . .' and which I have used in a wide variety of

French occasions ever since. I lectured in English in Norway, Sweden, Denmark, Finland and Iceland, and used my schoolboy French to join with the other expedition members in lectures in France and Belgium. The magic name of Everest attracted people to these lectures in their thousands and the funds of the Everest Foundation swelled appreciably. All the expedition members received the same pay for their services – travelling expenses plus £25 per lecture – and I was favoured with an extra grant to cover my living costs while out of New Zealand. We made no fortunes out of Everest – but then we didn't expect to and most of us considered our financial arrangements were quite adequate. It was from my first book *High Adventure* that I received sufficient funds to pay off my overdraft and start building myself a small but comfortable family home in Auckland.

Early in December 1953 we flew across the Atlantic for a lecture tour in America. It was an exciting moment when the great buildings on Manhattan Island loomed up out of the haze and hard to believe that we were actually going to stay in the Waldorf Astoria Hotel. I soon learned something about the hard facts of life in New York; I opened the door for a lady at Saks on Fifth Avenue and a hundred men went through before I could get inside. In one week I was forced to spend more on tips than I would normally have earned in a week at the bees. I suppose plenty of country visitors to New York have had the same experience.

In the penthouse on top of the Pierre Hotel our publishers held a great party to celebrate the launching of the expedition book. It was a very noisy and alcoholic occasion and I spent most of my time saying 'Pardon me?' as I tried to catch some question shouted across the din. Halfway through the function a waiter came up and presented me with a note. I opened it – it was the bill for the party – several thousand dollars. Fortunately our host saw me standing there rigid with shock and snatched the bill out of my hand. His comments to the waiter would have shrivelled the hide of a rhinoceros.

A very large and impressive man introduced himself as the head of a famous news agency. He told me that one of his staff had concluded a substantial contract with Tenzing for his autobiography. 'What sort of writer do you think he will be?' he enquired in rather worried fashion. Tenzing should produce a good book, I told him, his only trouble being that he couldn't read or write in English. I thought the man was going to explode from apoplexy. Later James Ramsay Ullman was commissioned to go to Darjeeling and work with Tenzing on the book and *Tiger of the Snows* was the result.

For six weeks we travelled through the North American continent lecturing almost every night and attending a succession of cocktail parties and press conferences. I doubt if we met any 'ordinary' Americans – only the well-heeled and the influential. In Cleveland we were invited to 'come around to the house and meet a few of our crowd.' The house was as large as Buckingham Palace and we shook hands with 400 guests.

The highlight of our trip was to be the presentation to us of the Hubbard Medal of the National Geographic Society and this was to be carried out by President Eisenhower in the White House. We certainly anticipated a great occasion – one of the greatest – and guessed it would be a slightly less formal rendition of the well-organised functions we had attended with other Heads of State elsewhere. John Hunt had come over from Europe for the occasion and we were all ushered into the White House and given a quick conducted tour by a cheerful gentleman who vaguely reminded me of a film star I had seen in days gone by. We were then taken into a large impressive oval-shaped room and lined up to await the arrival of the President.

When the President entered I was surprised to see how thin and tired he appeared – although he must have been only sixty-three at the time. He looked at us in startled surprise and it was quite clear he didn't have the vaguest idea who we were or what we were there for. He leaned down to one of his aides and after a lot of whispering he came forward with a smile and quickly went down the line of us shaking hands. He then asked us to follow him and we strolled down a passage and into a large room which was crammed with radio equipment, cameramen and press – it was to be a coast-to-coast hook-up. We were formed into a line with the President in the middle and John Hunt and myself on either side.

The National Geographic President gave quite a long introductory speech about his society and what it stood for, and he then invited President Eisenhower to present the Hubbard Medals. The President turned to John, as expedition leader, and said, 'Sir Edmund Hunt,' . . . Well, everybody else had been whispering in the President's ear so it seemed good enough for me too, and I leaned over and said rather loudly, 'Sir John Hunt!' The President quickly corrected himself and carried on to make the presentation to John. Then he turned towards me and immediately all the lights came on and cameras started grinding. The pressmen had told me when I suggested they interview John, 'You were the guy who got on top!' . . . so I was receiving the full treatment. The President said a few words and then handed me the medal – and we stood there under the floodlights with rather strained grins on our faces. It was certainly a considerable occasion for me as I hadn't done anything quite like this before.

We were just relaxing from the great moment when there was a loud shout from behind the cameras, 'Give it to him again!' There wasn't a flicker of change in the President's pleasant smile. He stepped forward, took the medal out of my hand, and duly presented it to me all over again.

I can't say that I enjoyed my first visit to the United States. We travelled too much and were worked too hard – and we met all the wrong people. We were being lionised by a class of society with which we had little in common. In those days every rich American expected foreigners to want to share the American way of life and they simply

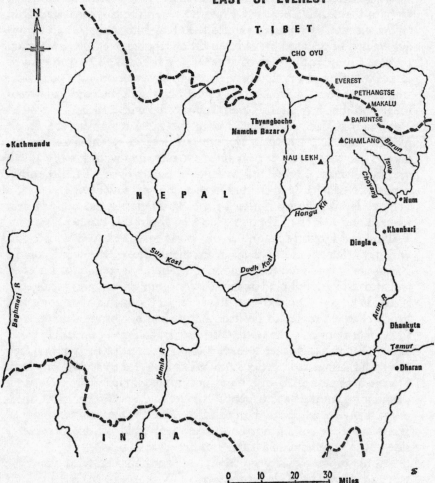

EAST OF EVEREST

couldn't understand it when I told them that I was content to remain a New Zealander. As we flew down through the Pacific, Louise and I agreed that it had been a remarkable experience but we wouldn't really care if we never went back to the United States again.

I didn't have much time to enjoy the calm routine of married life. Six weeks after our return to New Zealand I had to say a fond farewell to my wife and head back to Nepal. For someone who has always enjoyed my time at home I seem to have a flair for getting involved in things that take me away from it. I had agreed to lead a New Zealand Alpine Club expedition to the Barun Valley, east of Everest, and we had a dozen good mountains to climb and the Iswa and Choyang valleys to explore.

We gathered all our equipment in Dharan and trekked up the Arun river to the north. There was heavy snow on the pass into the Barun valley and while two teams pushed their way into the Iswa and Choyang valleys I organised the arduous lift of supplies over the pass and up to Base Camp at the foot of Makalu. I was elated to find the valley just as beautiful as I remembered it. High above us on both sides were tremendous rock precipices and jagged ice ridges, but the valley was green and the air gloriously fresh and scented with azaleas.

From Base Camp Wilkins, McFarlane and I set off up the Barun glacier with five Sherpas. Despite our lack of acclimatisation we hacked our way up an ice peak of 20,370 feet and revelled in the superb views of Everest, Lhotse and Makalu. In *East of Everest* I tell the first-hand story of what happened to us over the next few days.

Next day we moved farther up the Barun glacier and camped near its head at a height of about 18,800 feet. From this camp McFarlane, Wilkins and I set off to climb an obviously easy peak to the north-east which we felt would give us an excellent idea of the whole of the Barun neve. It proved to be more of a mound of rubble than a peak, and after a long, dull plod up shingle slopes and an easy snow ridge we reached the top – 20,300 feet. It was a very valuable viewpoint and Jim McFarlane regretted the fact that he had not brought his photo-theodolite along. To the north-east were several easily accessible passes and McFarlane was eager to have a look over one of them into Tibet. His enthusiasm was infectious and Wilkins agreed to accompany him. I wanted to return to camp and get things organised, for we were planning to commence our return trip down the valley the same afternoon. They roped up and headed off towards the pass, and with a final word that they should not be too late I plunged off down the easy side of the mountain and back to camp.

The afternoon passed very slowly. At four p.m. I crawled out of the tent and searched the glacier for signs of Wilkins and McFarlane, but I could not see anything. I felt a surge of anger. What could they be doing? I had told them to get back early and now the afternoon was nearly gone. We could not possibly go down the valley today. Feeling somewhat disgruntled, I crawled back into the tent. Time passed and there was no sign of them. My anger had changed to worry. The clouds were down around the peaks and the weather was dull and gloomy. I decided to set a deadline. If they had not turned up by six o'clock I would go and look for them. It was getting cold now and I crawled inside my sleeping bag and was soon snug and warm. At five thirty p.m. I heard a faint shout. It was one of the boys! I wriggled out of my bag and struggled through the door of the tent. Staggering into camp was Wilkins. He was alone. With a tight feeling in the pit of my stomach, I saw that his face was covered with blood.

'Where's Jim?'

'We fell down a crevasse. I got out, but Jim is still down there.'

We got Wilkins into the tent and gave him a drink, and he told me the story.

After they left me they had crossed over the head of the glacier and up on to a little saddle on the main divide. From there, much to their excitement, they had been able to look far out on to the high plateau and peaks of Tibet. After enjoying the view to the full they had turned to come home. They were tired and suffering a little from the effects of altitude, but the glacier seemed to have no crevasses and they plugged dully downwards thinking of nothing but reaching the camp and resting. Wilkins was leading, with only a short stretch of rope, thirty or forty feet, separating him from McFarlane. They were reaching a crest on the glacier where it dropped off rather more steeply, when suddenly without warning Wilkins stepped on a thin crust of snow which concealed a great crevasse. He had no memory of falling, but found himself squatting in deep, loose snow sixty feet down at the narrow bottom of the crevasse. Beside him was McFarlane. Wilkins examined himself and found that despite his terrific fall he seemed comparatively unhurt, although his snowglasses had cut his forehead and he was having trouble in keeping the blood out of his eyes. He examined McFarlane and found that he was having some difficulty in moving at all. It was obvious that he was either badly bruised or had broken something.

Wilkins set to work to try to make a way out: it was quite impossible to get out of the hole down which they had fallen. The crevasse in places was very wide and narrowed at the top with overhanging lips of ice. He started working his way along the crevasse to where it narrowed. Wriggling through small ice passages and scrambling along a snowy ledge which clung to the wall of the crevasse, he made considerable height. Above him the sky was cut off by a thin roof of snow. On every side great unstable-looking masses of snow and ice hung menacingly. It was a horrifying place, but he had to get out. Cutting steps in the walls of the crevasse he inched his way upwards, fearful that at any moment he might dislodge an avalanche that would sweep him to the bottom again. He was aiming for a point where there was a hole in the roof. After two hours of difficult and nerve-racking work he reached the hole and started dragging himself out. At the last moment he felt the snow giving way under him and frantically clawed his way to the surface, leaving his ice-axe sunk in the snow behind. He could do nothing for McFarlane, who was too injured to help himself. The only thing to do was to get help. Lying up on the edge of the crevasse was McFarlane's ice-axe, so Wilkins picked it up and then carefully and cautiously made his way across to the edge of the glacier. Tired and shocked as he was, his trip down the rough boulders beside the glacier must have been a nightmare. The climb up to the tents took the last of his strength.

I looked anxiously at the sky. The weather was still dull and night was not far off. I felt a great sense of urgency. We must get up and find the hole in the glacier before darkness fell. I shouted instructions at our five Sherpas and then quickly bundled together two sleeping bags, some ropes, food and water. I made sure the Sherpas had all their warm clothing, for I knew we could not be back until long after dark. We dropped down from the camp and started off up the rocks beside the glacier. The loose, rolling boulders made for tiring and exasperating travelling. To my worried mind they seemed to be deliberately hindering our progress. The light was already getting very dim and I raced on ahead of the Sherpas, impelled by the fear that we might not find the crevasse. I was searching anxiously now for some sign of tracks, and suddenly to my relief I saw Wilkins's hat on top of a boulder and a set of uneven tracks leading off into the dim whiteness of the glacier. I stifled my urge to follow them and waited impatiently for the Sherpas to catch up. We put on the rope and then I cautiously started along Wilkins's steps. They led far out across the glacier. The light now was very bad. It was almost dark and I berated myself for having arrived too late. 'Now we will never find him!' And then I noticed, fifty feet in front of us, a small, round, black hole in the snow. 'It must be the one!' I rushed over towards it, but the Sherpas were holding me firmly with a tight rope. Wilkins had warned me about the overhanging lips of the crevasse, so I lay down on my stomach and wriggled slowly over to the hole. I looked down into a black void.

'Hello, Jim!'

For one awful moment there was no reply and then, to my intense relief, a faint voice came from far below. I asked him how he was. His replies were strangely hesitant but seemed quite rational. He said he was quite comfortable, that he was not badly hurt at all, but he thought he had a broken finger. His main trouble was that he was feeling rather thirsty. I pulled my torch out of my pocket and shone it downwards. The cold, gleaming walls of the crevasse sprang into life, and with a shock I realised how deep it was. I could not see the bottom. McFarlane called up that he could see the light or the reflection of it. I told him I would lower a rope down. I crawled back to the Sherpas, got another rope and then returned to the hole. I was not very happy about my position, because with the torch I could see that I was lying on top of a thin corniced lip. If that broke off it would probably engulf McFarlane. I lowered the rope carefully down the crevasse. It disappeared out of the range of my light but still went on down. McFarlane did not seem to be able to get it. His voice sounded very weak now and at times rather aimless. I tried swinging the rope around desperately in the hope that it would strike him and he could get hold of it, but with no result.

I crept back from the hole and thought what to do. It was pitch-dark now. The wind was whistling over the glacier and it was bitterly cold. The Sherpas, despite all their clothes, were obviously unhappy and miserable. Their morale did not seem too high. I decided the only thing to do was to go down the crevasse myself. I explained this to them in detail in my faltering Hindustani. They would lower me on two ropes. When I reached the bottom I would tie McFarlane on one of the ropes and they were to pull him to the surface. Then they could pull me up. They obviously understood my instructions but tried to persuade me against going down. I ignored their pleas.

I tied the two ropes around me and wriggled once again over to the hole in the ice, and then with a hollow feeling of insecurity, I pushed myself over the edge and dropped into the hole. The ropes came tight and I hung free, unable to reach either wall of the crevasse. I immediately realised I had made a mistake. I had tied the ropes around my waist instead of taking most of the weight around my thighs or feet. Already the rope was cutting into me, crushing my chest and restricting my breathing, but I thought I could stick it out long enough to get down to the bottom of the crevasse. I yelled to the Sherpas to lower me, and slowly, in a series of great jerks, I dropped down. I seemed to go on for ever. The crevasse had narrowed now and I could touch one of the smooth hard walls. And then the Sherpas stopped lowering and I just hung there, gasping like a fish. With all my strength I yelled at them to lower me farther, but they would not move. I twisted frantically on the end of the rope to ease the strain. I knew I could not last for long and I started thinking, 'What a funny way to die.' The Sherpas still ignored my shouts to lower me farther so I called out for them to pull me up. At first there was no response. Then from below me McFarlane's voice joined in shouting, 'Uppa uppa', and like an answer to a prayer I started moving upwards. I must have transmitted something of my urgency to the Sherpas, for they were pulling with all their strength and I gained height rapidly. Then I jammed under the overhanging lip of the crevasse. The rope was cutting into the edge and held me immovably. The Sherpas panicked once again. Tugging like madmen, they tried to wrench me free. Something had to give and I could feel my ribs bending under the fierce pressure of the rope and a sharp pain in my side. I yelled to them once again to ease off a little, and after some long moments they obeyed. The smooth, slippery ice gave no purchase to my flaying hands, but with a tremendous wriggle I managed to get an arm over the top of the crevasse and my eyes rose above the edge. In the blackness I could see dimly the straining figures of the Sherpas, but I could not move any further. Still suspended from the rope, I could feel all my strength draining out of me. With an impassioned plea that would have done credit to Romeo and Juliet, I tried to persuade one of the Sherpas to come over closer so that I could grasp him with my hand, but they all refused to move nearer the edge. I started wriggling again and somehow got my other elbow above the surface. And then they pulled me out like a cork from a bottle. I have had few better moments than that – lying exhausted on the ice at 19,500 feet, feeling the air flood into my released lungs, with the chattering Sherpas pouring water down my throat.

It was not long before some of my strength came back and I started racking my brains to decide what next to do. The Sherpas were tired and cold, and their morale could not be relied on. It seemed as if our chances of getting McFarlane out were very slim ones. I slid over to the hole once again and shouted down to McFarlane:

'We may have to leave you down there for the night, Jim. If we lower down a couple of sleeping bags, do you think you will be all right?'

There was the usual long pause and then Jim's weak but cheerful reply that he would be quite comfortable. I tied the rope around two sleeping bags and started lowering them carefully over the edge. They seemed to go on for ever and soon disappeared out of the range of my torch. The rope came slack and I knew that they had reached the bottom. McFarlane called out that he had managed to get hold of them and that he had got the rope too. Why not pull him out then? I called down and asked him to tie the rope around his waist. I knew it was taking a risk because he might not be capable of tying it properly, but it was worth a try. It was many minutes before McFarlane's voice told me he thought he was safely tied on. I signalled to the Sherpas to start pulling in the rope.

They took in the slack and next moment McFarlane was on his way up. With growing excitement I grabbed hold of the rope and added my weight to the Sherpas! And then the rope stopped, McFarlane must be jammed under the overhanging edge. I crawled to the edge and peered over. The rope was cutting in deeply and I could not see anything. I tried jerking it free it, but to no avail, and then out of the darkness appeared McFarlane's questing hand. Stretching down, I just managed to touch it before it fell listlessly away again and some dreadful choking sounds came from under the ice. We must lower him down again! I shouted desperately at the Sherpas and, startled into life, they commenced lowering with a rush. In a minute the rope came slack and McFarlane was on the bottom again.

I crawled over to the edge and shouted down. It was a long time before he replied. His voice was weak, but seemed somehow indestructible and cheerful. He said he had had a few bad moments up top, but that now he was all right. He would have to spend the night down there. I told him to crawl into the sleeping bags and he said that he would. I waited a few moments and then asked him if he was getting into them; there was a pause and he said, 'Yes'. We anchored the end of McFarlane's rope solidly into the ice and then started slowly downwards. I felt bruised and weak and it was painful to breathe, but worse than this was the awful sense of shame in having to leave poor McFarlane sixty feet down in the ice. My only consolation was the two sleeping bags which should keep him safe and warm.

The trip back to the tents was a nightmare. The Sherpas were almost as tired as I was, and we slid and fell over the loose rocks. It took us a long time to get up to the tents. I crawled in beside Wilkins and got into the comfort and security of my sleeping bag. The thought of McFarlane dominated my mind and I felt sure I would never sleep. But Nature was kind and my head had barely touched my rough pillow before I had fallen into a deep sleep.

I woke with a start and looked at my watch. It was still dark and the wind was flapping vigorously at the tent. It was about four thirty a.m. I undid the zip and looked out – there was a swirling mist of light snow. My chest felt stiff and painful, but I knew we must get moving, for a heavy fall of snow could prove disastrous. I wakened the Sherpas and we started a cooker going. Wilkins was much refreshed. In the dim morning light we left the tent and started off into the driving snow. I was relieved to find it was fairly light, and did not think it would trouble us much. We were all travelling slowly and it was a long and bitter grind over the loose rocks, but as we went, it cleared, and when we reached the side of the glacier we could actually see the little black hole several hundred yards out.

Wilkins and I roped together. I think both of us had the same thought, but neither of us had uttered it. Would McFarlane still be alive? Wilkins carefully belayed me and I wriggled once again on my stomach over to the edge of the hole and looked down. In the morning light I could see the smooth hard shining walls of ice dropping down, but at the bottom it was still dark. I shouted a greeting. There was a long pause and then, to my intense relief, a faint reply – thank God, he was still alive! And then to my amazement McFarlane called out that he had had quite a good night, but he was feeling a little cold now and rather thirsty. 'It won't take us long to get you out, Jim.'

I conferred with Wilkins. We were still very much afraid of dislodging the corniced edge of the crevasse and engulfing McFarlane. Wilkins, with great courage, offered to descend by the very dangerous route by which he had made his escape and to try to get McFarlane through that way. On the end of the rope we made a sling to put under his thighs to take the weight and then, after arranging a code of signals, we watched him climb cautiously into the second jagged hole fifty feet to the right. He slowly disappeared from view. For an eternity we seemed to let the rope out, and well over a hundred feet had gone before he signalled that he had reached McFarlane. It was a long time before the signal came to pull in the rope, and we tugged and hauled with all our strength. But all that came to the surface was Wilkins himself. He had a depressing story to tell. He had managed to reach McFarlane, but only after great difficulty. The route was quite impossible for anyone not possessed of his full strength and agility. McFarlane was unable to help himself. Contrary to what he had told me, he had not got into his sleeping bags but had just draped them over his knees. He had taken his gloves off his hands and they were cold and stiff. It gave him a good deal of pain in the back to be moved and he was obviously suffering from concussion. This was bad news. Wilkins had tied a sling around McFarlane and he considered the only chance was to lower a rope straight down the other hole and hope that McFarlane could clip it on to the sling.

We moved to the other hole again and lowered the rope. McFarlane got it and called out that he had attached it. We started pulling him in. We were all much fresher and stronger now and the rope came in rapidly, and then it jammed. McFarlane was stuck under the overhang. Wilkins leaned alarmingly over the edge and tried frantically to release it, but it was useless, and we lowered McFarlane right down to the bottom again. We would just have to take the risk of cutting some of the edge away! Carefully held on two ropes Wilkins and Da Thondup chipped away the edge, trying to make the falling pieces of ice as small as possible. They cut it back about a foot without anything major falling off, so we decided to give it another go. Up McFarlane came. He reached the cornice and jammed once more. I leaned over the edge. There he was, only a short distance below me. Leaning hard out on the rope, I stretched down and managed to get a hand on the slings around his body. Exerting all my strength I pulled him outwards. He came loose and the next moment with a mighty tug he was pulled over the edge.

We carried him over to a bed we had made. His clothing was frozen and hard, so we dressed him in warm clothing of our own. His hands and feet were the greatest worry. His hands, which had been battered by the fall down the crevasse, were whitish-blue and frozen stiff like claws. When we removed his boots his feet were hard and lifeless, but in spirit he was as strong and cheerful as ever and he jokingly commented that he much preferred being carried down the glacier to walking. We knew we must get him down as quickly as possible – down into the denser air of lower altitudes and back to the ministrations of Dr. Michael Ball. We tied three pack frames together with a rope into a rough stretcher. On this we placed an inflated air-mattress. Jim was by now inside a sleeping bag and we gently lifted him on to the stretcher.

We dragged him over the glacier to the edge of the rocks and started carrying him down. It was terribly hard work. Carrying a man at any time is a difficult business, but at over 19,000 feet it was most exhausting. The five Sherpas worked magnificently, and Wilkins and I took turns as a sixth man on the stretcher. We rarely made more than fifty feet, slipping and crashing over the boulders, before we would have to have a rest and stop, gasping for breath. My chest was hurting me abominably and Wilkins seemed at the end of his tether. It was obvious that we could never reach our camp, so when we finally gained a flat stretch of gravel with a small stream running through it we left McFarlane there with Wilkins to look after him and the Sherpas and I crossed over and climbed slowly up to our tents. The first necessity was to get medical aid.

Four of the Sherpas set to work packing up all the tents to move the camp back to McFarlane. The remaining Sherpa, Kancha, and I had a quick meal and then, carrying light packs, started off down the valley. Spurred on by my apprehension, I set a fast pace down the terraces above the Barun glacier. It was snowing again and there was a strong and bitter wind, but the going was fairly easy. Then we dropped down on to the moraine of the glacier and had to jump from boulder to shifting boulder. With every jump my chest seemed to burst with pain, and I started dropping behind. I knew I could not get down to camp that day – it was much too far. Kancha was waiting for me on a little flat stretch of gravel beside some ice cliffs in the centre of the glacier. I decided to camp. We pitched our little tent and crawled inside. I was too tired to eat, and fell immediately into a deep sleep – dead to the world.

It was still dark when we started again next morning. I wanted to reach Base Camp by breakfast time, before the others had started off on any trips. We stumbled downwards. I was stiff and sore, and seemed unable to go quickly. It was eight o'clock when we forded the river and started climbing up towards Base Camp. There were some shouted greetings and I saw, with great relief, that there was a big crowd in camp. George Lowe's strong, confident figure came towards me and I felt a lifting of my burden. Everyone was there, all looking fresh and strong. I told them the whole story and then left the rescue operations in their safe and capable hands.

It took the party four hard days to carry Jim down the glacier to Base Camp. I rested most of the time as I was still having difficulty with my breathing. Each time I coughed or took a deep breath I felt a stab of pain – an X-ray later showed I had three broken ribs. Jim arrived at Base Camp in pretty good condition but his feet were badly frost-bitten and his fingers had been nipped as well. We decided to rest him up and get him strong before he had to face the long carry out to India.

Mount Makalu, 27,790 feet, wasn't one of our official objectives but we had been excited to discover that an approach from the north had distinct possibilities. We didn't have the clothing and equipment to go really high but the party threw itself into a vigorous reconnaissance. Camp III was established at 20,800 feet and Camp IV at 22,000 feet. A strong party under Charles Evans pushed to over 23,000 feet and things were going very well indeed. I couldn't bear to be left out and although my ribs were still troubling me I decided to join the assault. I travelled up through the camps without too much difficulty and it wasn't until I reached Camp III that I had any particular discomfort. But at this quite moderate altitude I had difficulty in breathing and every cough sent a sharp pain through my chest. I suppose I should have gone back down but I was terribly keen to go high again and both the expedition doctors had told me my ribs were bruised rather than broken.

When Evans returned with an optimistic account of the route ahead I decided to push home the attack. Hardie, Lowe, Wilkins and I would go up to Camp IV and then establish Camp V at 23,000 feet the next day. From Camp V we could undoubtedly reach the Makalu Col. I led off up the steep slopes above Camp III but to my disappointment I was completely lacking in my usual energy and I was thankful when George took over the trail breaking. It was none too soon for me when we reached Camp IV at 22,000 feet and I crawled thankfully into a tent.

I had a very uncomfortable night and in the morning I was too weak to move. The other members of the party did some work on the route ahead but the weather deteriorated and they were soon back in the tents. I had another bad night and in the morning I felt pretty terrible and knew I'd have to go down. I commenced dressing but didn't seem able to get my boots on. George suddenly noticed my deplorable condition and realised they must quickly get me down to a lower camp – we had no oxygen on the expedition. I managed to walk down the first long slope but then I came to an uphill grade and it was just too much for me – and everything went black. I had a period of terrible hallucinations and found myself clinging to the ice cliffs of Makalu with avalanches falling all around and people screaming for help ... I came back to consciousness to find George tying me into a makeshift stretcher. Then followed a long period of semi-consciousness, of heat and extreme discomfort, of swinging and bumping. It is the only time I can remember thinking that maybe it would be easiest just to die. When my mind cleared again I was lying in Camp III with Charles Evans examining me and telling me in his quiet steady voice that I would be all right – but even I could sense his great concern. I had a terrible feeling of suffocation and extreme dehydration. The three days it took the Sherpas to carry me down to Camp I seemed like three lifetimes.

In the thick air of Camp I, I started to recover – slowly at first and then with great rapidity – although the doctors never did quite discover what was wrong with me except possibly some complicated form of pneumonia. Ten days after my collapse I was able to walk comfortably down to Base Camp – but I was so weak that I knew my mountaineering was finished for the season. The other members carried on with a feast of climbing and exploration culminating in a spectacular success on Baruntse 23,570 feet. I turned down valley with McFarlane and a team of strong porters; at least I could do a useful job and get him back to hospital. It proved a considerable challenge in its own right and took twenty days of heat, rain, flies and mud before we emerged at the railhead at the Indian border and made our way slowly homeward.

Chapter 12

Southern Continent

FOR EIGHTEEN MONTHS I LIVED THE ROUTINE EXISTENCE OF A FAMILY man – or as near to it as I have ever achieved. I worked at the bees with my brother; wrote a book *High Adventure;* had my house built; did a first ascent of Mount Magellan in the Southern Alps of New Zealand – and was presented with a son. I turned down a tempting offer to lecture in Japan because I preferred to be at home. I was getting a great deal of pleasure from my family life and Louise and I had already achieved a cheerful comradship that looked as though it might last. We shared the responsibilities and the decisions and although Louise could be pretty fiery when she was provoked, it was always shortlived and mostly she was calm and kind enough to accept, and even encourage, my periodic restlessness. For my part, I knew I had been extraordinarily lucky and I can remember no occasion in the last twenty years that I would have wished for any other companion.

In the middle of 1955 I agreed to do a lecture tour in Africa with George Lowe as this was a place I had always wanted to visit. I was impressed with South Africa in particular. The winter climate was superb and so was the scenery. The people we met were very relaxed and friendly and the life they led was extremely comfortable. The only snag seemed to be the poor Bantu – and he was happiest, I was constant-ly assured, when being told precisely what to do and where to go. George and I realised that some of the local people had attitudes that were different from our own – we went walking down a street in Johannesburg with a man who called himself the 'unofficial New Zealand representative' and were obstructed by a thin elderly Bantu who was weaving from side to side in front of us. Maybe he was drunk or maybe that was just the way he walked but it certainly irritated our companion who kicked him firmly into the gutter. Our 'representative' was a whisker from being kicked into the gutter himself. The thing that impressed me most about this incident was the look of resignation on the Bantu's face – it was clearly the sort of treatment he expected. We were mostly meeting the English speaking section of the community and in those days many of them deplored the growing emphasis on apartheid and were still hoping that they could make some political changes – but instead their influence seemed to decline.

In Johannesburg on June 9th I received a telegram from New Zealand inviting me to lead an expedition to the Antarctic.

'The Last Great Journey in the World' was how the press in 1953 described the plans of Dr. Vivian Fuchs to make the first crossing of the Antarctic continent through the South Pole. Forty years before, Ernest Shackleton had set out to do this same journey but had failed when his small ship was crushed in the fierce ice of the Weddell Sea. Shackleton's memorable retreat over the pack-ice and through the terrible storms of the southern ocean had enthralled me when I was young . . . what a man he was! Now Fuchs wanted to try again using modern equipment and aircraft and carrying out a scientific programme. George Lowe was involved in the expedition and at Fuchs' request he had arranged a meeting between us.

Fuchs was a square, strongly built man with a formidable air of determination and toughness. His manner was quite abrupt and even awkward until he started talking about his plans and then the words flowed with eager enthusiasm. He detailed his intentions, using the stem of his pipe to point out the route on a large map of the Antarctic, and became completely immersed in the story although he must have told it a hundred times before.

It sounded a good trip, I conceded to myself, but what did it have to do with me? Even at this first meeting I felt that Fuchs and I had little in common – he was far more serious and dogged than I could ever be and he spent so much time emphasising the scientific worth of the journey and playing down the sheer adventure of it. As the plan unfolded my possible usefulness became more apparent – Fuchs wanted a supporting expedition to go to the opposite side of the Continent, south of New Zealand, to establish a base and lay out depots towards the Pole. It would help, he admitted, if he could get financial and material support from the New Zealand Government – perhaps I could influence opinion in New Zealand? Maybe I would consider leading the New Zealand party myself?

I left the meeting with great respect for Fuchs's determination and drive but quite sure I didn't want to fit into his plans. Maybe he was a good judge of character or perhaps things just developed the right way but in 1954 and '55 I became more and more involved in organising New Zealand support for his crossing and increasingly interested myself in the potential for adventure on the Southern Continent. Responding with some reluctance to public pressure, the New Zealand Government agreed to contribute £50,000 ($120,000) then later appointed the Ross Sea Committee to organise New Zealand's participation. It was the Ross Sea Committee that had sent the cable inviting me to lead the expedition – and I replied in the affirmative; but not without some worried thoughts for the welfare of my young family.

From South Africa I travelled to an international Antarctic Conference in Paris and later spent a month in London with Fuchs and his expedition members. I returned to New Zealand full of plans and enthusiasm but a little puzzled by the almost masochistic belief in the virtue of discomfort held by some of the traditionalists in the British party. I was determined that my expedition would be a lively, successful, and reasonably comfortable operation.

I found the Ross Sea Committee an easy body to deal with – or most of the members anyway. Although few of them had any expedition experience they were all successful men with wide practical knowledge in their own fields. We had a number of urgent tasks to tackle – the selection of parties; raising of funds; the chartering of a boat; the construction of base huts; and the accumulating of all the necessary equipment.

There was an overwhelming response from young people wishing to go on the expedition but it didn't prove too difficult to reduce their numbers down to a manageable level. Being enthusiastic and strong wasn't quite enough – everyone needed some qualification and had to fit some particular slot – or several slots. This was illustrated by the two experienced dog drivers who were joining us from Great Britain – Dr. George Marsh would also be our Base medical officer and Lieutenant Commander Richard Brooke was a competent surveyor and mountaineer.

A sub-committee had been appointed to assist in the selection of the party and the Chairman was Dr. Falla (now Sir Robert Falla) – a distinguished scientist and administrator and an experienced judge of character (he had understandable reservations, for instance, about my suitability as leader of the party). In general I was given a very free hand but a number of Dr. Falla's protégés were strong contenders for various jobs and in the end a certain amount of horse trading went on; I accepted a couple of his men in order to reduce opposition to my own, and this worked out fairly well in most cases.

In the specialist field the applicants' technical qualifications were assessed by experts before we made our decisions on personality. It was essential to have a competent person in charge of radio communications and a lot of work went into this selection. The final two men were both senior Petty Officers in the Navy with extensive experience. In the interviews, one of them tacked a 'Sir' on the end of each sentence when he answered my questions – then it was Peter Mulgrew's turn; he was polite, correct and enthusiastic and I can't remember a single 'Sir' being used. Peter was small and active, a keen tramper and climber, and although he had been told he would be confined to base at all times he constantly expressed his keenness to get out on field trips as well. I liked Peter's spirit – and although I was unaware of it at the time this was the start of a lifelong friendship.

The Committee asked the New Zealand Army to give us a thorough medical examination. Most of us passed without too much difficulty but Harry Ayres was turned down because he had varicose veins in his legs and no eulogies about his ability to cross rough country would sway the army doctors. After some acrimonious exchanges between the army and myself it was agreed to seek the opinion of an independent civilian specialist. This expert had fortuitously done an energetic cross-country trip with Harry the summer before and had a vast respect for his abilities – so Harry joined my party. Medical tests are certainly important – but so too is a recent history of proved performance. Harry later showed there wasn't too much wrong with his legs when he carried out extensive exploratory journeys with dog teams and he still gallops up the odd big mountain.

To help our finances we instituted a public appeal and several of us travelled around the country setting up fund-raising committees. Our leader was the Hon. Charles Bowden, Chairman of the Ross Sea Committee, and a retired Cabinet Minister and politician. Mr. Bowden didn't know too much about the expedition but he had a fluent tongue and a good memory. At the first public meeting in Christchurch he introduced the subject in general terms and I had the task of filling in the details. In Dunedin he delivered his own introduction and then gave my Christchurch address almost word for word – while I desperately thought up a new line to present. In Invercargill he was in great form – he gave his own talk and both of mine, and left me with little else to say but to agree with him. From then on I ensured that we went our different ways . . .

Fund-raising proved the toughest part of the whole expedition. We had a great deal of help from volunteer committees but it was still a struggle. I found the succession of talks in support of the appeal a heavy burden and so was all the travelling involved. On one particular day I gave four public lectures and drove 500 miles in the process.

Various methods were used by local committees to raise funds – one team decided to sweep all before it with a fireworks display. A suitable location was hired, large quantities of fireworks purchased, and extensive advertising undertaken. Unfortunately rain started falling an hour before the gates opened. A handful of people watched rockets disappearing into the murk and squibs fizzing miserably, while the rain got heavier and heavier. It took this committee several months of hard work to raise enough money to pay off their debts.

New Zealand certainly became aware of our trip to the southern ice although not everyone was quite clear what it was all about. In a small backcountry bar one farmer was overheard saying to his neighbour, 'Hey, Bill . . . that there Antarctic? How many sheep do they run to the acre?' But by and large there was great national interest and considerable public support.

The general plan had now taken shape. In the 1955/56 Antarctic summer Fuchs intended taking an expedition south into the Weddell Sea to establish Shackleton Base. A small party would stay on through the winter to complete the construction of the Base and get it ready for Fuchs to inhabit with his main party in the summer of 1956/57. In December 1956 I would sail south from New Zealand with my expedition and establish Scott Base in McMurdo Sound. Both parties would winter over and then start in the spring to move towards the Pole – Fuchs to complete the crossing and my party to lay a depot 250 miles inland. The crossing would be completed in February 1958 and the whole party withdrawn from McMurdo Sound by the end of that month.

Our New Zealand programme had been greatly strengthened by the decision of the Government to play a full part in the International Geophysical Year and we were now expecting to take south with us a scientific team of five men and a great deal of sophisticated scientific equipment. For my field parties I envisaged a wide programme of exploration, survey and geology in the mountains of Victoria Land. It was an exciting prospect as I saw us grow from a modest supporting role – very much the junior partner – into a major national operation.

I was well satisfied with the membership of my party and felt they could handle most of the problems we were likely to meet – but our main weakness was the lack of direct Antarctic experience. We still had a summer to use for this purpose and we were lucky to be able to arrange trips south for seven of our group. Harry Ayres went with the Australian Antarctic Research Expedition to their sector of the Continent and brought back twenty-five of their husky dogs. Dr. Trevor Hatherton, the senior scientist of our party, and Bernie Gunn a tough and competent geologist visited McMurdo Sound with the first American 'Deep Freeze' operation and examined possible base sites and access routes to the Polar Plateau. Lastly, three of us were invited to join Fuchs on the *Theron* to sail into the Weddell Sea. My companions were to be Bob Miller, my deputy leader and senior surveyor, and Squadron Leader John Claydon who was to be in charge of our RNZAF Antarctic flight.

We joined the 900 ton *Theron* in Montevideo and rolled our way southwards through stormy oceans. The skipper was Captain Harold Maro, a Norwegian of much the same age as myself, and he had a tough competent look about him. I felt we were in good hands but I was glad to reach the bleak mountainous island of South Georgia and have a break from the incessant rolling. We visited various Norwegian whaling stations and filled our tanks full with fuel. Then it was southward again into noticeably cooler temperatures and our first icebergs. I could feel a growing excitement at the thought of crossing the Antarctic circle.

I grew very friendly with Captain Harold Maro and learned to like and admire him. He was the champion sealer captain of east Canadian waters with a vast amount of experience in pack-ice but this was his first visit to the Antarctic. From him I learned about the unusual route we were steering into the Weddell Sea. Bunny Fuchs believed the Weddell Sea contained two great areas of floating ice rotating independently with the ocean currents. If we could strike the point where the two areas met, there would be a lot of open water and the chance of a quick passage to Vahsel Bay at the southern extremity of the Sea. Harold Maro wasn't very enthusiastic about this idea and would have greatly preferred to try the proven route to the east down the channel of open water that usually existed along the ice cliffs of the Caird coast . . . but he had accepted this new course of action and was hoping that Bunny's theory might prove right. I sounded Bunny out a few times on this plan but he didn't seem very keen to talk about it. It was a daring gamble which could save some time if it proved successful.

I was sharing a cabin with Bunny and had the uncomfortable suspicion that he regarded this as the most satisfactory way of keeping a firm and fatherly eye on me. I was treated with an unswerving friendliness but it was made very clear that I was only an 'observer' and I was never permitted to attend the regular meetings of his executive committee (although both of my expedition members were invited to these meetings on various occasions). I suppose I shouldn't have resented this, but I did. I felt an outsider – not to be trusted with expedition responsibilities – and this was probably an uncomfortable

ANTARCTICA

PACIFIC OCEAN

SOUTHERN OCEAN

FALKLAND ISLANDS
DEPENDENCIES

JAMES W ELLSWORTH
LAND

*Weddell
Sea*

*Filchner
Ice Shelf*

Shackleton
Base

ROSS DEPENDENCY
(NEW ZEALAND)

Ross Sea

Ross
Ice
Shelf

+ South Pole

THERON MTS
SHACKLETON
RANGE

QUEEN MAUD
LAND

Scott
Base

Ross Is
McMurdo
Sound

Beardmore Glacier

MT MARKHAM

Skelton Glacier

AUSTRALIAN
ANTARCTIC TERRITORY

ADÉLIE LAND (FRANCE)

AUSTRALIAN
ANTARCTIC
TERRITORY

KING HAAKON SEA

SOUTHERN OCEAN

0   200   400   600 Miles

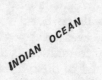

INDIAN OCEAN

foundation on which to build our association over the next couple of years.

It was very rough indeed on the morning of Thursday, December 22nd and few of us could raise much interest in our lunch. There were a number of icebergs around, and during the afternoon we entered an area of bergy bits and the sea became peppered with dancing chunks of ice. At six p.m. we sailed into our first light pack-ice. Almost miraculously the sea became calm, the weather improved, and all of us emerged on deck to chatter excitedly about every piece of ice we bumped. It was 63° 50′ S 30° 20′ W and we felt we were into the Antarctic at last. Captain Maro climbed up into the crow's nest and steered the ship from there, weaving in and out amongst the floes and giving us a demonstration of his remarkable ability as a helmsman in pack-ice. The air temperature had now dropped to 29°F and the sea temperature was much the same.

We sailed on for hour after hour making very good speed as Harold Maro led us through a series of great pools separated only by strips of pack-ice. When I went to bed at eleven thirty p.m. it was still quite light with excellent visibility. I awoke periodically to feel the ship vibrating under the steady thrust of her engine, with now and then a sudden quiver as she pushed aside a more substantial chunk of ice. All night and the next day we continued on south, chased along by a strong north-east wind. By the end of our first twenty-four-hour period in the pack-ice we had covered 160 miles.

For three more days over the Christmas period we battered our way southward, always hoping that an easy line would open up before us. On December 26th we entered a larger pool in the ice and our small Auster aircraft was lowered over the side and did a brief reconnaissance. John Lewis reported a number of leads of open water to the south but heavy pack elsewhere. As our ambition was still to get south as quickly as possible this was good news. The ship moved on once more, but our hopes for quicker progress were soon dashed. We struck very heavy pack, almost too much for our small vessel, and for one period we were stuck in the same position for at least three hours before Captain Maro could shake us free. Although we managed to find a few good leads of open water and made good time across these, it needed some very hard bashing to get through the ice between them. The farther we went the tougher this ice seemed to get and the slower our progress. The wind was now blowing very strongly from the east and this was perhaps one of the main causes of the trouble – the ice was packing in tight and rafting up, and proving an overwhelming opponent.

For five more days we battled with appalling pack making virtually no progress. We commenced the New Year well and truly stuck in the ice. The wind was from the south and freshening, and we hoped this might loosen the pressure and let us free. Instead, during the afternoon the pressure increased considerably and our vessel quivered under the strain. In the evening everything eased a little and we were able to push forward a few yards. But there was no room to move and we were soon jammed once more. I climbed to the top of the mast for a look around and could see nothing but tumbled ice stretching in every direction to the horizon, and dotted with icebergs. It was a sombre scene, and made me realise that quite apart from the annoying delay, the ship might be in some danger. Anything could happen if there was a marked increase in pressure as these huge masses of ice ground against each other.

During the next two days we weren't successful in moving an inch for the heavy pack had set solidly around us. I spent a good deal of time digging snow and ice away from the sides of the ship and first one, then two and finally half of the expedition were doing the same. Our two explosives experts let off four small charges around the ship but there still wasn't any movement. I think we all accepted now that Bunny's route was a failure and all we could hope to do was escape to the north into open water and try the traditional route further east. It didn't help to know that the Royal Society's *Tottan* which was also establishing a base in the Weddell Sea had found open water and easy going along the coast and was now ten degrees south of us with no problems ahead. It must have been a tough time for Bunny - I couldn't help admiring his stubborn refusal to admit any loss of confidence or to show the slightest sign of weakness.

I think in many ways I regarded January 4th as the turning point in the expedition. All the morning we remained wedged in and we more or less accepted it with dull resignation. But after lunch a few of us were leaning over the side of the ship discussing our predicament and wondering what we could do about it. We noticed that the ship was gripped by a mass of broken fragments of ice weighing from a few pounds to a few tons. These were all tightly jammed, but it did look as though it might be possible to prise some of them free and work them into the small pool created behind the ship by its propeller. It seemed well worth a try, so grabbing all the tools available we jumped overboard and set to work. With crowbars, picks, spades and boathooks we dug and levered at the blocks and rafted them away. It was hard work but we made a great clearance and before long almost the whole expedition was on the job. At various intervals Captain Maro started up the motor and tried moving the ship to test

The author's favourite picture of Louise Rose who became his wife.

The *Theron* stuck fast in Weddell Sea ice.

A Ferguson tractor in crevasse.

Scott Base after winter.

Travelling south over the Ross Ice Shelf.

Peter Mulgrew in Antarctica.

'The Old Firm' who went to the South Pole. Edmund Hillary, Murray Ellis, Jim Bates, Peter Mulgrew, Derek Wright.

Louise and Peter Hillary—
1956.

Louise and the children
camping in a park in
Virginia.

Edmund Hillary in 1960.

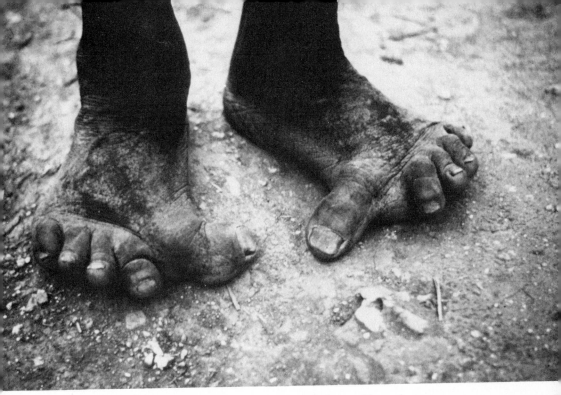

Feet of Nepalese with right-angled toe—like yeti.

Yeti skin—blue bear.

A yeti scalp and hand in Pangboche monastery.

Everest from Thyangboche.

Amadablam from Imja river.

Edmund and Louise Hillary with their son,
Peter, on Kala Pittar with Everest behind.

out our progress. To our great joy, late in the evening the ship finally broke free and moved forward from this spot where we'd been held for five whole days. At last we'd proved that it was possible to do something tangible towards our progress.

But progress was desperately slow over the next eighteen days as we battled our way to the north. We had a multitude of problems to meet and overcome – a bent rudder, a steel wire rope around the propeller, and immense pressure from thick ice. But now that we were moving I was actually starting to enjoy myself. Poling, hacking and blasting, we spent half the time over the side of the ship and every hundred feet we made seemed a considerable triumph. It is hard to know just how much contribution our efforts made to the northwards progress of the ship – possibly a day; maybe even a week – but it certainly helped my morale and the morale of many of the expedition members. We felt we were involved in the struggle and slowly winning.

At seven p.m. on January 22nd we broke through the last of the pack-ice and emerged into the open ocean – we had been thirty-two days in the Weddell Sea and were now back at our starting point again. Four days later we picked out a long line to the east of us which gradually enlarged into the cliffs of the Antarctic Continent. This was an exciting moment and we clustered at the rail and absorbed the remarkable sight of these great ice cliffs standing out white and glittering above the dark blue of the ocean. We turned down the wide channel of open water beside the cliffs, and although the way was freely dotted with icebergs and odd pieces of pack-ice, our ship was now throbbing with the familiar and unfaltering vibration of the open ocean, and our progress was completely unchecked.

On the morning of January 27th we reached 74°S and carried on down the coast through an area of huge icebergs. The sun came out and everything seemed far more beautiful than I had ever imagined. Stimulated by the superb scenery, we had a feast of photography and the day passed very quickly. In the evening we commenced a careful watch along the ice cliffs to ensure that we didn't overlook Halley Bay where the Royal Society Expedition had established its base. At nine p.m. we were just over 75° 30′S when someone noticed two black dots on the edge of the sea ice. Captain Maro swung the ship in towards them and we were soon greeting the other party. Our welcome was very warm indeed and we were impressed with the progress of their base hut and the obvious competence of their construction crew. Although they had left London after us they were now at least three weeks ahead of us in progress.

At two p.m. on January 28th we said goodbye to the Royal Society party and sailed off again down the coast. Our progress was almost uninterrupted as we cruised down the wide channel between the ice cliffs of the continent and the hundreds of miles of pack-ice that stretched to the west of us. For many hours we were passing the heavily crevassed face of the enormous Dawson Lambton Glacier, twisting in and out amongst the great icebergs that had split off it, and crossing only a few meagre strips of pack-ice. Once again the colouring was absolutely superb – the velvety blue of the sea and the lighter blue of the sky; the clean white snow and the sparkling white foam at our bow; the innumerable shades of green and blue in the icy cliffs above us and the icy chunks hiding in the water beneath; the black backs of the seals and penguins who indifferently watched us pass; and the bright galaxy of colours on board the *Theron* itself. I stayed up all night to watch it.

It was an exciting moment when we first caught sight of the black nunataks of Vahsel Bay – the first rock I had seen on the Antarctic continent. Twenty-eight miles further on the tall cliffs of the ice shelf sloped quite gradually down to the mile-wide strip of sea ice at their foot. This appeared to offer a reasonable vehicle route up on to the flat plateau on top of the shelf. From an aerial reconnaissance, Bunny considered that a feasible route existed off the Filchner Ice Shelf to the firm ice of the continental mass. So this site filled the most fundamental requirements – access to the ship and access towards the Pole. Bunny decided to build the base there.

We commenced unloading the *Theron* at eight a.m. on Monday, January 30th. Unfortunately our tractors and Weasels were well embedded in the hold so we had to start unloading without them. All my reading had indicated that stacking supplies on the sea ice which could break up in the event of a storm was the worst possible procedure – but we seemed to have no alternative. The equipment was lifted with the ship's crane onto some sledges and then we hauled it away by hand and rolled it off onto a clear piece of ice. Many of the crates were of considerable weight and this was hard work for our soft hands and unaccustomed muscles. When we completed work at eleven p.m. we were all very tired, but we could look with some satisfaction on a huge pile of equipment on the ice beside the ship – although my satisfaction was a little tempered by the fear of what might happen to it if the weather took a turn for the worse. But I was too tired to let such lugubrious thoughts keep me from my slumber and dropped quickly off to sleep.

I awoke next morning feeling a little stiff and sore, and when I emerged on deck I found the weather was rather bitter with a strong wind and a temperature of $+2°F$. I'd been rather slow to arise, but even so I was first on the job and it was apparent that the previous day's physical labour had taken its toll on the expedition. We had now unloaded enough to be able to get to the vehicles, and we occupied most of the morning in lifting out the two Ferguson tractors and the two Weasels. David Pratt and Roy Homard concentrated on getting them all operational and soon we had four vehicles dragging loads away from the ship to the foot of the cliffs a mile away and reducing the pile of gear we'd dumped off the previous day. The Weasels were excellent snow vehicles although they could be mechanically unreliable. The Fergusons on the other hand were only a modified farm tractor. As I expected my expedition to be using Fergusons I cornered one of these vehicles with the intention of thoroughly testing it out. Painted bright red, it was a very cheerful spot on the landscape and I soon found out its strengths and its limitations. On harder surfaces and where it was reasonably flat it operated very effectively but it soon bogged down in soft snow or on a steep slope. The steering was the main problem but after a while I became quite expert at getting around and I developed quite an affection for the vehicle.

One of our major worries was the lack of experience of many of our drivers. Not only had the majority of them never used a Weasel or Ferguson but some hadn't even driven an ordinary motor car. It was surprising therefore that by the end of the day quite a useful amount of our load had been transported to the far side of the sea ice at the foot of the cliff. But one Weasel was out of action and the spares for it deep in a hold that hadn't yet been opened.

I emerged sleepily on deck on February 1st to find much milder temperatures and dark and ominous skies to the north – the thermometer had climbed abruptly to +20°F. Bunny was very concerned about the immobilised Weasel and decided to make every effort to get it into action once more. He instructed the second hold to be opened and the equipment to be unloaded on to the ice beside the ship until the necessary parts were found. I asked somewhat dubiously if this was a wise procedure considering the look of the weather but my comments were brushed aside.

We concentrated on unloading the hold as quickly as possible and by mid-day, when the parts had been located, an astonishing amount of equipment had been moved overboard. By now the weather was looking most threatening and very little time was wasted at lunch. Early in the afternoon the wind became very strong from the north and there were fierce squalls of driving snow. The ship was heaving around in an alarming fashion and bashing against the edge of the ice. Large waves began to break over the ice edge and flooded amongst the stores. Working frantically we tried to sledge away what we could onto the airfield, which was halfway across to the hill, but soon most of the remaining equipment was lying in pools of water six inches to a foot deep.

I found it very hard to keep my tractor on course even though I'd gone to the trouble to place lines of stakes at close intervals along the track. I had to feel my way from flag to flag through almost nil visibility, and the driving snow was extremely painful on my unprotected face and eyes. About five p.m. the storm reached a crescendo of fury with the wind screaming off the sea and great waves breaking over the ice edge.

I was fumbling my way back across the airfield for another load when a figure loomed up ahead of me and I recognised George Lowe. He waved me to stop and then came over and shouted in my ear, 'The ship's tow-ropes have parted and she's had to steam away! Harold Maro will be back for us as soon as he can. We are leaving all the vehicles on the airfield and walking back to the ice edge!'

I nodded my agreement and then drove slowly over to join the other parked vehicles. Leaning into the wind we walked along the track towards the ice edge and were greeted by an awe-inspiring sight. Spray was dashing high in the air as the sea lashed around in fury and just off shore was the *Theron*, rising with each wave high above our heads and then sinking half out of sight. There were about eight of us left there on the ice and our predicament wasn't a pleasant one as we had no shelter or camping equipment. We realised we'd have to get on board somehow and we had great confidence in Captain Maro's ability to do something for us. It was certainly a desolate and frightening scene around us – the fury of the elements and the innumerable crates lying half submerged in sea water – but we made our way quite cheerfully to a rather higher promontory on the ice edge over which the sea wasn't breaking and from which we hoped we could step onto the ship. We had to wade through the surface water to get there.

We hadn't been there for long before a huge icefloe, driven by the wind, angled its way along the ice edge towards us and bumped the bay ice so heavily with each wave that our perch quivered in response. But this was the opportunity that Captain Maro had been waiting for. On the lee side of the floe the sea was quite tame and subdued. Guiding the ship with his usual deft touch he brought it right into the ice edge, nosed in behind the great floe and then swivelled the ship in towards our perch. Next moment the rail was bobbing and swaying above us, so, spurred by our emergency, we leapt for it and were dragged or fell onto the deck. In a few seconds we were all aboard and the ship was a hundred yards out from the spray-drenched shore and turning to head into the gale.

In the morning we were still several miles off shore in very angry seas, but during the early afternoon the wind switched around very suddenly. Quite miraculously the seas calmed. We sailed rapidly back towards the ice edge to find out what had happened to five men who had been left up at the hut site. To our great relief we saw figures on the ice as we approached and realised that all was well. We were soon alongside the old unloading point and hearing from the shore party the story of their very uncomfortable night. We set to work to move the wet stores to the foot of the hill and found them dripping with moisture and starting to ice up – later it was found that much of the contents had been ruined.

For three days we worked extremely hard, moving supplies to the cliff dump. A very jittery atmosphere reigned on board ship and a close watch was kept on the movements of the pack-ice to the north of us. Everyone was conscious of the fact that we were deep in the Weddell Sea, that the season was moving along, and that we were very much on our own. No one wanted to be caught in the ice and forced to winter over, as this would mean the abandoning of his Antarctic crossing for Bunny and a wasted year for Captain Maro. After lunch it became quite clear that a wide expanse of heavy pack and some moderate sized icebergs were moving in onto the ship once more. There was something of a panic and we were warned that we might have to pull out fairly soon. All afternoon we worked like madmen unloading the ship and shifting the gear to the foot of the hill. After tea John Lewis and Captain Maro went for a reconnaissance flight in the Auster and returned with the news that although things weren't as bad as they appeared, the ice to the north of us had increased a great deal. We went on working steadily until one thirty a.m., by which time the ship was completely unloaded except for ten tons of coal. We were just too tired to move this and as the pack-ice showed no signs of closing in on us we staggered off to bed.

When we started again on February 6th all our fears seemed to have been groundless for the weather was now clear and cold and the pack-ice had vanished. We were feeling very tired after our previous day's efforts and had to counteract strong feelings of lethargy as we unloaded the coal. By mid-day the ship was empty and the first big stage of our job was done.

The greater part of the supplies was now located in the first dump on the sea ice at the foot of the hill, and we concentrated on moving this up to the hut site. Here flags had been set out to indicate where the various piles of equipment should go, and a group of men was at work erecting the Sno-cat crate so that the wintering party would have at least some sort of shelter for their use, apart from their tents. The whole emphasis now was on transporting the hut parts so that the hut could be completed before the onset of winter. 'You can't build a hut in the winter but you can haul food and fuel,' was the motto expressed, and although

I had my doubts about such a philosophy we concentrated on moving hut parts and left most of the fuel and food in the depot on the floating ice. It was very cold when we knocked off for the night and frost smoke was rising steadily from the sea.

We had a very cold night and in the morning the temperature was down to —3°F. The weather was fine with practically no wind and the sea was covered with a thin skin of new ice. All morning we moved loads up to the base site, but when we returned to the ship for lunch we found that the wind had changed and that a great deal of heavy pack-ice was approaching from the north. This was sweeping up the new ice before it, and we had the astonishing sight of wave after tiny wave of new ice rolling up towards us and steadily increasing in thickness until it was six inches in places. This was the last straw and the word was passed around that we were sailing at three p.m. The wintering party hastily gathered all their gear together and threw it on to the ice. Farewells were said and last instructions given and then, with almost unseemly haste, we waved goodbye and sailed off. The ten men left behind looked a lonely and forlorn group – as they had every right to be. Few parties have been deposited in the Antarctic so late in the season with so much to do. They experienced many difficulties and setbacks. Most of the winter was spent cramped in the Sno-cat crate; a fierce storm cracked the sea ice and the depot at the foot of the cliff with nearly all the fuel on it disappeared out to sea; and survival became a desperate struggle. We on the *Theron* had it much easier – for two hours we struggled with the fast approaching pack-ice before we broke through and motored easily to the north.

I had a good deal to think about as we tossed our way back up through the Atlantic. I had the feeling we'd been a fairly amateurish operation – energetic but amateurish – and we'd made too many simple mistakes. The thing that we had all gained had been experience, and in many ways it was the best introduction I could have had to the Antarctic. I had learned at first hand about what to do and what not to do.

In retrospect, the gaining of experience was the main success of the *Theron* expedition. We contributed little to science, and Shackleton Base could just as easily have been established and built the following season. But all of us gained an enormous amount of much needed experience. By the time we sailed clear of the Weddell Sea we were an infinitely more competent and knowledgeable group. We were just about ready to tackle our major objectives.

Chapter 13

Winter on the Ice

I RETURNED TO NEW ZEALAND IN APRIL 1956 CONVINCED THAT I WOULD run my expedition in the way that seemed best to me. Putting a depot 250 miles south of McMurdo Sound for the crossing party could require quite a lot of effort but we should have plenty of time to carry out widespread exploration as well – and maybe even push further south towards the Pole. Finance, of course, might be a problem and I could hardly expect either Fuchs or the Ross Sea Committee to be happy about any substantial increase in the budget. I went through our lists of food and equipment in great detail and found it was possible to increase vital requirements without any obvious effect on our finances.

But vehicles were a different matter – and I wanted plenty of vehicles. There was no way we could afford the sophisticated and expensive Sno-cats to be used by Bunny – much as I would have liked them. The Ferguson tractors seemed our only chance. Three tractors were being lent to us by the manufacturers in Britain and with some gentle persuasion two more were generously donated by the local New Zealand distributor. Without much hope I instituted an enquiry to see if the Americans might have some snow vehicles to spare. I could hardly believe my luck when I received a message that Admiral Dufek, the Commander of the U.S. 'Deep Freeze,' was bringing two Weasels south for us – although this generosity proved to be typical of Admiral Dufek and his team.

Despite the efforts I was putting into increasing the expedition's vehicle force, I realised it was largely experimental in nature. We still worked on the basis that our various journeys and laying of depots would be done by dog teams supported by two small aircraft. Fuchs had suggested a route up the Ferrar Glacier from a base at its foot, and then a relatively short and direct line over the Polar Plateau to the furthest depot near Mount Albert Markham – a total distance of about 250 miles from base. To do this plus our own wide programme of survey and geology would require six dog teams with a total of about sixty dogs. We had quite a job getting the dogs together. We bred from some huskies in the Auckland zoo; obtained twenty-five magnificent dogs from the Australian Antarctic Base; and imported a dozen dogs from Greenland.

We constructed a compound for the dogs at the foot of the Tasman Glacier in New Zealand. George Marsh and Richard Brooke, helped by various other members of the expedition, began training dog teams there – hitching them at first to the chassis of an old motor car and galloping along the local roads. With the onset of winter snows they were able to continue the training behind sledges.

This activity with the dogs reached a peak when all the members of the expedition gathered together on the Tasman Glacier in August for a combined training period. Under its heavy layer of winter snow the eighteen-mile-long glacier gave us ample scope for landing our ski aircraft and for doing long training trips with our dog teams. All the members of the party had the chance to become thoroughly familiar with the equipment we planned to use down south and all of them spent some time driving Ferguson tractors.

By the middle of September the dogs had been completely transformed. Their podgy condition had disappeared and they were now sleek and strong and looking their magnificent best. Dragging laden sledges up and down the glacier for eleven or twelve miles a day had done them a world of good. The last few months before our departure were a period of intense activity. We had been making satisfactory progress with the accumulation of our vast quantity of stores and foodstuff but we suffered a major setback with the arrival in Wellington of the expedition vessel H.M.N.Z.S. *Endeavour*, laden with specialist stores for us from the United Kingdom. When we opened up the lower hold we were aghast to find that it had been flooded by sea water and that a large portion of the stores were completely ruined. Working around the clock we listed our losses, decided which of them could be replaced in New Zealand and then sat at the telephone for many hours and rang up concerns all over New Zealand to place new orders and ask for special priorities in delivery. Although our requests must have proved a considerable inconvenience to many firms, without fail we were assured that our requirements would be delivered in Wellington on time for loading on board ship – and without fail they were. Fortunately there weren't many things we couldn't replace from stock in New Zealand, but the rest had to be airfreighted from the United Kingdom.

This disaster created a vast amount of extra work but it did have some very beneficial results. In many cases we were able to replace the damaged equipment or food with much more satisfactory items and the fact that we had to purchase and pack all this gear ourselves made sure we knew what and where it was.

The eight months after my return from the Weddell Sea was probably the busiest I have ever spent. Lecturing and fund-raising; planning and training; buying and packing; it was a hectic period but an exciting and enjoyable one too. It was rather complicated for me as Louise produced a baby daughter and I was trying to get my new house and grounds into some sort of respectable order.

My team had swung into effective action – Bob Miller and Arthur Helm, secretary of the Ross Sea Committee, were everywhere organising and directing; John Claydon had the flying operations well under control; Jim Bates was surrounded by tractors and spares; Peter Mulgrew and Ted Gawn were packing radio equipment with meticulous care; we had dozens of willing experts to help us – architects, engineers, scientists, businessmen, plus the three armed services. The public was right behind us too and this in itself was a marvellous experience.

At the end of December we commenced loading the *Endeavour* (whose leaks by then had been repaired) and we took great care to see that our initial requirements were somewhere near the top of the hold. Up on deck, ready to go, were our Ferguson tractors plus the dog teams and sledges. Perched on the stern was our Auster aircraft.

On December 21st 1956 we finally said goodbye to New Zealand and I had my usual mixture of feelings at the start of a new expedition. There was relief that the preliminary organisation was behind me; a deep pleasure and confidence in my stout companions; excitement and yes, fear, at the challenges ahead, and a disquietening uncertainty about my ability to carry the plans through. I had refused to think about the separation from Louise and our two small children but now it could be put off no longer. As we pulled away from the wharf I watched my quiet little family fade behind us . . . and someone started singing the sad sweet strains of 'Now is the Hour'. . I was glad of the darkness to hide the tears on my cheeks. I'd be gone for sixteen months – what would become of them?

Our journey into McMurdo Sound was full of contrasts. For a time we had blue skies and sparkling water, and then the wildest storm I have experienced. We motored through hundreds of miles of easy pack-ice and then became jammed immovably in thick pressure ridges. Even our planned Base site on Butter Point proved inaccessible and hazardous – we were lucky to get our reconnaissance tractors safely back on board ship before the ice parted under a strong easterly wind. In the end this proved an advantage for we established Scott Base in a much better position – at Pram Point on Ross Island, only two miles over the hill from the American base at Hut Point.

Our unloading plan swung smoothly into action with two shifts around the clock. The supplies were winched straight onto the sledges and then dragged nine miles across the bay ice by our five Ferguson tractors and dumped on the gravel foreshore at Pram Point beside our tent camp. Each hut was removed from the *Endeavour* in its entirety and this enabled construction to go ahead with a minimum of delay. Our huts were made of large insulated panels which fitted neatly together and as they had all been assembled in Wellington before departure our builders were completely familiar with them. On the morning of January 14th the floor of the large mess hut was laid down, and by nine p.m. the same evening the hut was externally complete and we now had satisfactory shelter whatever the weather should do to us. It looked a fine solid building and we were very proud of it.

I received a message from George Marsh that his party had found the lower part of the Ferrar Glacier quite impracticable for dog travel. This was a serious setback, as our plans had been based largely on the use of this glacier as a southern outlet towards the Pole. On January 15th the assembling of our Beaver aircraft was completed and it was success-fully test flown. A few minutes later we were on our way across McMurdo Sound towards Butter Point. We flew back and forwards across the lower Ferrar Glacier seeking a chink in the defences, but in the end I had to admit defeat. The glacier was a continual succession of melt pools and ice pinnacles, and it was split by great ice trenches which carried turbulent streams down to the sea.

The unloading was progressing so satisfactorily and the buildings going up so smoothly that it was already quite clear that we would be ahead of schedule in the completion of Scott Base. This was counter-balanced by my concern about where we would find a satisfactory way through the mountains. I remembered Bernie Gunn telling mea bout a flight he had done in an American aircraft the previous summer. They had flown up the Skelton Glacier, which was some distance to the south of the Ferrar, and Bernie had thought it at least worth investigating as a route to the Polar Plateau. On January 18th I did a marvellous flight with John Claydon across the Ross Ice Shelf, up the great trench of the lower Skelton Glacier, over the broad crevassed snowfields at the glacier head, and out on to the wide snowy desert of the Polar Plateau. I saw crevasses and problems in plenty but none that looked impossible to overcome. I decided to carry out an immediate surface examination of the route using dog teams.

It would save time if we could fly two teams into the Skelton Glacier.

John Claydon, Richard Brooke and I flew to the glacier and searched from the air for a suitable depot site. We were pleased to see a snowy patch beside a strip of moraine about twenty miles up the glacier. We came down low several times and the snow looked excellent so John lowered the flaps of the Beaver and made a steady approach. I watched the snow coming smoothly up towards us and it wasn't until we were almost touching that our angle of vision changed and I was aghast to realise that the surface, which had appeared so smooth from above, was in fact liberally peppered with large sastrugi – some of them up to three feet in height.

We touched with a tremendous crash – the snow was as hard as iron – and crash followed crash as we lurched from one bump to the next and rocked violently around in our seats. It really seemed as if the aircraft must disintegrate around us. John reacted immediately. He swept the throttle open and tried to lift the plane off once more. The propeller clawed at the air, there were a couple more resounding crashes and then to our immense relief we floated up to safety. John looked fairly calm, but Richard and I were decidedly white about the gills and agreed that it had been a little too close for comfort. I was surprised to see that we had any skis left after the treatment they had received, but nothing appeared to be damaged. Although our confidence was a little shaken by this experience we flew to the mouth of the glacier where the surface looked exceptionally smooth and John landed us without a bump. It was an ideal spot for a depot and four of our dog experts and two teams were promptly flown into it. On January 28th they started up the glacier.

During the next ten days we completed the unloading of the *Endeavour* and flew large quantities of supplies into the Skelton Depot. We followed the progress of the dog teams with intense interest – their battles with weather and crevasses and deep soft snow. On February 9th they reached the Polar Plateau at 8,000 feet and could report that the Skelton route had been established. We flew both aircraft out to meet them and had little difficulty in finding their camp on the wide snow-fields and landing smoothly beside the sledges. It was quite a shock to step out of a heated plane into a fresh wind and a temperature in the minus twenties – but a tremendously exciting moment. The dog teams could now turn back down valley with their job well done but our pilots concentrated on flying supplies into the Plateau Depot with the maximum speed. By February 12th the Depot was completed and we had a substantial amount of food and fuel 290 miles from base.

On February 22nd the *Endeavour* sailed for New Zealand taking with it the construction party. We owed a considerable debt of gratitude to them, for as a result of their efforts Scott Base was now a very comfortable and well-appointed home. The onset of stormy weather with gloomy skies and shorter days indicated that winter wasn't far off and spurred us to complete our outside tasks while we could. On February 28th the weather relented, and we were successful in evacuating the dog teams and their drivers from the Skelton depot and for the first time our whole complement of twenty-three men was together at Base.

On March 5th we made our first radio contact with Shackleton Base and I had a long talk to Bunny Fuchs and George Lowe. It was interesting to get first-hand knowledge of their progress, as to date our information had come from the somewhat conflicting stories of newspapers and radio news. We were pleased to hear that they were well installed in their hut and were preparing everything for the winter. They had successfully established by air a small advanced base – which they called 'South Ice' – some 250 miles to the south of Shackleton and three men were installed there for the winter. They all sounded in great heart and well pleased with their progress. George Lowe's strong voice boomed out of the speakers giving us the sort of expedition gossip we all loved to hear; who was doing what; how the vehicles were going; problems they had struck; what they intended to do. We agreed to maintain a weekly radio schedule but I don't think we ever had one quite as successful as this again.

Winter was now approaching but I was determined to do one long trip with the tractors to give us added experience of handling them in difficult conditions. One of my favourite adventures had been the trip described in the book *The Worst Journey in the World* by Aspley Cherry-Garrard when in the winter of 1911 Wilson and his party manhauled their way in appalling conditions to Cape Crozier to visit an Emperor Penguin colony. I decided to do the same trip with two Ferguson tractors – linking them together with a very strong terylene rope for safety amongst the crevasses. Each tractor would tow two sledges laden with one and a half tons of freight and I felt that if we could safely accomplish this trip it would give us great encouragement for our southern journey.

It was March 19th and the days were getting short before our tractors were ready and Ellis, Bates, Mulgrew and I took them through the pressure ridges and out onto the Ross Ice Shelf. My tractor broke through into a crevasse and then we were held up by soft snow and bad visibility. At the end of the day we camped only twelve miles from Scott Base. The next day wasn't any more successful. We were crossing the infamous 'Windless Bight' which had given Wilson's party much trouble and I felt at times that the deep snow might well prove too much for us. By nightfall we had only another twelve miles behind us.

By the third morning we were feeling decidedly pessimistic as the soft snow seemed never ending. To our relief conditions started to improve and by the time we turned Terror Point – thirty miles out from Scott Base – the surface was hard and we were roaring along at six miles an hour in third gear. We thundered on for several hours at high speed until we entered a broad trough between the pressure ridges of the Ross Ice Shelf and the slopes of Mount Terror. Wilson's party had experienced considerable difficulty with crevasses at this stage so for a while we moved forward with extreme caution. The crevasses we found were not very devastating and in the end we got rather impatient and charged ahead at full power, clattering over a variety of crevasses but coming to no grief. An impossible section of broken ice forced us to climb up the icy slopes of Mount Terror and we slithered our way upwards becoming very conscious of the increasing drop on our right. Finally we could traverse no longer – we could only go straight up or return by the way we had come.

We turned upwards and crawled inch by inch up a very steep slope. My tractor was pulling the heaviest load and the surface became just too icy for it – the tracks were slipping futilely around. I remained poised there for some time, debating how quickly I could get out of the cab if my vehicle started sliding towards the Ross Ice Shelf some hundreds of feet below me. Meanwhile with some shrewd driving Jim coaxed his tractor over the top and was able to drop his sledges in a safe spot and come back to give me a tow. Late in the evening we reached a snowy basin about a thousand feet above the Shelf and pitched our camp at the foot of the Knoll. It was an exposed position but we made ourselves snug on a patch of firm snow and tied everything securely down against the wind and weather. We had completed twenty-three miles in the day and were now forty-eight miles from Scott Base.

All night our tents were battered by the wind; and next morning too. With reluctance we crawled outside to see if we could find the primitive stone hut that Wilson's party had built for themselves forty-six years before. We retreated back to camp after four hours having found nothing. Mulgrew and I re-read the relevant pages of *The Worst Journey in the World*. The hut must be somewhere near us, we decided, so out we went again. Finally we found it – only a few hundred yards away – perched in an exposed position on the side of a rocky ridge that thrust sharply out over the Ross Ice Shelf. All that remained were the rough stone walls embracing an old sledge, some test tubes, rolls of unexposed film, and other abandoned relics. What a grim home it must have been in the darkness of the Antarctic night!

Another windy night and temperatures below —30°F persuaded us to set out on the return journey – we were a long way from home and winter was fast approaching. It was difficult to dig away the four feet of snow surrounding our tractors and tents and we didn't move off until one thirty in the afternoon. For the descent of the dangerous ice slope we attached the four sledges behind my lead tractor while Jim Bates hitched on at the back with a long rope to act as brake. We crossed the bad slopes without too much trouble, for we were so well spaced that usually one or other of the vehicles was on a safe footing. Even so it was a relief to get down into the trough again and be able to make full speed towards Terror Point. The weather was now fine but getting steadily colder. By eight p.m. the thermometer showed −46F° and we were struggling with the deep soft snow of the 'Windless Bight'. For hour after hour we chugged on, stopping only for refuelling. To our relief the outward trail was still visible, and even when darkness descended we could follow it in the headlamps and feel confident that we wouldn't stray into any crevasses.

It became extremely monotonous as we travelled along, taking hour about on the driving, and the cold was starting to creep into our bones. It wasn't so bad when you were actually driving, as you got a little protection from the rough canvas cabs and a bit of warmth seemed to seep out from the engine. If you weren't driving there was nothing to do except sit on a sledge. When you became too miserable you jumped off and ran alongside the tractors for a while in your cumbersome clothes until you either warmed up or your lungs gave out. In these spells of 'resting', you had plenty of time to think and I resolved to build some sort of shelter to enable the passengers to travel more comfortably.

Just before midnight the fog descended on us and so did our misfortunes. It all started when the lights on my tractor failed and I had to follow along behind the other one through the darkness and gathering mist. About midnight we stopped to refuel and to our disgust Jim's tractor wouldn't start again – some water had frozen in the petrol line. Jim and Murray took drastic action. They lit a powerful blowlamp and played the flame on the fuel lines and petrol tank, and were successful in warming the fuel sufficiently to melt the blockage and permit a free flow again – Peter Mulgrew and I stood well back out of danger waiting for the explosion. The lights on Jim's tractor were now fading rapidly as the bitterly cold conditions prevented the battery from recharging, and in the dim light we lost the track time and again. We knew we must be fairly close to Base so we roped the vehicles for the last few miles through the crevasses of the pressure ridges. Somehow we found the track again and managed to keep on it, to creep into Scott Base just before four o'clock in the morning. It had been a long and tiring day and we had covered forty-eight miles in fourteen hours at one and three quarter miles per gallon. My confidence in the tractors had grown – and so had my confidence in the ability of my engineers to keep them going. We resolved to modify and improve the tractors even further and have them in peak condition to take on the trail in the spring.

The long dark Antarctic winter proved much less terrifying than its reputation. We had too much to do to be bored. Even the maintenance and operation of the Base took more time in the darkness and this was the period when our scientists were most deeply involved in their programmes. The dog men had weeks of work to be carried out on sledges and equipment and the dogs themselves required feeding and attention. The flying team kept active too and the Auster was flown on many moonlit nights with oil-wick lamps marking out the airfield.

Perhaps the biggest task during the winter was the preparing of our vehicles and sledges for the southern journey. Murray Ellis and Jim Bates completely overhauled three Fergusons; they constructed stout crash bars over the drivers' heads as protection in case the vehicles should roll over; and improved the canvas cabs to try and give the drivers a little more protection against the wind and drift. We did a great deal of work on the tracks and the tracking system, trying to get the maximum performance out of the vehicles in soft snow, and we removed the steel soles from the runners of most of our sledges and replaced them with the much more efficient bakelite plastic, Tufnol. Remembering the discomforts we suffered on our Cape Crozier trip I started the construction of a caravan on skis, we called it the 'caboose', with a framework of welded piping and angle iron, covered in a sheath of plywood and an outer skin of heavy green canvas. The internal dimensions were only twelve feet by four feet but we installed bunks, cupboards, a cooking bench with primus stoves and our radio equipment. Despite its ludicrous resemblance to a horse-box we were very proud of it. The garage was always the scene of extreme activity; of varying optimism and depression depending on our progress with preparations; and of restless energy as a constant programme of modification and adaption was pursued.

The general operation of the base quickly settled down into a comfortable routine. All of us did a share of the general duties – washing up, cleaning out the various huts, collecting snow and ice to be melted for water, and refuelling the heaters and stoves from our depot of forty-four gallon drums. For relaxation we had an adequate library, a radiogram, and a sufficient supply of alcoholic drinks. The mess-room was a noisy and cheerful place and there seemed to be a minimum of the pointless complaining that can go on under crowded conditions.

We had excellent radio communications with New Zealand and I spoke to Louise twice a week. Even so, many of us greatly missed our wives and children – I know I did. It was wonderful to hear about the family and all that was going on – but rather frustrating to hang up the telephone and suddenly realise that all was cold and dark outside, and that we were separated by a couple of thousand miles of stormy ocean. The only thing to do was to keep busy – and this we certainly did – but in any spare moments it was difficult not to feel lonely and homesick.

The weather during the winter was much better on the whole than I had expected – we had some beautiful moonlight periods with temperatures down to −60°F but we could walk around comfortably on the sea ice and even run the dogs for short trips. The storms were sometimes very violent and we had one period of five days when the winds rarely dropped below sixty miles per hour. I was very worried about the roof on our generating shed and we had to rope up and go outside in the fiercest part of the storm to lash a couple of safety lines over the top. The power of the wind sweeping out of the darkness of McMurdo Sound was quite awesome and I was glad when the storm passed and all the buildings had survived.

The field parties had proved so energetic and competent that I was determined to use their abilities to the utmost in the spring and summer. It was a marvellous opportunity with so many thousands of square miles of unvisited mountain country right on our doorstep. Our first responsibility would be to establish the depot that Fuchs had requested opposite Mount Albert Markham and this would be about 200 miles south of the Plateau Depot. I decided we should put in a further depot – Depot 700 – about 400 miles south of the Plateau Depot and only 500 miles from the South Pole. This would provide many advantages – our dog teams could then survey the mountainous area behind the Beardmore Glacier; it would be an extra safety factor for Fuchs; and it would be vital if I took the vehicles on any long inland journeys.

I sent an enthusiastic summary of my plans to the Ross Sea Committee – not to ask for permission (I considered the field activities were now my responsibility) but just to let them know what I had in mind and to ask for more fuel and supplies. To my surprise I received a reply from the Executive Committee forbidding me to carry out many of my objectives and demanding much greater precautions against possible but unlikely disasters. I had no particular desire to offend the committee but I was confident that the programme was well within our powers. I continued as though the exchange of messages had never occurred, made a few worthwhile modifications to the plans and reintroduced the idea of a push towards the Pole if I could get enough extra fuel at

Depot 700. It was becoming clear to me that a supporting role was not my particular strength. Once we had done all that was asked of us – and a good bit more – I could see no reason why we shouldn't organise a few interesting challenges for ourselves.

I spent many long but enjoyable hours working on the logistics for the summer operation. I spoke to Bunny Fuchs across the continent and his attenuated voice, speckled with static, sounded like someone from another planet. It was difficult to feel we were part of the same operation. I told him of my plans to put in Depot 700 and he seemed quite pleased with the idea. I asked for a list of the supplies he wanted left at the two furthest depots and he said he'd let me have it later. In fact I never did get this list and after a month or so worked one out for myself in my estimate of the performance of his vehicles. I suppose our difference in temperament made for difficulties in communication – I was always impatient for information and quick to make decisions and prepared to change them if something better offered; Bunny considered his plans with great care and stuck to them with dogged determination once a decision had been made. I found myself increasingly regarding my expedition as an autonomous operation – there was so much to do that I had little time left to worry about Bunny's problems.

The winter passed remarkably quickly and soon mid-winter's day had come and gone. We realised then how much there still remained to do and the tempo speeded up considerably. By August 1st, it was becoming quite light by the middle of the day and we were growing accustomed to a renewing pattern of day and night. As the month progressed we had wonderful displays of colour in the northern sky around noon; indications that the sun was fast returning.

On August 23rd it was a fine morning with a clear sky and a moderate temperature of −30°F. By eleven o'clock the western mountains were glowing with a glorious pink; and at one thirty p.m. the sea ice beyond Cape Armitage was alight and the sun was shining on Observation Hill. Scott Base was still in the shadow so we gravitated over to the sunshine like moths towards a candle. In imagination we could almost feel the returning warmth and revelled in the pleasure of seeing the great red ball skipping along the horizon. I could easily understand why many ancient people had worshipped the sun.

This was the signal for the tempo at Scott Base to reach its highest pitch, and long hours of work went into completing preparations for the spring journeys, which would serve to test equipment and vehicles and get men and dogs into training. At the beginning of September in the cold half light of the Antarctic spring we started our early journeys.

Depots were laid out, interesting corners explored, and hundreds of miles covered. Fitter and full of confidence we gathered back at base to repair equipment, modify plans, and tie up all loose ends. The six dog teams had tremendous trips ahead of them and thousands of square miles in which to explore, map and geologise. They would be supported and co-ordinated by our two aircraft and be in daily contact by radio with Scott Base – and with me in the field. Our two pilots were in effect our back-up group with responsibility for any search and rescue, and I had a lot of confidence in their ability to deal with any emergencies that might arise.

Our primary task remained the same – to get Depot 700 established as soon as possible. This depot would be beyond the direct range of the Beaver aircraft from Scott Base so John Claydon would have to establish an intermediate refuelling point on the Ross Ice Shelf. I became very concerned about what would happen to my plans if the Beaver should come to grief during one of these complicated operations. While the dog teams could travel considerable distances when supported by aircraft they had limited usefulness as load carriers. But by using the tractors we could be doubly sure of completing the task. I was convinced that by starting fully laden from the Plateau Depot we should be able to establish Depot 700 with the tractors alone.

My whole planning turned in this direction – the tractors would be the major thrust and the dog teams would be useful for reconnaissance and for support in emergency. Once the tractors reached the Plateau Depot we could head south fully laden with fuel and the establishing of Depot 700 would be assured. But first we had to get the tractors to the Plateau Depot.

During the winter four of us had became closely involved with the tractor operation – the 'Old Firm' we called ourselves – and it was the group that had driven to Cape Crozier; Jim Bates, Murray Ellis, Peter Mulgrew and myself. Peter had done a very good job running our radio communications at Scott Base but he was never satisfied with staying at home. Increasingly he infiltrated into field activities – and I think he had appointed himself to the southern tractor party almost before I was aware of it. Certainly his technical skill with radio equipment proved invaluable to me on long journeys and we were always able to maintain close communications with base and the outside world – at times I felt we were almost too efficient in this respect. Jim Bates was quite a contrast. Lean and hungry looking, Jim was an expert skier and had a notable disinterest in how he looked and dressed. Jim was something of a mechanical genius and a successful inventor and I have never met anyone with more imagination and resourcefulness in mechanical matters. Murray Ellis was large, strong and very reliable; an engineering graduate who might grumble a little at times but who would tackle any job however unpleasant it might be; a mighty useful chap to have around in unpleasant circumstances.

Very few people in McMurdo Sound had any confidence in the travelling ability of our tractors. Our neighbouring Americans and most of the people at Scott Base openly doubted that we would go fifty miles out on the Ross Ice Shelf before having to be rescued. And as for our hopes of getting up the Skelton Glacier ... not a chance! Even Murray and Jim lost heart at times but the more opposition we got the more determined I became to prove them wrong – and Peter Mulgrew was always murmuring, 'Let's go to the Pole, Ed'.

In the late afternoon on Monday, October 14th we waved goodbye to our friends and drove off in our four vehicles – one Weasel and three Ferguson tractors. Jim Bates couldn't join us until the Skelton Depot and Dr. Ron Balham was taking his place for the first sector. We had tremendously heavy loads and in the soft snow we had the greatest of difficulty in moving. A couple of miles out one of my sledges broke through into a crevasse and we had to unload the twelve drums of fuel, haul the sledge to the surface and load the 350 lb drums back on again. We changed sledges around between vehicles to distribute the load more effectively and struggled on for a few more miles. After five and a half hours we were only six and a half miles in a direct line from Scott Base. We camped within sight of Base and I wondered if the pessimists might not be proved right...

The second day started badly. We entered an area of really soft snow and were quite unable to drag all our loads together. For two hours we relayed the loads and covered exactly one mile. I decided on drastic action and rolled eight drums off the sledges. We started moving now, although slowly, but by the end of the day we had covered twenty-three miles. On the third day we did thirty miles; on the fourth thirty-two; and the fifth thirty-eight – even though we were having considerable trouble with overheating in the Weasel.

We were now only fifty miles from the depot we had established at the foot of the Skelton Glacier the previous autumn and we could already see the great mountains on either side of the glacier. Then the Weasel wouldn't start and Murray struggled with the problem all day. Soon after five p.m. the motor sprang into life. By six p.m. the tractor train was ready to leave and we determined to keep going all night and try and reach the depot without the motors getting cold again.

I was pointing my tractor towards the distant mouth of the Skelton Glacier and as I bumped along I looked out on a strangely beautiful scene. To the south of us the sun was a molten ball of fire on the horizon and its low rays brought into sharp relief the jagged sastrugi and transformed the hills and hollows into a mottled patchwork of flame and shadow. The whole sky glowed with a delicate purple while the great peaks standing all around us were dressed in crimson robes. We were swimming along in a sea of glorious colour and for a while I forgot even the cold and the discomfort.

By four a.m. we were approaching the entrance to the Skelton Glacier. From the aircraft I had taken a special note of the large areas of crevasses flanking the entrance on either side and knew that careful navigation would be required to dodge them. I fixed our position accurately from the local peaks with the astro-compass, and then changed direction in order to come squarely into the mouth of the valley. As we drove on over the rough hard surface I felt tired and cold, and knew that according to all the rules there was every chance of groups of concealed crevasses being somewhere in the vicinity. There was little we could do about it but keep a close watch and drive on, but I found that my muscles had quite unconsciously tensed as though preparing for some unexpected and violent encounter. By six a.m. we were safely through the entrance and I started looking ahead for the Depot. I soon picked up a black dot a little to starboard of our course and swung my vehicle towards it. As we rattled on over the hard surface the dot expanded and became two, and then three, and finally we could pick out the tent, the two dog teams, and the piles of stores. At seven a.m. we rolled into the camp to be greeted vociferously by eighteen dogs and handshakes from Bob Miller, George Marsh and Jim Bates who had all flown in the previous day. The fifty miles had taken us thirteen hours – but it was twenty-four hours since we'd been to bed and we were very tired. I checked the temperature – it was −34°F – wrote my diary and then thankfully tumbled into my sleeping bag.

The next two days were spent at the Skelton Depot while Jim and Murray worked on the Weasel. They discovered that the distributor drive was broken and it was a miracle the Weasel had kept going. Displaying their usual ingenuity they rigged up a bi-pod, lifted out the engine and repaired the broken piece, and reassembled the vehicle – all in temperatures below −30°F. Late in the afternoon of the third day we set off up the glacier carrying heavy loads. The surface was extremely rough and hard and we made excellent time. The dog teams had left early in the morning and we reached their camp at nine fifteen p.m. – they had done a very good effort and covered eighteen miles in the day.

The next day we were immobilised by mist and snow and by the following morning a terrific wind was blowing so we still couldn't move. Around mid-day on October 24th the wind was easing off and we prepared to start. We had no sooner got under way than the wind and drift returned but we decided to persist. We clattered up the glacier on very icy surfaces and soon came to an area of long narrow crevasses. Following the advice of the autumn reconnaissance we swung down to the right into a broad trough that ran up the glacier. There were just as many crevasses here but they were mostly only two or three feet wide. These crevasses might not have been very dangerous but I found it rather unpleasant to look back and see a series of gaping holes appearing behind my tractor.

It was a relief when the surface improved and we started climbing upwards amongst magnificent peaks and superb scenery. The wind had eased considerably and although it was still blowing a half gale it seemed almost balmy in contrast with what it had been before. We were now driving over firm wind packed snow towards a prominent rock feature we had called Clinker Bluff. To the left of Clinker Bluff a vast ice fall came tumbling down, criss-crossed with great crevasses. It was certainly no route for us and instead we swung right towards gradually ascending snow slopes which steepened some distance ahead and seemed to merge with the great buttresses of Mount Huggins. At eight p.m. we stopped and camped. We had done nineteen and a half miles of really tough travelling and this had certainly been our hardest day to date. It took all of us to pitch the flapping tents but soon we were snug and comfortable despite the wind and drift.

The autumn reconnaissance of the glacier had indicated we had now come to the crucial section with extensive areas of crevassing and a steep rise in altitude. Harassed by wind and poor visibility we struggled upwards for six days – constantly having to relay our loads up steep snow slopes and detour away from areas of open crevasses. The thought of crevasses was never out of my mind and I lived with a tense feeling in the pit of my stomach. By the night of October 29th we had reached an altitude of 8,000 feet and were only seventeen miles from the Plateau Depot. At six a.m. the next morning the wind was gusting to over fifty knots and heavy drift completely wiped out all visibility. At ten o'clock, in most unpredictable fashion, there was a rapid clearance.

The temperature was $-23°$F, and after the strong wind and thick drift the vehicles were well snowed up. We had a great deal of difficulty in starting them, but were away at eleven thirty a.m. and hadn't done more than a few hundred yards before we entered another area of particularly fierce winds. I was in the lead tractor and couldn't see a thing but ploughed on as I was fairly confident there were no crevasses in the area. The temperature had dropped to $-33°$F and the wind was increasing. The only thing that enabled me to keep going was the pale gleam of the sun barely visible through the mist above us. Steering on the sun with the astro-compass I battled on over the rough surface. It was impossible to see more than thirty or forty feet ahead and the surface itself was quite obscured. The cab of each Ferguson became a vortex of wind currents and drift and we were miserably cold. Finally I'd had enough and I stopped, waved to the others, and we all crawled inside the caboose and had a meal. It was pleasant to thaw out again and to get some warm food inside us. We had only covered two miles.

It was cold during the night with temperatures down to $-34°F$ and it was a terrible job getting our vehicles going next morning. We couldn't leave until eleven a.m. and we were soon back in another area of wind and snow on the crest of the pass – I was able to see just enough of the sun to steer an approximate course.

The surface here was very rough and we were climbing up and down over a series of quite steep folds. The vehicles were going particularly well, and were able to drag the sledges up the steeper slopes without the necessity for relaying. During the early afternoon the fog closed right in and obscured the sun, so we stopped and had a brewup and lunch. I estimated we were seven miles due east of the depot but was afraid we might miss it in this sort of visibility. Later on in the afternoon we were getting a few glimpses of the sun so I decided to move on again. I took over the lead tractor myself for the first hour and tried to hold a straight course. Whenever the sun appeared for a few moments I'd hastily swing the tractor back on to the correct heading, and when it disappeared I'd try and maintain the course by following the lie of sastrugi. We were weaving all over the place and I was hoping that the errors would cancel themselves out.

At the end of the hour Jim Bates took over the lead tractor and followed the same procedure. He'd only been driving for twenty minutes when the mist began to thin out and we emerged through the edge of it into clear visibility. I was in the Weasel at the back of the train and I saw Jim suddenly change direction a few degrees and he seemed to gain a new lease of life. I looked ahead, and there on the horizon several miles away was a tiny black triangle – a tent. It was the Plateau Depot.

I have never felt more relieved or excited. In an outburst of emotion I shouted and sang at the top of my voice. There had been so many uncertainties. So often we'd only just got through. But now we'd made it – despite all the doubts of the others and our own fears, we'd made it! It was one of the best moments I can remember.

Chapter 14

Race for the Pole

Sir Edmund Hillary, conqueror of Mount Everest, and his dead tired polar expedition reached the South Pole today and fell asleep on the spot. They were winners of an Antarctic race and the first men to treck to the Pole in 46 years.

Daily News, Chicago.
Saturday, January 4th, 1958

I WANTED THE TRACTORS AND DOG TEAMS TO LEAVE THE PLATEAU DEPOT with maximum loads and this meant that many flights of fuel and food would be needed. The weather followed an erratic and unpredictable pattern and there were long periods when no flying was possible. There seemed to be a bit of a jinx on the Plateau Depot – first Murray Ellis strained his back and had to be evacuated, and then Peter Mulgrew fell off the roof of the caboose and broke three of his ribs so he had to go out too. That left only two members of the 'Old Firm' – Jim Bates and me – which was a serious blow. We needed four drivers to be able to move so I recruited our second radio expert, Ted Gawn, and Derek Wright who was a film cameraman down for the summer. Bob Miller and George Marsh put full loads on their sledges and found their dogs couldn't move them so had to unload most of it onto the tractors. They departed with difficulty and then reported on the radio an area of very soft snow – and my optimism was starting to get a little strained.

The jinx at the Plateau Depot still hadn't run its course. I must have picked up the bug that had swept through the wintering party after the arrival of the first American aircraft and I developed a high fever with appalling aches and pains. When we moved off on November 12th my assistance was very spasmodic and as the snow conditions were extremely difficult our progress was minimal. We were pulling a total load of eleven tons and the Weasel was quite magnificent in the deep snow and frequently dragged five tons by itself. We can only guess what harm this overloading did to the Weasel's transmission. We discovered by experience the best way to use the three Ferguson tractors in soft snow. The lead tractor had no sledges but threw all its weight onto a tow rope attached to the second tractor. The second tractor had two sledges behind it and then a rope to the third tractor which had three sledges. The three vehicles were spread over such a distance that usually two of the three would find reasonable traction and could keep the lot going.

By the end of the fourth day we reached a cairn established by Bob Miller thirty-five miles out – we weren't exactly making the sort of pace we were aiming for.

We now turned onto a southerly heading and in firmer conditions we started making much better mileage – eighteen miles on November 16th, thirty miles on 17th and then a great struggle for twenty-two miles in a tough day of gale force winds and hard rough sastrugi. The weather relented a little and though temperatures were down to $-30°F$ we had excellent surfaces and covered thirty-four point one miles on November 19th and a more difficult thirty point three miles on the next day's run. These long drives in cold temperatures sapped our strength and we decided to have a short rest on the 20th. While I relaxed in my sleeping bag, Ted Gawn received two important messages on the radio circuit with Scott Base. One message was from Bunny Fuchs and indicated they would leave Shackleton with their main vehicle group on November 24th and that they hoped to average twenty miles a day. That should get them to Scott Base by March 9th and I found this rather devastating news as any further delay in their movements could result in another winter in the Antarctic for them, and me – which was the last thing I wanted to do. Leaving Shackleton this late was incomprehensible to me – we were already more than five weeks on the trail south and had 350 miles of our journey behind us. Even with their much faster and more powerful vehicles they couldn't afford to be too casual about the vast distances they had to cover. Bunny didn't seem to realise the weight and momentum we were getting into our journey south – he suggested we might like to put the Depot at 600 miles rather than 700 miles . . . or maybe he did realise and didn't want us to travel out too far. As we were only 250 miles from Depot 700 I considered our arrival there in some force was a foregone conclusion. It was what would happen beyond Depot 700 that occupied my thoughts and plans.

The second message was far more encouraging. There had been a meeting of the full Ross Sea Committee and their message said, 'If you are prepared to go for the Pole the Committee will give you every encouragement and full support following formal approval from London'. When we started up our tractors again we had only thirty-six miles to go to reach the position we had chosen for Depot 480 and I had every intention of doing it in one long haul. But things didn't turn out quite as well as that. We had to go back five miles for a drum that had fallen off a sledge; the weather and surface deteriorated and after a very trying and difficult day we had only covered eighteen miles.

November 23rd was a very stormy morning with a heavy snow fall and huge piles of drift snow around the vehicles and sledges. At eleven thirty a.m. conditions were still rather impossible but we felt it was better to push on rather than sit around doing nothing. Standing up in the lead tractor with my head over the front I managed to feel my way forward for a couple of miles over hummocks and through hollows, having great difficulty in steering any sort of an accurate course and making great alterations of direction whenever the sun appeared and let me get a true heading. When we ran into a dense fog I gave up and we all lolled around in the caboose and waited impatiently for it to lift. At the first glimpse of the sun we drove on again, but only managed to cover another hazardous half-mile in terrible lighting before we tipped a sledge over on a giant sastrugi which had been quite invisible from the tractor's cab. After a lot of digging and much tugging from the tractors we righted the two-ton sledge and dragged it to level ground. We hadn't done any damage but this was a sharp indication that this sort of travelling would do more harm than good. We sat around until nine p.m. and the radio schedule. Bob and his party were now forty-four miles *behind* us and being retarded by the same sort of unpleasant weather we had experienced. After the schedule, the weather was still as thick as ever so we had a leisurely meal. I had almost decided to abandon travelling for the day when, in tantalising fashion, the sun appeared again and it was possible to travel. We couldn't afford to waste any weather so we shrugged off thoughts of bed and drove on.

It was after midnight when we got away, and from the lead tractor I had no difficulty now in steering an accurate course although the cloudy skies gave us rather flat lighting on the snow. As we drove along the nature of the country started to change. We seemed to be climbing steadily upwards and in every direction ice hummocks were appearing, growing larger and larger the farther we went. Our course became a sinuous one, twisting in and out amongst the hummocks and even over them when no other way presented itself. As we only had about eighteen miles to cover to get to Depot 480 we pushed on as hard as we could and were delighted at the speed we were making. The only disturbing feature was the increase in size and number of the ice hummocks and far ahead they loomed up on the horizon in formidable proportions. In the first two hours we covered nearly ten miles. Jim Bates was now in the lead tractor and I was following along in the Weasel some hundreds of yards behind the Fergusons.

I started noticing that the vehicles ahead of me were breaking through a series of small crevasses and leaving behind them regular holes about six inches or a foot wide. These weren't big enough to be troublesome but they were an indication that we might be approaching a bad crevasse area. I accelerated in the Weasel to overtake the tractors and warn them, but Jim was in full flight and I had difficulty in making up the leeway on him. I shot around a hummock at full speed and then came to a halt as I almost overran the last sledge of the train. The three vehicles had stopped and I noticed that the middle one was leaning over at an unaccustomed angle. I parked the Weasel and walked carefully forward to join the others.

An unpleasant sight met my eyes. The lead tractor was now on firm ground but behind it was a great open hole – so big that it was hard to see how the tractor had managed to get clear of it. The second tractor was lying over at a sharp angle with one of its tracks deep in a crevasse. I carefully investigated the surface with my ice-axe and made my way up forward to join Jim at the lead tractor and to gaze with some dislike down the icy depths of the crevasse behind it. It had only been his speed that had carried him across.

The first thing to do was to get the lead tractor out of danger. I probed over a wide area of snow around the vehicle and soon discovered a number of other holes running in a regular pattern across our route. The bridges over many of these crevasses were very thin and we had strayed into a very nasty area. I carefully marked out a route across all the crevasses I could find and then untied the lead tractor from the rest of the vehicles and jumped aboard. With my nerves a little on edge I swung the tractor around and carefully inched my way back over the snow bridges, in imagination expecting them to crumble underneath me, but finally arriving safely back beside the Weasel.

The big task was now to get the number two tractor free. The left-hand track was deep into the crevasse, but it appeared that a really concerted pull by the other three vehicles might drag it clear. First we had to move all the laden sledges out of danger. Thoroughly investigating any new piece of ground and getting back into our old tracks as soon as possible, we made two trips and dragged all the sledges about a mile back on to safer ground. This constant passage over the same track was now opening up all the crevasses and the route was liberally supplied with them. Then we returned to the attack on the helpless Ferguson. With our thick Terylene ropes we hitched the three vehicles together and then attached them on to the trapped one. As we'd probably only get one chance it would have to be a good one and co-ordination would be all important. I gave the signal, let out the clutch of the Weasel, and accelerated forward as hard as I could go. The strain came on with a jerk, and for a moment the tracks skidded in the snow and I thought, 'We're not going to do it!' Then we shot forward again like a cork out of a bottle and I knew the tractor was out or the rope had broken. I jumped out of my vehicle and walked back to see what had happened. To my delight I realised that the third Ferguson was on an even keel again and that we'd succeeded in getting it free. We gathered around it but could see no particular damage.

Jim seemed rather excited and called out, 'Take a look at the hole we left behind'. To my amazement I saw that an enormous area had completely sunk away leaving a huge void large enough to absorb a house. We crept over to the edge and looked in. It was a most unpleasant sight with sheer ice walls dropping away to vast depths and enough room to put a hundred Fergusons. I realised how extraordinarily lucky we'd been in striking this crevasse at a narrow spot, for another ten feet to the left and there was no doubt that Jim's tractor would have plunged into this hole with certain loss of the tractor and only the tow rope to save Jim's life. As the bogged tractor came free it had dislodged the thin snow bridge over the wider part and had shown us what we had escaped. We were a subdued party as we drove our four vehicles back along our tracks to the sledges, and there was no doubt that our faculties had been sharpened by this close escape – too much so in fact and we were seeing crevasses in every direction.

We reassembled the tractor train and then retreated several miles back along our route before striking off in a north-westerly direction in an attempt to clear the crevasses and get on to better going. We travelled cautiously for some miles, watching the surface with great concentration, but didn't see any more signs of crevasses. As our confidence increased we started travelling more quickly again.

I was doing another spell in the Weasel, feeling a little more relaxed after the trying period we had passed through, when again I noticed narrow cracks across the tracks ahead – more crevasses. By the time we had all stopped we were in the middle of another bad area. We were too tired now to cope with it – we needed food and a good rest. I decided to establish camp.

In the clear sunlight after a long rest we tackled the problem with more vigour. Roped together we walked ahead prodding snow bridges and marking the route. With considerable trepidation I started up the lead tractor – it was up to me, I felt, to test out my judgment on the crevasse bridges ahead. I drove over the first few bridges with some nervousness, but was encouraged when there were only minor subsidences and I pushed on with more confidence over bridge after bridge. All went well, and I had soon reached the far side of the bad area. I stopped and went back to check with the others. I found it was the last tractor which had suffered the discomfort on this occasion. By the time the leading three vehicles had crossed the bridges they had been weakened considerably and usually the fourth tractor would punch a hole in the bridge and then lurch violently across as the irresistible weight of the other three vehicles came on the rope and dragged it to safe ground.

Six hours later we came over the crest of a long slope and entered a broad easy basin with a smooth surface suitable for aircraft landings. We drove our vehicles into position and pitched our tent to mark the establishment of Depot 480 – the end of the second stage in our journey – and undoubtedly the easiest stage of all.

We spent nine days at Depot 480 and very busy days they were too. All the vehicles had to be checked over and any problems corrected; quite a few of the sledges needed repairing; and the Beaver was relaying loads in from a depot on the Ross Ice Shelf. Best of all Murray Ellis and Peter Mulgrew had now recovered and were flown in to join us so the 'Old Firm' were all together again. Derek Wright made our numbers up to five and I persuaded our expedition Press correspondent Douglas Mackenzie to do the next sector with us too. This made six drivers and would ease the burden considerably.

On Tuesday, December 6th we moved on again leaving behind a well stocked depot and dragging sledges weighing eleven tons. The tractors responded magnificently and their performance had improved considerably after Jim's tune-up. When we stopped at midnight for a radio schedule and a meal we had covered twenty-five miles in six hours.

The food was good but I wasn't so happy about a message from the Executive Committee which insisted that, 'Depot 700 must not be left unmanned since experience proves this may make it impossible to find under certain climatic conditions'. I didn't know what experience they were referring to but I realised this message was the result of growing concern over Bunny's slow rate of progress. I did not consider that the manning of Depot 700 would serve any useful purpose and felt quite confident that Bunny would think the same. My fixing of our position with a bubble sextant had shown errors of up to six miles but Bob Miller's figures taken with his theodolite would be very accurate indeed. In a decidedly grumpy mood I got into the lead tractor and drove furiously on. Forty miles out we turned due south and when we stopped to camp we had covered fifty-two point three miles – the best run so far. The next day we did quite well too – forty-one miles were covered despite an uncomfortable period spent in an area of crevasses.

The strain of constant travelling was starting to tell on the Weasel. For six hours the next day Jim and Murray worked on its clutch. When we started off again there were still unpleasant noises coming from the transmission and we had the feeling our troubles weren't over. When we stopped at the end of our run we had only done twenty-seven miles but we were too tired to bother much about food and crawled into our beds. The alarm at two p.m. was sheer agony, and after I'd done a shot on the sun I spent a restless few hours tossing about until the alarm went again at five thirty p.m. for the radio schedule. I was rather worried about the condition of the Weasel. It seemed very likely that it could be a write-off at any time, and I doubted if our three tractors could pull the full load, especially if we struck soft snow again. Bob and George had asked me to establish a small intermediate depot for them about a hundred miles before Depot 700. I decided the only thing to do was to transform this into a full-scale depot and leave petrol and oil for the crossing party. This would relieve us of a considerable load in case we had to abandon the Weasel.

The dog teams had left several days ahead of us on this sector and due to our delays in the early part of the run they were still in front of us. Next day we struck their tracks and followed them to an area of large hummocks which showed many of the familiar signs of crevasse country. Twisting in and out we climbed to the crest of a long hill and there, amongst a group of prominent sastrugi, we saw a tall cairn with a flag on top. This was where Bob and George wanted their depot and here we established Midway Depot at midnight on December 9th. Its position was 81°30′S 146°09′E.

We unloaded six drums of fuel, eight tins of pemmican, two-man ration boxes, and a jerrican of kerosene. I also decided to abandon a sledge here, and we tipped this up on its end with a flag lashed to the drawbar so that it could be seen at a considerable distance. At half-mile intervals on either side we built five snow cairns with flags on them to help the crossing party locate the Depot when they came through. This took most of the day, so I decided to camp the night at the Depot and start off afresh with the ambition of doing fifty miles in each of the next two nights to reach D700.

It's amazing how plans go awry. We started off from Midway Depot all set for a good run but stopped after a couple of hundred yards as the Weasel was making disturbing noises. Finally it was analysed as a bearing gone in the differential and as we had no spares there was nothing we could do about it. We decided we'd run the Weasel till it dropped and then abandon it.

We moved on again, going quite well, but after ten miles we started breaking through into crevasses. Bob Miller had told us about these in a message which said 'Crevasse tracks ten miles south of cairn are harmless,' and we could see the marks of the dog sledges passing over flimsy bridges without difficulty. But for us the crevasses were far from harmless – they were deep, wide and very unpleasant. By cutting across them at right angles we reduced the danger but it wasn't very enjoyable. In one place we had to do a very sharp turn between two big crevasses and the track of one of the Fergusons caught on a towbar and broke. Perched in a rather uncomfortable position with big holes on either side, Murray and Jim tackled the mending problem with their usual determination but it took quite a long time. When we moved on we had some more frights breaking through other crevasses but generally the bridges we had picked held satisfactorily. We finally cleared this three miles of crevasses but it had been an eight and a half hour struggle.

We bowled merrily along over a flatish area for some miles then I pointed the lead tractor towards a knobbly looking slope that looked rather suspicious but was the only way to go. Sure enough my tractor lurched through another crevasse – and this seemed a good enough excuse to stop and camp.

For many hours Jim and Murray worked on the Weasel in a desperate effort to keep it going but it proved hopeless. The radio schedule had a lot of news – and good news too. Our northern party had discovered extensive seams of coal and some excellent fossils, and Bunny Fuchs was making better progress than expected.

With great reluctance we left the Weasel behind and transferred all the gear onto the sledges. We drove on with the three Fergusons pulling the full load of eight tons and the abandoned Weasel looked mighty lonely perched by itself amongst the sastrugi. I felt quite a sense of loss. The crevasses soon came to an end and we made good time despite our heavy loads. We camped only fifty-eight miles from Depot 700 and on the radio schedule we heard that Bob and George were only fifteen miles from the Depot. There was always a bit of healthy competition between the tractors and dog teams and I decided to put in one of our desperation runs and complete the distance to the Depot in a day. Despite the loss of the Weasel, I went to bed reasonably contented.

We were held up for a while by bad weather but then struck south-east with the idea of picking up Bob's dog tracks and found them after half an hour. We soon entered an area of very soft snow and started labouring mightily. It got worse and worse and we finally bogged down and had to start relaying. We floundered around for many hours not making much progress and sadly missing the Weasel. Finally we cleared the soft area and started climbing up a firmer knobbly slope. Then Murray punched a hole in the top of a very unpleasant crevasse and was lucky to get across. We searched out suitable bridges over four more large crevasses and brought the tractors safely through. At the end of the run we had only done seventeen point three miles.

We made quite good progress at first on the 14th but then struck soft snow for several miles and had to relay loads so wasted several hours and a lot of fuel. When we broke free of this we climbed up onto a plateau with softish snow and many sastrugi but we were able to keep going steadily. After thirteen hours' travelling we had covered thirty-three miles and were only ten miles from Depot 700. I was in the lead tractor and drove up a long hill with a firm surface and an increasing number of ice hummocks. These were some of the familiar signs of a crevasse area and Bob Miller had warned us to expect some here. This time I saw them before hitting them and asked Murray and Jim, who were having a spell off driving, to go forward and pick a route.

With careful prodding they identified crevasses and found suitable bridges across them and then waved me on to follow. I wound my way along their route, tiptoeing in imagination over the bridges, and making quite good progress. Then I stopped in front of a very wide crevasse. Murray and Jim were investigating it carefully to see if the bridge would support the weight of the tractor. They seemed to have some doubts about it, for their examination was a long and careful one and resulted in a good deal of discussion. Finally they waved me over but suggested I didn't linger too long in the process.

I gave the signal for the tractor train to start and then revved up my motor and headed towards the bridge. My nerves were tense with expectation as I clattered on to the near side and then into the centre. All seemed to be going well, when suddenly there was a thud beneath me and my tractor tipped steeply backwards. I almost fell out of my seat but had sufficient presence of mind to lean forward and flick the throttle full on. The bridge had gone and I was going with it! For a few awful moments we teetered on the lip of the crevasse, with the tracks clawing at the edge and the nose high in the air. Then the extra bit of power told and we seemed literally to climb up the wall of the crevasse and thump to a level keel on the far side.

Somewhat shaken I turned off the motor and scrambled out for a look. The hole was a beauty, big enough to take the tractor, and I couldn't quite see how I'd managed to escape from it. If the motor had stalled I wouldn't have had a chance. I found a more substantial bridge and brought the other vehicles across. We had been going for fifteen hours and covered thirty-three and a half miles and we were dead beat. I gave the word to camp – we'd tackle the rest of the crevasses the next morning. I never found it very successful to handle unpleasant problems when we were tired and scared.

Feeling somewhat stronger after a good rest I went ahead with Peter Mulgrew on the rope and prodded around to find crevasses and choose bridges over them. I think I was probably the best at this particular job but always felt a queer sense of guilt when I did it and then let someone else drive the vehicles over. We moved the tractor train across a flat area and then up a slope where the crevasses were bigger but better bridged. We came to the last crevasse which was a big one and the bridges seemed rather shaky. The only suitable crossing was a little doubtful but after a lot of prodding I decided it should do and waved Jim Bates in the lead tractor to come across.

Jim was almost over when the bridge collapsed and the tractor sank down into it with a rush. Luckily the back of the cab jammed on the side of the crevasse and there she stayed, tilting up into the sky with nothing underneath. Jim crawled out unhurt but he had been very lucky – the crevasse was a whopper with vertical ice walls dropping hundreds of feet into darkness.

By going far enough to the east we managed to get the remaining two tractors and the sledges across but we were nervous all right – I'd had just about as much as I wanted of crevasses by this stage. We dug a deep ramp down towards the front wheels, hitched on the other two vehicles and popped the Ferguson to the surface like a cork out of a bottle. Only a farm tractor could have stood the sort of treatment we were giving it.

We started off at a good pace over rough going. We were only seven miles from Depot 700 and we were anxious to get there as soon as possible. We drove up a broad high ridge keeping our eyes open for some indication of the dog camp. It was many hundreds of miles since we had seen a prominent land feature of any sort – only the wide rolling swells of the plateau – but now we were vouchsafed one last glimpse of a mountain. From the crest of the ridge we caught sight of a great massif far to the east – it was Mount Markham, 15,000 feet, on the south side of the Nimrod Glacier. A few moments later we saw before us a wide snowy basin – and some miles away the black dot of a tent.

A couple of miles from their camp we bogged down once again and had to resort to the ignominy of relaying. Dropping a two-ton sledge, we drove on again in low gear and ploughed a deep furrow towards the camp. We could soon pick out the figures of Bob and George coming out to meet us. It was great to see them again, and before long we were circling their tent in our tractors and picking a suitable place for our camp. The dogs gave us a vociferous welcome, and we all felt an enormous sense of satisfaction in having reached Depot 700 at last. In a way Depot 700 meant the end of our major task. It was the last depot for Bunny Fuchs – almost the reason why our expedition had originally started. To reach it in such force and in reasonably good time seemed to justify all our efforts and our plans.

Our first morning at Depot 700 seemed to have been specially chosen for us – it was gloriously fine and the temperature had risen to an astonishing $+3°F$. We had a radio schedule with Base and were told that bad weather in McMurdo Sound would prevent any one flying out to us. I snuggled back into my sleeping bag and felt more relaxed than I had for a long time. For two months now I'd been travelling with the tractors – I was the only one of the 'Old Firm' to have covered the complete distance – and I could feel the constant strain of worrying about crevasses, and petrol consumption, and Fuchs's progress – or lack of it. Now I could legitimately call it a day, return to Scott Base, act like an expedition leader . . .

I had planned a day of complete rest but instead it turned into a period of energetic discussion and some soul-searching. Bob and George had now completed their depot supporting operations and could be released for the more interesting work of survey and exploration. Bob was keen for us to use a couple of tractors to put in a subsidiary depot for him to the east, but I didn't want to spare the fuel or time. The two dog men were very much traditional Antarctic travellers – and good ones too – and didn't have too much time for tractors or my ideas of taking them further south. They accepted with reluctance a suggestion that their depot should be established by the Beaver even though this was a much more efficient method. I realised that it was a well meaning effort to divert me from continuing the journey with the tractors, and my determination hardened again.

Then, to round off a difficult morning, Murray and Jim came over from their tent to present their combined views. They were happier now about the way the Fergusons were going as long as snow conditions remained firm – but what if we struck plenty of soft snow and lots of crevasses? It was 500 miles to the Pole and we could easily run out of fuel. Was it wise to carry on beyond the effective range of the Beaver?

I felt pretty grumpy after all this and went and sat in the sun by myself to think it over. I could see our scruffy, pathetic tractors and sneered to myself in anger; weren't they the most inadequate snow vehicles that had ever been thought up? I seemed to be in a minority as far as my plans were concerned; should I just call it a day like everyone wanted me to?

In actual fact I was sure that my plans were feasible enough even if our margins were a little slim. In a pinch we would just have to drop one vehicle . . . or two. We would be carrying manhauling sledges and in an emergency we could complete the journey on foot – as Captain Scott had done forty-six years before. I was certainly getting a little obsessed about the whole business and probably the only action I never considered seriously was to turn back. I even worked out the logistics for heading south by myself with one tractor, although I was pretty sure that Peter Mulgrew would go with me whatever happened.

Despite my bad temper the day seemed to pass quite quickly and after a good meal and another night's sleep we were back to our normal selves again and there was no more discussion about our not going on. To our pleasure and astonishment we heard over the radio that Fuchs was now expecting to reach the Pole between Christmas and New Year which indicated that he was making a tremendous spurt forward. This certainly changed our whole outlook and made my fears of another winter look rather silly. I didn't think that we had a chance of getting to the Pole by New Year whatever we did, but we should be there soon after. As long as we could get within a couple of days from the Pole by the time that Bunny arrived, then I felt sure he would be agreeable to us finishing the journey. The newspapers were flashing great headlines about our 'race for the Pole' but it had never been my aim to get there before him. If we hurried we might get there on the same day and this would be a fantastic result that we'd work pretty hard to achieve – only the competitive Mulgrew really wanted us to get there first; or was honest enough to admit it anyway. I sent a message to Bunny expressing pleasure at his news and telling him we were planning to reconnoitre the route further south.

John Claydon arrived at Depot 700 in the Beaver after a superbly executed flight from Scott Base via a refuelling stop at the depot he had established on the Ross Ice Shelf. It was terrific to see him again and get our mail and all the news from Scott Base. On the third flight I was handed another message – Fuchs now didn't expect to *leave* South Ice until Christmas Day; he was still 555 miles from the Pole and had no chance in the world of reaching there by New Year. We felt thoroughly deflated; we seemed to be able to get good communications with everyone except the crossing party and now we were back to the old uncertainty. The Beaver departed after its last flight leaving a well-stocked depot and our little group of three tractors and five men. We were 730 miles from Scott Base and 500 from the South Pole and we were a quiet and subdued group as we watched the plane disappear over the eastern horizon.

We started rolling on December 20th carrying twenty 44-gallon drums – enough to get us to the pole at the one point seven miles per gallon we had averaged from Scott Base. But with nothing to spare. We steered south-west hoping to get clear of the crevasse areas that had been plaguing us. Our loads were much lighter than we'd been towing before but soft snow followed by rough sastrugi kept us to a minimum pace. Twenty-seven and a half miles out we bumped through a couple of big crevasses and managed to locate four more. We hadn't been to bed for twenty-four hours and it seemed a good time to have a rest. There was another message from Bunny on the five thirty p.m. radio schedule confirming that they'd had a lot of trouble with crevasses and that he expected to arrive at South Ice in one or two days. There was also a message from the Committee telling me in the meantime not to proceed beyond D700 which was now twenty-seven miles behind us. I sent the following message to Bunny:

Personal to Fuchs

Have completed stocking of depots as arranged. Left D700 yesterday with three Fergusons and twenty drums of fuel with the intention of proving the route out another 200 miles and then, if the going proves easy, doing a trip to the Pole. Did 27 miles yesterday in heavy going before being stopped by small area crevasses. Will scrub southward jaunt if vehicles and fuel can be used in any way to expedite your safe crossing either by a further depot or anything else you suggest. In the interim until I get a reply we will continue on out a hundred miles from D700 and will cairn crevasse areas . . .

Best wishes for a speedy onward trip from South Ice.

Ed Hillary

For two days we were too busy worrying about crevasses to think of anything else and we made small mileages. In one area of bad crevasses it was only by the greatest of luck that we didn't lose the caboose and possibly a tractor. On the third day we had turned onto a due south heading and things went much better. By eight a.m. on December 24th we had completed 46·1 miles and we hadn't sighted a crevasse for all that run. We were now 110 miles out from Depot 700.

The radio schedule on Christmas Eve produced a cheerful message from Fuchs saying they were leaving South Ice on December 25th and giving other details of their plans. I was pleased to get this for it gave confirmation of his position and asked for no further assistance or raised any objection to our move south. Just in case he should have second thoughts on the subject I decided to wait one more day and then push for the Pole.

The next twenty-four hours was very relaxed. Our spirits were high and we listened with great pleasure to a special Christmas broadcast from Radio New Zealand and heard the voices of our families. We even had a Christmas dinner and a tot of brandy supplied by Murray Ellis. We took advantage of the occasion to initiate Derek Wright as the permanent fifth member of the 'Old Firm'.

At seven p.m. on Christmas day we were ready to move on again – our whole objective now was to get to the Pole as quickly as possible. Twelve and a half hours later we camped after covering fifty-six point seven miles and only crossing one area of small crevasses. For the next two days conditions weren't quite so good. We climbed to an altitude of over 10,000 feet and there were many periods of poor visibility. But we still did forty-four and a half miles and forty-one miles and were now over halfway from D700 to the South Pole. We were so tired that we were past being pleased about anything. We had an immense feeling of isolation – if anything went wrong now no one would ever find us.

When Peter handed me another message from Fuchs I could hardly believe it. Bunny was just about to leave South Ice – and was worried about fuel. Would I put in another depot at an 'appropriate' distance from D700 and abandon the attempt to reach the Pole?

I didn't have to do much figuring. We had just enough fuel to reach either the Pole or back to D700. The only way we could establish a depot was to stop and sit where we were – and hope that Bunny would arrive before our food ran out. It would be a lot easier and safer to fly some more fuel into D700. Or get a few drums deposited at the Pole by the Americans. I had the unkind suspicion that this was an excuse to stop us going on to the Pole without actually telling us not to. I didn't fancy sitting out in the middle of nowhere for a month or more with rapidly diminishing supplies – and I doubted if my companions would have liked it either. I decided that I'd get the Beaver to fly more fuel to D700 – but that we'd head onto the Pole ourselves. I duly advised Fuchs of this.

(The crossing party did not in fact suffer from any shortage of fuel. We put fifty drums out for them at the Depots and by the time they reached Scott Base they had thirty full drums left.)

Almost numb with fatigue and cold we carried on – 44·2 miles the first day; 44·5 the next and 36·2 the third. We had climbed to an altitude of 11,000 feet and our engines were labouring with the effort. My sextant was getting difficult to use too – the levelling bubble was getting larger and larger as alcohol escaped from a leak in the fluid chamber and I was having trouble in getting good readings. How accurate would my position lines be?

Once again the alarm clock dominated our night, and we were a silent and subdued party when we started up our vehicles and drove off at seven p.m. into what had now become a familiar pattern – masses of soft snow! But this wasn't the ordinary soft snow! This was heart-breaking stuff, loose and bottomless, and the Fergies were almost helpless. Time after time we bogged down completely and had to unhitch vehicles and laboriously drag sledges and tractors to the surface once more. In six frightful hours we only travelled six miles, and our fuel supplies were shrinking before our eyes. I have rarely felt a greater sense of helplessness. Even when a tractor wasn't pulling a sledge it had considerable difficulty in moving around, and it was obvious that the snow conditions wouldn't have to get much worse before the tractors would be quite immobilised. This was an unpleasant shock, and it had come at a difficult time on the southern journey. We were now much too far from D700 to have any chance of getting back to it, and we had to go on even though the farther we went the worse the conditions seemed to be getting. I decided to have one more try before instituting drastic action. We dug our sledges out, hitched the whole train up again, and then at the crucial moment surged forward to-gether. But it was useless! For a hundred yards we churned away at the snow, and then came to an ignominious halt as the three vehicles dug their way deep down.

This was it. We'd have to dispense with reserves of food and kerosene and get rid of everything not essential. It came to a substantial pile. We hitched the remaining sledges and tractors together and it made a very compact little group. Three tractors, a caboose, and two laden sledges. Surely we'd be able to move this much? We tried every trick we knew to keep things moving and even thought out a few new ones. We changed sledges around, and tractors around, and finally ended up with a system in which we just managed to keep going but we were con-suming a horrifying amount of fuel. When we stopped after thirteen hours we had managed to cover twenty-two miles – far more than I had dreamed possible. The next day was a nightmare too but in over thirteen hours we covered 27·7 miles. We had four drums of petrol left and seventy miles to go.

I was loathe to abandon any tractors and even more reluctant to discard the caboose which I now regarded as the symbol of our tractor train. I had designed it myself and helped to build it, and its comfort and security had made our journey bearable. If we couldn't get through with all the Fergusons plus the caboose it was tantamount to failure, and I resolved to push things to the limit, before we aban-doned any of these.

It was a cold, bitter evening when we awoke, with a fresh wind and a temperature of −28°F. The drifting snow had built up around the sledges and in the tractors, and we had to preheat all the vehicles with a hot-air blower to get them going. This delayed our departure by over an hour, and was all the more annoying because we'd agreed to make a really big effort to get the trip over and done with – to keep going until we got to the Pole. At 8.14 p.m. we tugged our sledges clear and moved slowly off. Conditions weren't at all pleasant – it was cold and windy and we were plagued with cloud and mist. The sun played hide and seek with us, but we didn't lose it for long enough to put us too far off course, and we drove steadily on in low gear. After a couple of hours it became apparent that we were moving a little more easily, and a check on the altimeter showed we were starting to lose height – a good sign, for the Pole Station was at 9,200 feet. Periodically now we were able to change up to third gear with a consequent increase in pace. The problem of navigation had now became the dominant thought in my mind, and at every opportunity I shot the altitude of the sun and plotted a position line. To my relief all of my shots, taken with considerable care, were proving reasonably consistent, although the growing size of the bubble was making the centring of the sun's image increasingly difficult.

For twelve hours we drove grimly on, and by eight a.m. on January 3rd we had done thirty miles. We crowded into the caboose for a meal, and I noticed how drawn and weary were the shaggy faces of my companions. We were a subdued group as we quietly munched our unappetising food. At nine a.m. we had a schedule with Scott Base and afterwards we made our first direct voice contact with Bunny Fuchs in the crossing party. With his voice thinned out between the surging static Bunny gave us his position —84°30′S – still 380 miles from the Pole. 'Gawd! He's going backwards!' someone muttered, expressing our disappointment that an earlier message indicating greater progress had been inaccurate.

It was with a feeling of actual physical dislike that I clambered into the gloomy canvas cab and started up the motor again. I gave the wave to start, jerked harshly on the brake to swing my tractor back onto course, and then trundled gently forward with my engine roaring at maximum revolutions, tracks slipping in the deep snow, and the miles dropping very slowly behind. At two o'clock we stopped for a short meal and the 'noon' sight, and then we were on again, deadly tired now and having difficulty in keeping our eyes open. Only the Antarctic chill creeping up our backbones and freezing our extremities kept us from falling asleep. At seven p.m. I considered we must be something over twelve or thirteen miles from the Pole and started keeping a very good watch on either side for fear we might overshoot it. Several miles farther on I still hadn't seen anything – it was eight p.m. and time to change drivers.

I was just about to signal a halt when I suddenly noticed a black speck far in the distance a little to the right of our course. I blinked, and looked again and it was still there. Almost without thinking I swung the tractor over and headed towards it. 'Surely it's a flag?' I drove a few more hundred yards with growing excitement, and then stopped my tractor, jumped up on the seat and signalled furiously to the others. Then I ran madly back to the caboose to get my binoculars. A flag it was, and soon we identified a whole line of them stretching out to the left and to the right.

Our relief was enormous. I don't think any of us were thinking very clearly – we'd been driving for twenty-four hours and we'd covered exactly sixty miles.

'The flag is good enough for me!' I said. 'I'm going to bed.'

When we reached the Pole station next day, January 4th, we had twenty gallons of petrol to spare – enough for twelve more miles. What did we achieve by our southern journey? We had located the crevasse areas and established the route and we had been the first vehicle party to travel overland to the South Pole – that was something I suppose. But we had produced no scientific data about the ice and little information about its properties. We showed that if you were enthusiastic enough and had good mechanics you could get a farm tractor to the South Pole – which doesn't sound much to risk your life for. The press had a field day on the pros and cons of our journey but for me the decision had been reasonably straightforward. I would have despised myself if I hadn't continued – it was as simple as that – I just had to go on.

Bunny Fuchs arrived at the Pole Station on January 20th, 1958. Somewhat depressed by his lack of progress and not wishing to spend another winter in the Antarctic myself I had suggested he consider breaking the journey at the Pole Station and completing it the next summer. This Bunny had no intention of doing and he proved himself right.

Their group of four powerful Sno-cats covered our route to D700 in fifteen days (the same time we had taken) but they carried out a series of seismic observations and suffered damage to two of their vehicles in the crevasses to the south of the depot. I joined them at D700 and acted as guide and navigator for the rest of the journey. Much of the time we were able to follow the Fergusons' tracks sculptured out by the Antarctic winds – while I lay for days in my double sleeping bags in an unheated gloomy rear cab, pining for the warm caboose and almost dying of boredom. When bad weather intervened or we struck crevasse areas I was called forward and my local knowledge proved of some worth. On March 2nd we reached Scott Base just in time to catch the *Endeavour* north. I felt considerable satisfaction at the part I had been able to play in making New Zealand a force to be considered in Antarctic matters. We had established a good base and an effective operation which has been maintained and expanded ever since. But it was marvellous, now, to return to a quiet and peaceful life with my family – while Bunny and his team flew off to a heroes' welcome in London.

Chapter 15

How high can you go?

I HAD BEEN INVOLVED IN ANTARCTIC MATTERS FOR THREE FULL YEARS and felt it was about time I settled down to a more regular existence as a reliable family man. I had been rather shaken by the violent Press controversy I seemed to have generated in my 'race for the Pole' and I had no hesitation in deciding against doing an overseas lecture tour about the expedition. I concentrated on writing another book and returned to my work with the bees. Much of my spare time was devoted to getting my half acre of land into respectable order – it was an energetic life but a good one – as life can be in New Zealand if you enjoy outdoor activities.

The mountains still exerted a considerable attraction. Four months after our return, even though it was the middle of winter, Peter Mulgrew and I drove south towards the Alps accompanied by my brother and a pregnant Louise. We didn't achieve anything very exciting but it was tremendous fun and significant for me in the pleasure I got out of having Louise along. She had always been strong and energetic and had done quite a lot of mountaineering in her student days – but I'd never realised how much she really loved the mountains even though disliking dangerous climbing. One of our objectives was to climb a small peak called Scott's Knob in the mountains of Marlborough. It had been climbed before but not as far as we knew up the jagged ridge leading from the Branch River. We left the road late one afternoon and lugged heavy loads up the valley for a couple of hours before camping on a pleasant river flat with a good supply of firewood.

It was a very cold night and in the morning there was lots of ice on every pool and fringing the river. As the valley narrowed we were forced to ford the river time after time and it was sheer agony. In an attempt to escape crossing the river we did a difficult sidle over steep slopes in the bush but it wasn't very satisfactory and we went back to wading. We established our camp at the meeting of the Branch River and Silverstream. It was a lovely position and every shady place was a fairyland of hoar frost. When the sun disappeared everything froze again but we had lots of firewood. Peter had shot a wild pig and we roasted this over a blazing camp fire.

Peter and I set off at daylight to see how high we could go on Scott's Knob. It was a cool overcast morning and all the tops were in cloud. We climbed through steep forest and then out onto a long traverse split by a series of bluffs. Everything looked threatening and sombre in the gloomy lighting. After three hours we reached the crest of the ridge and started climbing up and down over a series of precipitous bumps. We came over one rocky tower and surprised fifteen chamois grazing on a steep ledge and watched with admiration as they leapt away with contemptuous ease.

Shafts of sunlight were now reaching towards us and it was incredibly wild and beautiful. Some of the climbing demanded particular care and we didn't reach the foot of the main face until nearly mid-day. A twisting ridge led up the face and we roped up for this and on occasions had to move one at a time. We crossed several exposed snow ridges and cut steps for a hundred feet up an icy gully.

It had now turned very windy and ominous and our enthusiasm started to fade. I was climbing a steep buttress and found all the holes covered in a thin layer of ice. We had a shouted conversation about what we should do. We were only a couple of hundred feet from the top but it looked a bit unpleasant and we didn't want to be too late back. Without any great sense of disappointment we turned downwards again.

Descending the face took us a long time and we kept the rope on down the ridge as the wind was blowing strongly. The light was fading as we reached the start of the traverse and we crossed it rather high and got bluffed – and had to retrace our steps and cross lower down. On the cliffs above us we could see chamois outlined against the evening sky. It was almost dark as we hit the lower ridge and black as pitch in the forest. We fumbled our way down, guiding ourselves by the sound of the river. Then we caught the smell of smoke and homed onto the camp – it was seven p.m. and we'd been away twelve hours. Louise had a terrific stew ready for us and we ate until we could eat no more – then lay in front of the fire and talked about climbing and life and anything that entered our minds. You could say the day had been a failure – but it was the sort of day you always remember.

A year of routine life passed by – I experienced the hopes and disappointments of another honey crop; the birth of a second daughter; the hard grind of writing a book (which I have never found easy); and the satisfaction of making smooth lawns out of overgrown jungle. I enjoyed it all, too, but I couldn't suppress the restless urge to get involved in something more demanding – possibly another expedition or some responsible position in business or society – maybe even politics? 'Don't worry', I was frequently told, 'you'll get lots of directorships and good Government jobs. They're sure to make you an ambassador or something!' I discovered that the ability to get a tractor to the South Pole didn't count for much in business. Mostly I was approached by people who sold cigarettes or hair cream and thought my title would look good in one of their advertisements even though I didn't use their products. I was in considerable demand for luncheon talks and as guest of honour at country balls but can't remember any other great opportunities being thrust my way.

In the middle of 1959 I received a letter from the editor of *Argosy* magazine in the U.S.A. They had instituted an annual 'Explorer of the Year Award' and I had been chosen to receive it. Would my wife and I come to New York at their expense, give a talk at an award banquet, and receive an appropriate plaque plus a cheque for $1,000? In those days few organisations in New Zealand would even think of reimbursing you for your travelling expenses if you gave them a lecture – the honour of being asked was regarded as being sufficient reward in itself.

Our trip to New York was very successful and we certainly got a great deal of publicity. I even had a telephone call from Chicago asking me to do a programme for educational television. Would I be prepared to spend a couple of days in Chicago? All expenses would be paid and a useful honorarium as well?

Field Enterprises Educational Corporation proved to be a huge company which published World Book Encyclopedia – the world's biggest selling encyclopedia – and a variety of other educational publications. They were very hospitable and kind to us and I was rather impressed with the editor and some of the other executives. The filming was very expertly handled and altogether it proved a pleasant and happy occasion. One evening we were entertained to dinner by John Dienhart, the Public Relations Director, who was a confident, talkative type of person. We started discussing my future expedition plans. I was in a convivial mood and without any ulterior motive I told John about my dream expedition – an expedition that would be a happy blend of science and mountaineering. We would tackle the secrets of high altitude acclimatisation with more effective techniques and equipment than had been used before; we would search out the Abominable Snowman and find out if he was a myth or a monster – or perhaps something in between; and we would climb and explore on some of the superb peaks in the Mount Everest region.

I really got quite carried away with this discourse and John Dienhart seemed to find it rather fascinating. Perhaps his Company could help with the expedition, he told me, it would be very good internal public relations and they'd be making history and not just recording it. He was so enthusiastic in fact that I became a little cautious – I find things that start with a rush can often fizzle out just as quickly. John saw us off at the airport and made me promise to send him a detailed report about the project.

When we got back to New Zealand John Dienhart and Field Enterprises seemed to fade into the past as though I had just dreamed about them – until I received a telephone call from Chicago asking what had happened to my report. I wrote down my ideas in some detail and posted them off. A week later I received a cable, '. . . can you come Chicago soonest our expense discuss expedition . . .' I flew to Chicago and presented my plans to the hard-headed Board of Field Enterprises and was closely questioned by the President, Mr. Bailey K. Howard. To my delight the Company agreed to contribute $125,000 to the programme.

This was by far the most complex expedition I had organised – we had many objectives, and people from many countries were involved – New Zealand, the United States, Great Britain, India, Nepal, Australia. We gathered in Kathmandu at the beginning of September 1960 with eighteen tons of supplies and plans to spend ten months on the job. We reorganised our loads and split everything into two groups – the Yeti party would start its search in the Rolwaling Valley near the Tibetan border while the main body of supplies would travel into the Everest region where the physiological programme was to be undertaken.

I had always been a little sceptical about the existence of the Yeti – the Abominable Snowman. It seemed inconceivable to me that such a large creature could live in open mountain country without being sighted by the keen-eyed Sherpas. Several expeditions had gone looking for the Yeti but hadn't been able to find it although they still expressed a firm belief in the existence of the creature. There was a scalp in the Khumjung Monastery and a bony hand at Thyangboche. What about the Yetis that had actually been seen by the monks at Thyangboche – gambolling in the winter snow in front of the monastery? And the many tracks that had been described and photographed? The best example was the track Shipton had seen on the Menlung glacier just over the border from the Rolwaling valley. I had to admit this photograph was a beauty – the footprint was fresh and clear although the other ones round about were much more blurred and indistinct.

Knowing what a cynic Shipton could be I had the feeling he might have tidied up that track a little, just for a laugh . . . !

My own experience was limited to inconclusive incidents. In 1951 a tough and experienced Sherpa, Sen Tensing, had related to me with great conviction how he had seen a Yeti and watched it for some time. The following year George Lowe and I found a tuft of black hair at 19,000 feet on a difficult pass and our Sherpas assured us this was Yeti hair – and threw it away in obvious fear. On the Barun Pass in 1954 some of our porters had cowered in fear inside their tents while they listened to a Yeti walking around their camp (and the next day in the same area I had a close view of a magnificent snow leopard moving easily through the snow). George Lowe and I had even been mistaken for Yetis when we descended a high valley from an unexpected direction – and two shepherds had fled in terror.

It would be interesting I thought, to examine all this evidence methodically and see what came out of it. We set off from Kathmandu in the tail end of the monsoon and walked for a hundred miles through rain and leeches to the Sherpa village of Beding in the precipitous Rolwaling Valley. We had two animal experts with the expedition – Marlin Perkins, Director of the Lincoln Park Zoo in Chicago, and widely known for his television programme 'Wild Kingdom'; and biologist Dr. Larry Swan who was an experienced Himalayan traveller. Their task would be to weigh and assess the evidence as it became available.

For eight days after our arrival in Beding we were immobilised by torrential rain and snow but made profitable use of the time to interrogate the villagers and the monks in the local monastery. Our Press correspondent, Desmond Doig, proved an unexpected asset. Artist, author, romanticist, he had a fluent grasp of the Nepali language and a remarkable ability to gain the confidence and liking of the local people. Like Sherlock Holmes he scoured the village for information and every day there was a new story and a new trail to follow. We didn't find any Sherpas who had seen a Yeti but several who had heard them – usually when the winter snowfalls lay deep on the ground and the villagers were confined to their houses. Then, it seemed, the sound of the Yeti was frequently heard during the night and tracks were seen by the frightened Sherpas next morning.

One day we received the news that there was a Yeti skin in the village – the prized possession of a monk and his wife. The monk was away and at first we met with determined refusal to even show us the skin. Only after much persuasion and some sordid chinking of rupees did the skin become ours. It was a fine specimen of the rare Tibetan blue bear – or so we thought, although all our Sherpas immediately identified it as Yeti and nothing we said could sway this belief.

We were interested to find that many of the local descriptions of the Yeti tracks indicated that the big toe was at right angles to the foot or sometimes even appeared out of the heel. This seemed hard to explain until we photographed a Nepalese porter with just such a deformity.

When the weather cleared in early October we moved up the Rolwaling Valley and commenced our search for signs of the Yeti. Several weeks later our efforts were rewarded by the discovery of many tracks on the Ripimu Glacier between 18,000 and 19,000 feet. These tracks were unhesitatingly identified by our Sherpas as having been made by a Yeti and they certainly seemed to fit some of the specifications. The best ones were large and broad with toe marks clearly defined. We followed a number of these tracks for considerable distances and saw nothing of the animals that were making them – but we did learn something about the tracks themselves. In the places where the footprints were continually in the shade of rocks or on a north facing slope the giant tracks would disappear and be replaced by the small footprints of a fox or wild dog grouped together as the animal bounded over the snow. We saw much evidence of the effects of sun on these small tracks, melting them out, running them together and making as fine a Yeti track as one would wish.

Early in November we crossed the formidable 19,000 foot Tashi Lapcha Pass into the Khumbu area at the foot of Mount Everest and carried on our investigations there. In the villages of Namche Bazar and Khumjung we obtained two more Yeti skins which also seemed to be those of blue bears. We carried out a thorough enquiry amongst the Khumbu villagers and monasteries and it became apparent that although most of the Sherpas accepted the existence of the Yeti it was almost impossible to find anyone who under careful questioning would claim to have seen one. Even in the Thyangboche Monastery – traditionally the source of much Yeti lore and Yeti sightings – we were unable to find anyone who had seen a Yeti. In fact the two oldest monks who had lived in the monastery since its foundation some forty years before both said they had not seen a Yeti and knew of no case in which a monk in the monastery had.

The Head Lama of Thyangboche was an old friend of mine. He showed us dramatic paintings of the Yeti with fearsome teeth, sharp claws, and pointed scalp. 'I have not seen one, myself,' he told me 'but we know they exist. You will never be able to see one as Yetis do not like the smell of foreigners and if you approach they will make themselves invisible.'

I questioned Sen Tenzing again in the conviviality of his own home. He still clung firmly to the story he had given us in 1951 but I was able

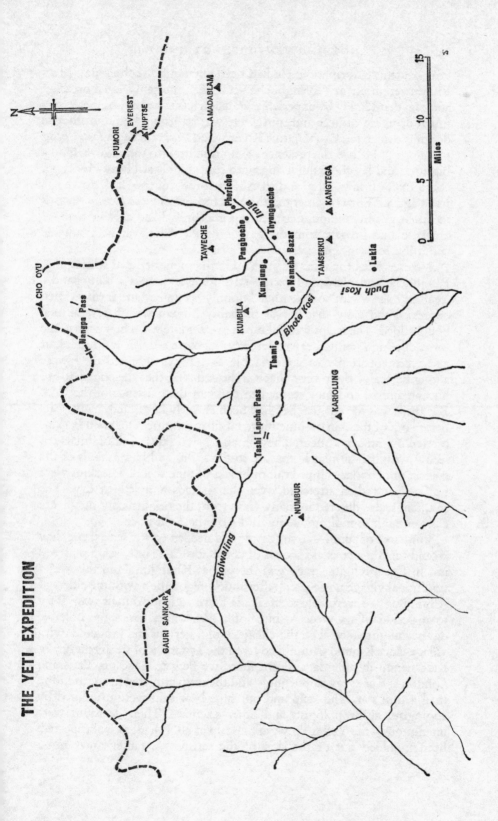

THE YETI EXPEDITION

to get further information. He had been attending the three-day Mani Rimdu ceremony at Thyangboche – a most important annual occasion and one that I knew by experience ended in a carnival atmosphere with much drinking of beer and spirits. He was returning home to Phortse down the steep track to the Imja River when he saw a Yeti approaching up the path. He had the presence of mind to drop to the snow behind a big rock and lay there quivering with fear as he heard heavy footsteps come towards him, stop, and then after some time go back down the track again. When he emerged the Yeti footprints were clearly defined in the bright moonlight. Sen Tensing is a shrewd and capable man – I am sure that he saw something, but doubt if he was in a suitable condition to judge precisely what it was . . .

We examined the relics of the Yeti in the monasteries at Khumjung, Pangboche and Namche Bazar. At Pangboche there is a bony hand – long and slim with some rather knobbly sections. Our medical men expressed the view that it was probably human with a few animal bones added. The scalps were of much greater interest. They were in the form of a high pointed cap covered with coarse reddish and black hair and were apparently of considerable age. If we accepted they were authentic scalps their very shape indicated that they belonged to no known animal and they seemed to confirm the existence of the Yeti. But there was the chance they had been cleverly fabricated many years before out of the skin of some more familiar creature. Doig and Perkins carried out an experiment. They obtained two skins of the Himalayan serow with hair similar in texture to the scalps and had moulds of the correct dimensions chipped out of blocks of pine wood. The skins were softened and then stretched over the moulds and left to dry. The resultant scalps differed in many ways from the originals but they were close enough to indicate we might be on the right track.

Some sort of authoritative answer was needed on the scalps, else they would remain a constant source of conjecture. The only scalp that was not in fact a religious relic was the one at Khumjung and this was a traditional village possession. After much negotiation with the elders of Khumjung we were able to persuade them to lend us their scalp for a total period of six weeks – but not a day longer else some horrible disaster might descend on the village. Doig, Perkins and I together with village elder Khunjo Chumbi covered the 170 miles of steep country to Kathmandu in nine days. From there we flew to Chicago, Paris and London and at every stop Khunjo and the scalp attracted more attention than a film star. The scalp and our blue bear skin were examined by zoologists, anthropologists and other scientists. Their decisions were unanimous – the Yeti scalp wasn't a scalp at all. It had, as we suspected, been moulded out of the skin of the serow – a rather uncommon

Base Camp on floating ice with Mount Herschel in the background.

Junbesi school.

Sherpa children in
Khumjung school.

Distilling *rakshi* on the banks of the Sun Kosi river.

Tawas blow trumpets during Mani Rimdu at Thami *Gompa.*

Stamping out Lukla airfield.

Chaunrikarka school.

Mani Rimdu ceremony at Thyangboche.

Last big rapid on Sun Kosi before Kathmandu road.

Camping on Great Barrier Island, New Zealand.

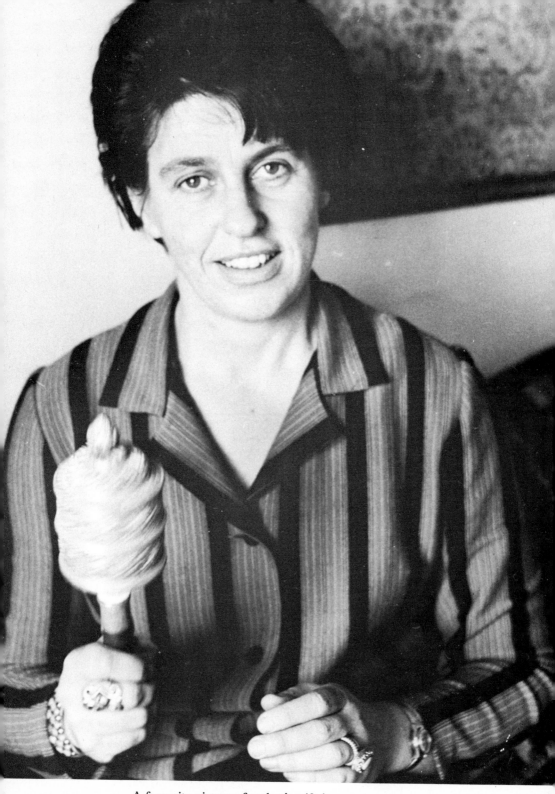

A favourite picture of author's wife in recent years.

Sir Edmund Hillary receiving an Honorary Doctorate of Laws in Victoria B.C., Canada.

member of the antelope family. Our Yeti skins were confirmed as Tibetan blue bear.

There was still much remaining to be explained. Our theory on the tracks could not cover many other types of footprints which have been seen in mud as well as snow. We were not able to give a satisfactory answer to the noise of the Yeti which many Sherpas claim to have heard. But the evidence we uncovered had a normal and mundane explanation.

People go on looking for the Yeti for the creature has a fascination that is not lightly abandoned. Stories still come in of footprints, of encounters, of disasters from the length and breadth of the Himalayan chain. There seems good reason to believe that the blue bear is to blame for many of the Yeti sightings – and someday perhaps one will be photographed in the deep forests of Bhutan or on a high Himalayan pass. But people will still not be satisfied – they want to believe in a strange, completely unknown creature and will not be happy until they can observe it in all its horror from the comfort of their television chairs. Despite our investigations the Yeti remains part of the tradition and mythology of the Sherpa people although most of the young Sherpas now just laugh when you question them. I am inclined to think that the realm of mythology is where the Yeti rightly belongs.

The search for the Yeti had been an interesting and entertaining part of our expedition but it was not our major undertaking. The thread which tied the whole expedition together was physiological research. I had always been interested in the problems of altitude and the reasons why some people seemed to operate much better than others. Everyone gets affected to some extent when first going above ten thousand feet but after a period of acclimatisation most of us make some adjustment and it becomes possible to live and perform in reasonable comfort. What are the specific reasons for this adjustment? Could it be improved by long periods of living at considerable heights? What was the maximum height at which people could live for long periods?

These were questions I had puzzled over in my own mind. Dr. Griffiths Pugh the physiologist of our '53 Everest expedition examined the same questions from the viewpoint of a scientist and was just as eager to get an answer. Together we worked out a programme. It was impracticable to expect scientists to do satisfactory work while sitting in a small alpine tent at 20,000 feet so we decided an insulated hut was essential. This would enable the research programme to be carried out independently of the bad weather during the Himalayan winter. It was my belief that a graded programme of acclimatisation could get our party so well adjusted to altitude that they would be able to tackle severe climbing at considerable heights. We intended to test our theories on Mount Makalu 27,790 feet. Makalu had already been climbed by a very competent French expedition but they had used lots of oxygen and we wanted to try it without. Men had been as high without oxygen on the north side of Everest but that was relatively easy terrain. Could we do it on Makalu? I thought we could, but Griff Pugh wasn't as optimistic, although he regarded it as a magnificent chance to experiment.

Our party was a large one with physiologists, builders, scientists and Sherpas – and they formed an energetic and experienced group. I had chosen the Mingbo Valley on the south side of Amadablam as the best location for our scientific bases. From my recollections of the place I thought it possible to establish an intermediate hut (the Green hut) at the terminal face of the glacier around 17,000 feet and the main scientific hut (the Silver hut) on the Amadablam Col at 19,600 feet. Norman Hardie whose feats included the ascent of Kangchenjunga – the third highest peak in the world – took a team with several hundred porters into the Khumbu and despite extremely heavy monsoon snows, started getting a route established up the Mingbo and organised the carrying of loads to 19,000 feet.

I had my first trip to see what he had done on November 3rd. We had been staying in the village of Chanmitang and we crossed the river at Pangboche and climbed the hill into the entrance to the Mingbo Valley. We walked up to Base Camp and then continued over deceptively steep surfaces before striking rough moraine and bare ice. The Green hut was at 17,500 feet and I was enormously impressed with the work the men had already done. The hut was snug and warm and seemed capable of withstanding the coldest temperatures and the strongest winds.

The next morning we set off up the glacier, following Hardie's route along ice cliffs and gulleys and around crevasses. We trudged over the snowfield at the top of the glacier to the foot of the steep face running up to the Col and admired the large pile of hut sections that had already been carried there. We roped up and climbed the steep fluted slopes and emerged on the Col, 19,600 feet, into a terrific wind. It was bitterly cold and we had a tough job pitching our tents. Hardie and I examined possible hut sites but weren't impressed with what we saw and feared the Col might be cut off by dangerous winter snows. It was now blowing like fury and we were happy to retreat into our flapping tents. Four of us spent a poor night on the Col and were very glad when morning came.

We decided to abandon this camp so left early, cramponing steeply down the fluted ice. After a careful search we decided on a pleasant location for the Silver hut on a small snow field with excellent access to the Green hut and protected from avalanche danger by a large open crevasse. Its altitude of 19,100 feet was rather lower than we had hoped but still high enough for our purpose. We spent the next day making a substantial snow platform, assembling the foundation beams, and carrying all the hut sections into position.

On November 7th we left the Green hut early and trudged back up the glacier. We expected a busy day as the Silver hut must be completed before nightfall. We started immediately on the job of assembling the hut sections. With remarkable smoothness and efficiency the shell grew rapidly into a giant drainpipe. We made firm use of the sledge-hammer to join the sections together tightly and were delighted how much more professional we had become since our trial assembly at the manufacturer's in England. The end walls were fitted into place and by evening the whole shell was completed and safely tied down. We returned to the Green hut with a glow of pride – it had been an important day for the expedition.

I descended into the valley and discovered a storm was brewing. I had known Griff Pugh for ten years and had enjoyed his company and his conversation. I looked on him as being pleasantly eccentric but regarded this as an asset rather than a disadvantage. On some topics he had very strong opinions and far from scientific detachment. I had been present on separate occasions when both Eric Shipton and John Hunt had experienced a Pugh tongue lashing.

I was not excluded from this experience. Griff approached me, opened his notebook, and reeled off a long and detailed list of my various weaknesses and inadequacies. My incompetence as a leader was beyond belief but what could you expect from someone without a suitable background of culture and education? Griff had put plenty of thought into his presentation and it was a frightening declaration – like God summing up on Judgment Day.

This was a most devastating criticism and I had been largely unaware of my transgressions. When I examined the matter conscientiously I realised that Griff had some basis for his dissatisfaction. He had been closely involved in the designing of the Silver hut but because he hadn't been up the glacier with us I had not thought to consult him on its final location or its erection. I determined to give more consideration to his wishes and feelings as long as they didn't conflict too much with the need to get the job done quickly.

Several of us returned to the outside world in early January to organise a second lift of supplies in the spring. The physiological programme continued efficiently and well under Griff Pugh's direction and much profitable research was carried out in the Silver hut.

At this time large numbers of refugees were crossing the border from Tibet in order to escape from Chinese troops. Many of the refugees were in rather pitiful condition and the International Red Cross was anxious to help them with food. The Red Cross had a Pilatus Porter aircraft with an outstanding high altitude performance and the ability to operate off very small airstrips – but there was nowhere in the Khumbu for it to land. Could I recommend a suitable area? I remembered the long slopes in the little valley above Mingbo and we agreed to co-operate on building a strip there.

The wintering group put a team of men on to levelling the site at 15,000 feet – chopping off the frozen clumps of snow grass, filling in the worst of the holes, and rolling away the large boulders. Snow sometimes restricted their activity but it rarely lay for long once the sun was shining again. When the strip had been cleared to 400 yards the first landing was made – and the aircraft damaged its tail wheel on a rock and had an unscheduled stay of some days while being made airworthy again. Work on the strip continued for some months and we finally enlarged it to 500 yards and generally improved it.

At the take-off end were two huge boulders weighing many tons and standing six feet above the ground. We had no explosives and the boulders were singularly unresponsive to the blows of our sledgehammer. The problem was finally solved in a highly ingenious fashion by our Sherpas. They dug enormous craters beside each boulder and then used long heavy poles as levers to tip the boulders out of the way into them. Altogether we paid Rs.7,000 Indian currency ($900) for the labour used on building this strip which possibly made it one of the cheapest as well as one of the highest airfields in the world. Due to the skill and experience of Captain Schrieber, the Red Cross pilot, large quantities of refugee food was transported safely in to the Mingbo and we were helped considerably with the rapid freighting of personnel, scientific equipment and a school building.

I returned to Nepal in February 1961 with large quantities of supplies for the restocking of the Mingbo Valley and the mounting of the assault on Mount Makalu. With me was a temporary addition to the team – my wife Louise – and several other wives accompanied their husbands too. Our journey into Thyangboche was a source of great pleasure to me. It was Louise's first visit to the Himalayas and I saw this familiar route afresh through her delighted eyes. More than anything it was the flowers that made our days so wonderful. The crimson rhododendrons were in full bloom and our path would often cling to a hillside which was a blaze of colour in every direction. As we climbed up to each pass the air would be heavy with the scent of daphne and the grass was hidden by a thick carpet of primulas. The magnolias were just coming into bloom; and in many shady spots were clusters of graceful orchids.

At a camp beside the Dudh Kosi River I received a message that team members Mike Ward, Mike Gill, Barry Bishop and Wally Romanes had reached the summit of Amadablam. From the climber's viewpoint this was wonderful news – a triumph for the expediton. Amadablam had seemed impossibly steep and difficult. But at the back of my mind was a nagging worry. The Nepalese Government had recently instituted a system of permits and peak fees for mountains – something quite new to the Himalayas – and we certainly didn't have permission for Amadablam. I had agreed that expedition members should carry out acclimatisation trips on the slopes of Amadablam and other peaks – this was well within the bounds of our expedition permission – but not for a moment had I thought it likely they would actually reach the summit.

On March 22nd Griff Pugh flew into the Mingbo airstrip from Kathmandu with disturbing news. The Nepalese Government was getting very difficult about Amadablam – they required an official explanation. A moment's reflection and I realised I would have to return to Kathmandu and clear the matter up. I snatched my satchel of papers and joined the expedition wives on the plane.

We were loaded to the maximum. Captain Schrieber started up the motor and revved it fiercely but we were held firm by two large rocks under the wheels for the brakes were insufficient on this steep slope. Now that the engine was warm the large rocks were removed and we rolled forward onto two smaller ones. The motor was given full throttle and the plane shuddered with power as the wheels inched over the small rocks and then rolled suddenly down the other side. With the motor blaring like a demon we surged into our take-off run.

To my startled eyes the short strip ahead of us seemed quite inadequate for our needs and the hill at the end loomed up with frightening rapidity. At the last moment Captain Schrieber pulled back on the stick and we lifted sluggishly off the ground. Next moment he had tipped us onto one wing to dodge the hill and we were slipping through the gully to the left, to be precipitated out into free air as the river valley dropped sharply away beneath us. With a sigh of relief I unclenched my hands as we soared high over Thyangboche and set course for Kathmandu.

The news in Kathmandu couldn't have been worse – the Government was instructing us to withdraw immediately. We were to be punished as an example to others. For nine days I trudged around Government buildings seeing officials and ministers and trying desperately to change the decision. If it had served any useful purpose I was ready to crawl through the Government offices on my hands and knees. It was an enormous relief when the Government finally relented and allowed us to continue after payment of a modest fine – but I had spent the worst nine days I can remember and I was emotionally exhausted.

By the time I returned to the Mingbo on April 5th we had lost two weeks of valuable time and to have any chance of climbing Makalu we would have to apply all the pressure we could. This wasn't going to be easy as our approach to Makalu was a technically demanding one. All previous expeditions to this mountain had brought their main supplies along the Arun River and then into the Barun Valley on the west side of Makalu – the route pioneered by Shipton, Lowe and myself in 1952. But I planned to use a high level approach. By going from the Mingbo over the 19,600 foot Amadablam Col, then across the Hongu Glacier, over 20,000 feet passes on either side of the high Barun Plateau and finally down to the Barun Glacier we could cover the distance in three or four days. It was a formidable route over which to take 200 loads of sixty lbs each but certainly a feasible one – although I was a little worried about the consequences of a heavy fall of snow on the steep passes.

For ten days we concentrated on getting all the loads into the Hongu and then up the very steep face of the West Col at 20,000 feet. Our Sherpas and the expedition members worked magnificently under difficult conditions. At times I had forty-seven Sherpas carrying loads on one sector or another and by April 16th we had 133 loads on the West Col.

The next day we started the second phase of our plan. With a large group of climbers and Sherpas we left our base on the Hongu Glacier, climbed the fixed ropes to the West Col, trudged slowly across the broad Barun Plateau to the East Col and then descended abruptly down a tributary valley towards the main Barun Glacier. It was a tremendously hard day with heavy loads and by five p.m. we were still 500 feet above the glacier and looking desperately for a camp site. An hour later I was down on the glacier and still hadn't found anything suitable. I was feeling terribly tired and knew the Sherpas were tired too – I decided we'd just have to camp on the uneven moraine and look for a better place in the morning. Then our luck changed. As the Sherpas came slowly down to join me they stumbled over a pleasant hollow containing a small stream of fresh water – and Camp I was established.

We commenced relaying loads from the West Col down to Camp I. I had promised myself a few days of rest to recover from my efforts in Kathmandu and on the high route but problems had arisen in the

Mingbo that needed urgent attention. With Peter Mulgrew for company I did a mad rush back to the Green hut and then returned to Camp I with some more loads. I seemed to be travelling as well as anyone – but felt very tired on the completion of this trip. On April 25th we brought the last loads down from the West Col and Camp I was fully stocked. It was time to issue high altitude equipment to our Sherpas and ourselves.

All our attention was now devoted to establishing and stocking the camps on the flanks of Makalu. By May 1st Camp III at 21,000 feet was in full use and the route had been pushed through to nearly 23,000 feet using the steep couloir we had pioneered in 1954.

Wally Romanes and I set off to complete the route to Camp IV. We made good time across the terrace and worked hard on the couloir cutting steps and putting in fixed ropes to complete the work done by a previous day's team. The sense of exposure in the couloir was quite terrific as it drained out over a thousand foot precipice. In thick fog and driving snow we came to the top of the couloir and although I was feeling rather tired we pushed on to find a suitable place for the camp. After a steepish traverse we dropped over a little ridge onto a flat piece of snow which seemed an ideal location. The altitude was somewhere around 23,000 feet. We returned in thick visibility and heavy snowfall and there was three inches of new snow around Camp III. The wind battered our tents and it was just like the Antarctic with drifting snow and high sastrugi. I was awake most of that wild night with a miserable headache which seemed reluctant to go away.

Despite the weather, Camp IV was established next morning and over the next two days many loads of supplies were carried up. On May 5th we watched with great excitement as Mike Gill and Mike Ward forced their way onto the Makalu Col at 24,300 feet. We had made great progress on the mountain despite the initial delays and we would soon be tackling the final few thousand feet – we had good grounds for optimism.

The pains on the left side of my forehead and face wouldn't go away so I decided I'd better go down to Camp II for a breather at lower altitudes. Mike Ward and Mike Gill deserved a rest too as they'd been working very hard. We had an easy trip down and I had a reasonable night's sleep although I didn't feel particularly comfortable in the morning. During the day Jim Milledge and John West staggered down in a heavy snowstorm with Aila who was suffering from pulmonary oedema and had to be put on emergency oxygen.

I felt rather poorly all afternoon. In the evening I had a frightful pain on the side of my head and face. When a Sherpa came to give me my evening meal, I couldn't get him to understand that I didn't want it. I was sort of helpless, divorced from my limbs, and although I seemed perfectly rational I discovered that when I tried to say something it just came out as gibberish – which was most unpleasant. The pain was pretty grim and I managed to shout for Mike Ward who finally came. He and Jim Milledge did a stout job on me. They put me on oxygen for the whole night and gave me a shot of pethadine but it wasn't a period I enjoyed too much. I went off to sleep in the latter stages of the night and when I woke I was human again – but rather fumbling in speech, shaking in hand and poor of balance – also seeing double.

Mike Ward called it a cerebral vascular accident and there was a certain amount of talk about altitude and thick blood. Mike gave me a rather brutal discourse on what might happen to me if I didn't get down lower – or even if I did get down. I had a terrible urge to see Louise again and also my mother; I suppose I wanted consolation of some sort.

I lay there for quite a while thinking about what it would be like to end up a cripple or a cabbage – and decided I would never return home in that condition. I'd rather be dead, and I was completely determined about this. I was pretty sure it had all been the result of my frantic efforts to catch up on everything after the Amadablam business. Makalu certainly had always been bad luck for me.

I got a lot stronger during the morning and as the doctors were anxious for me to be carried down to lower altitudes I decided I could walk if I had a couple of Sherpas to help me. I didn't in fact need any help although my balance was still a bit affected and my face and eyes were sore and bruised. The same day twenty-one loads were carried up to the Makalu Col in a highly successful effort so everything was now ready for the top camp – I felt rather depressed that I was staggering down the mountain in the other direction.

Over the radio there was a lot of talk about my condition and some pessimistic forecasts by Griff who insisted I should be helicoptered immediately to Kathmandu. I had no intention of returning to Kathmandu but agreed to do the long walk around to Mingbo via the Arun River so as to keep at altitudes below 15,000 feet. Dr. Jim Milledge very generously agreed to abandon his chances on the mountain and come around with me. I recast my assault plans and handed them over for Mike Ward to use, and consoled myself with the thought that my work on the mountain was largely done anyhow – the camps were established up to the Col with plenty of supplies and we had excellent Sherpas and a good bunch of climbers. What could go wrong?

In actual fact quite a lot went wrong and I think my presence would have been quite useful at times. However quite a lot went right too. An excellent physiological camp was established on the Makalu Col and all sorts of useful experiments were undertaken at this very considerable altitude (24,300 feet). On May 13th Gill, Romanes and Ortenburger established Camp VI at 25,800 feet. The following day was a very bad one with strong winds but they pushed on with great difficulty and struggled up to 26,300 feet. Carrying loads and working hard in bad weather without any oxygen was an exhausting procedure. Rather than establish a camp they just made a depot of the supplies and then turned downwards. It was a pretty grim struggle back to Camp VI in the heavy wind and Gill and Romanes had a fall which could have been disastrous. The weather was still rather appalling next morning so they battled their way back to the Col. This was May 15th – the day I had hoped this party might be on the summit.

After a lot of discussion the attack continued with Nevison and Mulgrew as the next assault team and Harrison and Ortenburger standing by for a third assault. Nevison and Mulgrew with six Sherpas climbed to Camp VI in improving conditions and spent the night there. When they started next morning the Sherpas carried the loads and broke trail to save the strength of the two climbers. The Sherpas were tied together on one rope and had almost reached the Depot when one of them slipped and pulled the others off – and away they went in a devastating slide. By sheer chance two of them broke through a bridge into a crevasse and this pulled the whole team up with a jerk – otherwise they would all have fallen to their deaths. Two of the Sherpas had been rather battered but felt they could get back to Camp VI by themselves. The two climbers and the remaining four Sherpas continued to the Depot, shared out the loads and carried on upwards, going very slowly. At 27,000 feet they established Camp VII on the edge of a crevasse and Nevison, Mulgrew and Annullu stayed there while the others descended.

They had quite a restful night's sleep in this spectacular position. When they started in the morning they were moving very slowly indeed and after four hours were only 400 feet above the tents – but this meant only 400 feet from the top. They continued on again, determined to reach the summit when suddenly Mulgrew's strength ran out. He doubled up and collapsed on the snow – it was discovered later he had a pulmonary oedema in his right lung which probably should have killed him at this altitude. Somehow Nevison and Annullu got him down to Camp VII and by then Annullu was very weak too as he'd broken a rib in the Sherpa fall.

Mulgrew's second night at 27,000 feet was a bad one and he coughed up quite a lot of blood. Yet in the morning he was able to move slowly downwards with Annullu and Nevison belaying him. He only got to 26,300 feet before blacking out and here Nevison decided they would have to stay. He sent Annullu down to Camp VI for help. Late in the afternoon Pemba Tenzing and Passang Tenzing arrived with a tent and food, and the rescue operation slowly got under way.

How Mulgrew managed to survive the trip down the mountain is hard to know. It was a nightmarish operation with desperate efforts by many men spearheaded by Leigh Ortenburger and John Harrison. Urkein and his Sherpas were absolutely magnificent. Somehow Peter reached Camp I more dead than alive and was helicoptered back to Kathmandu. During the descent he had suffered severe frostbite to his feet and fingers. But his spirit kept him alive and he emerged from hospital many months later almost as good as new but minus his feet which had been amputated. Peter's efforts since then have become quite a legend in his own country. He has succeeded resoundingly in business and despite his two artificial legs he has become a leading skipper of ocean racing yachts.

The expedition failed to climb Makalu without oxygen – but only just. That the summit can be reached there is no doubt – even the summit of Everest is not beyond the capacity of an unassisted man – but the risks are enormous. At times I find myself planning Everest assaults without oxygen – the support party putting in all the camps, establishing the route, doing all the hard work, the summitters getting fit at more enjoyable altitudes then moving up Everest with a rush, minimising deterioration and saving strength for the final thrust. It could work and I have no doubt that some day it will be tried.

For me this was perhaps the most difficult expedition I had organised and in many ways I was dissatisfied with my own efforts. But there had been a host of enjoyable and exciting activities. We'd had problems of temperament and problems with Government; altitude had taken its toll and some of us would never be quite the same again; there had been a multitude of challenges and difficulties some of which we had tackled more successfully than others – but we had some solid results to show for our efforts and many great moments that I am not likely to forget.

It took Jim Milledge and me fifteen days of vigorous walking to reach Mingbo again and by that time I was as fit and normal as I ever am. When the party returned off Makalu we saw them safely on the way to Kathmandu and then concentrated on dismantling the Silver hut and bringing all the equipment down from the Mingbo. Wally Romanes, Desmond Doig and Bhanu Banerjee stayed behind with me and together we tackled our last project – a school for Khumjung.

Eight months before on the Tolam Bau Glacier the idea had first seen the light. We'd been talking about the future of the Sherpas and what help we could give them. It was Urkein Sherpa who first suggested that the greatest need in Khumjung was a school – and it seemed an ideal way for me to repay the Sherpas for the help and pleasure they had given me. Mr. Bailey K. Howard and World Book Encyclopedia generously responded to the request for money; the Indian Aluminium Company donated a building; and the Red Cross flew it into Mingbo. We had recruited an experienced teacher in Darjeeling and he was already on the job. In misty monsoon conditions we assembled the aluminium building ready for occupation.

The opening ceremony was a remarkable occasion. Surrounded by clouds and fog, with frequent showers of rain, the villagers celebrated this important function with great enthusiasm. The Head Lama of Thyangboche and his musical entourage carried out the official blessing and I was invited to cut the ribbons and open the door. The forty pupils had grubby hands and smelly clothes – but their rosy cheeks and sparkling eyes were irresistible. It was a happy and satisfying occasion. When I left Khumjung on June 13th I little realised I was leaving behind what was to become a new way of life for me.

Chapter 16

You are very lucky!

I HAD AGREED TO LECTURE FOR A YEAR IN NORTH AMERICA IN RETURN for the massive support I had received from World Book on the expedition. A couple of days after Christmas 1961 the family and I packed our bags, let our home, and flew to Honolulu en route to the U.S.A. We moved into a house in a pleasant suburb of Chicago and Louise was warmly welcomed into the local community. With the regularity of a businessman going to his office I departed by jet plane each Monday morning to a series of cities in the U.S.A. and Canada. After a luncheon engagement on Saturday I'd fly back to Chicago again. During the year I did 106 banquet lectures in eighty different cities and innumerable other talks plus television, radio and press interviews. It was an exhausting procedure – but an interesting one in many ways.

Although I had become friendly with senior executives of the Company I had little idea of their business activities except that they published and sold a very successful encyclopedia. During the year I learned a great deal more about the Company and their unique use of part-time sales people to demonstrate books in their own communities. In the many meetings I attended the managers worked hard to create an emotional and excited atmosphere. Considerable emphasis was placed on the quality of their products; on the service that was being rendered to parents and children; and on the importance of honesty and an ethical approach to selling. Strangely enough there was very little mention of money which must have been a major factor in attracting people to do this work. Judging by the enthusiastic response the philosophy was being accepted with an almost religious fervour. Someone calculated that I shook hands with 17,000 of the 'World Bookers' as they called themselves – mostly teachers or housewives – and although I started off feeling rather cynical about the business I ended up being very impressed with the calibre and devotion of the people concerned, and in the quality of the products they were selling.

For the first time I was meeting some of the ordinary people of America and I found it easy to like their warmth, generosity and interest. In these groups I sensed an almost desperate need for social recognition and financial independence. They felt that World Book was giving them the chance to break out of the routine, to meet and be accepted by a cheerful group of like-minded people, and to make extra money and yet feel that they were giving a much needed service. In the process many of them were prepared to sink their individuality in a common philosophy – a Company philosophy – and this produced widespread feelings of belonging and in many cases instant economic success.

Soon after our arrival in Chicago I was invited by the colossal American operation, Sears Roebuck and Company, to join their Sports Advisory Staff as an expert on camping equipment. Sears were making a vigorous attempt to improve the quality and status of their sporting gear and for this purpose they had recruited a famous baseball player, Ted Williams, who was also a fishing and hunting enthusiast. Various other experts were added in a wide diversity of sporting activities – skiing, athletics, football, swimming, tennis and so on – and they formed a redoubtable group, dripping with Olympic gold medals and famous names.

Endorsement by a renowned sporting figure isn't always much of a recommendation – sporting heroes can become depressingly human when money and principles are involved. However I learned that the members of the Sears Sports Advisory Committee were actually meant to work on the design and testing of their equipment so I agreed to become part of the team. It has been a happy and successful arrangement for me and over the years I've been involved in the production of some pretty good tents – and tested them, too, on all sorts of expeditions and in many parts of the world.

In June 1962 we took a summer vacation – and I certainly needed a holiday by that time. From Chicago we drove across America, up to Alaska, and then back across Canada. Behind our large Ford station-wagon we towed a small 'camper trailer' – an ingenious device that opened into a large and comfortable tent. The children were now three, six and seven years old and this became our first major family adventure. We camped in the beautiful mountains and forests of Colorado; raced at eighty miles per hour across the wide deserts of Nevada and looked open-eyed but unenviously at the throbbing gambling towns. Lake Tahoe was very beautiful and so were the other lakes in the Sierras but often we had to admire them from a distance as their shorelines were usually the private preserve of the rich. San

Francisco was a beautiful city, but we were not interested in cities and drove happily north to mighty redwood forests and great volcanic cones.

I had been commissioned by the U.S. Secretary of Agriculture to produce a report on the camping grounds of the National Forest Parks. They had asked an experienced Antarctic traveller, Mat Brennan, to look after us and make sure the camp grounds gave us full co-operation. We enjoyed the company of Mat and his family but I think they found our camping and travelling habits something of a strain. Following the routine of our Himalayan trekking we were up at daylight, loaded the sleeping children into the back of the station wagon, packed up camp, drove past the sleeping Brennan tent, and dashed on for three or so hours through the cool of the morning. When the children complained of hunger we'd stop in some beautiful place for a leisurely and substantial breakfast. By mid-afternoon we had usually covered 300 or 400 miles to reach our destination and the children had plenty of time to play and explore while we set up camp. We were very impressed with the National Forest camp grounds which were roomy and peaceful – in marked contrast to the crammed conditions in the National Parks.

America must have been incredibly beautiful in the halcyon days before the white man arrived to tame and develop it. It is still beautiful despite the despoilation and the garbage. The new awareness of ecology and conservation may help it return to some of its former glory although the battle has hardly yet begun – too many powerful economic interests still equate progress with access roads, hamburger stands, and housing developments. Nature needs time for growing and sleeping, free from automobile fumes and massive tractors, away from the cacophony of snowmobiles and trail bikes. There are plenty of tamed wonders for all to goggle at through vehicle windows – we must also retain our wilderness areas where nature can develop in its own calm way and where only those humans who are prepared to walk and sweat a little qualify to go.

In Vancouver we loaded our vehicle on the *Princess Louise* and sailed north up the Inside Passage towards Alaska. We had glorious weather and revelled in the calm waters and the innumerable pine-clad rocky islands. In the Juneau area we watched glaciers carving icebergs into the sea and fished for trout on mountain lakes. In the fiords I caught a fourteen lb silver salmon on a rod and line heavy enough to land a swordfish, and helicoptered over rocky mountain summits and deep crevasses. On a high mountain pasture we buzzed a huge bear who reared upright and waved his mighty paws at us in anger.

At Haines we joined a Sears filming crew and drove together across

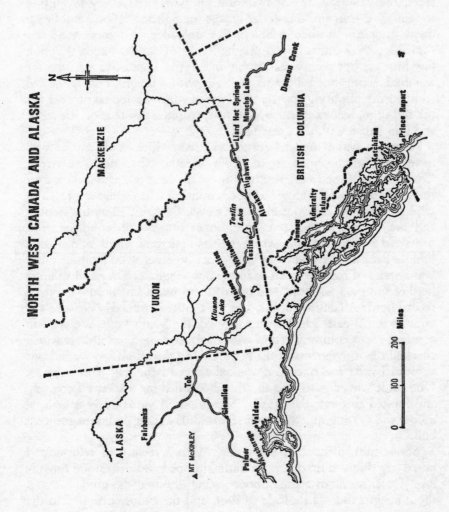

NORTH WEST CANADA AND ALASKA

N

MACKENZIE

BRITISH COLUMBIA

Dawson Creek

Liard Hot Springs
Muncho Lake
Liard River

Teslin Lake
Teslin
Alaskan Highway

YUKON

Kluane Lake
Haines Junction
Whitehorse

ALASKA

Fairbanks
Tok
Glennallen
MT McKINLEY
Palmer
Anchorage
Valdez

Juneau
Admiralty Island
Ketchikan
Prince Rupert

Miles
0   100   200

Alaska to Anchorage. They were a pleasant and agreeable group and we enjoyed their company as they filmed us around the camp fire and on the road. In Anchorage a train was chartered to carry our vehicles and ourselves inland to Fairbanks. I doubt if I will ever have another train trip quite like it. We rattled over the tundra through forests and lakes, marvellously free of man and his works. At every promising stream we'd stop and thrash the waters for fighting salmon and beach them on clean washed pebbles. We unloaded our cars at Mount McKinley Park and camped on the flanks of the mountain – seeing few humans but plenty of caribou and bears. There was no time for mountaineering but I did a plane flight with a famous bush pilot and climbed the mighty glaciers and ridges in super-heated comfort. I felt the old urge, half excitement, half fear, to pitch my tent on the snow and join battle with the great peak.

Fairbanks was a modern American town which could just as well have been on the outskirts of Chicago rather than near the Arctic Circle. It had little to interest us and we drove south again. As a treat the film team had organised a moose hunting trip – although truth to tell I get little pleasure out of hunting even though I enjoy the scenery and the company. In a two-seater Piper Super Cub equipped with oversized wheels we flew across the roadless tundra and landed on a shingle bank in the middle of a meandering river. The hunting camp was a series of battered tents – simple but adequate. They had found a herd of moose, I was told, and one of them was a fine head – maybe a record head? All day we drove over the tundra in tracked Weasels – the same as the Weasel I had driven towards the South Pole. We were in constant radio communication with our reconnaissance aircraft which checked the movements of the herd. Late in the afternoon we hid our vehicles beside the river and walked forward for half a mile or so. Our guide waved us to stop and then beckoned me forward. I crept up and looked through the brush. Two hundred yards away a herd of moose was grazing quietly – and in the middle of them was a magnificent bull.

'Shoot him,' instructed the guide. With a feeling of reluctance I raised my rifle and fired . . . the animal jumped and then stood quivering. 'Quickly, shoot again! Shoot again!' shouted the guide . . . and shoot again I did – a fusillade of shots and the moose dropped to the ground.

I knelt beside the animal holding up the noble head and the great spread of antlers so they could take my picture. It was forty-eight inches across I was told – very good indeed – but not quite a record. I felt no triumph – only shame and disgust with myself. What right had I to destroy such a beast? We had used aircraft and tracked vehicles to chase it down. What courage, strength or skill had I shown? I resolved never again to carry out such senseless and cold blooded slaughter in the name of sport.

We said goodbye to the film team and drove into the Yukon and down the gravel road of the Alcan Highway. We loved the feeling of wide open spaces and the beautiful lakes and mountains. Names like Dawson City, Klondike, Whitehorse reeked of adventure and romance. Banff National Park was superb. Our camp in the forest was visited by bears and I had to crawl reluctantly out of bed to drive away a cub that was pushing its nose into Peter's small tent. Beside Diamond Lake a fall of snow warned us that summer was over. We headed east across the Canadian prairies, covering vast distances each day. We were drunk with the joys of camping and travelling. We had established our simple routine, life was free and unpressured, and nature very beautiful. We could have gone on for ever – it was with immense reluctance that we drove down the expressway into Chicago and accepted that our dream was over. It was back to work – me to lecture and Louise to write a book on our adventures called *Keep Calm if you Can*.

Towards the end of 1962 I completed my lecture programme and we finalised our plans to return home. It had been a marvellous experience and we had made many new friends. We had even learned to love Chicago. But it was good to be going back to our peaceful and beautiful New Zealand.

There was much in America that was stimulating and exciting, yet so much that puzzled and distressed me. I disliked the constant appeal to my baser instincts, the pressure to do things and buy things and read things which would be of little real use to me. The great American machine was churning out so much wealth and useless luxuries – it seemed too materialistic, pleasure seeking, and aggressive – even the few churches I visited had facilities and philosophies that put little strain on body or conscience.

I admired the enormous vitality and the creativeness; the basic desire to do the right thing; the growing dislike of war and hypocrisy. I listened on TV to a famous French philosopher saying that America was producing the new revolution and that most other countries were on the sidelines. Perhaps he was right – most of us are happier to observe than to be involved. If it is really possible to produce a satisfactory and just society out of aggressive capitalism then America might do it – but maybe it is the capitalism that must change.

My visits to America remain exciting affairs. I feel I am in the front line, where the action is. And yet, as I slump in my aircraft seat at the start of the long flight back over the Pacific, tired with anticlimax, I wonder about all I have seen, and heard and done; and I feel a deep sadness for the future of America – and the world.

Field Enterprises decided to investigate the possibility of entering the Australian market and I was invited to assist in the initial survey. I visited Australia with the Executive Vice-President, Mr. Donald McKellar and talked to parents, educationalists, and Directors of education. We found a number of encyclopedias were already being sold in Australia but the questionable sales methods being used had created a bad public image and strong reactions from Government departments. It seemed an unpropitious time to commence a new operation but we felt our material and methods could overcome this reputation.

Field Enterprises established a subsidiary based on Sydney and I was appointed a Director. During the next ten years we achieved a dominant position on the Australian educational scene. I had little to do with the day-to-day operation but helped ensure that the company steered a sound and reputable course. Their material was of the highest quality and I was confident that most families could benefit greatly from it – as long as we insisted that the products were presented in an honest and fair manner by the right type of person.

Reports from Khumjung had indicated that the new school under headmaster Tem Dorje was proving a tremendous success. Petitions kept coming in from other villages asking for help with more schools and with water pipelines and bridges. Both Field Enterprises and Sears Roebuck showed sympathy for these projects so with their backing I returned to Nepal in March 1963. My expedition tackled these new problems with vigour and we completed schools at Thyangboche and Thami, and laid a mile-long pipe to bring fresh water to Khumjung. We had a strong climbing team from New Zealand and the U.S.A., and although we were forced to abandon the climb of Taweche when the assault party was only 200 feet from the top, we succeeded in getting a team to the summit of the mighty Kangtega (22,300 feet). A successful film 'High in the Himalayas' came out of the expedition and I also wrote a book *Schoolhouse in the Clouds*. Our work with the Sherpas became more widely known and I was not only able to obtain more finance from World Book but also the increasing support from companies, Service clubs, schools and private donors. I was back again in 1964 with a large and experienced party and a very ambitious programme – to establish an airfield; build three schools; construct a difficult suspension bridge; and attempt the formidable mountain Tamserku 21,730 feet.

To my admittedly prejudiced eye the mountains and valleys of the

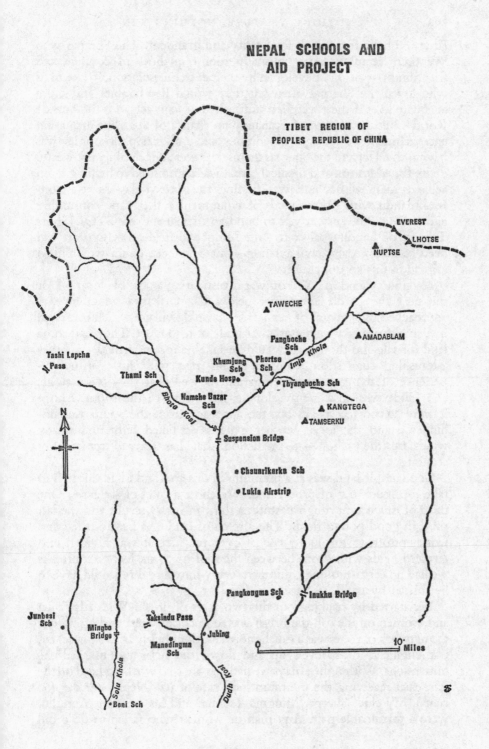

NEPAL SCHOOLS AND
AID PROJECT

TIBET REGION OF
PEOPLES REPUBLIC OF CHINA

EVEREST

LHOTSE

▲ NUPTSE

▲ TAWECHE

Pangboche
Sch

▲ AMADABLAM

Imja Khola

Tashi Lapcha
Pass

Khumjung
Sch

Phortse
Sch

Thami Sch

Kunde Hospe

• Thyangboche Sch

Namche Bazar
Sch

Bhote Kosi

▲ KANGTEGA

▲ TAMSERKU

N

Suspension Bridge

• Chaunrikarka Sch

• Lukla Airstrip

Pangkongma Sch

Inukhu Bridge

Junbesi
Sch

Mingbo
Bridge

Taksindu Pass

Jubing

Manedingma
Sch

0   10 Miles

Solu Khola

Dudh Kosi

• Beni Sch

Khumbu have few equals for beauty and grandeur. The Sherpas who live there seem to have unusually robust qualities of courage and friendliness – possibly developed by their extreme isolation. Those of us who loved the Sherpas often felt they would live happier and more adequate lives if they were left untouched by contact with the outside world – but there was unfortunately no chance of this. The increasing encroachment of foreign expeditions and political philosophies was having its effect and the Sherpas themselves were developing a powerful desire for education and medical care. I was committed to helping them achieve their wishes and was finding the sixteen day march from Kathmandu with porter loads of equipment rather time consuming and tedious. The answer was to build an airfield and use STOL (Short Takeoff or Landing) aircraft. Our Mingbo airfield at 15,500 feet had been condemned by civil aviation – but where else could we build an airfield in this abrupt country?

My good friend Jim Wilson was investigating a possible location for me near the Dudh Kosi river below Chaunrikarka when he was approached by a group of farmers from Lukla village which is located in a small tributary valley at an altitude of 9,500 feet. They had some land for sale and thought it would be suitable for an airfield – a rather astonishing suggestion from mountain men with little or no experience of flying. Our investigation showed that they were right; . . . Lukla was on a gently sloping fan facing to the south. Above it were 20,000 feet peaks but the approach from the south was unhindered and the local weather experts predicted light and steady winds up the valley – a prediction that has proved remarkably accurate.

Good arable land was at a premium in this area and I had no wish to take too much out of production. We chose a total of six acres. One third of this was in rough pasture; a third in heavy scrub; and the last third in good potato fields. This stretch of land was far from flat and from bottom to top had a rise of over 100 feet. It was divided into terraced fields with drops between them of up to six feet or more. As we had no earth-moving equipment every shovel of dirt would have to be shifted by hand.

We started by hacking out the two acres of brush. With fifty men and women on the job the brush was soon cut down, but digging out the network of roots was a much more laborious business. Don Mackay, our engineer, took levels up and down the field and marked the dimensions. Within three days we had 160 Sherpas working hard on the job, each receiving the premium local rate of Rs6 Nepali per day (60 cents). My chief Sherpa, Mingma Tsering, and his assistant, Annullu, were a formidable pair. Any man or woman who failed to do a full day's work was immediately paid off and replaced by someone stronger and more willing.

Through trial and error we discovered that 110 workers were the most efficient number to handle. One group would be digging out soil and small rocks and shovelling it into wicker baskets; another team would carry this away and dump it onto the places requiring filling, and a third group of strong men would be handling the larger boulders that periodically came to light. These boulders were dug out and then rolled and dragged with levers and ropes to the side of the airfield. The few giant boulders we unearthed were buried in the same method we had used at Mingbo. The Sherpas are always cheerful workers but they found it hard to compete in this respect with a dozen stalwart Tibetans. These men were tireless with a shovel and they worked in unison – shovelling in time to attractive Tibetan folk songs. However hard they worked they always seemed to have breath for singing and they set the pattern for song and laughter throughout the construction period.

By the end of two weeks the general form of the airfield was taking shape and we speeded things up by using four simple ploughs pulled by two cows each to loosen up the surface so that it could be more readily shovelled into baskets. All the dips and hollows were filled with tons of earth and rock and every hillock was chopped up and removed. Don Mackay was an energetic and conscientious supervisor. He roamed the airfield like an avenging angel and woe betide anyone who was digging earth from the wrong spot or dumping his load in an unauthorised position.

I completed negotiations with the five owners of the land named Aila, Chocki, Passang, Ongal and Ila Tenzing. An impressively official document was written out in Nepali by our Liaison Officer Mr. Rai who was a deputy Superintendent of Police when carrying out his usual duties. Each document acknowledged receipt of the appropriate money and made it clear that the land was becoming the property of the Nepalese Government – for this was the agreement we had made in Kathmandu. Each man signed with his thumbprint as none of them could write in Nepali. One man offered to sign his name in English but this was brushed aside as quite unconstitutional. I should perhaps make it clear that all the property owners were shrewd capable farmers and that the fact they couldn't sign their name was no reflection on their intelligence or resourcefulness – it simply indicated a lack of opportunity. For the six acres of land I paid a total of Rs. 6,350. ($635).

The pressure of work now intensified. The first flight would soon be arriving so time was getting short. Don Mackay obtained a colossal piece of timber, twenty feet long and one foot square, to be used as a grader. He attached a rope to each end and then had two cows hitched onto each rope. Alas for his grand ideas of mechanisation – the cows persistently headed off in opposite directions and the timber remained stationary. Men had to take the place of the cows and this was much more satisfactory. With a dozen laughing and cheering Sherpas pulling at each end of the timber it was dragged backwards and forwards, and up and down the field compacting and levelling at the same time.

I was not entirely happy about the top surface of the field which was still rather soft. Don departed for some climbing on Tamserku and I was able to abandon his much prized log. I instructed fifty Sherpas to link arms and stamp their way backwards and forwards across the field. Sherpa dancing involves a great deal of vigorous stamping and before long a very festive mass dance resulted and the earth received a most resounding thumping. I helped things along by providing a good supply of the local *chung* (beer). Two days of this had somewhat lessened the Sherpas' enthusiasm for the dance but pounded out a firm and smooth surface. We were now ready for the first landing. We had an airfield 1,150 feet long and 100 feet wide clearly marked by painted boards. The grade was one in ten – quite steep for an airfield – but the surface was excellent. Altogether I had paid out a total of just over Rs. 20,000 ($2,000) for land and labour.

The morning of October 26th was fine and clear but I had spent a restless night. Two civil aviation representatives, perhaps with memories of Mingbo airfield, were coming in on the first flight and their judgment would be final. The windsock was drooping down under the negligible wind breathing up the line of the airfield. Above us the icy summits were rigid against a blue Tibetan sky. By eight o'clock Sherpas were gathering for the occasion and it was the sharp ears of a Sherpa who first heard the dull roar of the engine and pointed out a black speck approaching rapidly up the great gorge of the Dudh Kosi river. In a clamour of sound the aircraft circled overhead and we hastily chased the last of the children off the runway. Then the plane wheeled and with flaps down swung towards the bottom of the strip. Holding my breath I watched as the wheels touched in a brief cloud of dust – and then the plane was coasting to a rapid halt. It took full power for the plane to taxi up the hill to the end of the runway and swing to a stop in a whirlwind of dust. The cheerful smiles and friendly waves of the crew and passengers gave little doubt that our Lukla airfield was now in commission – almost four weeks to the day since work had commenced.

Lukla quickly became one of the major internal airports of Nepal. Over the years thousands of tourists, trampers and expedition members have flown into the airfield as well as lots of Nepalese and vast quantities of freight. Later we extended the airfield to 1,400 feet and sowed the surface with a hardy grass.

Lukla has hastened the onset of officialdom and tourism into the Everest area. Already the Khumbu has received many of the 'blessings' of civilisation – forests are being denuded; rubbish is piled high around the camp sites and the monasteries; and the children are learning to beg. The Sherpas have a hospital and half a dozen schools, and more work is available to combat the galloping inflation – but is this sufficient recompense? At times I am racked by a sense of guilt. My only consolation is that the traditional Sherpa way of life was doomed in any case, few societies can overcome the temptations that the civilised world has to offer. We have helped the Sherpas retain their individuality – enabled them to compete in their new society. And if contact with the west has made them lose their traditional hospitality, their religious motivation, and their community spirit – who cares? Foreign money, they tell me, is a powerful panacea for such ailments.

With a gentle sweep of his slim brown hand the Head Lama of Thyangboche monastery waved me to the seat of honour beside him. I had arrived for afternoon tea, but our surroundings could not have been duplicated in any drawing room. Spread out on the grassy sward in front of the monastery was a large table laden with food and drink, and on every side towered great ice-clad precipices and rocky pinnacles. At the head of the valley was Mount Everest with a long plume of snow blowing from its summit.

'I am glad to welcome you again to Thyangboche,' said my old friend the Head Lama, 'and I am very pleased at the new schools you are building at Namche Bazar and Chaunrikarka. I have however a problem to discuss with you.'

I sipped gingerly at my cup of Tibetan tea – flavoured with salt and yak butter – and waited for the main point of his discourse.

'Your schools have brought knowledge to the Sherpa people,' continued the Head Lama, 'and this is good. But my young trainee Lamas must not be left behind and I consider it is essential they learn more Nepali and English.' He pointed at a beautifully constructed rock and wood building behind us which had no roof. 'With help from many sources we have built our own school, but we still lack glass for windows and a good roof – and most of all we need a well-trained teacher. Can you help us with these?'

I glanced at the calm face of the Head Lama – and noticed the slight smile at the corner of his mouth. Bowing to the inevitable I murmured that I would do what I could – and was immediately conducted by the Head Lama around the school to take the necessary measurements and draw an appropriate plan.

In the ten years before 1964 eighteen men and women died on bridges over the turbulent mountain rivers of the Khumbu region. Some died in the construction of new bridges, others when old ones collapsed. One of the most notorious spots was where the Bhote Kosi (Tibetan River) entered the main stream of the Dudh Kosi at a height of 9,500 feet just below the important village of Namche Bazar. In the deep gorge the track wound its way up and down on narrow ledges and wooden ladders – and it was heartily disliked and feared by the local people. After many requests the Nepalese Government granted a sum of money to make a more direct route by bridging the two rivers near their confluence. The 100 feet wide Dudh Kosi was a major problem. Rock walls were built out into the stream to carry a wooden structure and the bridge was finally completed just before the monsoon – the season of heavy rains. Alas, the builders of the bridge had been imported from outside the district and completely underestimated the force of the Dudh Kosi in flood. One day of heavy rain in the mountains was sufficient – the bridge was washed out on the east side and completely destroyed. The temporary bridge over the narrower but equally vigorous Bhote Kosi had a sadder ending. A Sherpa woman and a Tibetan man from Khumjung village were crossing the bridge when it tilted under their feet and the two were thrown into the foaming waters and drowned.

In 1964 my expedition planned to take a new look at these bridges to see if we could succeed where the local people had failed. We could not afford the finance for an elaborate western suspension bridge but I was convinced we could use the basic Sherpa wooden cantilevered type and extend its practicable length by suspending the central portion from two light stranded steel wire ropes. This would be a very economical form of construction and would not involve us in carrying vast quantities of equipment over the long walk from Kathmandu. In fact only six loads of sixty pounds each contained all the bridge equipment we brought in with us.

By mid-October the Dudh Kosi had subsided sufficiently from its monsoon levels to enable us to work on the approaches to the bridge. I established a construction camp in the depths of the gorge and a cold and windy spot it proved to be with only three hours of sunlight each day. On careful examination I was somewhat aghast at the width and ferocity of the river but I was determined that this time the bridge foundations would not succumb to the monsoon rain. From the precipices above the river we prised off scores of great boulders weighing many tons each and dropped them into the foaming water near the east bank. At first the rocks disappeared out of sight in the deep water but slowly they built up on each other and forced the fierce current out into the middle of the river. With a group of tough Sherpa workmen we rolled huge rocks into place to form the base of the eastern embankment which would bear the brunt of the monsoon floods. We made baskets of strong wire-netting four feet square and filled them with rocks – then tied them firmly to the bank with heavy wire. After ten days of hard labour we had a well-protected embankment rising ten feet above the highest flood level.

Meanwhile we had thrown a temporary bridge across the river – a crazy, shaky structure of insecurely perched logs zigzagging from rock to rock over a hundred and twenty feet of terrifying rapids. Despite our efforts to stop people from crossing this structure it soon became the trade route for hundreds of heavily laden porters. After seeing many near escapes from disaster I strung a wire rope across the gap to serve as a safety line in case the bridge collapsed. Even so, crossing this bridge was always something of an adventure.

Each day teams of Sherpas climbed the steep bluffs above the bridge to find trees we had felled and trimmed five months before. These trees were dragged and dropped down the cliffs to the river below. A thirty-five foot long tree trunk plunging downwards in uncontrolled fashion from 200 feet above is an impressive sight but somehow the Sherpas managed to escape injuring themselves – only a series of shattered logs testified to the ones that had got away.

We were now joined by Don Mackay, the expedition engineer, who took over the more technical task of stringing the suspension ropes across the river. From either side we pushed out wooden logs in cantilever form and weighed their ends down with piles of rock. Those cantilevers bridged over twenty feet from each bank but in the middle there still remained a gap of more than fifty feet. Mackay and his helpers tackled this job with ingenuity and determination. High above the river on the east bank holes were laboriously drilled into the solid rock and steel bolts concreted firmly in. It became a familiar sight to see Mackay's group festooned with ropes and equipment swinging like a group of agile monkeys across the vertical face. On the flatter western bank they bolted together a tall tower of pine logs and we securely weighed it down with many tons of boulders. Two stranded wire ropes were then stretched across in great sweeping loops and firmly attached at each end. We constructed a stout wooden cradle to hang from the ropes and this was dragged out into the middle to form an island onto which we could rest the end of the final bridging timbers.

Perched crazily above the river but always clipped safely onto the wire ropes by waist loops and karabiner in good mountaineering fashion we laboured mightily to haul the six heavy twenty-eight foot beams into place. It was a great moment when they were finally in position and we could balance our way across from bank to bank. It took only a few hours to hammer on the three foot wide decking. The $\frac{5}{8}$ inch diameter wire ropes seemed very thin but we knew they could carry many times the load that would ever be put on them.

The second bridge over the Bhote Kosi – only 300 yards away – had progressed equally quickly. This was a simpler structure – a stout Sherpa type bridge could span this lesser sixty feet gap – but we had to move huge quantities of rock to protect the embankment against the constant erosion of the swift flowing river.

By the early days of December the two bridges were completed and already carrying hundreds of heavily laden travellers each day; loads of oranges, rice and kerosene for Tibet in one direction and Tibetan rock salt and wool in the other. Our confidence in the suspension bridge was fully confirmed when we watched three heavily laden yaks gingerly picking their way across at the same time.

On December 7th we gathered at the bridges again. It was a bitterly cold day and a howling gale was roaring through the gorge of the Dudh Kosi. With us was the Head Lama of Thyangboche who had come to bless the bridges. Clad in glorious silks and brocades and seemingly unaffected by the freezing weather he intoned prayers and cast handfuls of rice into the waters as he strode vigorously across the bridges in a swirl of flapping garments and smoke from ceremonial fires. It encouraged us to see our bridges withstanding the gale with hardly a flutter and we were interested to note the confidence our Sherpas displayed in the Head Lama's blessing. 'When the rains come,' said Annullu, a tough Sherpa of vast experience, 'the floods will listen to the voice of the Head Lama and leave the bridge alone.' He thought for a moment and then spoke again in his limited but effective English.

'You are very lucky for us, Sahib. Three schools built, an airfield and two bridges . . . and nobody deaded! You are very lucky!'

From a camp at 9,500 feet in the little Sherpa village of Benkar we crawled out of our tents at five a.m. into a clear and beautiful morning. With a cup of tea and some biscuits to sustain us we started climbing up the very steep walls of the Dudh Kosi valley, clinging to the stunted shrubs and pine trees and zigzagging around vertical rock bluffs. The air was crisp, and perspiration was soon rolling down our faces as the energetic young mountaineers in the party set a torrid pace. At eight a.m. we threaded our way across a tumbling mountain waterfall and emerged onto a small grassy meadow at 12,000 feet.

The views were almost unbelievable. Far below us the thin thread of the Dudh Kosi river twined its way through steep bush-clad gorges towards the distant plains of India. At the head of the valley loomed the mighty bulk of Mount Everest – liberally plastered with the late monsoon snows but minus its habitual summit plume. Filling the whole horizon to the east were the vast unclimbed precipices of Mount Tamserku 21,730 feet – and Tamserku was mainly what we had come to see. With binoculars we scanned the mountain and assessed the expedition's chances of climbing it. We had now looked at the mountain from every side and generally agreed that the easiest route appeared to be the south ridge, although the term 'easy' was only relative for the south ridge reared up in terrifying fashion.

In 1953 on our way to Everest we had looked at Tamserku and agreed that the mountain was virtually impossible. But the surge forward in technical skill over the following decade had been phenomenal and little was 'impossible' any more. Lolling at ease in the warm sun we ate a hearty breakfast and glued our eyes on the mountain.

Where should the first camp be? And the second? Was there anywhere on that narrow ridge to put a third? From our viewpoint there seemed only one feasible route to follow – 2,000 feet up a steep snow valley scoured with deep avalanche grooves. Could the dangerous places be dodged by climbing on the ice fluting to the left? The route would then emerge onto a small snow saddle on the south ridge which might give room for a camp, and then over a sharp snow peak with a depressing loss of height on the north side. Next came the worst looking section of the climb; several hundred feet of almost vertical rock capped with a huge ice bulge, bleeding off in frequent avalanches to the west, seamed with deep crevasses and terrifyingly steep. If the top of this could be reached there was certainly ample room for a camp – but could it be reached? And then there was another giant step of vertical rock and ice leading to the final summit ridge – half a mile of wafer-thin snow perched uneasily at over 21,000 feet, a fretwork of giant overhanging cornices, ice towers and ragged gaps. Was it even worth starting?

Base camp for Tamserku was established in a pleasant hollow in the glacier moraine at 16,600 feet and thirty days of food, tentage, and climbing gear was carried into position. There were thirteen men in the climbing party – Wilson, Farrell, Crawford, Mackay, McKinnon and Stewart plus seven strong Sherpas under the leadership of Mingma Tsering.

After a week of toil up an icy gully of unrelenting steepness they reached a saddle on the ridge where we had optimistically expected a good camp site – but it proved to be a razor's edge of snow. They had no option but to camp there so dug their tents deeply into the mountain. One tent was so deeply intombed that it was completely invisible from five yards up the ridge. All movement had to be made while clipped onto a lifeline but for two weeks the camp served its useful purpose.

They scratched their way up the rock face to the bulging ice which capped it, knowing this would be the crux of the climb. At first glance it looked almost impossible and even the redoubtable Peter Farrell, a brilliant technician, predicted it would take three days to climb. But when they moved in to the assault, it yielded its worst pitches to Farrell in a day. On two pitches he used etriers – small rope ladders – but on the rest, near vertical though it was, he hacked and clawed his way up using only pitons for safety. It was brilliant climbing at a lung seering altitude of nearly 20,000 feet. Periodically the enormous ice cliffs would quiver with movement and the party's nerves would quiver in response.

McKinnon and Stewart completed the route to the top of the bulge next day. The party had agreed they could risk their own lives on this unstable ice but it would not be fair to risk the lives of their Sherpas. So while Mingma and his men maintained the lower part of the route, the six climbers proceeded to carry and haul their own loads up the cliff. On a flat piece of snow they pitched two small green tents face to face.

Next day they tackled the second big step and to their relief found it one of the easiest sections on the mountain although still formidably steep. Beyond lay the ridge and they were appalled by the giant mushroom cornices which festooned it. In a daring lead Farrell and Crawford forced their way under several of the mushrooms and gained a toehold on the ridge. They battled their way along, frequently being forced by the cornices out onto the snow fluting on the almost vertical west face. When they stopped they could see ahead of them a possible point for a bivouac.

Wilson, the assault leader, and Mackay who had worked very hard on the route, unselfishly agreed to act in a support role. Next day the other four men returned along the ridge carrying camping gear and carved out a tiny platform for their single tent. It was an incredibly exposed position and a storm could have been the end of them. The four men crushed into this tiny haven and although they were now protected from the wind they were all miserably cold. They prepared a simple meal on a small pressure stove and then dozed and tossed the night away.

It was very windy and cold in the morning and the men were haggard and lethargic. Even the unbelievable view failed to stir them. They slowly made their preparations and then crawled out of their tent – straight onto difficult climbing. Three bulging cornices had to be negotiated and these took a long time. A subsidiary summit gave them quite easy climbing and then they had the steep final summit ahead of them – needle sharp. The wind was strong and bitter and time was running out – but they moved confidently upwards. Cutting and kicking steps with professional strength and skill they fought against the altitude. At two p.m. they traversed the last steep face and with a tremendous sense of achievement stepped onto the top. It was a classic summit with room for only one man at a time – a fitting apex to an 'impossible' mountain.

In 1966 I achieved one of my greatest ambitions – to build a hospital for the Sherpas. The happy image of the Himalayan people free from stress, eating simple health-giving foods and living to a ripe old age certainly didn't apply to the Sherpas. Despite their toughness and strength they suffered from much the same ailments that we did, and without the benefit of medical care possibly half the children did not reach the age of twenty, and far too many young mothers died in childbirth.

We instituted a fund-raising campaign in New Zealand and succeeded in accumulating $30,000 for the hospital, plus substantial quantities of building materials, food, clothing and medical supplies. With the additional funds and equipment supplied by our traditional supporters in the U.S.A. we were in a position to get the project under way. Twelve tons of supplies were shipped to Kathmandu, flown in small aircraft to Lukla airfield and then carried on porters' backs up the hill to Khumjung. Our selected location for the hospital was in the neighbouring village of Kunde at 12,700 feet.

The hospital took six enjoyable but energetic weeks to build. At six a.m. each morning a cheerful Sherpa face would push through the tent door and a cup of tea and biscuits would be firmly placed beside you. Few of us had the strength of mind to emerge from our tents into the hard frosty world before the sun reached our camp at seven fifteen. Then everything changed. We crawled easily out of our sleeping bags, quickly dressed, raced to the cook tent for a little warm water for washing, then sat around the table in the sun to enjoy a substantial breakfast – usually cereal or porridge followed by a plateful of french fried potatoes and a precious egg. On two mornings we watched a great snow leopard cross the rocky slope a thousand feet above us.

Then it was off to work – laying out the foundations, nailing on the floor, assembling the framework, completing windows which framed magnificent views of great ice mountains.

Pembertarkay, Phudorje and Tenzing Niendra had become very expert assistants – tackling the building with the same fire and zest they had shown on the big mountains. Pembertarkay, for all his size and strength, moved as gracefully as a cat and tacked wallboards into place with neatness and despatch; Tenzing Niendra was the quiet one of the trio but his sense of responsibility was a steadying influence; Phudorje was the complete clown, telling wicked stories or making naughty suggestions he had all the Sherpas – and us – in fits of laughter. Phudorje did nothing by half measures – each time he wielded a hammer we cringed with the fear that he might drive it right through a wall or roof.

On December 5th, we had a touch of winter. During the night four inches of snow fell and we awoke to a white and beautiful world. We had little inclination to stir from our warm sleeping bags but our Sherpas had no mercy and prompted us into action by vigorously shaking the snow off our tents. It was exciting to see snow on the roof of our new Khumjung hospital and to find that inside the building it was warm and comfortable.

The snow brought to an end two weeks of sunshine with frosty nights and clear sparkling days. A transformation had been produced in the hospital with the outside virtually completed and much of the internal painting and finishing done as well. We had installed a hot water system heated by a wood-burning stove and there was a constant stream of Sherpas visiting the kitchen to turn on a tap and see hot water flowing – something they had never experienced before. There was an even greater transformation amongst the thyroid patients being treated by our medical group under Dr. Kay Ibbotsen. Huge goitres had shrunk, dull and cretinous young faces had brightened. One rather slow young man had responded so positively to iodine that he speeded up his normal shambling gait beyond his sense of balance and ended up with a broken collarbone. Many hundreds of Sherpas had received injections of iodine bearing oil and our doctors were forecasting the end of goitres and cretinism in the new generation of Sherpas.

We took a two-day break from hospital building and medical work to climb to the monastery at Thyangboche for Mane Rimdu, the main religious festival of the year. Hundreds of Sherpas gathered at this lovely spot with its tremendous view of Mount Everest and all were in their best and gayest clothing. The Head Lama of Thyangboche opened the festival in an out-of-doors ceremony. He was dressed in magnificent brocade and sat with legs crossed on his carpeted throne, radiating calmness and dignity. With untroubled authority he led his Tawas in the chanting and prayers which farewelled the old year and welcomed in the new. At the conclusion of the ceremony all the Sherpas swept forward to be blessed and all made offerings of money or food towards the upkeep of the monastery. The brilliant colouring, the deep-voiced chanting of religious scriptures, the clang of cymbals and the bellow of huge trumpets – all blended into the tremendous mountain backdrop to make an uncommonly impressive scene. It was only when the sun dipped behind a cloud that the chill air reminded us we were at an altitude of over 13,000 feet in the early days of winter.

In the centre of Khumjung village stood the *Gompa* (Temple), surrounded by a clump of handsome juniper trees. The *Gompa* filled a variety of purposes. It was used for religious gatherings, as a community centre where important village meetings were held, and as the site of all local festivals. The Khumjung *Gompa* had a particularly fine library of Tibetan religious books, many virtually irreplaceable, and these were suffering damage during the monsoon rains. We had agreed to help the village with a new roof and Neville Wooderson and I took over this job.

An air of cheerfulness and hilarity is always present at Sherpa working bees but plenty of work is done, too, and with great speed the huge flat rocks were removed from the roof and the ancient and rotting wooden shingles thrown to the ground. The rafters stood revealed and looked strong enough for another half century – although mighty uneven to our critical western eyes. Nailing new timber across the rafters to carry the roofing wasn't an easy job. Some rafters needed wood chipping off and others required chunks of timber nailed on to level them up. At each blow of the hammer a cloud of dust billowed up from the *Gompa* attic below – a fascinating place crammed with old Buddhist relics and flat wooden boards painted with religious symbols.

Neville and I had been using some of the more faded boards as chocks on the rafters and we enquired as to their purpose. Mingma Tsering explained that it was the custom on the death of a relative to have a suitable holy painting made by a local artist and then placed in the *Gompa* attic with due ceremony. The departing soul would then receive many blessings on his or her last journey. Neville and I felt decidedly guilty after this explanation as on many occasions we had driven a six-inch nail right through the centre of a painted board. With a twinkle in his eye Mingma told us not to worry 'as long as the painting had its head upwards and not downwards.' Great was our relief to discover that despite many nails through their middles all heads were upwards as recommended.

The corrugated aluminium roof was duly finished after three days of energetic work and there was much local rejoicing. To honour our contribution the villagers decided to hold a party and all houses were asked to contribute five rupees each. On the night of the function we were escorted to the *Gompa* and welcomed by the local dignitaries. In the temple we were led to carpeted seats with huge statues of the Buddha and Guru Rimpoche smiling benignly down upon us. The local firewater, *rakshi*, was then produced out of bottles of many shapes and sizes (mostly bearing old labels of well known Scottish products) – and the party was on! A huge meal of the Tibetan dish, *tukpa* (noodles and stew), was then produced and, of course, more *rakshi*. Before long, dancing was under way with the women at one end and the men at the other end of a long line. The expedition members were invited into the line and the building shook and quivered with the thump of expedition rubber soles and Tibetan style felt boots. It was a wonderfully happy occasion. As we walked back up the hill in the frosty moonlight I doubt if there was one of us who didn't feel a warm glow of affection and respect for our tough, vigorous and cheerful hosts.

By the middle of December the hospital was completed and already giving much needed attention to the sick people in the area. On December 28th we said goodbye to our Sherpa friends. We left the hospital in the competent hands of Dr. John McKinnon and his wife Dianne who had volunteered to remain behind and supervise operations for the first two years.

The contribution by the McKinnons to the welfare of the Sherpas was quite remarkable. I was back at Kunde Hospital when they concluded their two years of volunteer activity. Those last few days of farewell are something I will always remember – and it wasn't me that was being farewelled. There were dignified speeches, simple gifts to the McKinnons, and expressions of thanks from the many who believed that their lives had been saved. More than anything it was the tears from these rugged people – floods of tears. I wonder how many of us will have a whole community weep in sorrow at our departure?

Chapter 17

Family Frolics

LOUISE AND I HAD ALWAYS BEEN DETERMINED THAT AS SOON AS THE children were old enough they should be given the chance to share our adventures and meet the people who had given us so much pleasure over the years. The financial effort involved would be worth any sacrifice – if sacrifice it could be called when the presence of the children would be giving us great happiness.

In 1966 the time seemed appropriate for them to come to Nepal. Peter was now twelve; Sarah was ten; and Belinda was seven years old – they were physically robust and already experienced campers with a love for the out of doors. On December 7th they flew into Lukla with Louise, together with Lois Pearl and her three charming daughters – Ann fourteen, Lyn twelve, and Susan ten. Dr. Max Pearl and I were there to meet them and quite a group of Sherpas too. The welcome from the Sherpas was quite overwhelming – I think they appreciated the fact that we would *want* to bring our families into their country. The children responded with equal enthusiasm – which isn't hard to do when you're being thoroughly spoiled by people you expect to like.

The temperatures at Kunde were very cold and it took a while to adjust to the climate and the altitude – but before long both families were eating and sleeping well. My aim was to take everyone up to Everest Base Camp which I hadn't visited since our successful expedition thirteen years before. After ten days at Kunde everyone seemed well acclimatised so we set off up valley. It was a cold and sunny day as we did the first stretch to Pangboche but the views of Everest and other great peaks were quite superb. Snow was whipping off the high ridges but this was the only indication that life in winter above 20,000 feet would be miserable and hazardous. It was a cold night at Pangboche but squeezed into small tents we were comfortable enough inside two sleeping bags.

Our Sherpas woke us early with a cup of tea and biscuits and we started up valley at seven thirty a.m. The sun was still some distance away and every stream and pool was frozen hard. A cold wind drifted down the mountains and forced us to snuggle into our padded jackets. The children were very quiet at first and it was hard to get warm even with the vigorous exercise.

After two hours of stiff walking we started climbing a long hill and swung into the entrance of the Khumbu Valley. An easy half mile brought us to the deserted village of Pheriche – bathed in warm sunshine. Sheltering out of the wind behind rock walls we ate a substantial breakfast and I was pleased to note that the altitude of over 14,000 feet didn't seem to be affecting the children's appetites – or their enjoyment and laughter.

Then we carried on to the base of the Khumbu Glacier and climbed steeply up for 1,000 feet to the lateral moraine on the western side. Most of a recent snow fall had disappeared but all streams were solid sheets of ice and demanded considerable care when being crossed. At three p.m. we walked rather wearily into a summer grazing alp at Lobuje, 15,500 feet, and pitched our tents for the night. Headaches and nausea – the common complaints of altitude – were already present in both children and adults and there was a heavy demand for aspirin. When the sun dipped behind the mountains at four p.m. the temperature dropped in startling fashion and we retired to the only warm place we could find – our sleeping bags. We passed the time quite pleasantly with singing and corny jokes . . . then quietly drifted off to sleep.

The third morning was superbly clear but it was so cold that we didn't move from our tents until the sun had warmed the valley. Then we walked for several miles up easy going beside the glacier and climbed abruptly up onto a huge pile of moraine rock covering a tributary glacier. After a long scramble over loose boulders we reached the far side and looked down into a wide sandy bowl containing a small lake – frozen and shining. This was Gorakshep, 16,300 feet, and here we planned our highest camp. The frozen lake gave the children great entertainment. I investigated the ice and found it was a foot thick and quite safe. Before long everyone was slithering and sliding from side to side in great glee.

After a quick lunch, Louise and I set off with Peter to climb an 18,000 foot peak, Kala Pittar, for a good view of Mount Everest. A long scramble over loose rock was tedious and time consuming and I was surprised how much of the route I had forgotten after thirteen years. The last thousand feet was energetic scrambling up good rock and there was much heavy panting in the thin air – and twelve-year-old

Peter in particular was finding out what hard work altitude could be. We emerged on top to a superb view. Towering above our heads was the sombre summit of Everest with snow streaming out in the high wind. We could see the South Col, 26,000 feet, where I had spent three miserable nights in 1953, and the broken turmoil of the ice fall and the Western Cwm. It seemed a lifetime away.

Next morning we were heavy-headed and lethargic. The weather was still fine, but vigorous gusts of cold wind made conditions less pleasant. We set off on the long walk up the glacier to Base Camp. I was a little concerned about seven-year-old Belinda but my fears proved groundless – hand in hand with Mingma Tsering or Siku she danced her way up the moraine and the ice. Fierce gusts of wind whipped down from the summits and whirled amongst the tall ice pinnacles. With growing excitement we threaded our way under the towering ice until we reached 17,000 feet and came onto signs of the early Everest expeditions – rusty tins, bamboo marker poles, old batteries and the like . . . careless relics of some magnificent moments. Looming above us were the shattered ice cliffs leading into the Western Cwm and an avalanche thundered off Nuptse. It was a wild and impressive spot in such wintery conditions.

Chilled by the wind we started down the glacier again. Belinda squeezed out a tear or two and said she was tired and cold. At a word from Mingma Tsering, Siku swung her up onto his broad back and went off down the glacier at a half trot; a delighted Belinda smiling with pleasure. Half a mile later she had completely recovered and was dashing down the glacier clinging firmly to the flying Siku's hand. That was the last we saw of her until we tramped tiredly into camp. The wind came into camp with us and sent twisting spirals of frozen dust high over the lake. Our tents flapped and billowed all through the long night and we were glad we were departing next day.

We left in the hard cold before the sun was up and even the tough Sherpas were glad of every piece of clothing. Our spirits rose as the sun warmed us and our energy increased with each fall in altitude. We breakfasted enthusiastically at the terminal face of the glacier and then pushed on with determination towards Thyangboche – a long walk away.

We were tiring as we reached Pangboche but had a late lunch in the warm sun while the village elders plied us with *chung* and *rakshi* and gently mentioned their need for a new roof on their ancient *Gompa* – the oldest monastery in the Khumbu area.

We expended our last energy climbing up the shaded snowy slopes to Thyangboche monastery and Belinda's hand was dragging a little in mine. The Head Lama welcomed us in his beautifully decorated room and gave us food and drink. As we walked back to the monastery guest house we could see Mount Everest sharp and clear in the bright moonlight and noticed fierce wind clouds racing across the sky. It was Christmas Eve, and the children huddled around the fire singing Christmas carols. We were tired but very content.

Early on the morning of December 28th we said our final goodbyes to our Sherpa friends in Khumjung. There was an air of gloom about the party and even a few tears were shed. With many white scarves of farewell around our shoulders we turned sadly down valley. Ahead of us we had a hundred miles of stiff walking. At Lukla the snow that had been threatening for several days caught up with us and dusted the peaks around – but only spread an inch or two on our camp. In cold misty weather we climbed the track high above the Dudh Kosi river and pushed on without resting through an eerie mossy world of fog and snow.

We fumbled our way over two passes and then dropped sharply two thousand feet to dryer and warmer levels. Our camp on a grassy ledge in the forest was a haven of comfort and we luxuriated around a huge fire fed with giant tree trunks by Sherpa Phudorje. The children were happy to go early to their sleeping bags but we adults lingered on around the glowing warmth of the fire.

Next morning was fine – but cold – and we plunged down towards the Dudh Kosi river for three hours, losing thousands of feet of height and moving from winter into spring. Our breakfast place beside the river at Jubing was only 6,000 feet and the air was warm and balmy despite the fresh snow on the mountain tops. All afternoon we climbed upwards again – past the lower Rai villages; past a higher Chettri village; up through a Sherpa village and finally to a deserted yak pasture at 10,000 feet – and back into frosty winter. The children seemed tireless but their parents covered the last thousand feet on weary limbs. The incense of burning rhododendron logs and a hot cup of tea gave us renewed vigour.

The evening view from the yak pasture was beautiful beyond belief. Deep in the valley night had fallen but the great peaks still glowed crimson and gold. The stars were sharper and brighter than they ever can be in our stuffy cities – and a man-made satelite went streaking across the heavens.

Tragedy is never too far away in Nepal. A Sherpa came into camp seeking medical aid. On his back in a bamboo basket was a twelve year old lad, weak and pale. Our two doctors examined him and diagnosed a serious kidney condition plus extreme anemia. The boy was very close to death and only blood transfusions and hospital care could save his life. The nearest clinic was three days' walk away but it was the only hope. We hired a porter to help carry the boy and then sent the family off on a desperate race over the mountain ridges to try and reach hospital in time. The boy's calm patient eyes seemed to know that the race was already lost.

We crossed a steep little pass into the district of Solu – a high and lovely valley with fertile soil and many Sherpa villages. Below us like a jewel set into the wall of the valley was the famous monastery of Chewong – respected greatly by all Sherpas and Tibetans. We approached it by a narrow zigzag track up steep bluffs. The buildings seemed perfect in their setting and the view was quite breathtaking; not the usual view of great Himalayan peaks but a more peaceful outlook. The deep Solu valley with its patchwork of farms and villages was spread out far below us and seemed to sleep in the mid-day sun. Far to the south the hills decreased in height and blended with distance into the hot plains of India. Even the chanting of the Lamas at prayer was soothing and restful. Some day I resolved I would return to Chewong and pitch my tent in the sun, and just sit for a week and drink in its peace and tranquillity.

In New Zealand I am President of Volunteer Service Abroad – a similar organisation to the American Peace Corps. As we travelled back through Thailand it was an excellent opportunity to visit some of our volunteers in the north-east of that country. This was a period when both the Thai and the United States Governments were firmly denying that United States military aircraft were using Thai airfields for bombing raids on Vietnam.

On a train we met an officer from an Australian fighter squadron operating from the military airfield at Ubon and he persuaded us to visit his camp to help celebrate the Australian National Day. It proved to be an astonishing experience for all of us. The children refused to go to bed – they carried seats to the side of the runway and watched enthralled as every twenty minutes throughout the night two USAF Phantom bombers roared off with after-jets blazing and set course for Vietnam.

Inside the officers' mess things were almost as noisy with a cheerful jostling crowd of young pilots. I was introduced to the Commanding Officer of the Phantoms – a strongly built, handsome man with a multitude of decorations (I later saw his face on the front of a *Time* magazine). Late at night we leaned on the bar and he told me about his problems. He was nearly at the end of his tour of duty and admitted to being very tired and even a little shaky. He had no time for his politicians back home he assured me. Each time he flew his bomb-laden aircraft over North Vietnam the people down below in the darkness were firing rockets at him and the politicians wouldn't let him and his 'boys' fire back.

'It's not much fun having a heat seeking rocket chasing up your tail pipe,' he confided to me gloomily. I had no difficulty in agreeing with him – he was a formidable figure and I could understand his concern.

It cannot be over-emphasised that only motorists familiar with the procedures and difficulties of outback motoring in Australia should consider attempting the Birdsville Track.
Automobile Association Bulletin.

'Are you familiar with outback motoring in Australia, Daddy?' said Sarah – now eleven years old. My response was slightly defensive.

'Well, I was brought up in a farming area and learned to drive in the mud . . . and then I've driven down the Alaska Highway as you well know . . .'

'But have you driven in the desert?'

'I drove a tractor to the South Pole,' I said weakly . . . and then admitted the truth – that although I'd driven in all sorts of unusual places I hadn't done much on unformed roads in a hot sandy desert area.

The Hillary family was planning a camping holiday – several weeks of travelling and living in central Australia and a drive up the famous Birdsville Track. Peter, aged thirteen, Sarah, and Belinda now nine were full of excitement at the thought of such a journey and the family was buzzing with plans and preparations.

Equipment should include the usual selection of vehicle spare parts, spades and matting to overcome bogging in sand, and a magnetic compass. The party should be fully self-sufficient with food, water and petrol supplies.
AA Bulletin.

The five Hillarys plus two grandparents and two friends – a total of nine of us – gathered in Sydney, Australia, at the beginning of May. Stronger parties no doubt have set out on such an adventure but none more inspired by enthusiasm and keen anticipation. We had two well equipped automobiles and a handsome trailer camper. Shovels, ropes, planks and compasses abounded. We had maps galore, ample reserves of food and fuel, large sun hats and light clothes for the blazing desert days and warm sleeping bags for frosty desert nights.

The weather reports were rather ominous! Central Australia had experienced its heaviest rain for many years (in some areas it was the first rain for many years) and many roads were cut by flooded rivers. But 'she'll be right by the time we get there', was our motto as we drove a thousand miles to Adelaide in South Australia. From the jam packed roads of Sydney we passed through the organised beauty of the capital, Canberra; the lush green of the fertile Riverina; hundreds of miles of isolated and desolate sheep country; the magnificent orchards and vineyards of the Murray River valley; and the stately parks and gardens of Adelaide itself. Camping was no problem – we could pull off the road almost anywhere – and we soon developed a quick and efficient camping routine.

'Conditions are drying out up north,' we were told by the Automobile Association in Adelaide 'and if there is no further rain the Birdsville Track should be open. But if more rain comes get out as quickly as you can.'

We drove north towards the central deserts passing through the rugged Flinders Ranges with their dramatic red colourings and magnificent gum trees. The roads were badly scoured by the recent rains and we were constantly dipping through rough watercourses, now dry. Our heavily laden trailer camper took a pounding on the sharp rocks and there were innumerable resounding clangs on the heavy steel sheets protecting our engine sumps and gas tanks. We saw kangaroos and emus in plenty, and a host of colourful Australian birds. Somehow the sight of a kangaroo loping easily along the road beside us was so much more exciting than a cloistered and smelly zoo exhibit.

WARNING: The greatest danger to travellers on the Birdsville Track is the 'ground Haze' which is a common occurrence in the sandhill country south of Birdsville. When this becomes bad it is very easy to become lost, particularly on the flat featureless claypans where the faint wheelmarks showing the way ahead become difficult to detect.
AA Bulletin.

Seventy miles south of the Birdsville Track in a vast desolate windswept area one of our trailer tyres succumbed to ill treatment and we shuddered to an involuntary halt. At almost precisely the same moment the rains came in earnest. Clad in waterproof parkas and drooping sun hats we made a damp wheel change and then drove on over rapidly deteriorating roads in miserable visibility – at that moment we'd have given anything for some blazing desert sun or even a touch of 'ground haze'.

The police sergeant at Leigh Creek had bad news for us – the road ahead was now impassable with deep mud, and the Birdsville Track was cut by flooded rivers. 'And if this rain keeps up we'll be cut off here too,' he announced.

The small town seen through a veil of rain had little to attract us so we brushed aside our disappointment and turned south again. The sky was darkly threatening but it wasn't raining when we drove off the road and camped on a terrace above a broad dry watercourse. It was a lonely spot in the middle of a wide barren plain but we spent a cheerful evening planning a new programme and sipping a bottle of good red Australian wine.

I woke at midnight to the sound of torrential rain drumming on the roof of the camper trailer. Gradually another sound intruded – a low murmur that grew into a vigorous rushing sound. I crawled reluctantly out of bed, opened the door and shone my flashlight into the murk – the creek bed was now a brown turgid flood that was visibly rising as I watched. We were well above the river but were we high enough? For another hour I lay listening to the river and by now its thunderous roar was almost drowning out the rain. I knew the road above would be a much safer place but wasn't sure we could get there up the slippery wet ground. At one thirty a.m. I had another look. It was a terrifying sight! The ground was running with water and the raging torrent below seemed very close. I decided on action.

Louise was already awake – she'd been listening to the river as I had – and we sent our two sleepy girls sloshing through the rain and darkness into one of the cars. Peter helped us pack the camper trailer and hitch it onto a vehicle. We searched out the best route with flashlights, and then with everyone pushing we slithered and churned our way to the crest of the gravel road. A quick look along the road confirmed my fears – we were marooned by impassable water both ahead and behind. There was nothing to do but go back to bed. We re-established camp in the middle of the road and settled down to wait out the long hours of darkness.

By daylight the rain had eased but the skies were still heavy and threatening. The river ahead of us had subsided a great deal from its overnight peak but it was still much too deep to ford. During the morning it dropped another two feet and shrank to a mere 150 feet wide. I carefully waded across the river, bracing myself against the swift current. We had been warned that rain in this area usually washed snakes and scorpions down the streams. When a leafy branch wrapped

itself around my leg I almost leapt clear of the water in startled surprise.
The footing was rocky and uneven but the depth was only a few inches
over my knees.

Camp was dismantled and fan belts removed to prevent water
spraying over the electricals. Then it was all aboard and into the
river – not too fast to wreck the suspension on the rocky bottom or too
slow to let water seep in under the doors. There was an excited cheer
from the children as we surged out the other side and the trailer came
clear in a sheet of spray. With fan belts replaced we drove on. In the
next forty miles we crossed many flooded streams and battled through
a dozen long stretches of water and mud. Our progress was slow but
at least it was progress – until we came around a corner and saw the
road disappearing under a half mile of sweeping flood water.

We camped the night on the soggy edge of the road – tired but in
good spirits. Our food was holding well and although the main road
was cut we still had another route to try – a narrow winding track
through the mountains. A few stars came out as we went to bed and
seemed to refute the radio's sombre warning of more rain to come. We
woke to a chilly morning and our camp was bathed in sunshine –
though clouds towered high over the mountains. Even the muddy road
seemed easier as we slithered our way towards the foothills. When the
track entered a narrow high walled gorge it became hard to follow as it
zigzagged up the stream bed for several miles. It certainly wasn't a
place to be caught if another deluge came, and big black clouds were
coming closer . . .

I bumped over the first river without any real difficulty and then
bogged down in a long stretch of wet silt. Some brisk shovelling around
the wheels of the car and trailer, a cheerful push from the family and
we were free. Somehow the sun had transformed the almost desperate
struggles of the previous day into a picnic jaunt. Three more fords, each
one more difficult than the last failed to subdue our spirits, but the
next one brought us up with a jolt. The river, here only two feet deep,
surged along the bottom of a scoured out channel with twenty-foot
high vertical walls.

'This is it! We'll never get across!' said Louise in desperation. A
touch of rain on my cheek spurred me to renewed effort. Out came
the shovels and we concentrated on digging away the shingle walls and
making a steep ramp on either side. Any movable boulders were rolled
away from the stream bed although some of the worst of them couldn't
be shifted.

'It's about as good as we can get it,' I suggested. 'Let's see if the
station wagon will go across unladen.'

The vehicle was eased up to the wall and the front wheels dropped over the edge. Sliding and scraping on locked brakes it dipped straight down into the stream until the bonnet was under water and with heartrending crashes on the rear end came to an even keel in the middle of the river with water washing around the bottom of the doors. Jerking and bumping on the rough surface it got sufficient speed to tackle the other steep wall and with our united pushes it churned over the top and onto safe ground – accompanied by much laughter and cheering.

The car and heavy trailer were going to be more difficult! Another half hour on the shovels eased the worst parts of the descending ramp. Then I climbed into the car and drove it over the edge and straight down into the river. The extra weight of the trailer increased my speed and I hit the water with a rush and sent up a sheet of spray. There was a violent bumping across the stream bed and then an abrupt halt as a trailer wheel jammed against a large boulder. I was mildly surprised that the car and trailer were still joined together.

We waded around in the water, talking and looking, and everyone had different suggestions on what to do. With a great effort we managed to unhitch the trailer and then tie the two vehicles together with our long tow-rope. At the signal to go, motors roared and wheels spun; there was an awful smell from a burning clutch and then my car slowly climbed up the steep bank and came to rest on firm ground.

The trailer looked rather lonely by itself in the middle of the river, and we knew it would take a maximum effort to get it out. The towrope was attached and men, women and children went into the stream and took a firm grip on the trailer, supporting the drawbar and guiding the wheels. I drove the car forward in low gear, everybody pushing furiously, and like a reluctant bucking bronco the trailer jerked convulsively over boulders and holes and swivelled wildly up onto the firm road – showering everyone with water. We were through . . . !

Sarah stood in the water with a patch of mud on her long fair hair. On her face was a grin of sheer delight . . .

'Let's do the Birdsville Track again next year, Dad!' she said.

Big expeditions are rarely as much fun as small ones – the logistics tend to overshadow the good fellowship and the personal involvement. I have enjoyed all my small expeditions but never more so than when my family has been along. Nowadays they may well protest in embarrassment at such a statement – but it is true! We have adventured in small ways together around the world and shared many marvellous occasions and people. Even when I was absent from home for long periods, Louise kept me alive in the family's thoughts and on my return I slipped easily back into the comfortable routine. As the children entered their teens I had to learn how to understand them afresh; to listen rather more and be dogmatic rather less. We still share many adventures but inevitably and rightly our paths will separate, although I hope we will continue to get together on the trail as the years go by.

Chapter 18

Adventures Galore!

'THERE'S NOTHING LEFT TO DO!' IS A COMMON CRY YOU HEAR FROM ALL sorts of young people and it's sad in a way because you know the speaker must be closing his eyes to the adventurous opportunities that still abound. The world is full of interesting projects – if you have the imagination and resourcefulness to seek them out. Finding new adventures has never been a problem in my life – the big difficulty is finding time to do them.

For years I had been sketching out plans for a return to the Antarctic – not for another mighty effort but with ideas of a cheerful compact Himalayan-type expedition. The Antarctic mountains vary from lonely nunataks on the Polar Plateau to the Vinson Massif 16,860 feet. Many are squat in shape with a capping of ice, but all are defended by inaccessibility, cold temperatures, and rings of deep crevasses. On the northwest shore of the Ross Sea were a group of steep and slender summits with ice fluted faces and narrow soaring ridges. Queen of the area was Mount Herschel, rising 11,000 feet out of the sea across the bay from Cape Hallett and surely one of the most beautiful mountains in the world.

An attempt on the unclimbed Mount Herschel would be a tremendous challenge and there was plenty of geology, surveying, and topographical exploration to carry out – but permission and support were hard to come by. It took a few years before everything clicked into place and I obtained the approval of the New Zealand Antarctic division and the U.S. Deep Freeze operation. Then we had a mad rush to equip and finance ourselves – two snowmobiles (motorised toboggans) and special tents from Sears; monetary grants from the Everest Foundation and the New Zealand Alpine Club; a useful amount of cash from the sale of Press rights; every source had to be approached, persuaded, thanked.

We left Christchurch on October 18th 1967 and vibrated our way south for nine and a half hours in an old four-engined Constellation. It was cramped and boring until we saw pack-ice flecking the ocean and then everything became exciting again. Soon a solid sheet of white stretched towards the horizon. The great bulk of Mount Erebus loomed up ahead and we commenced our long descent towards the ice airfield at McMurdo Sound.

We pulled on our warm clothes before stepping out of the aircraft and the cold was solid and tangible. We scrambled inside heated tracked vehicles and were driven over bulldozed snow roads towards the familiar buildings of Scott Base on Pram Point. It was nine years since I had left the Base and I had a strange reluctance to return – even the warmth of our welcome failed to eradicate this feeling. Late in the evening I went for a stroll outside. The snow was hard frozen and the light fading. To the west the mountains glowed pink and blue in the midnight sun. I felt a deep sense of nostalgia and sadness – a conglomeration of all the fears, hopes and loneliness I'd experienced in my long stay many years before. I was glad to go inside and lose my thoughts in the warm activity of a well-run base.

I had many old friends in my party. There was Norman Hardie of Kanchenjunga fame and Murray Ellis who went with me to the South Pole; there was Dr. Mike Gill who had shared many adventures with me in the Himalayas and three other climbing 'tigers' – Bruce Jenkinson, Dr. Peter Strang and Mike White – they made a formidable quartet. Our senior geologist Dr. H. J. Harrington (who happened to be my brother-in-law) had previously led a very successful expedition to the mountain area south of Cape Hallett so knew the area as well as anyone. His assistant geologist, Graham Hancox, already had two Antarctic trips to his credit.

On October 21st we loaded 6,000 lbs of supplies on a U.S. Navy ski-equipped Hercules aircraft and took off for Hallett Station, 360 miles to the north. For the first hour we flew over cloud and then with dramatic suddenness the skies cleared and we could see the mighty Tucker Glacier and giant peaks stretching 100 miles to the north and west. We soon identified Cape Hallett thrusting out into the broken pack-ice and the glorious summit of Herschel standing clear above the surrounding ranges.

The closer we got to Herschel the more impressed I became. We had hoped to put a party on the east face but we could now see that this route would involve 3,000 feet of gleaming ice topped by a couple of thousand feet of vertical rock. Nowhere was there room for even one camp – let alone two or three. Our most hopeful route – up the north-east spur and then along the north ridge – showed itself to be far steeper than we had anticipated with formidable stretches of hard ice and jagged rocks. The Hercules landed smoothly on the floating ice in Edisto Bay and we were a quiet and subdued expedition as we unloaded our vehicles and supplies.

My snowmobile started at the first pull. With a jerk I shook the heavy sledge free of the ice and pointed my vehicle in the direction of Herschel, fifteen miles away across the bay. Almost immediately we struck hard pressure ridges with hollows of deep soft snow between them. A dozen times our heavily laden sledges bogged down and had to be dragged to the surface. By the end of the first day we had covered only eight miles.

The second day was even more frustrating. We entered a relatively windless area and the snow lay soft and thick – when you stepped from a sledge you sank thigh deep. Our gallant little snowmobiles performed marvellous feats but time and again they almost disappeared out of sight. We became expert at driving them at high speeds between the ice hummocks, planing on the surface of the snow, compacting a trail over which we could drag heavy sledges. Later we started dipping through hollows containing sea water; and Weddell seals were wallowing in the tide cracks nearby. It wasn't a very stable area – but here on the third day we established our Base Camp and parked the snowmobiles.

Our first obstacle lay directly ahead of us – a hundred-feet ice cliff stretching endlessly around the bay, clean cut and frequently overhanging. Most mountains lead you gently to their harder defences, but not Mount Herschel – the climbing was starting in earnest at sea level. We poked our way up a deep crack where the ice of the Ironsides Glacier gouged into the floating shelf. We passed tide cracks, melt pools, and mother seals with new-born babies. Finally we discovered a break in the cliff barrier – a complex route leading up and down over tumbled blocks of ice, deep crevasses and ice walls. Fixed ropes were laid over the most unpleasant sections – and by the end of the fourth day we had reached 100 feet above sea level.

A reconnaissance ahead into a long narrow valley showed that it gave steep access towards the north-east spur. The snow everywhere was soft and deep and the slopes shuddered and snapped with internal tension as we passed over them. Snow avalanches aren't common in the Antarctic but I had already noticed the debris of two large windslab avalanches nearby. Could we rely on these steep slopes not to avalanche, I wondered?

On the sixth day we had our first big breakthrough. Our four 'tigers' climbed the side valley up a very steep ice fall and reached the crest of the north-east spur at 3,400 feet. They reported that it hadn't been easy and that the snow was deep and soft. I decided to waste no time. The weather had been consistently fine and cold but I didn't know how long it would stay that way. Eight of us would carry in a camp next day with enough food and tents for a higher camp, and Mike Gill and Bruce Jenkinson would stay up top and work on the route ahead.

For three nights at Base Camp I had been suffering from nightmares – vivid and terrifying. I woke each morning tired and depressed and was reluctant to get to grips with the many problems that faced us. Why should I be so affected, I asked myself. There were difficulties and dangers ahead but no more than I'd struck a hundred times before. Then I remembered some sleeping pills that Mike Gill had given me. Apparently they were a new type – could they be having a strange effect? I stopped using the pills and the nightmares immediately ceased; my morale returned to normal.

Groaning under heavy packs of fifty-five to sixty-five lbs we climbed up through the ice cliffs to the ice shelf, and then strapped on our skis. For hour after hour we zigzagged our way upwards skirting vast crevasses and, despite our skis, sinking deep into the snow. When a relatively gentle slope gave a sharp complaining rumble at our passage it was difficult not to be alarmed. The air temperature was −10°F and there was no wind. We were stifling hot as we dragged our loads upwards and peeled off layer after layer of clothing. Perspiration dripped off brows and noses only to freeze into knobbly bumps on our scraggy beards.

At 1,500 feet we reached the foot of the ice fall leading to the ridge and my middle-aged bones wilted at the thought of getting a load up this next steep 2,000 feet. We left our skis here and, roped in pairs, started plugging our way laboriously upwards, traversing steep slopes over gaping crevasses, dodging vertical ice cliffs and leaving behind us a deep track that would have done credit to a herd of wild elephants. Every half dozen steps we'd break through thigh deep and an incredible effort was needed to drag yourself and your load to the surface again. On one steep slope there was a shuddering 'boom' and the whole slope quivered violently – and a cornice snapped off and fell with a plop into a crevasse. We hesitated in startled alarm, then carried on.

The last thousand feet was a very great trial for me. The slope was terribly steep and my pack seemed to have doubled in weight. The final sixty feet to the overhanging crest of the ridge was almost vertical and we moved cautiously, one at a time. A laborious scramble on hands and knees under the cornice for thirty feet out to the left, an energetic move over the last ice wall, and we were on the crest of the spur – seven and a half hours from Base Camp and at an altitude of 3,400 feet.

The ridge was broad and flattish with plenty of room for tents. Above us the east face of Herschel was an awe inspiring sight and the summit vastly remote. The view to the north-east over the sea ice was superb and we could see long leads of open ocean near Cape Hallett. We stayed to help pitch a tent, then said farewell to Mike and Bruce and dropped over the edge and plunged down the long slopes back to Base Camp. When I crawled into my sleeping bag I was dead tired but elated that we had achieved a well stocked camp with two formidable climbers in position.

In the assault camp the two men slept fitfully. There were many uncertainties about the climb. Should they concentrate on just establishing a route to a higher camp or should they push themselves to the limit and go for the summit? Their camp was only 3,400 feet and the summit an estimated 11,000 feet – a very considerable lift in height. Would the weather hold? A storm when they were on the summit could be disastrous – they'd be too far away for anyone to give them any help.

At five-thirty a.m. they left their tent with the sun lightening the ridge above but the pack-ice still in deep shadow. Their loads were relatively heavy. They had food, a vacuum flask of hot coffee, a primus stove for more drinks higher up, spare clothing, ice pitons, an altimeter, a movie camera and a still camera. Right from the start it was hard work with powdery snow a foot deep and as the angle steepened they were slithering on underlying hard ice and rock. In spite of the cold they started sweating with the effort and their snow goggles fogged up.

It was eight a.m. before we were able to locate them with binoculars from Base Camp. They had already climbed the first prominent snow peak on the ridge and were ascending a very steep looking slope towards a great ice wall which completely barred the way. Even from below we could see the wicked gleam of polished green ice. We saw them approach the ice wall and then disappear. . . They had entered a giant split in the face. For hours they laboured with great effort in the bowels of the mountain – hacking steps up a series of exposed ice walls and struggling in the depths of crevasses.

It wasn't until noon that Norman Hardie located them again – two tiny black dots crossing the great north shoulder of the mountain onto the north ridge. They had surmounted the ice wall and then clawed their way up the steep 1,500 foot slope above. When their ankles had tired from the constant strain of clinging on with crampons they had scratched steps in the hard surface in long zigzags. At twelve thirty p.m. they reached the rock which marked the top limit of the slope and we lost sight of them against its black background – and we weren't to see them again for another ten hours.

They had a long rest, more than an hour, while they brewed several cups of sweet coffee and munched biscuits and chocolate. Then they climbed up the narrow broken north ridge with the immense east face dropping away thousands of feet on their left and steep ice slopes on their right. They had three hours of this without any relief before they reached the foot of the final rock pyramid. They traversed across onto a snow basin on the west face of the mountain and then directly up the steep 1,500 feet towards the summit. The tension inseparable from difficult climbing was accentuated as the rock steepened and snow and ice filled every crevice. Worse still, the rock seemed to rear up ahead of them at an ever increasing angle. They seemed to have no thought of turning back (I envied them their courage and determination) – but suddenly it was all over. At seven p.m. they were standing on the sharp rocky spike of the summit.

At Base Camp, time had passed agonisingly slowly. Our relief was enormous when at ten thirty p.m. we saw them appear over the shoulder and descend the steep slopes below. We picked them up again as they came off the ice wall. They reached their tent soon after midnight – desperately tired after nineteen hours of difficult technical climbing. It had been a remarkable display of skill and endurance.

On the following day Strang and White made their push for the summit. They found the technical problems no less difficult and it was twenty-five hours before they were back in the tents again, completely exhausted but with the sweet satisfaction of victory. Next day we climbed up to meet them and helped carry all the gear off the mountain. In Base Camp Hardie produced bottles that had remained liquid despite the temperature, and we huddled together in our largest tent around the feeble flame of a pressure stove. It was as good a celebration as I can remember. I crawled out of the tent for a breather and came face to face with a Weddell seal . . .

Our expedition had achieved its major objective – we could now relax and get on with exploration and science.

The Antarctic continent is covered with an enormous thickness of solid ice and only occasional rock outcrops and peaks push through. Although it looks as if the ice has always been there such is not the case. Seams of coal and fossilised trees show that in some era of time parts of the continent had climates sufficiently temperate for forests to flourish. The theory of 'Continental Drift' was gaining widespread support as an explanation of how such phenomenon as forests in the Antarctic could have occurred.

Dr. Larry Harrington believed that some of the critical evidence about 'Continental Drift' could be found in Robertson Bay on the north coast of Antarctica. Our next move was to try and get to Robertson Bay separated from Cape Hallett by thirty miles of sea ice, twenty-five miles of crevassed glacier, and the steep slopes of Adare Saddle. We heartily disliked camping on the sea ice or travelling over it for long distances. The annual breakout of the ice was quite unpredictable and you had little hope of survival if you were swept out to sea. But to go north from Hallett you had to cross the ice of Maubray Bay and that's all there was to it.

We reconnoitred a route through heavy pressure ridges and grounded icebergs – thirty-two miles of winding, twisting track, bumping over hard ice and through soft snow. Murray Ellis dragged an abandoned Weasel off the scrap heap at Hallett Station and somehow got it going. He nursed it for thirty miles and then left it as a reserve vehicle for the retreat back over the ice. We camped on the sea ice for a couple of days of bad weather and could hear seals bubbling beneath our tent floors. We were glad to cross the tide cracks and establish a safer camp on the thick ice of the Maubray Piedmont glacier.

I organised reconnaissance parties to go ahead on skis prodding for crevasses and flagging a safe route. Then we followed with snow-mobiles and sledge loads and moved the party sixteen miles up the Maubray glacier to a camp at 1,300 feet. Above us were lines of great crevasses and steep slopes – would we be able to handle them? I had two men go ahead and flag a route for the snowmobiles. With motors roaring we charged through the flags like racing skiers . . . I felt a snow bridge subside slightly beneath me then was safely over. A turn to the left, a sharp swing to the right, a dozen crevasses behind, and we were clear with wide open snow slopes leading towards Adare Saddle.

With a feeling of exhilaration we pounded up the long slopes. The last half mile was peppered with hard sastrugi and warned us of constant vigorous winds. Suddenly we were on the crest of the saddle and a tremendous view opened out in front of us – the ice covered surface of Robertson Bay, 2,600 feet below us; the long Adare peninsula sweeping away to the north; the distant ocean crammed with great icebergs, stretching towards the far shores of my native New Zealand.

The inhospitable crest of Adare Saddle offered few desirable camping sites. On an easy slope to the west, the snow was a little softer and here we dug in two tents and parked the vehicles. Then we set off to climb a rocky peak above camp. The scale of the area deceived us and it was three hours of vigorous walking up crevassed slopes and some steepish cramponing before we reached the summit of Point 140 at about 5,000 feet.

There was hardly a breath of wind and the view was incredibly beautiful. We relaxed in relative comfort and enjoyed the tremendous spread of mountain, glacier and ocean – all tinted and sculptured by the late evening sunlight. Norman Hardie set up his theodolite and started another survey while we eagerly discussed the mighty mountains grouped around Mount Minto and Mount Sabine. Below us was Robertson Bay – as wild and lonely a spot as I have ever seen. It was at Cape Adare, clearly visible to the east, that Borchgrevinck in the summer of 1894/5 made the first recorded landing on the Antarctic Continent. Borchgrevinck was back again in 1899 with another expedition. He built a hut at Cape Adare and his party wintered over – the first such wintering on land in the Antarctic.

While our geologists hammered furiously at the rocks, Mike White and I climbed out to another outcrop – the thick vertical neck of an ancient volcano gloriously coloured in reds, browns and blacks. From here the view down onto Duke of York Island and the Murray Glacier was quite stupendous. The contorted ice of the glacier split around the flanks of the island and thrust remorselessly out into the pack-ice covering Robertson Bay. We shivered as the wind freshened but couldn't tear ourselves away. Around our heads like disembodied spirits drifted half a dozen snow petrels, incredibly beautiful birds with an amazing ability to survive in this harsh environment.

Frozen from their long sojourn on Point 140 the survey party had packed up and were descending the mountain on their way back to the old camp on the other side of Adare Saddle. Mike White and I soon followed towards our closer camp, our fur hoods crusting with ice as we pushed into the keen wind. Only the two geologists remained – wielding their rock hammers vigorously and clumsily taking notes with gloved hands. I admired their tenacity but didn't envy them their task. It was good to reach camp again and thaw out with a mug of hot soup.

The geologists returned, laden with rocks and pleased with their efforts. One of their discoveries interested all of us. We had noticed the prominent reefs of quartz on the ridges of Point 140 and Dr. Harrington told us these were very similar to saddle reefs of quartz in the goldfields of Victoria, Australia, and on the west coast of New Zealand. Furthermore he thought he had detected specks of gold in the quartz with his hand-lens. Included in their rucksack were samples of the quartz for assay.

During the next two days we had storms and poor visibility. Our efforts to reach sea level in Robertson Bay were frustrated and we were driven back by fierce winds and drifting snow. We packed up our camp and weighed down with fifty lb of rocks retreated back over Adare Saddle in a complete whiteout, fumbling our way along and not knowing quite where we were.

Dimly seen through the mist on either side of us were gaping crevasses that I didn't remember. The two Mikes went probing ahead on a rope and within a few minutes one of them was up to his waist in an unpleasant crevasse. Then someone caught a glimpse of a flapping flag – thank heavens for that! Cautiously we moved over to the faint signs of our upwards tracks. Great gaping holes loomed up on either side and then disappeared in the whiteout. Soon we were rushing down the last hill to the camp.

To our surprise Norman Hardie and his party weren't there. A note said they'd left at three thirty a.m. in good weather to climb a steep peak nearby and do a survey station. The clouds and drifting snow blotted out the view and we wrestled with our two tents to get them firmly pitched before the storm gathered too much force. By three thirty p.m. we were very concerned indeed. The strong wind and complete lack of visibility boded ill for the four climbers. Then occurred one of those temporary, almost miraculous, lulls in weather that can sometimes occur. For half an hour the low cloud lifted and the ridge could be dimly seen ... but still no sign of our four climbers. Then we heard Peter Strang's exuberant shout and they came tramping over the crest of a snow hump. Their beards were crusted with ice, they were battered and weary, but the clearance had enabled them to pick out the camp and rejoin us.

For three days the storm raged – each violent gust of wind being succeeded by an even more violent gust. It seemed impossible that the flimsy nylon of our tents could stand up against it. Drifting snow hammered against the tight stretched fabric like heavy rain on a tin roof. The first night I lay waiting for our Sears experimental tents to collapse but gradually my confidence grew. Our food and kerosene diminished and we reduced our rations – would the wind never cease?

At ten p.m. on the third night there was a sudden easing in the wind strength. I crawled outside and could see some crevasses half a mile away. We had to get down lower, I felt, in case the storm returned. Digging out the three feet of drift snow around the tents and sledges was a considerable effort. The snowmobiles started magnificently and at one a.m. we were away with full loads guessing our route by the dimly seen sides of the valley. Alas, the fresh snow was too deep for our heavy sledges and we bogged again and again. We split the food and the loads and Norman Hardie and four others pitched their tents again. Murray Ellis and I tied the two snowmobiles together and pulled a single sledge. Bruce Jenkinson and Mike White were towed on skis behind.

The further we went the better the surface became and we made good time. Murray was in the lead snowmobile and driving in a very dashing fashion. Suddenly there was a dull rumble and the snow started subsiding under his vehicle. Somehow he clawed his way up the other side. A great hole appeared in front of me and I swung my machine violently to the right and stopped. Crevasse!

More than a little shaken we crawled over to investigate the hole. It was ten feet wide with straight sided walls going to unimaginable depths. Luck had been with us or Murray's vehicle would have dropped like a stone and dragged mine in as well. Cautiously we drove half a mile out into the centre of the glacier. Then we twisted through our flagged crevasse areas and back to the camp on the Piedmont. The bay ice was still there although the tide crack was ominously wide and unstable.

The weather deteriorated again and we made only laboured progress in collecting the rear party. One of the vehicles broke a drive shaft and more crevasses were discovered. Finally with a combination of relaying and manhauling the whole party returned to the Piedmont camp. We felt we were racing against time – the ice could go out at any moment. Working around the clock, we transported loads over the tide cracks using makeshift bridges. Then in a long day of considerable effort we limped back towards Hallett with one snowmobile and the battered old Weasel. Somehow everything kept going and we bumped slowly over Edisto Bay leaving behind a trail of wheels, nuts and washers. It was mighty good to drive over the tide crack onto the solid land at Hallett. Sixteen days of hard, often desperate, work had netted us one precious bag of Robertson Bay rock.

When you get inside the hills of east Nepal it is surprising how little the country has changed over the last twenty years. There are still no roads once you leave the flat Terrai near the Indian border, and there are only a handful of mountain airfields. If you want to go anywhere it doesn't matter if you're a Government official or a heavily laden porter – you have to walk. And if the steep terrain is not enough of a problem you always find the great rivers of east Nepal – the Arun, the Dudh Kosi, and the Sun Kosi – barring the way. In places you can cross the rivers by modern suspension bridges, but the old traditional types are much more common – the best of these hang from hand-forged iron chains and the worst from twisted ropes made from *lianas* out of the forest. More common are the ferries; dugout canoes with vigorous crews who paddle furiously across wide stretches of fast flowing river, always keeping one eye on the ugly rapids below. The local villagers delight in telling of boats and crews that weren't quite lively enough . . .

Many of us would possibly prefer to see the hills of Nepal left the way they are – insulated by terrain from the benefits of the civilised world. But all over Nepal a spirit of change is abroad. The unsophist-icated villager has heard of education, medical care, a less arduous way of life and he wants these things for his children. Ultimately, I believe, he will get them.

Large rivers with many violent rapids make formidable natural barriers. It wasn't until I came into contact with jet boats that I realised the possibility of using these rivers as transport arteries into Himalayan country. I was introduced to jet boating by fellow New Zealander Jon Hamilton, son of the original inventor, and a famous driver of these boats (included in his feats is the first and only ascent of the Colorado river through the Grand Canyon). My first exhilarating journey with Jon up a wild rock-strewn mountain river completely converted me to the sport.

The jet boat is really a simple enough contraption – a strong fibre-glass hull capable of withstanding bruising contacts with rocks (and able to be quickly mended if a hole should result); a powerful and reliable inboard engine; and, instead of a propeller and rudder, a highly developed water pump! Water is sucked in through a flat grating in the bottom of the boat and projected violently out the back to supply propulsion and steering. There is nothing hanging down below the keel of the boat, so that at high speed it only needs three inches of water to operate – and it is incredibly manoeuvrable.

The jet boat, I felt, could be the answer to the rivers of Nepal and I determined to organise an expedition and test out my theories. Our main objective was to be the Sun Kosi River which twists across Nepal from Tibet to India in a succession of rapids, deep gorges and abrupt mountain slopes. With its tributaries it forms a giant river system where hundreds of thousands of hill people live. From June to September the monsoon rains drench the area and movement is restricted by slips and washouts on the mountain tracks. Even in the drier seasons it is a long walk of many days to get produce to market in Kathmandu.

I estimated there was 200 miles of river to cover from the Indian border to near Kathmandu, the capital. I flew by helicopter down ninety miles of the Sun Kosi following each twist and turn from only a hundred feet altitude. I photographed each rapid (and there's one almost every mile) and had the pilot land us on a number of occasions to look at the river from ground level. The flight was done in the driest season and the river carried the minimum of water, much less than it would during the monsoon, but I saw only two places that looked really difficult. There was still a hundred miles of the river I hadn't seen and there might be many more obstacles to be overcome but this uncertainty seemed to add something to the challenge.

In July 1968 I arrived in Kathmandu and was joined by various members of my expedition – Jon Hamilton, engineer and chief driver; Dr. Max Pearl, medical officer; and Neville Wooderson, builder and plumber. Dr. John McKinnon was already in the Everest area running our small Sherpa hospital, and Dr. Michael Gill and Jim Wilson would be arriving later with the jet boats.

But no expedition to Nepal, even on the rivers, would be the same without the presence of a few of our Sherpa friends. Mingma Tsering as usual was our *sirdar* – the man who could be relied on to find the answer to any problem be it obtaining food where there wasn't any or getting fifty men to carry a boat around a waterfall. Pembertarkay and Phudorje were there too with their unfailing cheerfulness and enormous strength. Peeling potatoes around the camp fire or carrying heavy loads at 26,000 feet they were unshakable and indestructible.

Exploring rivers with jet boats wasn't our only reason for being in Nepal – we had another school to build, an airfield to enlarge, and the hospital to restock with drugs and medical supplies. Kathmandu was awash with monsoon rains and heavy clouds over the hills made impossible any penetration into the mountains by aircraft. So we had to walk. With 200 heavily laden porters we trekked across country for fourteen days climbing over high ridges and descending steeply into the valleys. Torrential rain was a constant test of our tents and our camping techniques, and the hard-packed dirt tracks were slick and treacherous.

For a month we became builders and engineers – enlarging the mountain airfield at Lukla, now closed by the monsoon rains; and doubling in size the village school at Khumjung. Brief clearances in the weather gave us magnificent views of Mount Everest and the other great peaks around us, but the clearances were all too few. I visited our other schools in Sherpa villages – Thami near the Tibetan border; Phortse on a sloping ledge high on Mount Taweche; Chaunrikarka at the relatively low altitude of 9,000 feet; and Pangboche 13,500 feet at the foot of Mount Everest. In each village we received a warm welcome and discussed problems with the village councils. The raw local whisky flowed very freely and it was impossible not to believe that our modest efforts on their behalf were greatly appreciated by the Sherpas.

By the end of August our task was largely done and we could turn our thoughts back to jet boats. Bad weather was still making any flying in Nepal a hazardous business and we couldn't risk any more delays. I decided that once again we should walk. For twelve days we headed south towards the Indian border over some of the steepest country I had crossed in Nepal. From camps at over 10,000 feet on the crest of a narrow ridge we had some of the most extensive and beautiful views of the Himalayan peaks I have experienced – mighty Kangchenjunga far in the east; Makalu, Everest, and Cho Cyu to the north, and the giant mountains of west Nepal. As we dropped height down into the hill villages we carried out another of our objectives – a survey of the incidence of goitre which is an appallingly common infliction. There was plenty of other work for our doctors to do. Beside the track we found a distressed father and his eighteen-year-old son. The boy had a compound fracture of his right leg, suffered some three weeks before, and he was in a weak and deteriorating condition. Surrounded by interested villagers, my two doctors operated on the boy, cutting away the infected flesh, straightening the limb and putting it all in plaster. Massive doses of antibiotic gave him a chance for survival and we organised people to carry him to the nearest medical clinic, three days' walk away over the mountains.

On September 12th lean and fit, we arrived in the town of Biritnagar on the Indian border. It was incredibly hot and there was no sign of our jet boats. Impatient and frustrated and with virtually no way of contacting the outside world, we waited for day after day finding the heat and humidity a considerable trial after the cool clear air of the mountains. On the sixth day, when we were reaching the end of our tether, two bedraggled trucks drove into the border town and Mike Gill and Jim Wilson were waving us welcome. They had just driven non-stop from Calcutta in thirty-five hours and had a long tale of frustrations and delays on the Calcutta wharves. But at least we were now all together and could get on with the job.

We stood on the banks of the Sun Kosi river and watched the muddy violent water roll by – a hundred thousand cubic feet a second the local engineer had told us – far larger than the river had any right to be in late September when the monsoon rains usually ease in the Himalayas.

Our two gleaming jet boats *Kiwi* and *Sherpa* were on the bank beside us. Fifteen feet long and powered by 140 h.p. V6 engines driving jet units they were specially designed for fast flowing and rocky rivers. Somehow they look puny instruments for such big waters as these and I felt a sharp jab of pessimism. With much grunting and sweating we manhandled *Kiwi* down the thirty-foot bank into the river. A turn of the key brought the engine into swinging life and Jon Hamilton drove out into the swift current and next moment was sweeping along at thirty m.p.h. and making the river look easy.

We transferred all our equipment and fuel eight miles up the river to the green oasis of Tribeni where three great rivers meet – the Sun Kosi, the Arun and the Tamur. Here we established a comfortable base camp in beautiful and pleasant surroundings – a considerable improvement from the crowded and smelly streets of the border town. The weather adopted a set pattern – torrential rain at night and somewhat cloudy but pleasant days. The river rose and fell in quite remarkable fashion and many times we crawled out in the middle of the night to drag our boats above rising flood waters. We poked our noses up the steep Tamur River but only made three miles before the rapids became so difficult that we were in danger of risking the boats – so we turned back.

We turned our attention to the Arun – a mighty river nearly as big as the Sun Kosi and carrying water all the way from the Tibetan side of Mount Everest. I had walked beside the central section of the Arun river on several occasions and crossed the river by dugout canoe and swing bridge. I had even floated a section of it. I had seen no really bad rapids but the map indicated an ominous rise in height over the first fifteen miles – a part I had not visited – so we could expect some lively travelling.

We set off up the Arun with a good deal of confidence and determination. After the heavy rain the river was in full flood but the first three miles provided spectacular but easy travelling. Then the gradient steepened and we met a succession of big rapids up a long deep gorge. The river was foaming down with giant waves in the middle and no easy water at the sides. Only by determined and skilful driving were Jon Hamilton and Jim Wilson able to make any progress at all. Each time we swung through the steep central waves we took a battering and the further we went the harder the effort became. On one difficult corner Wilson was thrown violently backwards by the river but recovered and doggedly plunged through again. At any moment, we felt, we must come to easier water and we became so engrossed in the struggle that the dangers were forgotten.

Twelve miles on we were still battling up a long rough stretch and making very hard work of it. Mike Gill was in the back of our boat watching *Sherpa* plunging through the waves a couple of hundred yards behind. His yell, 'She's sinking, she's sinking,' snatched our startled attention. I looked around just in time to see the other boat toss completely over in a couple of great waves that seemed to have risen out of nowhere.

Horrified, we swung around and charged back. Already the boat had gone and I could see three heads in the water – where was the fourth member of the crew? Jim Wilson and Max Pearl, riding high in their life jackets, were striking out strongly for the shore so we swept past them. To my relief the last head divided into two and we saw that John McKinnon was dragging Sherpa Ang Passang slowly towards the bank. Handling the boat brilliantly in the rough water Jon Hamilton swung us about below the pair and we hauled the two of them over the side.

We gathered at the bank to lick our wounds and get back our confidence. Jim Wilson told us of the frightful moment when the boat sank and he hadn't been able to locate Ang Passang. He had dived under the water and found the jet boat floating down the river a few feet under the surface. Still sitting in the engine compartment was Ang Passang – holding his breath and hanging on like grim death. Jim was able to attract his attention and get him to the surface.

Our retreat down the Arun was not one of the better moments of the expedition. Half of the party had to walk the twelve miles back to the camp. The rest of us had a wildly precarious roller coaster ride back down the rapids. In one bad section we shipped two huge waves and only a lightning reaction by Jon to swing us into the slightly calmer water behind a giant boulder prevented us from taking in more water and possibly sinking. It was half an hour before we had the boat pumped out and dry again. A floating section of seat and a few pieces of other debris were all we saw of *Sherpa* and showed that the boat must have been torn to pieces on the rocky bottom of the river. We were a very subdued group that night. Our major task was still ahead of us and we had only one boat left. Plans must be changed, some of the party would have to be left behind – was it even worth persisting with the effort?

In due course our natural optimism returned – we could still achieve our main objective. I resolved that Jon Hamilton, Jim Wilson, Michael Gill, Mingma Tsering and myself would try and reach Kathmandu with the remaining boat. It took us several days to complete our preparations and by the evening of September 24th, we were ready to go. As if to challenge our determination, the heavens opened and we had the heaviest night's rain I have ever experienced. A sheet of water several inches deep flowed through the bottom of our tents and the beach was gouged by deep channels, each a maelstrom of thundering floodwaters. The Sun Kosi, a third of a mile wide in front of our camp, rose ten feet during the hours of darkness and in the morning was a mighty torrent indeed. We decided to push on regardless. The boat was loaded, we climbed aboard and with Jon at the wheel we got under way.

The current in the Sun Kosi was swift and powerful but for six miles we had smooth and easy going between steep bush-clad hills.

Skimming along through the superb scenery at thirty m.p.h. was tremendously exhilarating and our confidence was rapidly growing – perhaps it was all going to be like this?

Then a large side stream created a turbulent rapid and a little further on the whole river cascaded over two giant boulders. We managed to creep around the side in a patch of calmer water. A third big rapid had giant waves racing in every direction. There was nothing for it but to charge through as best we could, tossing violently on every upsurging wave and dropping with resounding crashes into the hollows.

Leaping white foam warned us of more trouble ahead – an appalling rapid this time with the whole river thundering down a steep incline and waves in the middle being pushed up ten feet or more. Once again we eased around to the left where the current was travelling almost as fast as we were. Thrusting out from the bank was a huge dead tree with a wave breaking over it three feet high . . . the only way was to the right under the curl of the first giant wave. Even a hesitation in our motor at this stage could have been the end of us. Slowly we inched our way over the crest and then hastened to safer waters.

As if to placate us the river became calm and easy and we covered many miles of beautiful travelling with dense bush and monkeys jumping around on the banks. Then the valley narrowed and we plunged into a steep and sombre gorge with racing water and big toppling waves. It was five miles before we emerged from the gorge and by then we were weary from the constant jarring crashes and violent swerves – and at no time had we seen a place where we could have escaped in an emergency up the rock walls.

We had now completed fifty miles and it was time to camp. We drove around another corner seeking a suitable beach and came to still another rapid – a foaming fury of big water. Battling against the current we drove up the left side of the river and found the full force of the water poured over a rock ledge – a most uninviting spot. 'I don't like that,' muttered Jon and spun us around. A hazardous crossing of the great central waves to the other side proved a waste of time as it was even worse there. So back up the original route we went to aggressively smash across the outside edge of the ledge and then charge up to the lip of the rapid. Three huge waves barred our way and after a great deal of jumping and crashing we lurched through them to calmer water. We camped on a white sandy beach beside the tributary Rasua Khola – it was peaceful and very beautiful.

Halfway point was the entrance of the Dudh Kosi river another forty miles up. Carrying a light camp and plenty of gasoline, we set off on a reconnaissance, charging through each rapid as we found it, and making fast time over long easy stretches. We plunged into a deep gorge split by a narrow trench carrying the cold glacier waters of the Dudh Kosi river straight from the slopes of Mount Everest. We couldn't resist turning up the Dudh Kosi and battling with its fast and turbulent flow.

High above us on the steep cliffs, huge apes were swinging across precipitous slopes with a speed and skill far beyond that of any human mountaineer. The valley widened a little and we pulled into the bank beside a small village and were soon surrounded by an excited group of people – most of whom had never seen a European or an engine before. I noticed a comely maiden with a young baby on her hip take its small hand and touch it to the boat and then to his forehead – as Sherpas do with something holy in the Khumbu.

We returned to the Sun Kosi hoping for a few more easy miles but turned a corner to find our way blocked by a severe obstacle – two rapids, four hundred yards apart, bristling with rocks, and with a substantial drop in height. Feeling thoroughly subdued, we tied up to the bank and went ashore for a closer examination. It was clear that the 'Twins' as we called these rapids were going to be a problem. Although the river here didn't carry as much water as lower down, it was still a mighty stream and the drop in each rapid was severe. I could see possible routes through both of the rapids but they were badly restricted by large boulders. Only Jon Hamilton, I felt, would be able to tackle such a problem.

We set up camp on a pleasant stretch of green grass and the afternoon was devoted to bringing another load of supplies up the river. It was a glorious evening as we lay in front of our tents and ate a substantial meal of chicken stew and rice. To the north we saw flashes of lightning warning of possible rain in the headwaters. Overhead a satellite streaked across the sky and reminded us of the more complex world outside. We seemed a long way from anywhere. If we sank the boat in these rapids, I warned myself, it would take us ten days to walk to the nearest road.

In the morning we tackled the problem of the Twin rapids. We emptied the *Kiwi* of everything we could move and backpacked the luggage a rough mile to open water. Jon spent a long time on the bank studying every wave and rock. Then he headed into the bottom Twin using full power against the steep racing water and taking advantage of the slacker water behind each great boulder. The last few waves threw him about in alarming fashion but he held his course and broke through into the easier central section. The upper Twin was less steep but had far more rocks to dodge. At full speed Jon hit the rapid like a skier on a slalom course, zigzagging between boulders, bouncing off great waves and sliding in behind protecting rocks. It was a masterly effort of jet boat driving and a great moment when he finally charged over the crest in safety.

For another eighty miles the Sun Kosi gave us delightful boating – rapids in plenty but none of them capable of stopping us for long; beautiful forest and the vivid green of terraced fields clinging to the mountainsides; wide peaceful valleys with tree-shaded camp sites. And everywhere we went we met cheerful and friendly people who commented on the virtues of our craft with the sober judgment of experienced river folk. We saw fishermen casting their nets in the shallows and villagers distilling whisky in great copper bowls on the river's edge. We tried the local brew straight from the pot and found it hot and raw.

Only twelve miles from our destination we met our last severe obstacle – a ferocious rapid in the depths of a precipitous gorge. For a moment it seemed we might be frustrated even at this late stage. All Jon's skill was needed to get us safely through! Then it was on at full speed. We swept around the last corner and saw the road to Kathmandu and a group of friends waving. It was good to nose into the bank and turn off the engine – and to be able to forget the jumping water and cruel rocks that had been waiting for us around every corner.

We had demonstrated that the Sun Kosi could be ascended by a skilled driver in a jet boat – but far more work would be needed over all seasons to assess the economic potential of river transport in Nepal. It is a task I would love to undertake but it would need plenty of time and ample funds. None of my adventures have left me with more exciting or enjoyable memories and I have a feeling that the rivers of Nepal will see our jet boats again.

Chapter 19

What to do?

FOR TEN YEARS MY LIFE HAS ASSUMED A MORE REGULAR ROUTINE – NOT
quite nine to five – but more predictable than it used to be. Each year I
make a couple of visits to the U.S.A. and three or four to Australia; I
spend several months building schools in the Himalayas and many
months raising funds for them. There is always lots of talking and walking; writing and camping; flying and driving; planning and organising.
I walk or jog a few miles each day to try and keep vaguely fit, and I take
Louise with me on trips whenever it is possible – and the family too at
times. They have been very happy years for me.

I have never devoted much time to worrying about the future or
been concerned about increasing years. There has always been so much
to do and you can adjust your contribution to your physical capacity.
But as my fiftieth year approached I woke one morning and took a
good look at myself. I had a mild hangover from a surfeit of good food
and wine, my discarded clothes reeked with other people's tobacco
smoke – and I realised with despair that I was becoming increasingly
involved in business and social activities and devoting less time to
energetic and health giving pursuits. Almost unconsciously I was
slipping into the easy habits of most of the well-meaning, self-indulgent,
and well-heeled members of our society. If I became too physically
soft I would be worth nothing to myself or to anybody else.

On the pad beside my bed I wrote a short list of resolutions – all
thoroughly selfish, perhaps – but things I had wanted to do for years
and which would at least help keep me reasonably fit and adventurous.
The first three tasks on the list are now completed to my reasonable
satisfaction.

To escape from the telephone and the concrete jungle I have built a
cottage on the cliffs above the Tasman Sea, surrounded by native trees
and facing the setting sun. There is no telephone – the thunder of the

surf on this wild coast is the dominating sound – and it is incredibly beautiful and peaceful. When the great westerly storms sweep in across the ocean and hammer at the windows we snuggle up to a warm fire and feel a contentment which we rarely experience in our comfortable home in the city.

I had greater doubts about my ambition to do a Grand Traverse of Mount Cook – a glorious route enjoyed even by the 'hot shots' of the younger generation – possibly it was now beyond my capacity? Then the chance came and with a mighty group of climbing friends we went up and over. It was an exhilarating day – one of the greatest for me not even marred on our descent to discover that a young man from another party had fallen to his death from the Summit Rocks.

My third resolution – to improve my skiing – probably proved the easiest to achieve. Helped by some good snow years and the increasing competence of my children, I learned to ski more expertly (if with less verve) than I ever did in my youthful days. I may have little opportunity for skiing in the next few years but this really doesn't matter – I have made the step forward I wanted.

I am working at the other resolutions on my list – and the list has grown considerably larger ...

Few things give me more pleasure than camping in tents – despite the vast amount of it I do. Every year I devote a great deal of time to thinking up new tent designs and in improving old ones. My work with Sears brings me in close contact with a group of manufacturers, research engineers, buyers and salesmen and we do an adventurous camping trip together each year to share our knowledge and experience and to get to know each other better. We have floated down the Green River in Utah; fished for giant salmon on Kodiak Island in Alaska; paddled canoes through La Vendraye Park in northern Quebec – nothing very heroic, of course, but good hard fun for all of that.

One of our early ventures was to float in a pontoon boat down the Middle Fork of the Salmon river in Idaho. This was a wild and furious river with a considerable reputation amongst American sportsmen. When we reached the river we found it in tremendous flood as the weather had been very mild and much of the snow had melted in the mountains. I expressed my doubts to our two young boatmen but they assured me it would be quite safe – I don't suppose they wanted to appear chicken-hearted.

It was quite a trip. The first day we ploughed through a dozen violent rapids and tore most of the bottom out of the boat. The second day was much livelier. Soon after launching we struck a big pinnacle of rock and tore off most of our superstructure and wallowed on down the river completely out of control.

After a desperate mile or two we were swept in towards the right-hand bank. Our two boatmen each grabbed a rope and leapt overboard – hoping to hitch onto a tree or rock. But the current was too strong. It dragged the ropes out of their hands and we carried on down the river leaving our experts behind. Another violent mile went by and we were thrown in towards the other bank. I leapt over with one rope and Carl Van Peenan went over with the other. Van Peenan slipped on a wet rock and fell flat on his face. I had managed to get my rope around a slender tree trunk when the pontoon swung around into the rapid, the rope came tight with a twang . . . and my tree snapped. The rope was torn out of my hands. The pontoon with the three most senior executives on board disappeared in lonely splendour down the next rapid. One of these men was Carl Lind – National Merchandise Manager with Sears Sports Department – and I could see my happy relationship with Sears departing down the river with him.

Van Peenan and I chased down the river bank, aghast at what disastrous sight we might find around the next corner. After two heated miles we were able to stop in relief. There on the other bank was the boat safe in an enormous backwater, swept in there by the current. We were in a wilderness area and a long way from anyone. Somehow or other Van Peenan and I had to cross the river and join up with what was left of our food and camping gear. I decided there was only one thing to do – jump in the river about a half mile upstream, swim like crazy for five minutes and let the current sweep me into the same backwater as the boat. I climbed onto a rock and leapt out into the foaming water – it was bitterly cold – then swam furiously, tossing around like a cork, until I could see I was being carried into the backwater. Somewhat to the surprise of our senior executives I popped up beside the damaged raft. Van Peenan wasn't as accustomed to such activities as I was, I suppose, but with considerable courage he jumped into the torrent and battled his way over.

We gathered our team together and limped slowly down the river – the whole trip had now turned into a survival operation. Unbeknown to us a number of people had been drowned in the river over the previous few days and the Park officials had already declared the river closed until the waters subsided. Our battered pontoon was losing air and it was almost impossible to control. We were relieved to reach a small airfield in the forest, to beach our unwieldy craft and to be evacuated by air. Although our trip had been great fun it had changed from a lighthearted test of equipment to a considerable test of men.

When I go back each year to Nepal to work on the hospital and schools I see many changes. A combined Japanese/Nepalese company obtained permission to build a luxury hotel in a magnificent position twelve miles from the foot of Mount Everest, only a short distance from Khumjung school and Kunde Hospital. The plan was to fly the tourists into the hotel – but the only easy location for an airfield was right through the potato fields and houses of Khumjung village. The company put great pressure on the Government and the local people. If they permitted the airfield to be built then the company would not only pay substantial compensation but they'd fly in from Kathmandu enough food to compensate the owners for the loss of production from their potato fields. A very reasonable and generous suggestion it sounded – and some of the Sherpas seemed tempted by the short-term benefits.

What they overlooked, of course, was the long-term effect it would have on their community and lives. I decided I couldn't let them be talked into something they'd later regret. I organised a meeting of the villagers and explained what was being proposed. I asked them a few questions; if they gave up their village for an airfield what would happen to their pride and their independence? They were now the focal point of a hundred thousand vigorous tough people – did they want to become a dependent bunch of pensioners, lining up each week for handouts of food?

My discourse seemed to strike a chord with the Sherpas and swept away any temptation they might have felt. After this not one of them would agree to sell his land – or even discuss the possible selling of it. A strong petition was taken down to the capital, Kathmandu, and it is to the credit of the Nepalese Government that they refused to override the wishes of the local people. I received a little abuse in the Japanese papers for obstructing the airfield but some encouraging support from Japanese mountaineers.

What was the sequel? A safer airfield has now been completed on another site, equally handy to the hotel but on more difficult terrain. It has cost a little more but no potato fields or houses are being destroyed. Khumjung retains its pride and personality – and will still have all the benefits of the hotel – if benefits they prove to be.

Invitations to deliver lectures are never ending – the world is full of worthy souls who have to produce a speaker each week for their organisations. Increasingly my lectures reflected my own growing interest and involvement in the problems that face our world – racialism, the population explosion, conservation of the environment, foreign aid programmes, the increasing gap in wealth between the rich and the poor nations.

We had a very conservative type of Government in New Zealand which had been in power for a long time. We seemed to be passing through a phase of political and moral stagnation with too much emphasis on national growth rates and sporting success, and a reluctance to acknowledge that social problems existed. Anyone who raised his voice in protest was attacked as one of the 'irresponsible minority'. It was a frustrating time for those who felt that New Zealand should be more active and independent in the international sphere.

The Auckland Rotary Club invited me to speak to a gathering of senior students from all the high schools in the city. I expressed the hope that their generation would tackle the social problems of our society with more courage and determination than my generation had shown. I went on to say,

> There's another thing I hope your generation can do . . . bring a little more honest to God morality into politics and Government at all levels nationally and internationally. Expediency and just plain dishonesty of utterances are recorded in our newspapers every day.
>
> It horrifies me the way a Head of State can one moment deny vehemently that his country is carrying out some particular action – and then a couple of days later, and with complete calmness admit the whole thing . . . Perhaps your generation can bring a little more honesty into these sort of things.

Statements such as this are common-place in any society but for some reason this was given wide publicity in New Zealand and brought an energetic reaction from the Prime Minister and the Government. My comments were directed at the world in general rather than New Zealand in particular – although the credibility gap was pretty wide in New Zealand at the time – but it was taken very personally indeed by our politicians. The battle was joined with enthusiasm by the news media and my participation became relatively incidental. For a week it was on the front pages and produced editorials and political comment from one end of the country to the other and then to my relief it faded away and disappeared.

I had other minor clashes too. I suggested a larger share of our national purse should be devoted to assistance to the poorer countries and our well-nourished Minister of Finance neatly commented, 'I think Sir Edmund knows as much about the New Zealand economy as I know about mountain climbing'. My suggestion that 'a free trip and a dollop of glory' was the motivation of a rugby football team making a controversial sporting visit to South Africa brought a burst of criticism from devout rugby fans and an equally energetic wave of support from those who rejected apartheid.

In general I dislike controversy and prefer a friendly and peaceful environment but it is sometimes better to speak up and suffer criticism than try to conserve a lukewarm friendship. I have been slapped on the back by a number of Prime Ministers in cheerful comradeship – when I finally asked for a little financial help for a Himalayan hospital the backslapping stopped and the finance never eventuated. I am thankful for the change of Government in New Zealand (1973) and for the idealism and responsibility that is creeping back into our foreign policy. I am also thankful for the substantial help I am now getting to build a new hospital in Nepal.

I get swept into many activities and become closely involved with few of them. I was not only President of V.S.A. but Patron of a Ski Club, an Outdoor Pursuits Centre, and a Race Relations Council. I am a Vice-President of the Youth Hostel Association and of an Abortion Reform Society; I am involved in Family Planning, a hearty supporter of conservation campaigns, and oppose Atom bomb testing in the South Pacific – and everywhere else too. I am not a formal member of any political party or Church although both politics and philosophy interest me a great deal. I believe the family unit is worth encouraging if it isn't socially exclusive; and that the police should be supported if they are honest and fair and don't try to push anyone around.

On occasions I have been associated with criticism of politicians and yet I am fully aware of the difficulties of their job and have the greatest respect for those who tackle it with courage and idealism. They are dealing after all with large numbers of us, the public, and we are not notable for selflessness, tolerance or honesty. Yet we can demand, I believe, certain standards from our lawmakers and refuse to stomach those who hide meagre principles behind a smokescreen of words.

On television I followed the first landing on the moon; the walk on the surface; the final glorious lifting off to a docking with the mother ship and a safe journey home. It was a triumph of technology, of incredibly complicated mechanisms and of men who could use them, so calm, so technically competent, so professional in their environment. Their only reaction to danger was an increase in pulse rate but not the slightest change in the intonation of their voices. How terrible it must be to have every emotion seen or heard by a hundred million people.

I lift my hat to the new explorers – they are the men of the tech-nological future with the Universe ahead of them. In many ways I regret I can't be one of them – but I was never competent enough, and I'm not very good at taking orders. Some day, I wouldn't mind betting, there'll be room in space for a different type of man – perhaps a little more like me – enthusiastic, resourceful, even a little irresponsible. They'll be found in all sorts of strange corners and they won't always have official permission. But when the pressure comes on I'm inclined to think they'll perform, achieve, and die with the best there is.

If my life finished tomorrow I would have little cause for complaint – I have gathered a few successes, a handful of honours and more love and laughter than I probably deserve. In a sense my life has been strung together by a series of friendships – Harry Ayres, George Lowe, Peter Mulgrew, Mike Gill, Jim Wilson, Max Pearl, Mingma Tsering – and most of all, Louise – the list goes on and on and I would have been nothing without them. I should be content I suppose. Yet, I look at myself and feel a vast dissatisfaction – there was so much more I could have done. And this is what really counts – not just achieving things . . . but the advantage you have taken of your opportunities and the opportunities you created.

Each of us has to discover his own path – of that I am sure. Some paths will be spectacular and others peaceful and quiet – who is to say which is the most important? For me the most rewarding moments have not always been the great moments – for what can surpass a tear on your departure, joy on your return, or a trusting hand in yours?

Most of all I am thankful for the tasks still left to do – for the adventures still lying ahead. I can see a mighty river to challenge; a hospital to build; a peaceful mountain valley with an unknown pass to cross; an untouched Himalayan summit and a shattered Southern glacier – yes, there is plenty left to do.

Index